Actionable Django

with examples and
hands-on exercises

WEBUCATOR

Version: DJG-101-1.0.2

The Authors

Nat Dunn

Nat Dunn is the founder of Webucator (www.webucator.com), a company that has provided training for tens of thousands of students from thousands of organizations. Nat started the company in 2003 to combine his passion for technical training with his business expertise, and to help companies benefit from both. His previous experience was in sales, business and technical training, and management. Nat has an MBA from Harvard Business School and a BA in International Relations from Pomona College.

Follow Nat on Twitter at @natdunn and Webucator at @webucator.

Justin Dunn (Editor)

Justin Dunn is a high school student with an eye for detail and a knack for learning new technologies. He is not only terrific at catching all of his father's extra and missing commas, he also serves as an excellent test reader for new programming books. His father is incredibly grateful to him for his editing help.

Class Files

Download the class files used in this book at https://www.webucator.com/class-files/index.cfm?versionId=4904.

Errata

Corrections to errors in the book can be found at https://www.webucator.com/books/errata.cfm.

Acknowledgments

- to **the phenomenal trainers** at Webucator.
- to **our many students**, who make it possible for us to keep playing with the technologies we love and learning to love new ones as they emerge.
- to **Dan Salamida** for designing the book cover.
- to **Will Vincent** and his excellent Django books and tutorials (available at learndjango.com).
- to all the hard work the Django team does. You can join Webucator in supporting them at `https://www.djangoproject.com/fundraising`.

And Thank You!

We appreciate you reading this book. We have some bonus material for you:

Go to `https://offers.webucator.com/actionable-django` to download a PDF with color images of all the screenshots used in this book.

Who is Webucator?

Customized Instructor-Led Training Services

The *Actionable* books are based on courseware Webucator has used since 2003 to train tens of thousands of people from thousands of organizations. For a partial list of our clients, see www.webucator.com/about-us/client-list.cfm.

Private Classes

Webucator offers onsite training throughout the world. We send an expert instructor to your location to deliver the class in person. Our classes can be customized to meet the specific needs of your team.

For disperse groups within an organization, Webucator can deliver private live online classes via a web conference.

Public Live Online Classes

Webucator's public instructor-led online classes provide the opportunity to learn the latest technologies from top experts without leaving the home or office. Most of our public instructor-led online classes are delivered from 10:00AM to 5:00PM Eastern Time via a live web conference.

Classes are hands-on. For each lesson, the instructor explains new concepts, shows a demo and answers questions. Then, students do an exercise with the instructor available for help. During the exercises, the instructor can (with your permission) see your computer, so they can provide one-on-one assistance as needed. After students complete the exercise, the instructor reviews the solution and answers questions. The process is repeated for each lesson.

Benefits

Webucator training stands out from the competition.

- **All Classes are Guaranteed-To-Run.** Classes never cancel. Classes run with one student.
- **Small Class Size.** We keep classes small. Public classes typically have 3-6 students.
- **Free Retake Options.** Students can come back to retake their class again at no charge. There's no time limit. Come back anytime and review!
- **Customization Options.** Our instructors tailor the class to meet students' needs. In public classes, instructors often discuss extra topics or stay after class to offer one-on-one help. For private classes, you may create your own custom outline from our class listings at no charge.
- **Post-Class Training.** We include free self-paced courses with many of our classes, enabling students to continue their learning after class.
- **Microsoft Certified Partner (CPLS).** We offer hundreds of Official Curriculum and Microsoft-approved courses.
- **Registered Education Provider (R.E.P.) with PMI.** PMI certification prep classes are available and PDUs can be earned by taking Webucator classes.
- **Competitive pricing.** Webucator offers high-quality training within your budget.

Actionable

adj.

1. ~~Giving cause for legal action: an actionable statement.~~
2. ~~Relating to or being information that allows a decision to be made or action to be taken.~~
3. **Capable of being put into practice.**

Source: https://ahdictionary.com/word/search.html?q=actionable

In this book, we cover material that you will be able to immediately put into practice.

Table of Contents

HOW TO READ THIS BOOK
(DON'T SKIP THIS)

"That Anne-girl improves all the time, ...she makes me love her and I like people who make me love them. It saves me so much trouble in making myself love them."

– *Anne of Green Gables, Lucy Maud Montgomery*

I believe that you will feel about Django, like Miss Barry feels about "that Anne-girl" – that you didn't have to work hard to make yourself love it. Django does so much of the work for you that *it* makes you love it. My hope is that this book will also play a role in building that relationship.

While I hope this book will eventually serve as a good reference for you, I didn't write it with that intention in mind. Rather, this book is a "course" on Django. The idea is for you to start at the beginning and work your way through to the end.

This is a Django book for Python developers. The better you know Python, the easier it will be to learn Django. Conversely, one of the great things about learning Django is that it will help you improve your Python skills. The Django framework is written beautifully and you have full access to the source code. We encourage you to dig into that code to see why things work the way they do and to learn how you can customize your site to work exactly how you want it to work.

Django is magical. That magic makes it easy to get started quickly. But it also can make it easy to get a little (or a lot) confused about how things happen. And when something goes wrong, it can be hard to figure out why. I don't promise that learning Django will always be easy. Some parts are pretty easy and some parts are pretty hard. Be patient with yourself. Pretend you're the teacher as well as the student. When the student fails, the good teacher doesn't insult or chastise. The good teacher encourages. The good teacher knows that failure is a part of learning and that overcoming failure is exciting and leads to more learning. So, be a good teacher and treat yourself well.

But be a good student too. When reading this book, you should be sitting at your computer. When you first begin, plan to spend at least three uninterrupted hours. You should do your best to get through the **Getting Started with Django** lesson in the first sitting. Go through the book slowly and methodically. Read every demo carefully. Work through every exercise. You cannot learn to code through reading alone. You must practice.

❖ What You Should Know Before You Read This Book

Django is used to create websites, and a website is created using many different languages and frameworks. As I already mentioned, you should know Python before tackling Django. If you don't know Python, check out my `Actionable Python` book on Amazon.

In addition to Python, experience with the following technologies will serve you well as you learn Django:

- HTML
- CSS
- JavaScript
- Bootstrap
- SQL

All of these technologies are used in parts of this book. Prior experience with them is not required, but it will come in handy.

LESSON 1

Setting Up Your Computer

Topics Covered

☑ Getting the demo and exercise files.

☑ Installing software.

The mechanic, who wishes to do his work well, must first sharpen his tools.

– *Confucius*

We're here to help!

Setting up a computer for development can be frustrating. If you run into problems during the setup, email actionable@webucator.com. Please include specifics (e.g., your operating system details and any errors you are getting). Screenshots of the error you're getting can also help us to diagnose the problem.

1.1. Demo and Exercise Files

To get started, create a new folder named `Webucator` on your computer wherever you want, but make sure you remember where it is. Then, download the demo and exercise files[1] that you will use throughout these lessons and unzip them into the `Webucator` folder you created.

This will create a `ClassFiles` folder in the `Webucator` folder. Rename the `ClassFiles` folder `Django`.

1. `https://www.webucator.com/class-files/index.cfm?versionId=4904`

The structure should look like this:

- `Webucator`
  - `Django`
    - `projects` – This folder just contains a placeholder file. You will create some Django projects within it.
    - `solutions` – This folder contains completed code for each lesson. When you finish a lesson, you can compare your code with the code found here.
    - `starter-code` – We will often reference files in this directory. In most cases, this will be to save you typing out long pieces of code. These references will usually be in footnotes, so be on the watch for them.

1.2. Visual Studio Code

We use Visual Studio Code for Django development and we recommend that you do too, at least while working through these lessons, as it will make it easier for you to follow along with the many demos and exercises.

1. Visit `https://code.visualstudio.com` and download Visual Studio Code for your operating system.
2. Install Visual Studio Code:
   A. **Windows instructions**: `https://code.visualstudio.com/docs/setup/windows`
   B. **Mac instructions**: `https://code.visualstudio.com/docs/setup/mac`
   C. **Linux instructions**: `https://code.visualstudio.com/docs/setup/linux`
3. Create a folder somewhere on your computer for storing Visual Studio Code workspaces. Name the folder `vs-code-workspaces` or something similar.
4. Open Visual Studio Code.
5. From the **File** menu, select **Save Workspace As...**

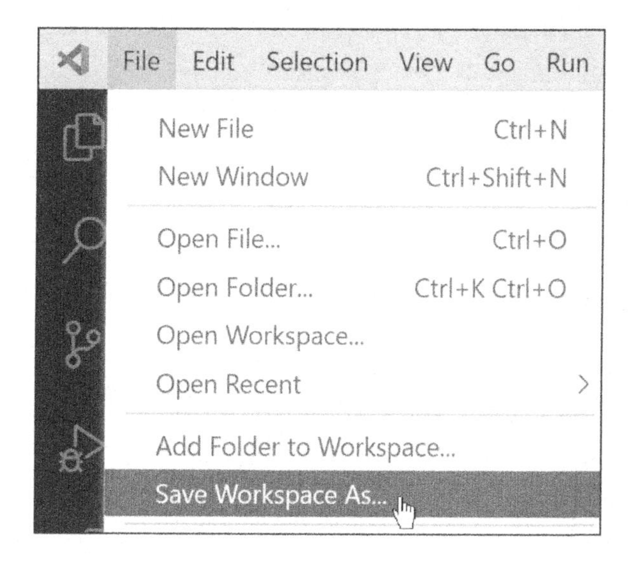

6. Save the workspace as `webucator-django` within the workspaces folder you created earlier:

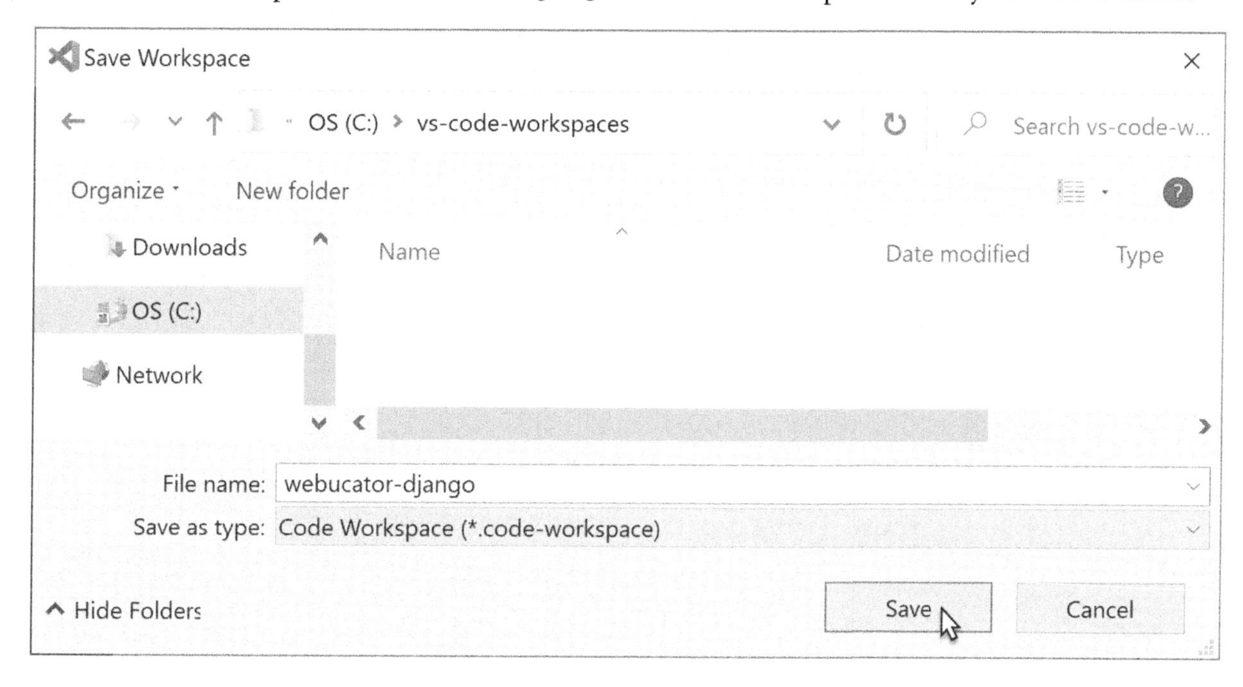

7. If Visual Studio Code's **Explorer** panel isn't open, open it by clicking the files icon in the upper left. Then click the **Add Folder** button:

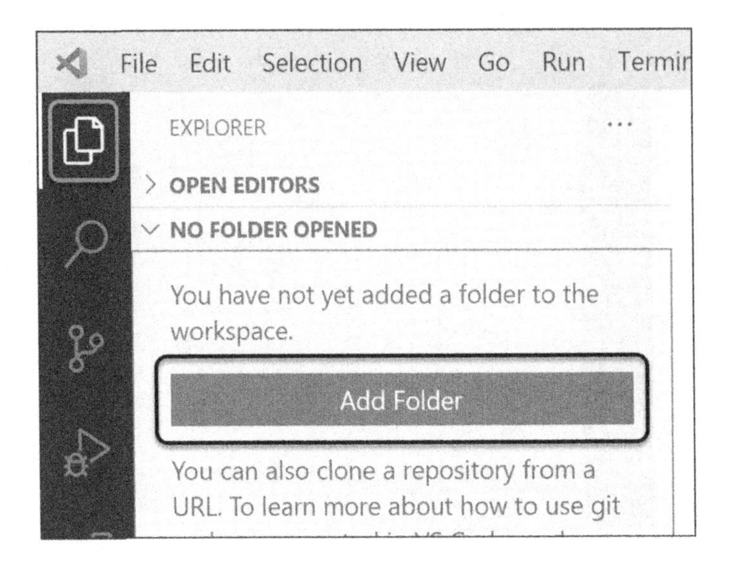

8. Select the `Django` folder (the one you renamed from `ClassFiles`) and click **Add**:

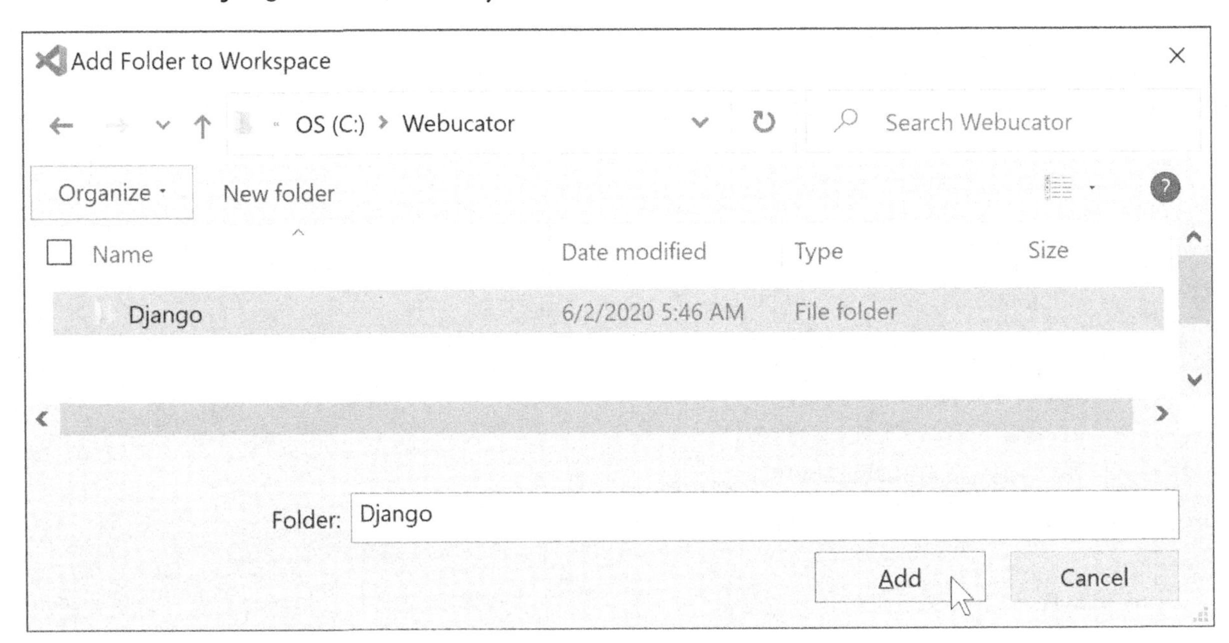

9. You will now see the `Django` folder in Visual Studio Code's **Explorer** panel:

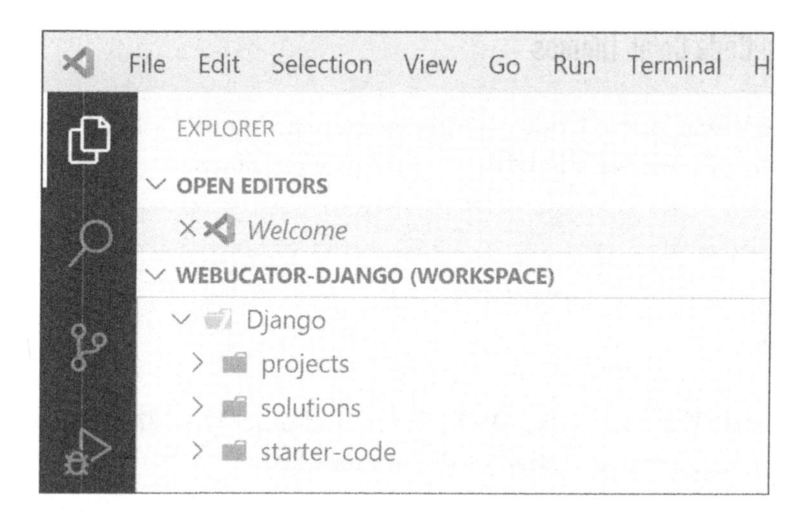

❖ 1.2.1. The Python Extension

Visual Studio Code has many freely available extensions for different programming languages. Python developers should install Microsoft's Python extension. As shown in the screenshot that follows:

1. Click the **Extensions** icon (below the bug) on the left of the **Explorer** panel.
2. Search for "Python".
3. If it doesn't show that the extension is already installed, click the **Install** button.

❖ 1.2.2. Visual Studio Code Color Themes

You can customize the Visual Studio Code color theme by selecting **File > Preferences > Color Theme**. The default is a dark theme. We use a light theme for our screenshots.

1.3. Running Python

Python runs on Microsoft Windows, Mac OS X, Linux, and other Unix-like systems. The first thing to do is to make sure you have a recent version of Python installed:

1. Open the terminal in Visual Studio Code by pressing Ctrl+` or selecting **New Terminal** from the **Terminal** menu.
2. Run `python -V`:

```
…/Webucator/Django> python -V
    Python 3.8.5
```

If you have Python 3.7 or later, you are all set, though we recommend you get the latest version, which is 3.8.5 at the time of this writing.

You can download Python for free at `https://www.python.org/downloads/`. After running through the installer, run `python -V` at the terminal again to make sure Python installed correctly.

Python Versions on Macs

Your Mac will likely have a version of Python 2 already installed. After you install Python 3, you may find that running `python -V` still shows the Python 2 version. In that case, try running `python3 -V`. That should output the version of Python 3 that you have. If it does, then you should use the `python3` command instead of the `python` command to run Python 3.

If you would prefer to be able to use the `python` command for Python 3 (and who wouldn't), visit `https://www.webucator.com/blog/2020/02/mapping-python-to-python-3-on-your-mac/` to see how you can map `python` to `python3`.

Conclusion

Although there will be additional software to install later on, your computer should now be all set for viewing and editing the files in this book.

LESSON 2

Getting Started with Django

Topics Covered

☑ Setting up a virtual environment.

☑ Installing Django.

☑ Creating your first Django website.

> And that he should be stirred by it marked the completeness with which he harked back through the ages of fire and roof to **the raw beginnings** of life in the howling ages.
>
> – *The Call of the Wild, Jack London*

Introduction

In this lesson, you will create a virtual environment and install Django within it. You will then create your first Django website.

2.1. Welcome to the Server-side

If you are already familiar with server-side web development and how web servers work, you can skip to Creating a Virtual Environment (see page 15).

Django is a Python web framework, which means that it's just Python. When you create a Django application, you will be using the Python language and any languages used in the static pages you send to the client: usually HTML, CSS, and JavaScript. Before learning Django or any server-side programming framework, you should be familiar with creating basic static websites using HTML and CSS. These client-side programming languages are executed by the browser, but the browser needs to get those pages somehow. Generally, they are delivered by a server. For static websites, the server will simply fetch and deliver those pages. For dynamic websites, some magic gets done on the server, which could affect the content of the pages returned.

❖ 2.1.1. What is a web server?

The first step to understanding server-side programming is to understand how a web server works. The following diagram shows how a web server delivers static pages, such as HTML, CSS, JavaScript, image, audio, video, and PDF files, all of which browsers have a built-in way of handling; and other files that can be downloaded but not handled by the browser, such as Microsoft Word documents, zip files, and executables. All these files, the ones the browser displays and the ones it downloads, are *static*, meaning they are fetched by the web server and returned to the client without any processing on the server.

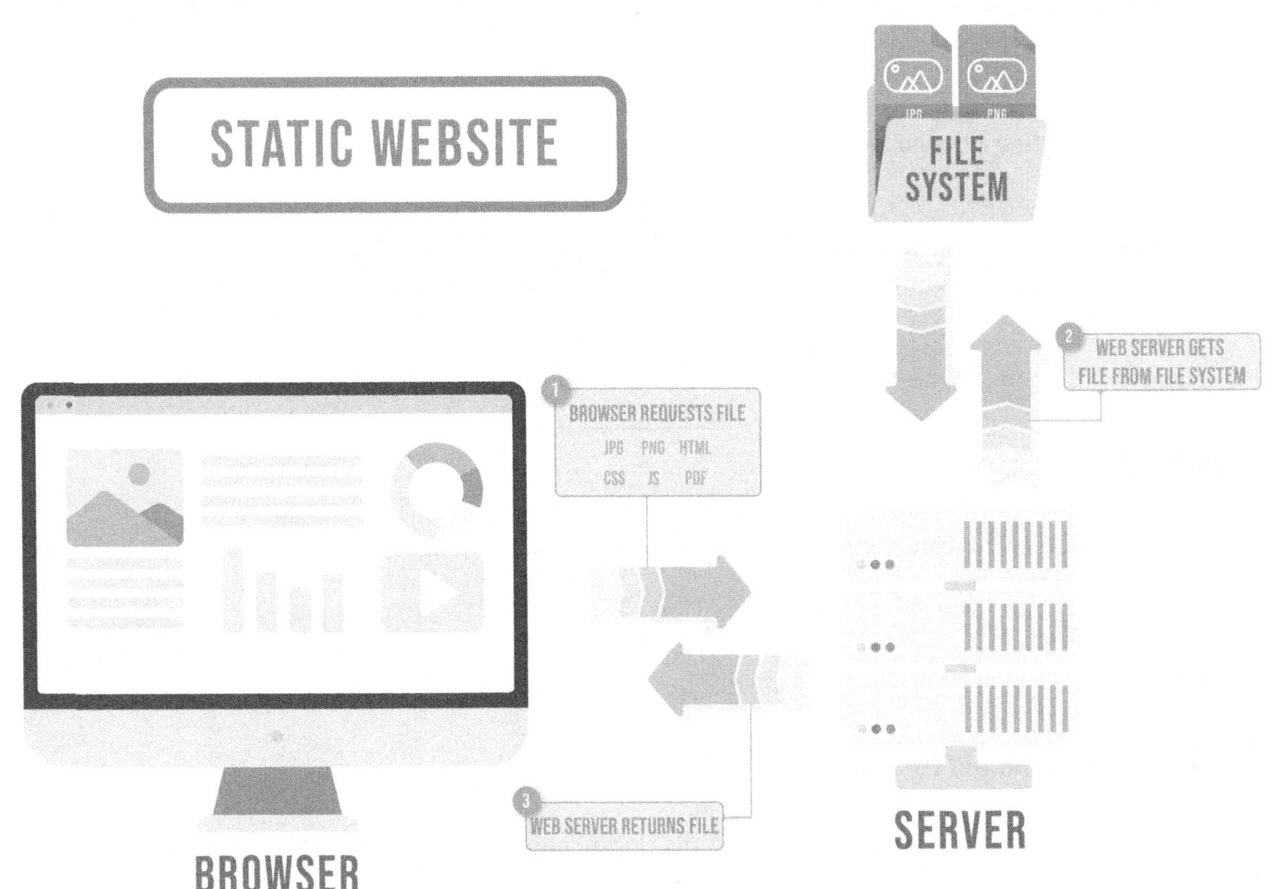

❖ 2.1.2. Dynamic Websites

Dynamic websites do more than just fetch and return files. They have software on the server that reviews the client request before deciding what to do. Depending on the client request, the server may just return a static file or it may perform any number of processes before returning a dynamically created file to the client. Here are some examples of what a dynamic site might do when it receives a request:

1. Perform a database search and return a list of search results.
2. Log a user into a website by checking the database for the user's credentials.
3. Redirect the user to a login page if the user requests a members-only page.
4. Record a user's support request in a database, email the user a friendly we-will-be-in-touch-soon message and the auto-generated support ticket number, email the support team letting them know a new request has come in, and return a dynamically created HTML page with a friendly we-will-be-in-touch-soon message and the auto-generated support ticket number.

Web servers can have access to all sorts of software on the computer on which they sit and can even reach across networks to make requests of other servers, so the variety of tasks they can perform is infinite. Follow the numbers in the following diagram to see how a dynamic website works:

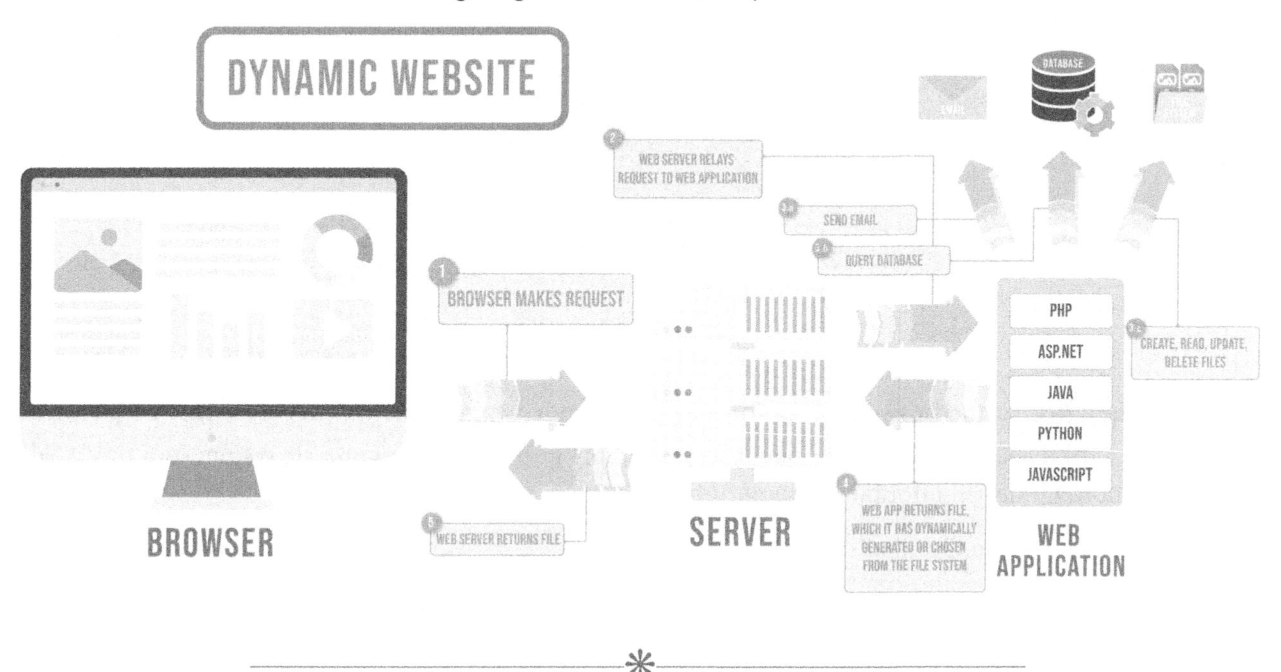

2.2. Google Chrome DevTools: Network Tab

The Google Chrome DevTools' **Network** tab shows which files are delivered when the browser makes a request. Let's first take a look at what it shows when you request a file from your local file system without going through a server:

1. Open `starter-code/getting-started/no-server/hello-world.html` from your class files in Google Chrome:

   The URL in the browser's location bar should not begin with "`http`." If it does begin with "`http`," close the file and re-open it by navigating to the folder in your file system (not in Visual Studio Code) and double-clicking on it.

2. Open Chrome DevTools:

   A. Click on the three-vertical-dots icon in the upper right of Google Chrome.

   B. Select **More Tools**.

   C. Select **Developer Tools**.

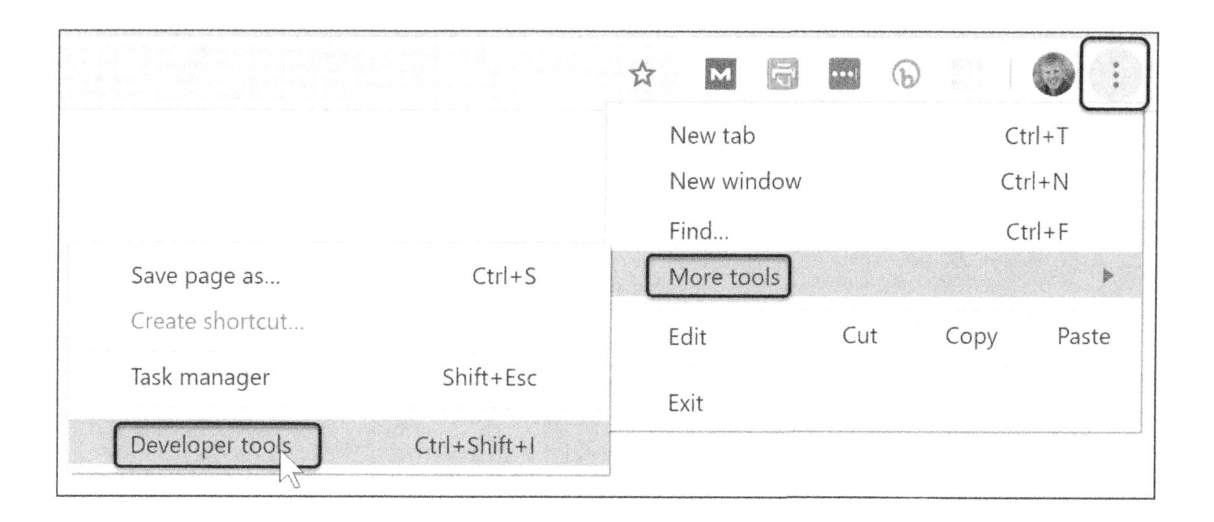

3. The tools will usually be docked on the right or bottom of your screen. Select the **Network** tab:

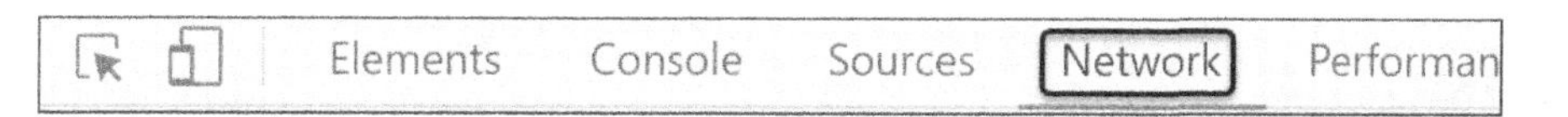

4. Now reload the page and look at the **Network** tab (make sure **All** is selected):

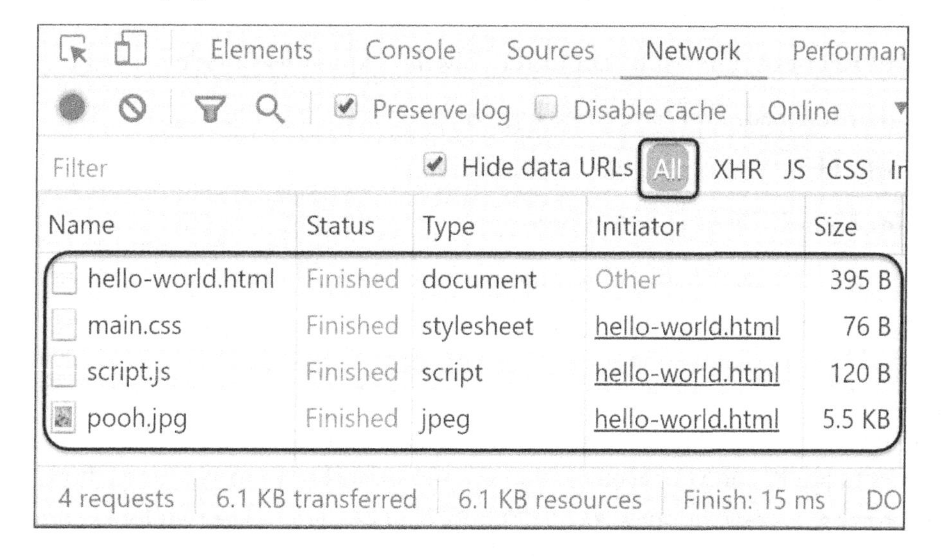

This shows what documents were delivered to the browser, their status, what type of documents they were, and what initiated the delivery.

5. By way of comparison, here are the same static files delivered from a web server:

Name	Status	Type	Initiator	Size
hello-world.html	200	document	Other	712 B
main.css	200	stylesheet	hello-world.html	390 B
script.js	200	script	hello-world.html	449 B
pooh.jpg	304	text/plain	hello-world.html	243 B

The only difference is the **Status** column. The web server sends back a status code to let the client know the status of the file. The `200` status code means that everything is fine. The `304` status code means that the file hasn't been modified since the last time it was requested, so the browser can use the version it has in cache if it has one.

❖ 2.2.1. Status Codes

Here are the most common status codes returned by a web server along with their meanings:

- `200` **OK**.
- `301` **Moved Permanently**. The file used to be at this URL, but it isn't anymore.
- `304` **Not Modified**. The file hasn't changed from the last time it was sent to the client.
- `400` **Bad Request**. Something about the way the request was made has baffled the web server.
- `401` **Unauthorized**. You have to be logged in to access this file.
- `403` **Forbidden**. You can't have this even if you are logged in.
- `404` **Not Found**. There is no file here.
- `500` **Internal Server Error**. Something went wrong on the server.
- `503` **Service Unavailable**. The web server is down or overloaded.

As the server-side developer, you have the ability to return these status codes and to decide what pages get returned with them. For example, it is common to return a special "404 Page Not Found" page when the user navigates to a URL on your website that doesn't exist. For example, to see how Google handles 404 pages, visit `https://www.google.com/nopage`. You will get a page that looks something like this:

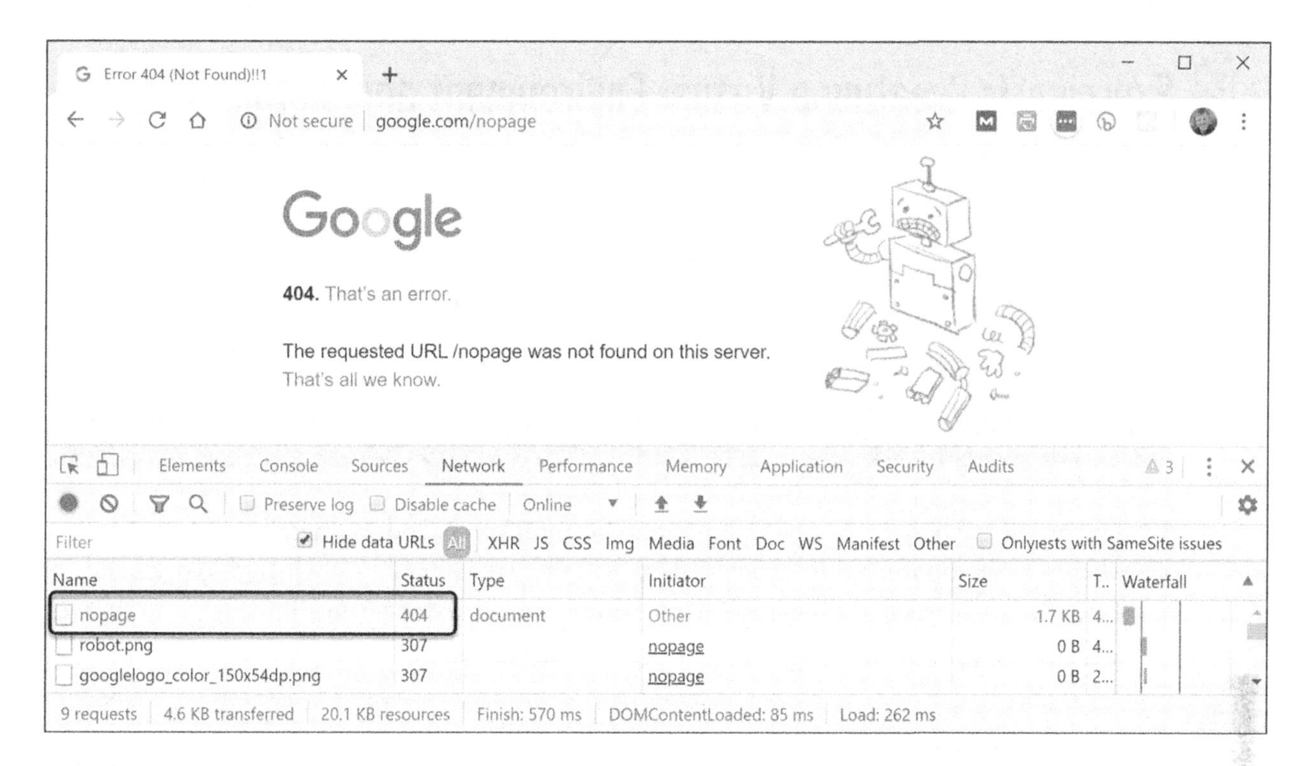

Notice the `404` status on the **Network** tab.

2.3. Creating the Virtual Environment

A virtual environment provides a self-contained directory tree with its own Python installation and additional packages necessary for the project(s) being done in that environment. As such, scripts can be run in a virtual environment that have dependencies that are different from those in other development projects that may be running in the standard environment or in separate virtual environments. As you are likely to work on Python projects that do not involve Django, when working on a Django project, you should install Django within a virtual environment.

Exercise 1: Creating a Virtual Environment and Installing Django

15 to 25 minutes

To create a virtual environment, you will use Python's built-in venv module.

1. Open a terminal at the root of your Django workspace in Visual Studio Code by selecting **New Terminal** from the **Terminal** menu.

Prompt Text

The prompt text varies by operating system, terminal type, and settings. To make it clear where you should run a command from, we will show the directory at which the command is run, preceded by that directory's parent directory, preceded by an ellipsis (e.g., …). We will end the prompt with right angle bracket (>) as follows:

```
…/parent-directory/current-directory> command arguments
```

Run the following to use the venv module to create a virtual environment in a .venv[2] folder:

```
…/Webucator/Django> python -m venv .venv
```

This will create and populate a new .venv directory.

2. Take a look at the directory contents, which should look something like this:

Windows

```
.venv
    Include
    Lib
    Scripts
    pyvenv.cfg
```

2. The period before the folder name is used to indicate that this is a special folder that is not part of the code you are writing yourself.

Mac / Linux

- .venv
  - bin
  - include
  - lib
  - pyvenv.cfg

The contents will differ by operating system. Included in this directory is a `Scripts` (Windows) or `bin` (Mac) folder that contains the `python` executable file and scripts for activating the virtual environment.

3. To work within your virtual environment, you must first activate it. The command for activating a virtual environment varies by operating system. At the terminal, run one of the following:

Windows

```
…/Webucator/Django> .venv\Scripts\activate
```

Mac / Linux

```
…/Webucator/Django> source .venv/bin/activate
```

4. When the virtual environment is activated, its name will always appear enclosed in parentheses before the prompt. For example:

```
(.venv) …/Webucator/Django>
```

If you don't see the virtual environment name in parentheses before the prompt, you are not in the virtual environment.

5. You can now invoke the Python interpreter and/or install additional packages (using `pip`) within the virtual environment. Install Django:

```
(.venv) …/Webucator/Django> pip install django
```

6. Check to see what version of Django you installed:

```
(.venv) …/Webucator/Django> python -m django --version
3.1
```

7. Django is a standard Python package, which you can import in Python just like any other Python package. Open Python interactive mode (by running `python` at the terminal) and use Django to check the version:

```
>>> import django
>>> django.get_version()
'3.1'
```

❖ E1.1. VS Code: Selecting the Python Interpreter

Now that you have created a virtual environment, you want to instruct Visual Studio Code to use this virtual environment for this workspace:

1. From the **View** menu, select **Command Palette** and enter "Python: Select Interpreter"

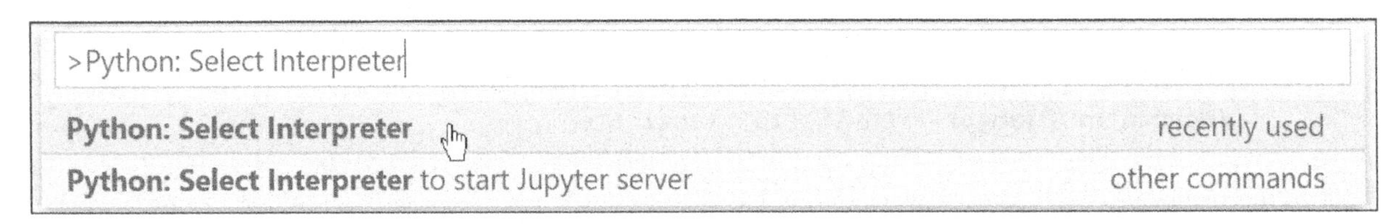

2. If you are given an option to select the folder or the entire workspace, select the entire workspace:

3. Select the interpreter for the virtual environment you just created:

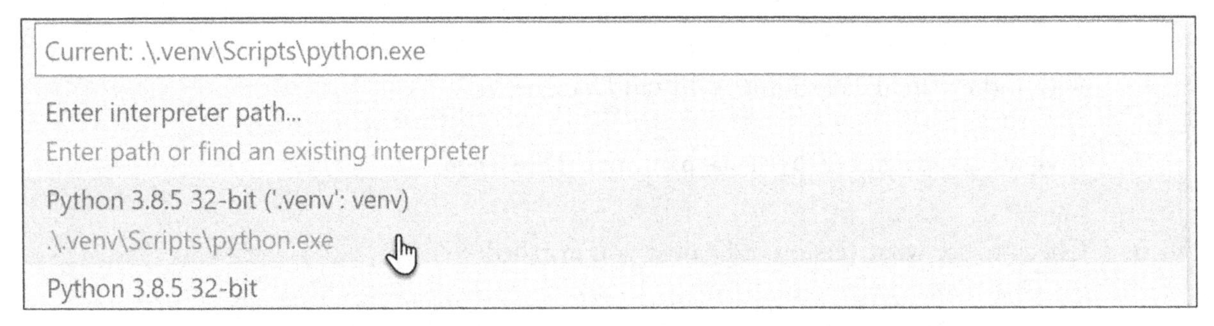

The Python interpreter in your virtual environment will now be used in new terminals.

2.4. Exploring the Django Source Code

Django is written in Python and the code is well documented. We will reference the Django source code throughout these lessons. The Django library is located within your virtual directory. When we point you to the Django source code, you should navigate to this directory:

- `.venv`
  - `Lib` (Windows) or `lib` (Mac)
    - `site-packages`
      - `django`

2.5. Creating a New Project

Django comes with `django-admin`, a command-line utility used for administrative tasks, such as creating a new project.

The steps for creating a new project in Django are (**Don't do this yet. Just read.**):

1. Create a new project directory. The name of this directory is unimportant.
2. Open that directory in the terminal.
3. Run:

    ```
    django-admin startproject package_name .
    ```

    where `package_name` is the name of the Python package for your new project.

Don't Forget the Dot

The dot (`.`) at the end of `django-admin startproject package_name .` indicates that the project should be created in the current directory. If you leave it off, a new project directory will be created with a nested folder that has the same name, which can be confusing.

It's time to create your first project!

Exercise 2: Hello, Django!

15 to 25 minutes

When a user browses to a page on a Django-based website, Python communicates with file systems, databases, and email servers as necessary, and then provides the web server with content (generally HTML) to return to the browser. Let's build your first Django project to see how it works.

1. Create a new `hello_proj` folder within the `projects` folder.
2. Open the new folder in the terminal and run the following command. **Be sure to include the dot at the end!**:

   ```
   (.venv) …/projects/hello_proj> django-admin startproject hello_django .
   ```

   This will create a new project within the `hello_proj` directory. The `hello_proj` folder will now contain the following:

   - `hello_proj` – The project folder.
     - `hello_django` – The Python package for your new project.
       - `__init__.py` – An empty file that turns the directory into a package.
       - `asgi.py` – An entry-point for ASGI-compatible web servers. We will not be using this.
       - `settings.py` – The project's settings file.
       - `urls.py` – The project's root URL configuration file, also known as a *URLConf* file.
       - `wsgi.py` – An entry-point for WSGI-compatible web servers. It is the interface between the web server and the Python/Django application you create. While this file is essential, you won't have to do anything with it. Just leave it be and let it do its magic.
     - `manage.py` – The Django administration file for your project.
3. Run the following command to start up the server:

   ```
   (.venv) …/projects/hello_proj> python manage.py runserver
   ```

4. In your browser, visit `http://127.0.0.1:8000` to see the default page for your new project. A quick way to open that page is to **Ctrl+click** on the URL in the terminal:

```
August 04, 2020 - 05:57:37
Django version 3.1, using setti Follow Link (ctrl + click) tings'
Starting development server at http://127.0.0.1:8000/
Quit the server with CTRL-BREAK.
```

The page should look like this:

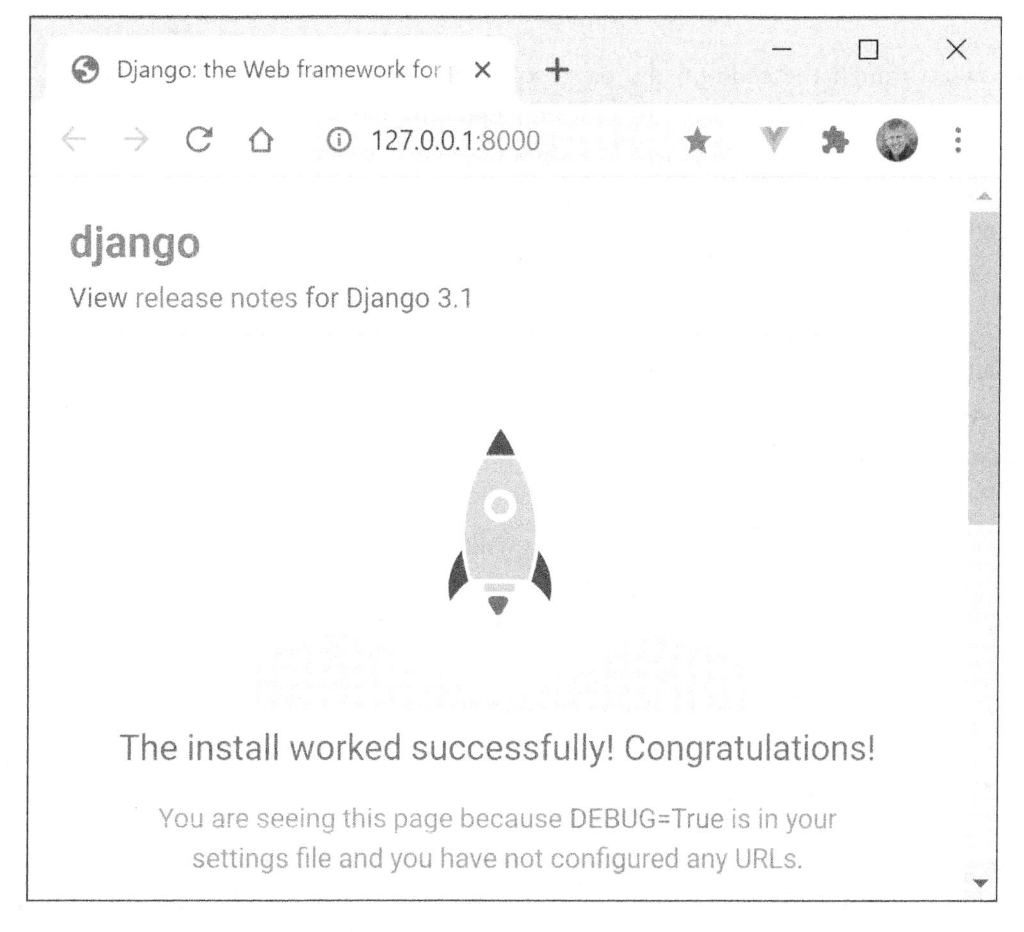

Where does this page come from? It was installed as part of the Django installation. Let's find the file…

5. In your editor, open `default_urlconf.html` from:

```
Django/.venv/Lib/site-packages/django/views/templates/
```

The file begins like this:

```
{% load i18n %}
<!doctype html>
{% get_current_language_bidi as LANGUAGE_BIDI %}
<html{% if LANGUAGE_BIDI %} dir="rtl"{% endif %}>
    <head>
        <meta charset="utf-8">
        <title>{% translate "Django: the Web framework for perfectionists…
```

6. Browse through the code on the page. You will see that it is a standard HTML page with embedded CSS. In addition, it includes Django template variables (denoted with double curly braces) and Django template tags (denoted with curly braces and percentage signs).

   Django Template Variable

   ```
   {{ variable_name }}
   ```

   Django Template Tag

   ```
   {% tag_name %}
   ```

   You will learn more about both later.

7. Search the file for "Congratulations!" You will find it in an `h2` element:

   ```
   <h2>{% translate "The install worked successfully! Congratulations!" %}</h2>
   ```

8. On the line above that `h2` element, add the following code:

   ```
   <h1>Hello, Django!</h1>
   ```

Never do this!

In practice, you should never change any of the files in the django package. We are doing this here only to demonstrate how it works.

9. Save the file, and return to the browser where `http://127.0.0.1:8000` is loaded. Refresh the page. It should have your "Hello, Django!" header:

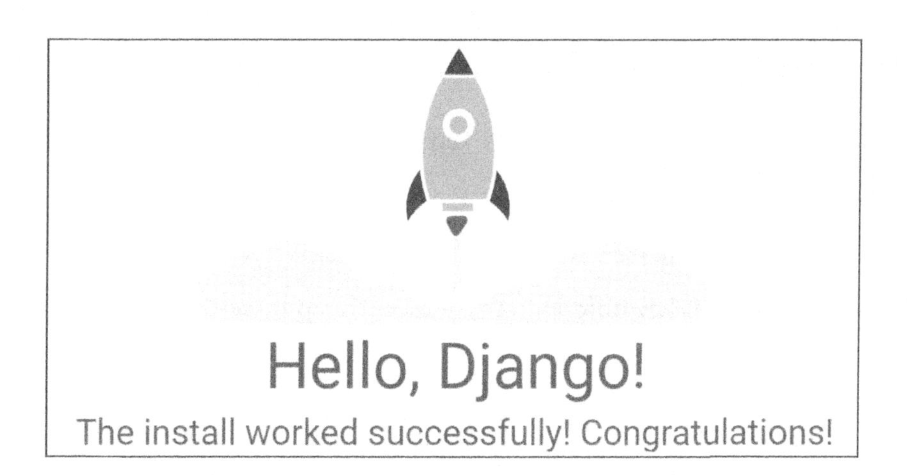
Hello, Django!
The install worked successfully! Congratulations!

10. Close the `default_urlconf.html` file. You won't need it anymore.
11. At the terminal, press Ctrl+C to stop the server.

❖ E2.1. Under the Hood

One of the great things about Django is that it makes difficult tasks easy. It does this by hiding a lot of magic "under the hood." We've shown you how to modify the default home page only to demonstrate how some of that magic is happening. In practice, you won't change `default_urlconf.html` or any of the files within the Django library itself. Instead, you will create new "apps" within your Django project. Each of these apps will represent a portion of (or serve a specific function for) your website. Every Django project has at least one app.

2.6. Settings

Each new Django project comes with pre-defined settings, which are stored in the `settings.py` file within the Python package folder. For your project, that's `hello_django/settings.py`. Open that file in your editor and browse through it. Notice that it contains a series of Python constants.[3] By default, the `settings.py` file contains no logic, but it is a standard Python file, so, as you will see later, you can add logic to it.

3. Python doesn't have real constants. These are really variables that aren't meant to be changed after they are set.

❖ 2.6.1. Default Settings for New Django Projects

Here, we provide a brief description of each of the settings included with new Django projects. We will cover many of these in detail later on.

- `BASE_DIR` – The absolute path to the project directory.
- `SECRET_KEY` – A secret key unique to the project. Keep it secret!
- `DEBUG` – Set to `True` to display detailed errors in the browser. In production, `DEBUG` should always be set to `False`.
- `ALLOWED_HOSTS` – A list of domains or IP addresses that can serve this site.
- `INSTALLED_APPS` – A list of apps in the project.
- `MIDDLEWARE` – A list of components that affect Django's input/output processing.
- `ROOT_URLCONF` – The import path to the root URL configuration file. In the project you just created, this is set to `hello_django.urls`, which means it points to:

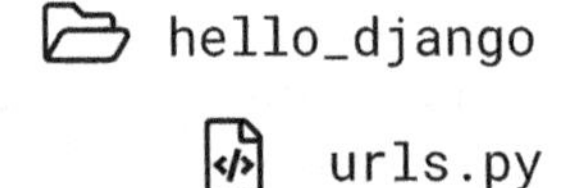

- `TEMPLATES` – A list of dictionaries containing settings for the template engines used by the project. More on this soon.
- `WSGI_APPLICATION` – The path to the WSGI application object used as a gateway between the application server and your Python code. You will typically leave this as is.
- `DATABASES` – A dictionary containing the databases used by the project. By default, a SQLite database is used. Later, you will set up a PosgreSQL database.
- `AUTH_PASSWORD_VALIDATORS` – A list of validators used to check new user passwords.
- `LANGUAGE_CODE` – The language code for the project.[4]
- `TIME_ZONE` – The time zone. In new projects, this will be set to "UTC".
- `USE_I18N` – Set to `True` to enable Django's translation system.
- `USE_L10N` – Set to `True` to use localized formatting of data (e.g., date formats[5]).
- `USE_TZ` – Set to `True` to use timezone-aware datetimes. This is generally what you want.
- `STATIC_URL` – The URL to use when referencing static files, such as CSS and JavaScript files and images.

---

4. See `http://www.i18nguy.com/unicode/language-identifiers.html` for a list of language codes.
5. `https://en.wikipedia.org/wiki/Date_format_by_country`

❖ 2.6.2. The Shell

As Django is used to create websites, you will often view the results of the code you write in a browser. However, it can be useful to interact with your Django code directly in Python interactive mode. To open a Python interpreter that is aware of your Django project, run:

```
(.venv) …/projects/hello_proj> python manage.py shell
```

With the shell open, you can import modules from your project. For example, to import all the settings variables in `settings.py`, run:

```
>>> from hello_django.settings import *
```

You can then look at different settings:

```
>>> BASE_DIR
WindowsPath('C:/Webucator/Django/projects/hello_proj')
>>> LANGUAGE_CODE
'en-us'
>>> ROOT_URLCONF
'hello_django.urls'
```

You will use the shell regularly throughout these lessons.

2.7. Django Apps

Before creating your own app, let's take a look at the apps that are included by default with a new Django project. You can print these out at the shell using Python. If it's not still open, open the Django shell:

```
(.venv) …/projects/hello_proj> python manage.py shell
```

Run the following code to loop through and print the apps in `INSTALLED_APPS`:

```
>>> from hello_django.settings import *
>>> for app in INSTALLED_APPS:
...     print(app)
...
django.contrib.admin
django.contrib.auth
django.contrib.contenttypes
django.contrib.sessions
django.contrib.messages
django.contrib.staticfiles
```

These apps come from the INSTALLED_APPS constant in `settings.py`. The following screenshot shows where the referenced apps are located in the Django library:

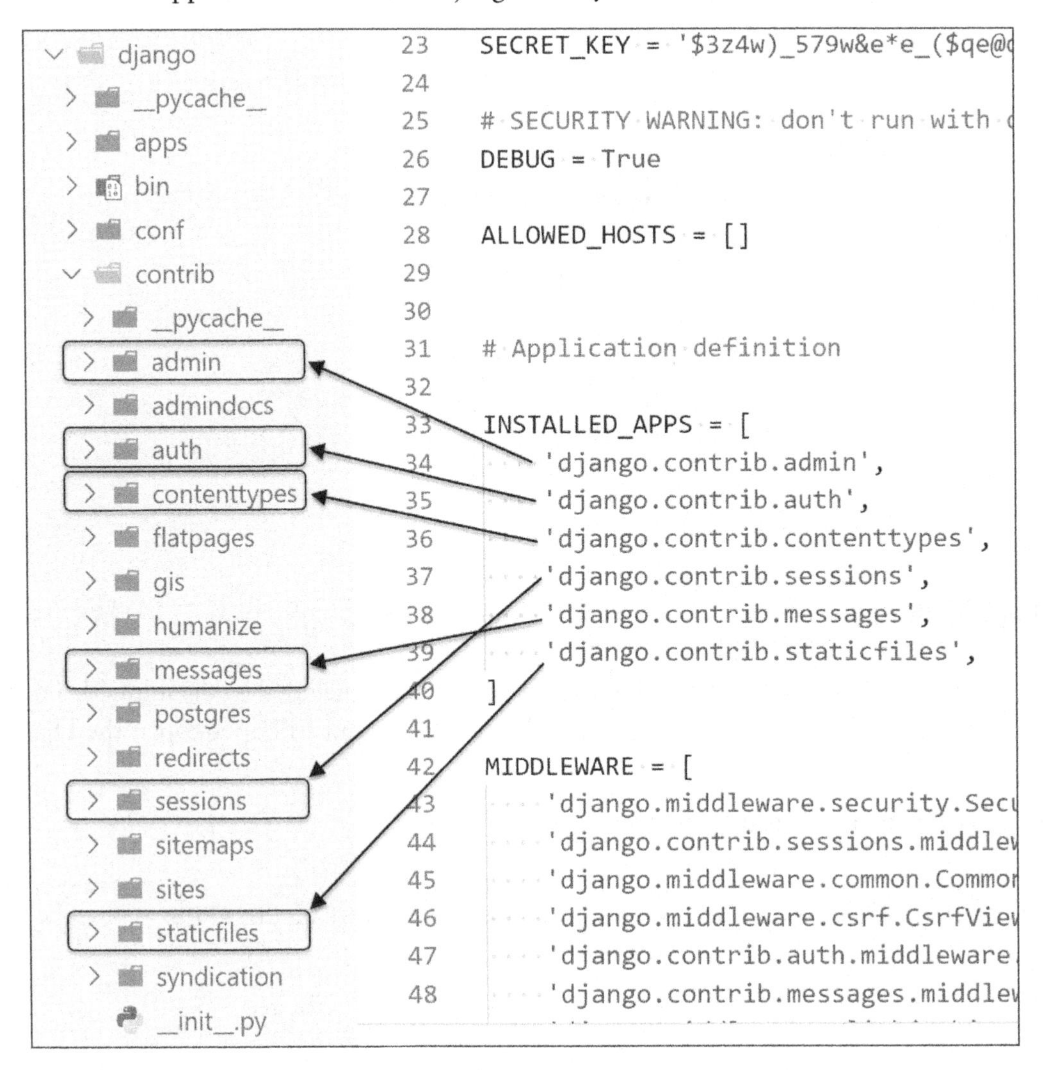

As you will soon see, each app that you create must be added to the `INSTALLED_APPS` list.

Exit the Django shell by running `exit()`:

```
>>> exit()
```

2.8. Creating a New App

The initial steps for creating an app in a Django project are (**Don't do this yet. Just read.**):

1. Create the scaffolding of the app by running:

   ```
   python manage.py startapp app_name
   ```

   where "app_name" is the name of the app.
2. Add the new application to the `INSTALLED_APPS` list.
3. Create one or more views. A view determines what happens when a user visits a page on the website.
4. Configure URLs. This is where you connect URLs to views, where you say: *when a user visits this URL, run this view.*
5. Create any necessary templates for the HTML code that renders the page. Most views will specify a template for rendering the page that is returned to the browser.

With those steps in mind, let's create your first app.

Exercise 3: First Django App

15 to 25 minutes

E3.1. Scaffolding

Make sure that you are in the `hello_proj` directory in the terminal and that you're not in Python interactive mode. Then run:

```
(.venv) …/projects/hello_proj> python manage.py startapp pages
```

This will create a new `pages` directory within `hello_proj` with the following contents:

- `pages`
  - `migrations` – Holds migration files that *automagically* update the database model based on changes in `models.py`.
  - `__init__.py` – An empty file that turns the directory into a package.
  - `admin.py` – For writing admin code.
  - `apps.py` – For writing application registration code.
  - `models.py` – For writing the data models.
  - `tests.py` – For writing tests.
  - `views.py` – For writing views.

E3.2. Installed Apps

You must add your new app to the `INSTALLED_APPS` list in the settings file. This will be your first modification to the settings file. As you modify this file, you should add comments to make it easier to read later on. It's a good idea to differentiate between what you have added and what was already there. Go ahead and add your new **pages** app to the `INSTALLED_APPS` list along with comments separating the built-in Django apps from the apps you created:

```
INSTALLED_APPS = [
    # Built-in Django apps
    'django.contrib.admin',
    'django.contrib.auth',
    'django.contrib.contenttypes',
    'django.contrib.sessions',
    'django.contrib.messages',
    'django.contrib.staticfiles',

    # Local apps
    'pages.apps.PagesConfig',
]
```

Notice the list ends with a comma. This is not required, but it is a common practice in the settings file to make it easier to add additional items to a list.

Legacy Django Projects (and tutorials)

If you work with Django projects that were written a while ago, or reference older tutorials or documentation, you may see local apps added to `INSTALLED_APPS` using just the app name (e.g., `'pages'` instead of `'pages.apps.PagesConfig'`). That was the old way, and while it still works, you should use the full dotted path to the `AppConfig` subclass.[6]

❖ E3.3. Views

Views are responsible for taking a web request, doing some magic, and then returning a web response. Views are created in the `views.py` file in the app folder.

1. Open `pages/views.py`.
2. By default, `render` is imported from `django.shortcuts`. It is a more common practice to use Django's built-in generic views, which are class-based. So, replace that import line with:

   ```
   from django.views.generic import TemplateView
   ```

6. https://docs.djangoproject.com/en/3.1/ref/applications/#configuring-applications

3. Below that, add the following class, which inherits from `TemplateView`:

   ```
   class HomePageView(TemplateView):
       template_name = 'home.html'
   ```

   This tells Django to load the `home.html` template when rendering the `HomePageView` view. The complete `views.py` file should now look like this:

Exercise Code 3.1: pages/views.py

```
1.  from django.views.generic import TemplateView
2.
3.  class HomePageView(TemplateView):
4.      template_name = 'home.html'
```

❖ E3.4. URLs

You want to render the `HomePageView` view when the user visits the root of your website, which is locally hosted at `http://127.0.0.1:8000/`. You are concerned with the part of that URL that follows the forward slash trailing the domain or IP Address (and port if specified). For the home page, that's simply an empty string:

URLs are configured in a *URLConf* file. The root (and currently only) URLConf file for your project is the `urls.py` file in the `hello_django` folder as specified in `settings.py` with the `ROOT_URLCONF` setting:

```
ROOT_URLCONF = 'hello_django.urls'
```

1. Open `hello_django/urls.py` in your editor. Notice that it contains the following list, which currently just has one item:

   ```
   urlpatterns = [
       path('admin/', admin.site.urls),
   ]
   ```

This path identifies Django's built-in admin site, which we will explore later (see page 199). At the top of the file, `admin` is imported from `django.contrib` and the `path()` function is imported from `django.urls`:

```
from django.contrib import admin
from django.urls import path
```

2. You need to add your own URL configurations to the `urlpatterns` list. There are different ways of doing this. The simplest approach is just to add a new path to the list. Add the following highlighted line of code:

```
urlpatterns = [
    path('admin/', admin.site.urls),
    path('', HomePageView.as_view()),
]
```

   This specifies that when a user visits `http://127.0.0.1:8000/` (with nothing trailing it), the `HomePageView` should be rendered as a view.

3. To make the `urls.py` module aware of `HomePageView`, you need to import it. Add the following line of code below the existing imports:

```
from pages.views import HomePageView
```

   You can remove the long comment at the beginning of the file.

4. The complete `urls.py` file should now look like this:

Exercise Code 3.2: hello_django/urls.py

```
1.  from django.contrib import admin
2.  from django.urls import path
3.
4.  from pages.views import HomePageView
5.
6.  urlpatterns = [
7.      path('admin/', admin.site.urls),
8.      path('', HomePageView.as_view()),
9.  ]
```

Give it a try to see how it works: if you have stopped the server, start it back up again by running the following command from the `hello_proj` directory:

```
(.venv) …/projects/hello_proj> python manage.py runserver
```

5. Now, navigate to `http://127.0.0.1:8000/`. You should see an error page like this one:

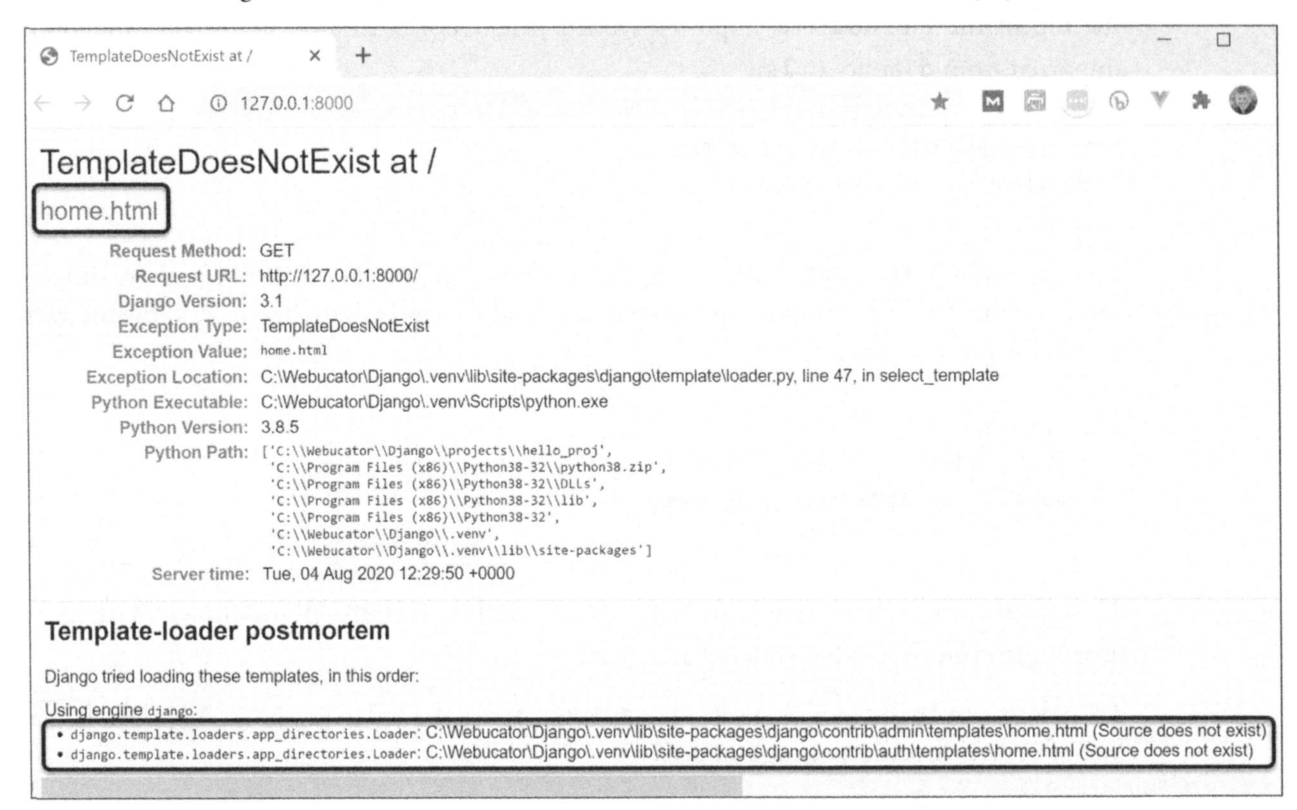

That tells you that Django has found your view and looked for `home.html`, but couldn't find it. It even tells you where it looked for the template – in the **admin** app and in the **auth** app:

- …`\.venv\lib\site-packages\django\contrib\`**`admin`**`\templates\home.html`
- …`\.venv\lib\site-packages\django\contrib\`**`auth`**`\templates\home.html`

You need to create the template and tell Django how to find it. You will do that in the next exercise.

Exercise 4: Templates

30 to 45 minutes

The settings file contains a `TEMPLATES` constant, which contains an empty `DIRS` list and an `APP_DIRS` boolean set to `True`:

```
TEMPLATES = [
    {
        'BACKEND': 'django.template.backends.django.DjangoTemplates',
        'DIRS': [],
        'APP_DIRS': True,
        ...
    },
]
```

The empty `DIRS` list, which you will soon add to, tells Django where to look for templates. If `APP_DIRS` is `True`, Django will also look in each app folder for a `templates` directory, which is what you want.

You want to create a project-level `templates` directory and tell Django to look for templates there too.

1. Create a new `templates` folder in the `hello_proj` directory.
2. Within this `templates` folder, create a `pages` folder. The project should now look like this:

```
hello_proj
    hello_django
    pages
    templates
        pages
    db.sqlite3
    manage.py
```

3. Within the new `pages` folder, create a `home.html` file with the following HTML code:[7]

7. **Don't want to type?** Copy from `starter-code/getting-started/home.html`.

Exercise Code 4.1: templates/pages/home.html

```
1.   <!DOCTYPE html>
2.   <html lang="en">
3.   <head>
4.   <meta charset="UTF-8">
5.   <meta name="viewport" content="width=device-width, initial-scale=1">
6.   <title>Hello, Django!</title>
7.   </head>
8.   <body>
9.   <p>Hello, Django!</p>
10.  </body>
11.  </html>
```

4. Add the following to the DIRS value of the dictionary in TEMPLATES:

```
'DIRS': [BASE_DIR / 'templates'],
```

To understand exactly what this does, open the shell in the project directory in a new terminal:

```
(.venv) …/projects/hello_proj> python manage.py shell
```

VS Code Tip

In Visual Studio Code, right-click on a folder in the **Explorer** panel and select **Open in Integrated Terminal** to open a new terminal:

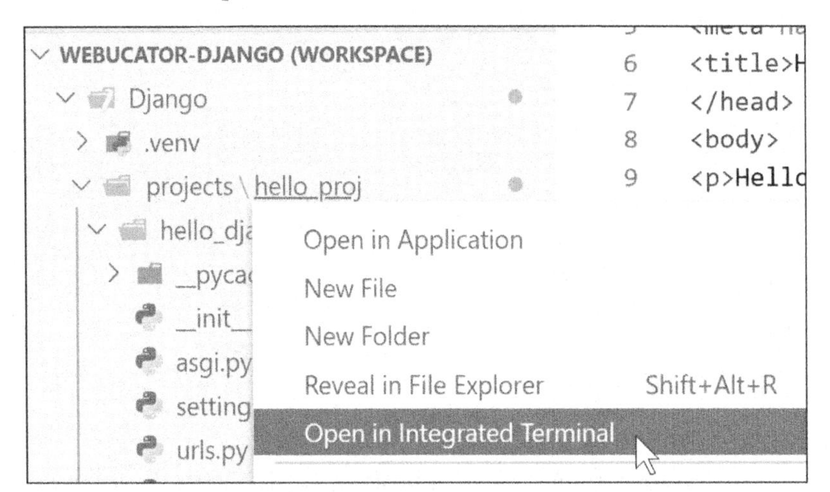

That way, you can leave the website running in the original terminal. You can then toggle between the two terminals using the dropdown menu:

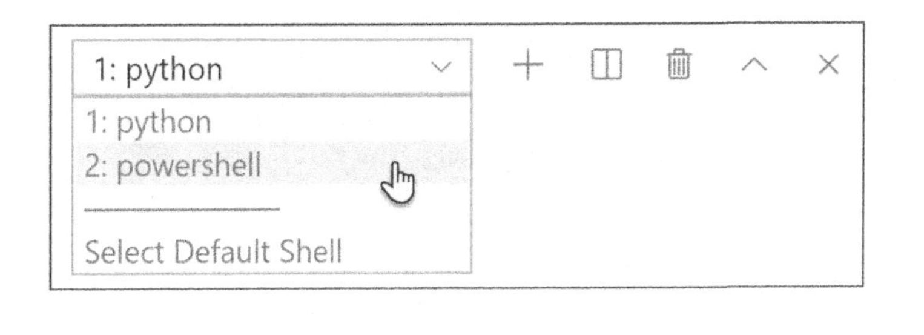

Then, import all the settings and inspect `TEMPLATES[0]['DIRS']`:

```
>>> from hello_django.settings import *
>>> TEMPLATES[0]['DIRS']
[WindowsPath('C:/Webucator/Django/projects/hello_proj/templates')]
```

The output will differ by operating system, but it will show the absolute path to the `templates` folder you just created. It will now search this directory for templates.

5. Return to the browser and refresh the home page. It will still return a `TemplateDoesNotExist` error, but now it shows that it also searched for the template in the new `templates` directory you specified in the settings:

   ```
   …\projects\hello_proj\templates\home.html
   ```

   It isn't finding the template, because you nested `home.html` within a `pages` directory within the `templates` directory. You did this to avoid conflicts, in case you create another app or include a third-party app that also has a `home.html` template.

6. To fix this, open `views.py` in the editor again and change the value of `template_name` to `'pages/home.html'`:

Exercise Code 4.2: pages/views.py

```
1.  from django.views.generic import TemplateView
2.
3.  class HomePageView(TemplateView):
4.      template_name = 'pages/home.html'
```

7. Return to the browser and refresh the home page again. It should now look like this:

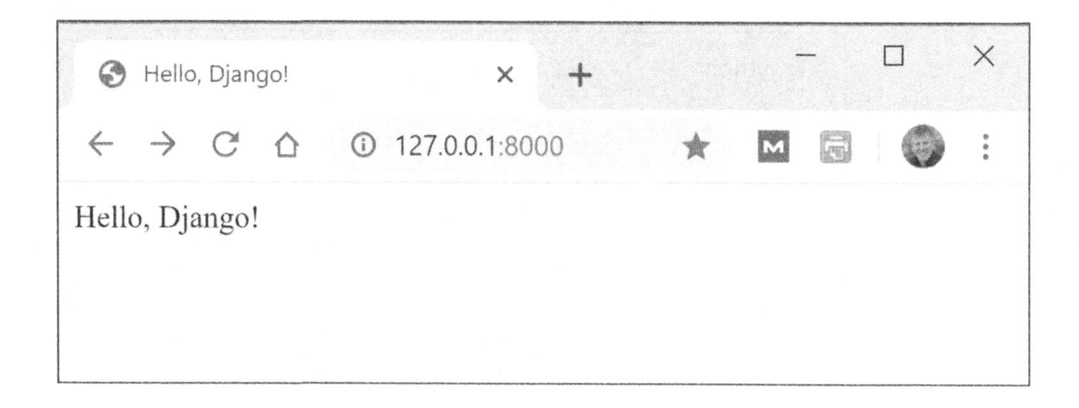

❖ E4.1. Template Inheritance

Django allows you to create a base template with named blocks that can be overridden by child templates:

1. Create a new `_base.html` file directly in the `templates` folder and copy and paste the code from `home.html` into it. The underscore in `_base.html` is used to indicate that this template is not meant to be used directly; instead, it is meant to be extended.
2. In `_base.html`, change the paragraph to an `h1` element and add a few `block` tags:

Exercise Code 4.3: templates/_base.html

```
1.  <!DOCTYPE html>
2.  <html lang="en">
3.  <head>
4.  <meta charset="UTF-8">
5.  <meta name="viewport" content="width=device-width, initial-scale=1">
6.  <title>{% block title %}{% endblock %} | Hello, Django!</title>
7.  </head>
8.  <body>
9.  <h1>{% block header %}Hello, Django!{% endblock %}</h1>
10. <main>
11.   {% block main %}{% endblock %}
12. </main>
13. </body>
14. </html>
```

Notice the file has three blocks defined and that only the `header` block contains default content:

A. `{% block title %}{% endblock %}`

B. `{% block header %}Hello, Django!{% endblock %}`

C. `{% block main %}{% endblock %}`

3. Replace the contents of `pages/home.html` with the following:

Exercise Code 4.4: templates/pages/home.html

```
1.   {% extends "_base.html" %}
2.
3.   {% block title %}Home{% endblock %}
4.   {% block main %}
5.     <p>Thank you for visiting our site!</p>
6.   {% endblock %}
```

4. Return to your browser and refresh the page. It should now look like this:

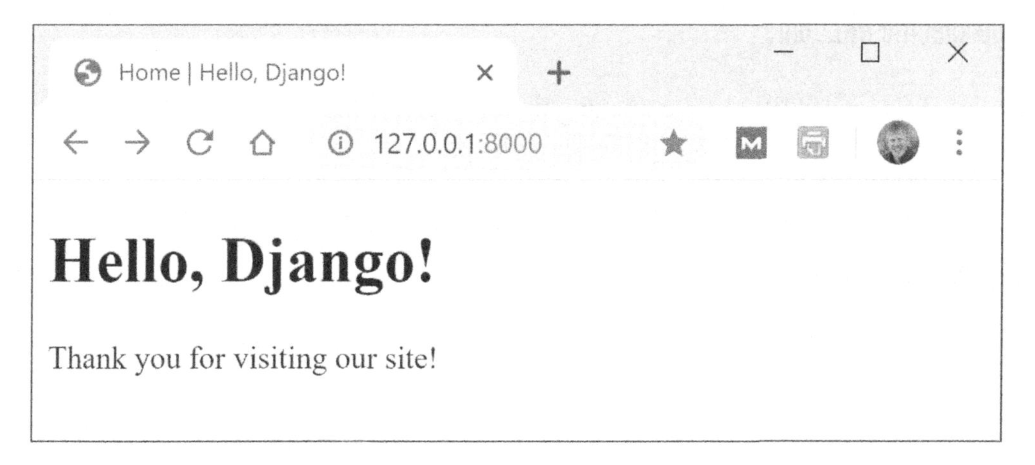

Notice that the `title` and `main` blocks are replaced with content from `home.html`, but the `header` block from `_base.html` is used as is, because there is no `header` block overriding it in `home.html`.

5. Add a `header` block to `home.html` between the `title` and `main` blocks:

```
{% block header %}Welcome!{% endblock %}
```

6. Refresh the page again. "Welcome!" should have replaced "Hello, Django!" like this:

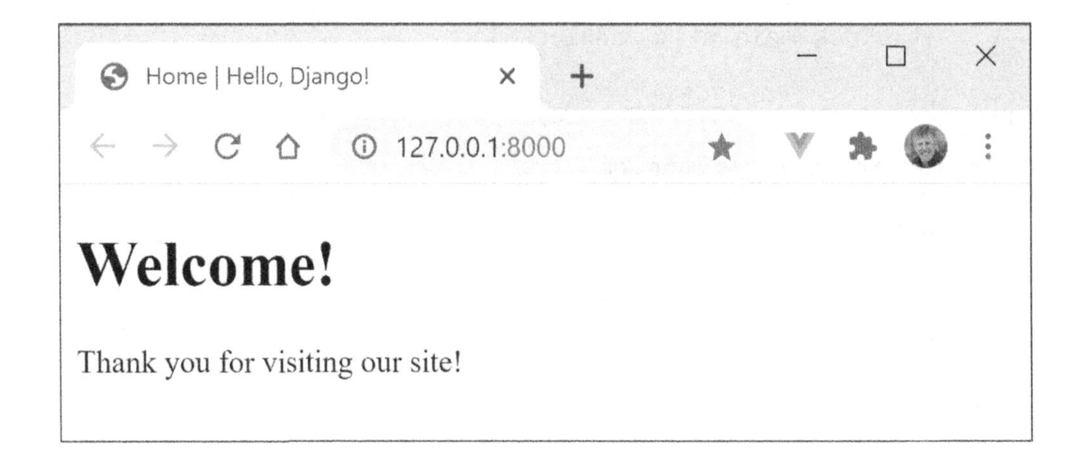

❖ E4.2. App-specific URLConfs

A website can have a lot of URLs and managing them all in one file can quickly become unwieldy. It is a common practice to create a URLConf file for each app.

1. Create a `urls.py` file within the `pages` directory with the following code:

   Exercise Code 4.5: pages/urls.py

   ```
   1.  from django.urls import path
   2.
   3.  from .views import HomePageView
   4.
   5.  app_name = 'pages'
   6.  urlpatterns = [
   7.      path('', HomePageView.as_view(), name='homepage'),
   8.  ]
   ```

   For the most part, you have just moved some of the content from the root URLConf file to your new app URLConf file. You have also added a new line of code:

   ```
   app_name = 'pages'
   ```

   This adds a *namespace* to the URLConf. The namespace is used to avoid conflicts when paths from different apps within your project have the same name. More on this in a moment.

2. Modify the `urls.py` file within the `hello_django` directory as follows:

   A. Import the `include` method from `django.urls`:

   ```
   from django.urls import path, include
   ```

B. Remove the line of code importing `HomePageView`.

C. Replace:

```
path('', HomePageView.as_view()),
```

... with ...

```
path('', include('pages.urls')),
```

This tells the file to look to the `urls.py` file in the `pages` directory for all URL patterns except those that begin with "admin/". Note that the order is important as it provides the sequence in which Django will look for matches.

Here is the complete file:

Exercise Code 4.6: hello_django/urls.py

```
1.  from django.contrib import admin
2.  from django.urls import path, include
3.
4.  urlpatterns = [
5.      path('admin/', admin.site.urls),
6.      path('', include('pages.urls')),
7.  ]
```

3. Return to your browser and refresh the page. It should look the same. If you get any errors, review your code to make sure it matches the code in the instructions.[8]

8. If you have found an error in our code or our instructions, please visit `https://www.webucator.com/books/errata.cfm` to see if we have posted a fix, and if not, please let us know by emailing actionable@webucator.com.

Exercise 5: Creating an About Us Page

15 to 25 minutes

Now that you have your **pages** app, follow these steps to create a new *About-Us* page:

1. Create the view in `pages/views.py`:

Exercise Code 5.1: pages/views.py

```
1.  from django.views.generic import TemplateView
2.
3.  class HomePageView(TemplateView):
4.      template_name = 'pages/home.html'
5.
6.  class AboutUsView(TemplateView):
7.      template_name = 'pages/about_us.html'
```

2. Add a new template at `templates/pages/about_us.html`:

Exercise Code 5.2: templates/pages/about_us.html

```
1.  {% extends "_base.html" %}
2.
3.  {% block title %}About Us{% endblock %}
4.  {% block header %}About Us{% endblock %}
5.  {% block main %}
6.    <p>Very interesting information about us!</p>
7.  {% endblock %}
```

3. Configure the URL in `pages/urls.py`: import `AboutUsView` and add the `path`:

Exercise Code 5.3: pages/urls.py

```
1.  from django.urls import path
2.
3.  from .views import AboutUsView, HomePageView
4.
5.  app_name = 'pages'
6.  urlpatterns = [
7.      path('', HomePageView.as_view(), name='homepage'),
8.      path('about-us/', AboutUsView.as_view(), name='about-us'),
9.  ]
```

4. If you have stopped the server, start it back up again by running the following command from the `hello_proj` directory:

```
(.venv) …/projects/hello_proj> python manage.py runserver
```

5. Visit `http://127.0.0.1:8000/about-us/` in the browser. You should see a page like this one:

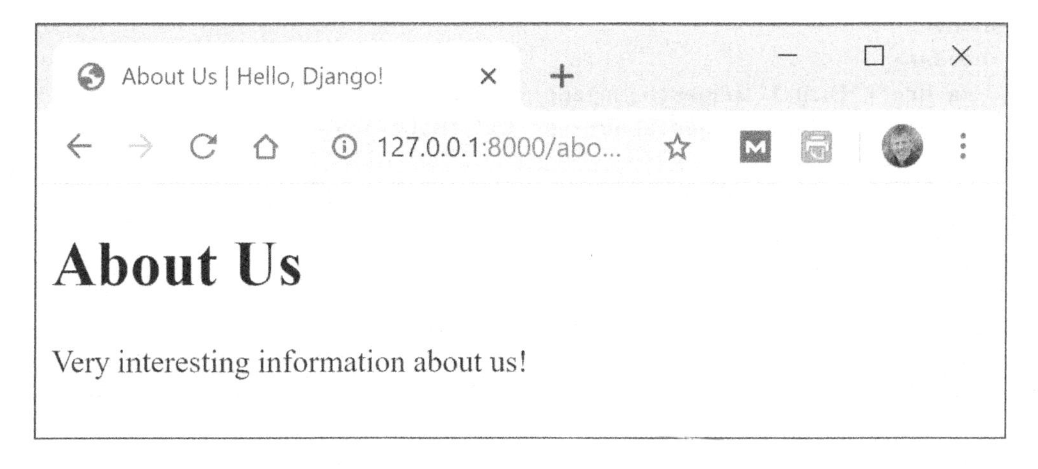

You may have noticed in `pages/urls.py` that the `path()` method that defines the URL patterns takes a `name` argument:

```
app_name = 'pages'
urlpatterns = [
    path('', HomePageView.as_view(), name='homepage'),
    path('about-us/', AboutUsView.as_view(), name='about-us'),
]
```

This allows you to link to these pages by referencing their names in Django template tags instead of hard-coding the URLs in links. This way, if you change the paths in your URL patterns, you won't need to modify your HTML links.

1. Open `templates/_base.html` in the editor.
2. Add a `header`:

Exercise Code 5.4: templates/_base.html

```
1.   <!DOCTYPE html>
2.   <html lang="en">
3.   <head>
4.   <meta charset="UTF-8">
5.   <meta name="viewport" content="width=device-width, initial-scale=1">
6.   <title>{% block title %}{% endblock %} | Hello, Django!</title>
7.   </head>
8.   <body>
9.   <header>
10.    <a href="{% url 'pages:homepage' %}">Home</a> |
11.    <a href="{% url 'pages:about-us' %}">About</a>
12.  </header>
13.  <h1>{% block header %}Hello, Django!{% endblock %}</h1>
14.  <main>
15.    {% block main %}{% endblock %}
16.  </main>
17.  </body>
18.  </html>
```

Notice the syntax of the URL tags:

```
{% url 'namespace:url-pattern-name' %}
```

where `url-pattern-name` is the name given to a URL pattern and `namespace` is the namespace given to the URLConf.

3. Return to the browser and refresh the **About Us** page. Notice the links at the top:

4. Click on the **Home** link. Notice the home page also has the links. That's because you added the header to `_base.html`, which `home.html` and `about_us.html` both extend.

We will cover the URL tag and other Django tags in detail in later lessons.

Conclusion

In this lesson, you have learned to install Django within a virtual environment and have created your first Django application. The completed project for this lesson is available in `solutions/getting-started/hello_proj`.

LESSON 3

Git, GitHub, and an App with a Model

Topics Covered

☑ Git and GitHub.

☑ Django Models.

☑ Migrations.

> "You don't know how good I feel! Wouldn't it be nice if it could last? I believe I could be a **model** child if I were just invited out to tea every day.
>
> – *Anne of Green Gables, Lucy Maud Montgomery*

Introduction

In this lesson, you will create a full `jokes` app and learn to use version control to back it up. You will touch on many different pieces of a Django application and learn the major steps in building a Django app. In later lessons, we will dig deeper into each of the individual pieces.

*

3.1. djangojokes.com

Throughout these lessons, you will build an app that is based on `https://www.djangojokes.com`:

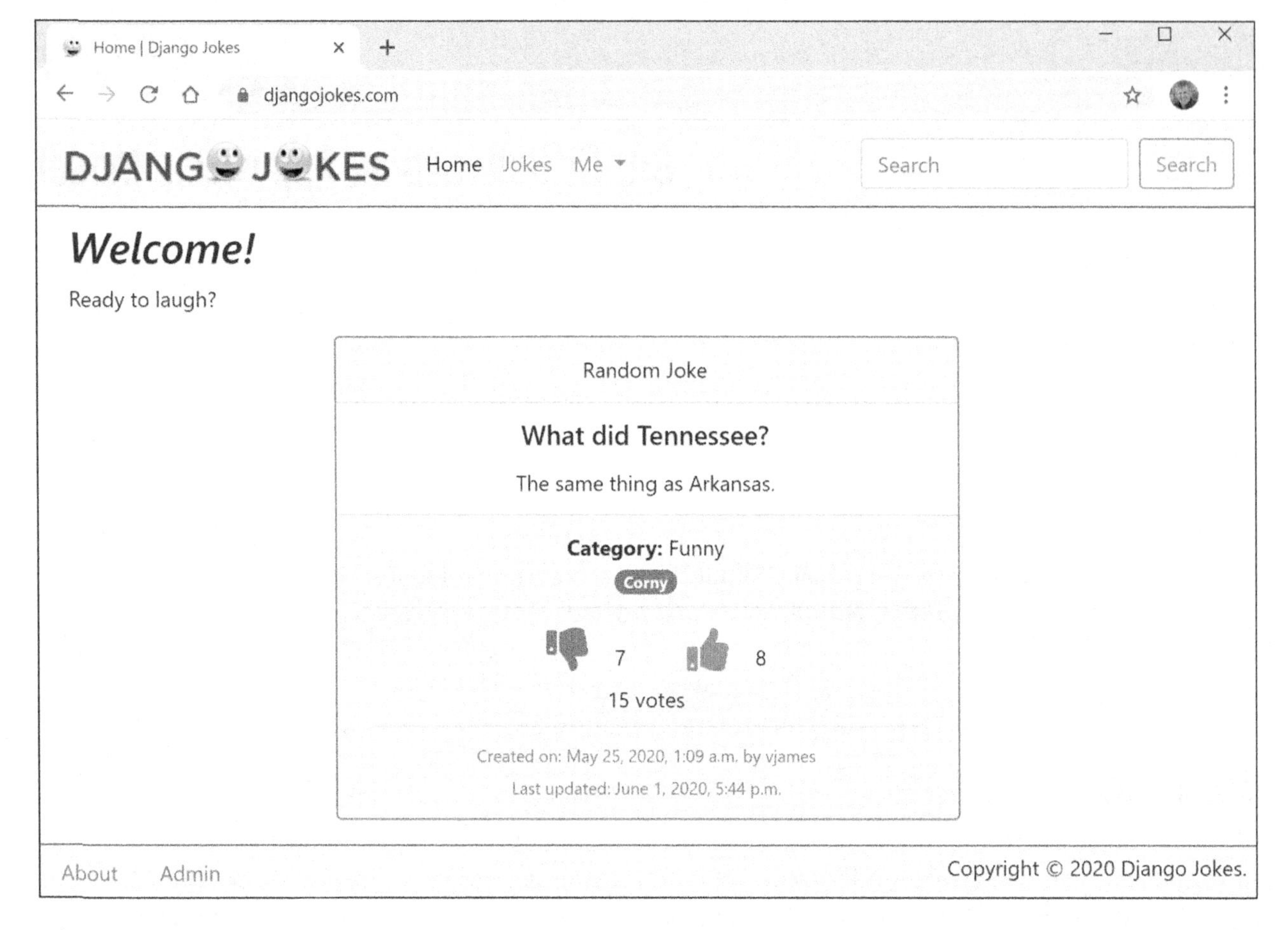

The site you build will be almost identical to the one you see there. Familiarize yourself with its features:

1. Visit the home page at `https://www.djangojokes.com/`. Refresh the page a couple of times and notice it outputs a random joke each time. You will implement this functionality in the Template Filters and Tags lesson (see page 163).
2. Click the **About** link in the footer. You will create a simplified version of this page. You will create a basic home page and about-us page in this lesson.
3. On the **About** page, click the **Work for us** link. This takes you to an application form, which will generate an email letting us know that someone has applied. Notice that it includes a `Resume` field. The user will be able to upload a resume. As this is a private document, we will teach you how to make sure it is not publicly available. You will also learn to prevent people from uploading dangerous files.
4. Click the **Jokes** link in the header. You will see a tabular list of jokes, each of which has a category, zero or more tags, a creator's username, and a rating with the number of votes.
5. Click on the **Joke**, **Creator**, or **Category** heading to sort by those fields. Click again on the same field to sort in the opposite direction.

6. Use the **Order By** form at the top to sort by other fields.
7. Click on a category (e.g., Play on Words), a tag (e.g., Animal or Money), or a username (e.g. askinner) to filter jokes:

8. Use the **Search** form at the top to search for jokes.
9. Open a joke and try voting on it. You will get a message saying only logged-in users can vote.
10. Back on the **Jokes** list, click the **New Joke** button. Notice that you are taken to a login form. Only logged-in users can create jokes.
11. Click the **Register** link below the login form or the **Sign up** link in the header to create an account and complete the registration process, which includes confirming your email address.
12. When you log in, notice that you have the chance to reset your password if you forgot it. Try it if you like.
13. Now that you are logged in, click the **New Joke** button again. Add a really funny (but clean) joke. Because this site is live, we have a joke approval process, so your joke won't immediately be public. Only you will see it, and there will be a "Pending Approval" note at the bottom.
14. Notice the **Update** button. You can update jokes you create.
15. Go back to the **Jokes** list, and open a joke (not the one that you created). Notice that you can now vote on it. Vote a few times on the same joke. Notice that it lets you change your vote, but doesn't register multiple votes by the same user for the same joke.
16. From the **Me** menu in the header, click **My Django Jokes**. It will show your added jokes.
17. From the **Me** menu, click **My Account**. Notice that you can update your profile and add a profile picture (an avatar). Do this if you wish. You will learn to allow users to upload profile pictures. You will also learn to validate the uploaded file, making sure that the file is an image and that it isn't too big.
18. You will also learn to use and customize Django admin, Django's built-in administration interface, to manage all the data.

This covers just some of what you will learn to do as you create the Django Jokes website. Unfortunately, we cannot teach you to write funny jokes. As you will see, we haven't yet learned that ourselves.

3.2. Version Control Systems, Git, and GitHub

A version control system is a piece of software for keeping track of changes you (and your team) make to source code. When you use version control, your development process (at its most basic) works like this:

1. Make changes to your code.
2. Stage your changes.
3. Commit your changes to version control with a short message describing them.
4. Push the commit to the master branch[9], so other developers have access to your changes.

9. Most sites will have additional branches for adding features and testing.

 Exercise 6: Setting Up VS Code, Git, and GitHub

45 to 60 minutes

In this exercise, you will:

1. Sign up for a GitHub account and create a repository.
2. Create a new workspace in Visual Studio Code.
3. Download and install Git.
4. Get the **GitHub Pull Requests and Issues** extension for Visual Studio Code.
5. Clone the GitHub repository you created on your local machine.
6. Make a change to a file in the repository.
7. **Stage that change.** When you stage changes, you are indicating that those changes are ready to commit. This does not mean that they are ready for production. It only means that you are ready to commit those changes to version control for safe keeping.
8. Make your first **Git commit**. Your files will be added to version control.
9. Push your changes to the *master* branch. The *master* branch is the main branch – the one that will be used in production. You can create other branches off of *master* that allow you to work on new features without affecting production, but for our purposes, we will just stick with the one branch. After you push your changes to *master*, you will be able to see them on GitHub.

❖ E6.1. Create a GitHub Account and Repository

1. Follow the instructions at `https://bit.ly/github-signup` to sign up for a new GitHub account. For our purposes, the free tier will work fine.
2. Once you have created you GitHub account, log into it.
3. Next to the **Repositories** header on the left, click **New**:

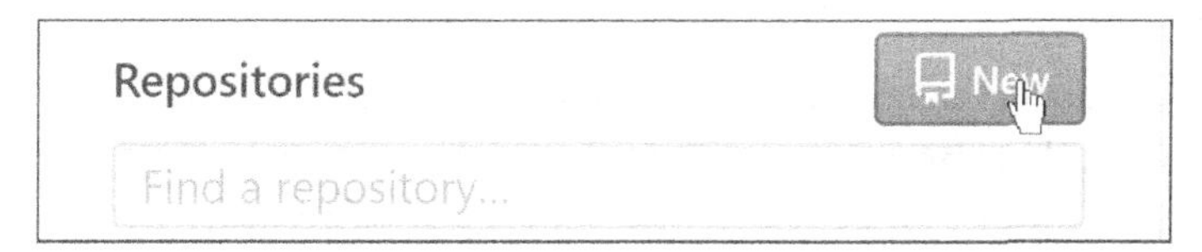

4. Fill out the **Create a new repository** form:

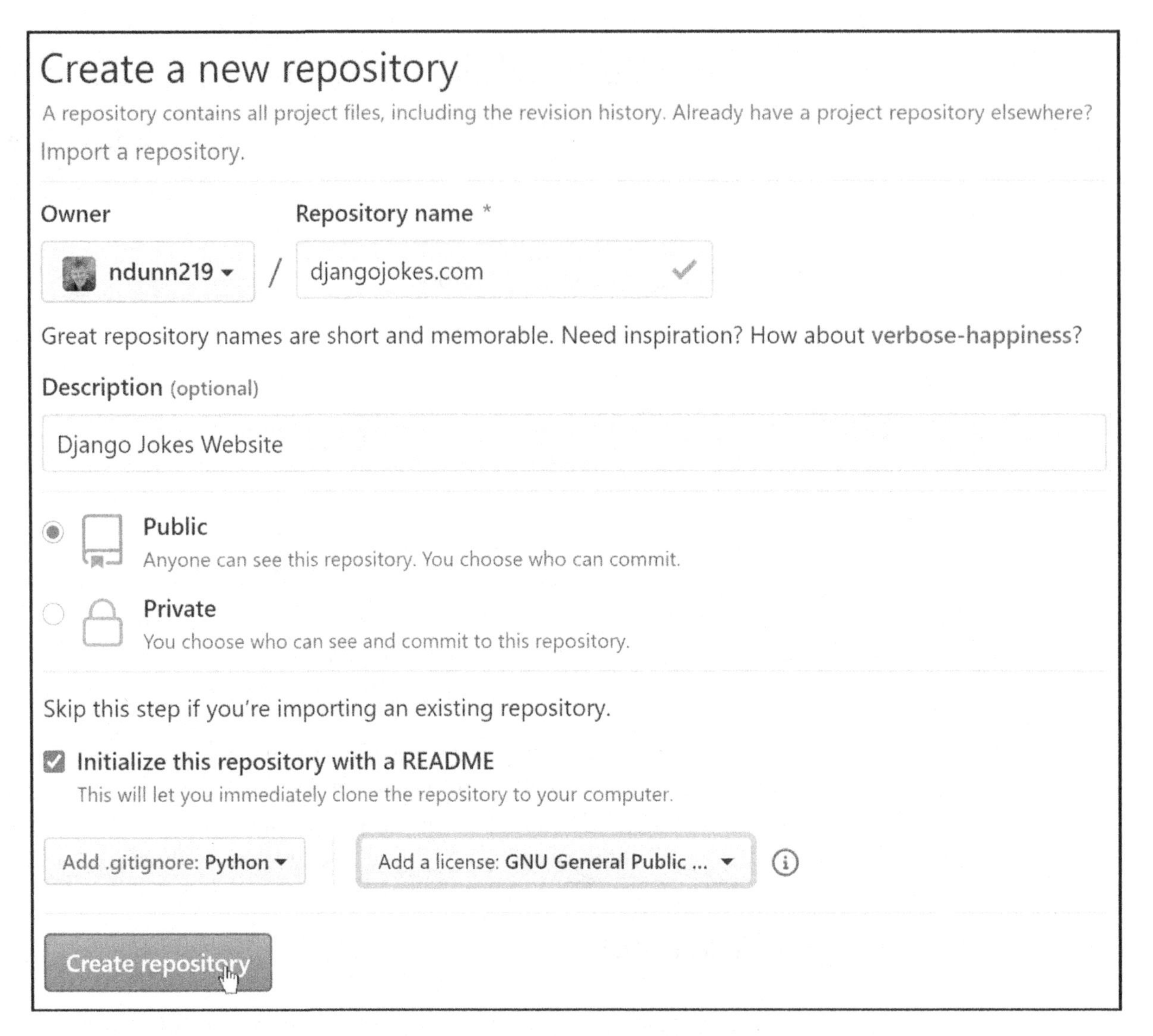

A. Enter "djangojokes.com" for the **Repository name**.

B. Enter "Django Jokes Website" for the **Description**.

C. Select **Public**. Only paid accounts can have private repositories.

D. Check **Initialize this repository with a README**.

E. Select **Python** from **Add .gitignore**. This will create a `.gitignore` file with a list of file paths that should not be kept in version control. The list is long and includes files in `__pycache__` directories, `db.sqlite3`, and `local_settings.py`.

F. Choose whatever license you wish or none at all.

G. Click **Create Repository**.

When you're finished, you should see your new repository:

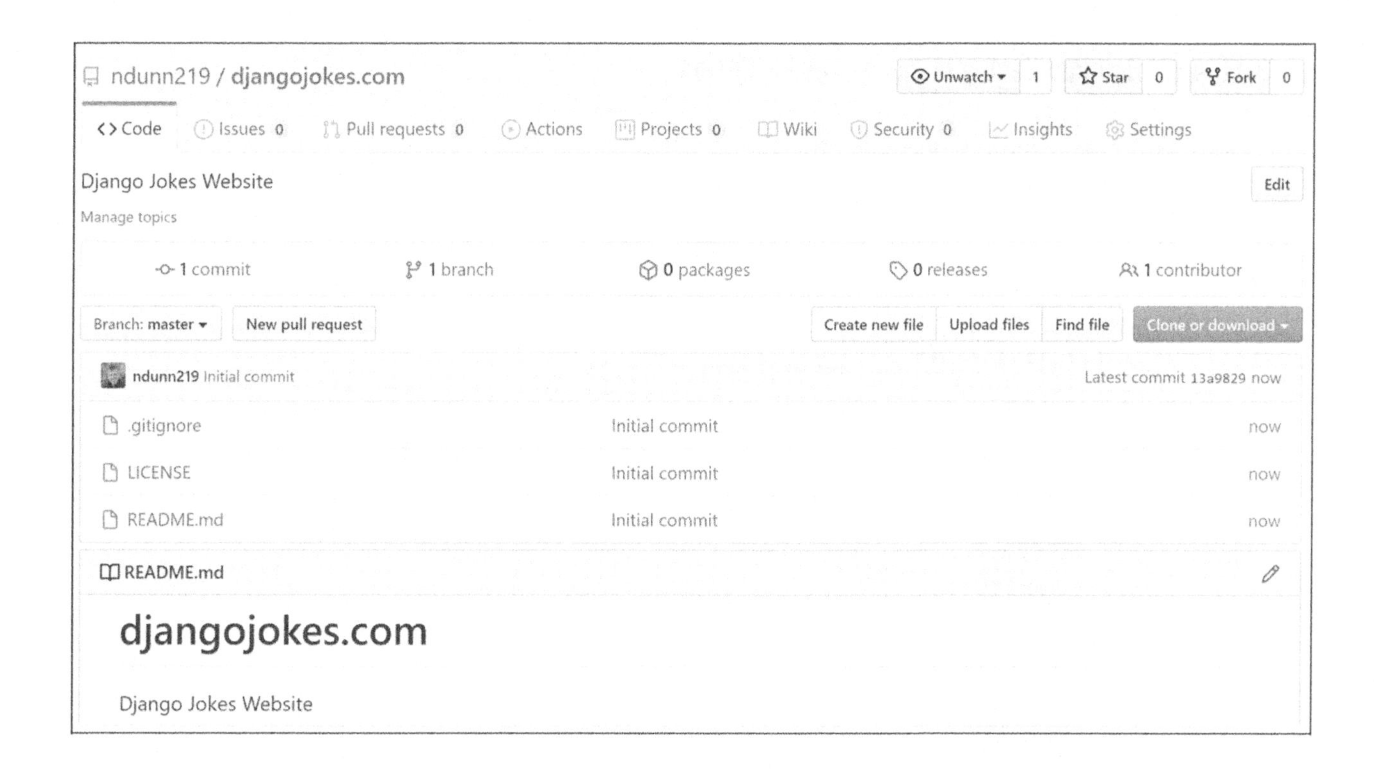

❖ E6.2. Create a New Workspace for djangojokes.com

1. Open Visual Studio Code.
2. If there is a workspace open, close it (**File** > **Close Workspace**).
3. Select **File** > **Save Workspace As...** and save the workspace as "djangojokes.com" in the workspace folder you created when doing the initial Visual Studio Code setup.

❖ E6.3. Download and Install Git

Before installing Git, check if you already have it by running `git --version` at the terminal:

```
…/Webucator> git --version
git version 2.28.0.windows.1
```

If you do not have Git installed or the version you have installed is older than 2.22, you should download and install the latest version for your operating system at `https://git-scm.com/downloads`. During the installation, you can select all the defaults, or when asked to choose the default editor used by Git, you can select Visual Studio Code.

❖ E6.4. GitHub Pull Requests and Issues Extension

1. In Visual Studio Code, click the **Extensions** icon:

2. Install **GitHub Pull Requests and Issues**:

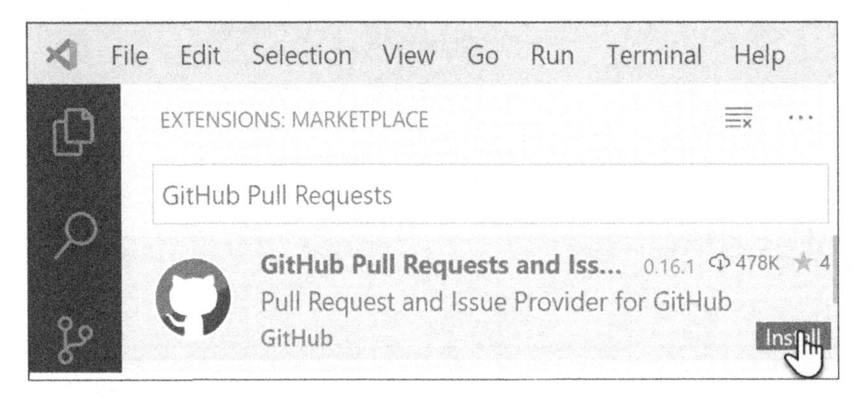

3. In the bottom left of Visual Studio Code, click the Accounts icon and select **Sign in to use GitHub Pull Requests and Issues (1)**:

   A page will open asking you to authorize Visual Studio Code to access GitHub. Click **Continue**.

4. If you get an **Open in Visual Studio Code?** prompt, click **Open Visual Studio Code**.
5. If you get an **Allow an extension to open this URI?** prompt, click **Open**.

You are now set to use the GitHub Pull Requests and Issues extension.

❖ E6.5. Clone Your GitHub Repository

1. Copy the URL of your GitHub repository:

2. In the Visual Studio Code **Explorer** panel, click the **Clone Repository** button:

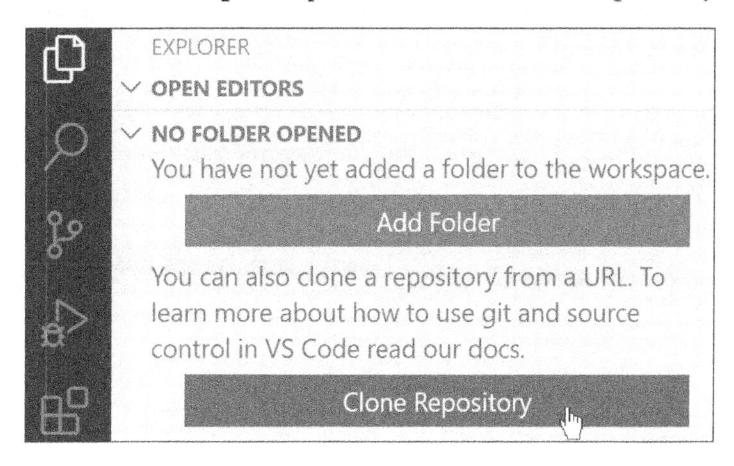

Paste in the GitHub repository URL and click **Clone from URL...**:

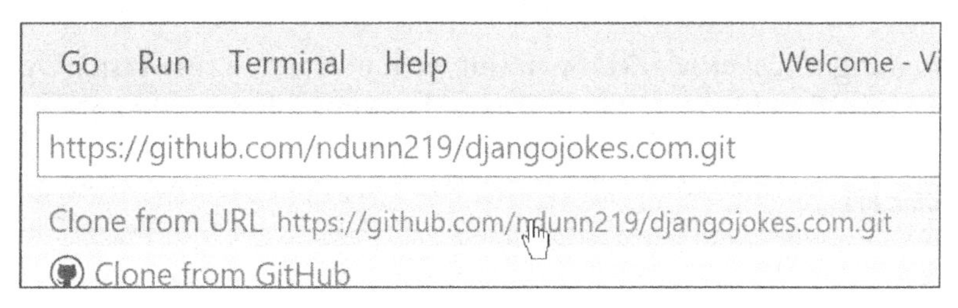

3. Select the folder in which to clone the repository (choose the `projects` folder inside of your `Webucator/Django` folder):

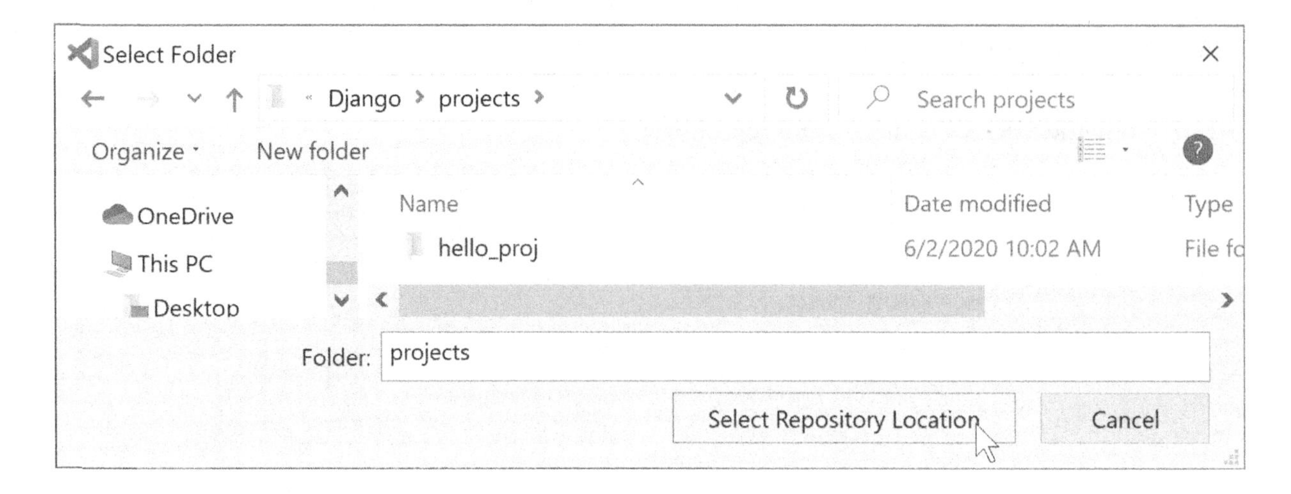

4. A prompt will pop up in Visual Studio Code asking you what you want to do with the repository. Select **Add to Workspace:**[10]

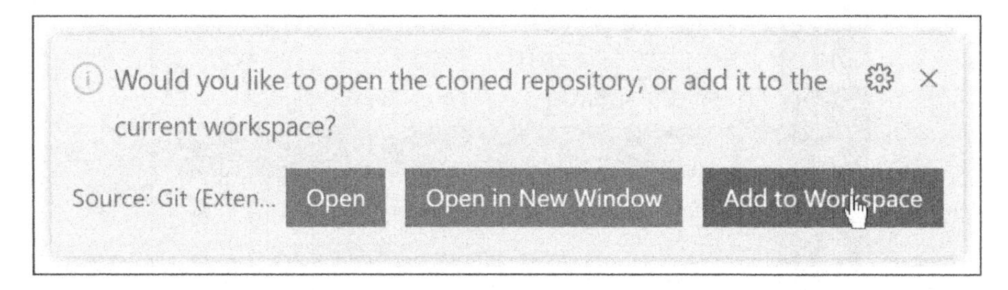

❖ E6.6. Your First Git Commit

The language used to create GitHub `README.md` files is called MarkDown.[11] It is a simple formatting language. We are not going to cover MarkDown, but we'll give you a tiny taste. Open `README.md` and add the following text, which will create a second-level heading followed by a paragraph with a link:

Exercise Code 6.1: README.md

```
1.  # django-jokes
2.  Django Jokes Website
3.  ## Practice Site for Learning Django
4.  I am using this site to learn. It is based on
5.  [Django Jokes](https://www.djangojokes.com).
```

10. If the prompt doesn't appear or it disappears before you have a chance to interact with it, select **File > Add Folder to Workspace…** and navigate to the cloned `djangojokes.com` repository.

11. `https://guides.github.com/features/mastering-markdown/`

Now, stage and commit the change to the repository:

1. On the far left of Visual Studio Code, notice that the **Source Control** icon has a circle with a "1" in it. That indicates that there has been one change. Click on that icon:

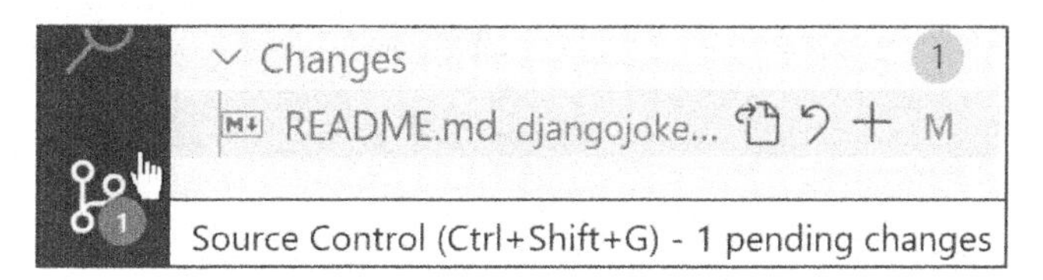

2. You can now click on the plus sign (+) next to the `README.md` file to *stage changes* for that file. When you stage changes, you are indicating that those changes are ready to commit. You can also hover over the bar just above it to get the option to **Stage All Changes**:

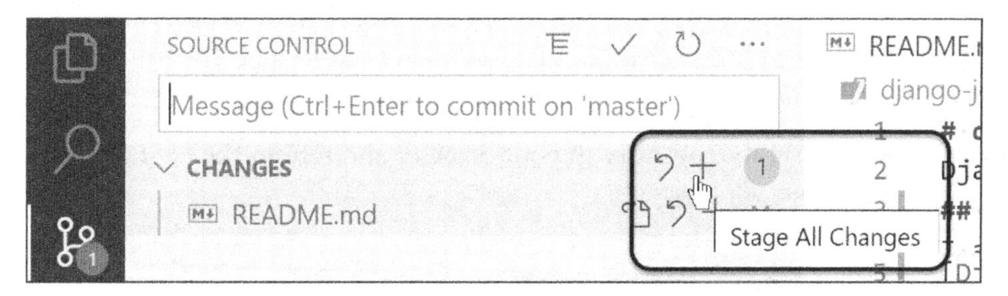

   In this case, you have only one change, so there is no difference between staging all changes and staging just the one. Click either plus sign to stage the changes.

3. Now that you have staged changes, you can commit those changes to source control. Enter a commit message (e.g., "My First Commit - updated README"), and click on the check mark to the right of the "SOURCE CONTROL" text:

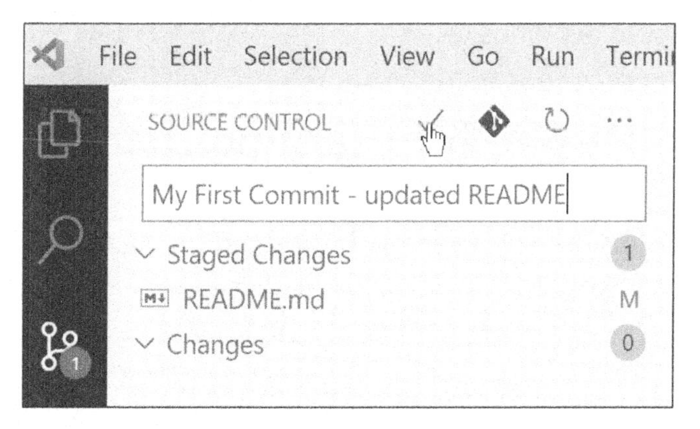

   Your changes are now in version control.

4. Go to your GitHub repository in your browser and refresh the page. Notice that the `README.md` file there is unchanged. That's because you have not yet pushed the change.

5. Push your files to the *master* branch by clicking on the ellipsis (three dots) to the right of the "SOURCE CONTROL" text. Then, from the submenu, select **Pull, Push** and then **Push**:

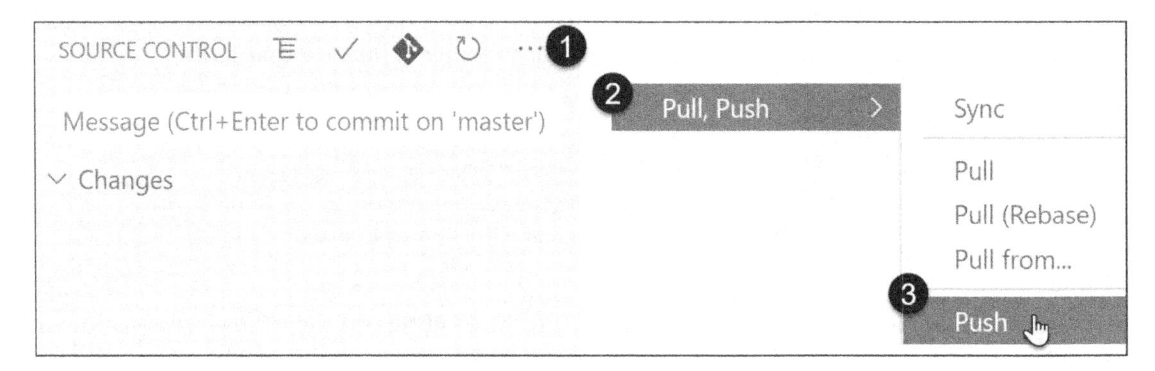

   You may get a prompt asking you if you would like Visual Studio Code to periodically fetch changes. This is generally only relevant if you have multiple developers working on the project as others might have pushed changes that you then need to pull. In that case, you will want to choose **Yes**. For now, you can select **Yes**, **No**, or **Ask Me Later**.

6. Return to your GitHub repository in your browser and refresh the page. Now, you should see the updated `README.md` file:

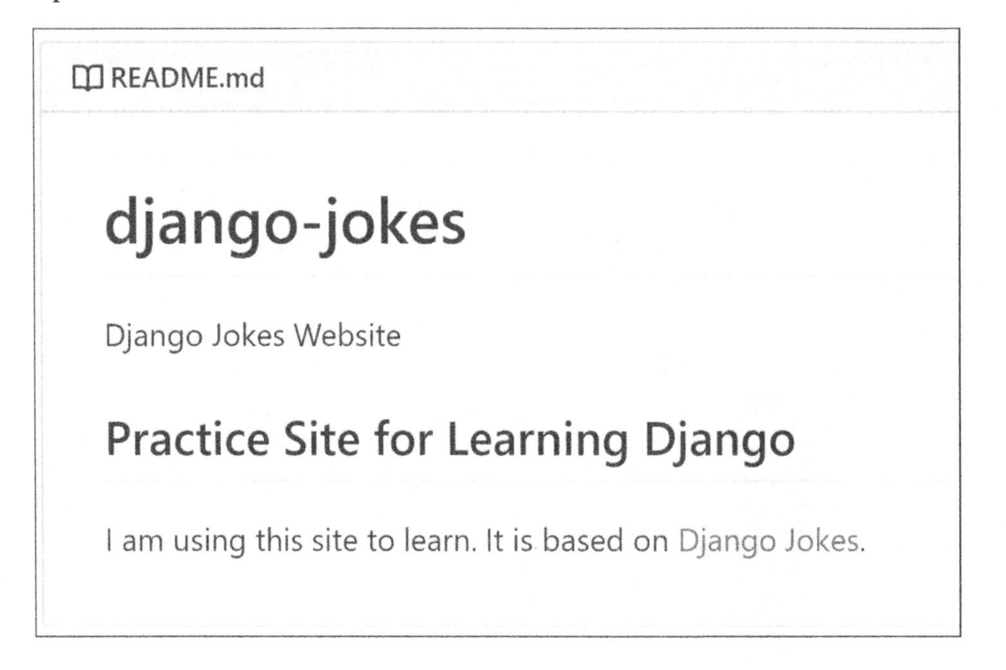

A few additional things to note:

1. If you were working on a team of developers, you would pull changes they made to your local machine using the **Pull** command:

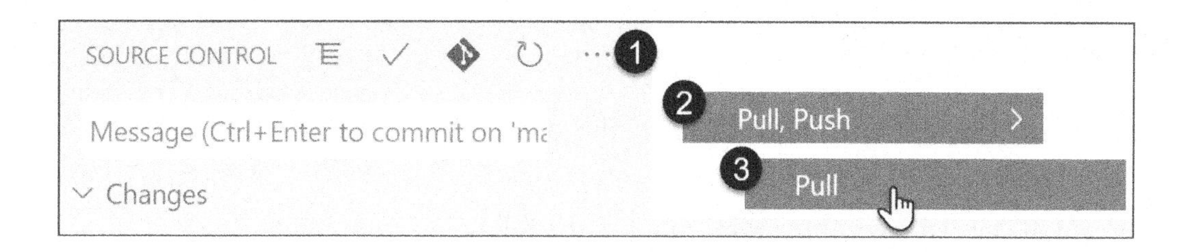

2. In a team environment, and even when you're working alone on a larger project, you might have multiple branches. In this case, you could use the **Push to...** command to choose the branch to push to:

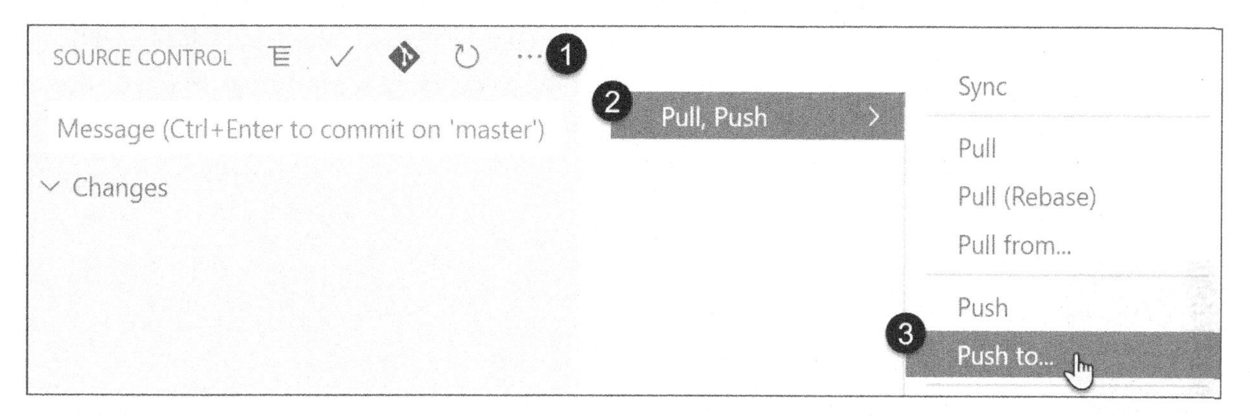

3. If you don't want to have to explicitly stage your changes before committing, you can skip the staging step, and just click on the **Commit** check mark. The first time you do it, you will get a prompt like this one:

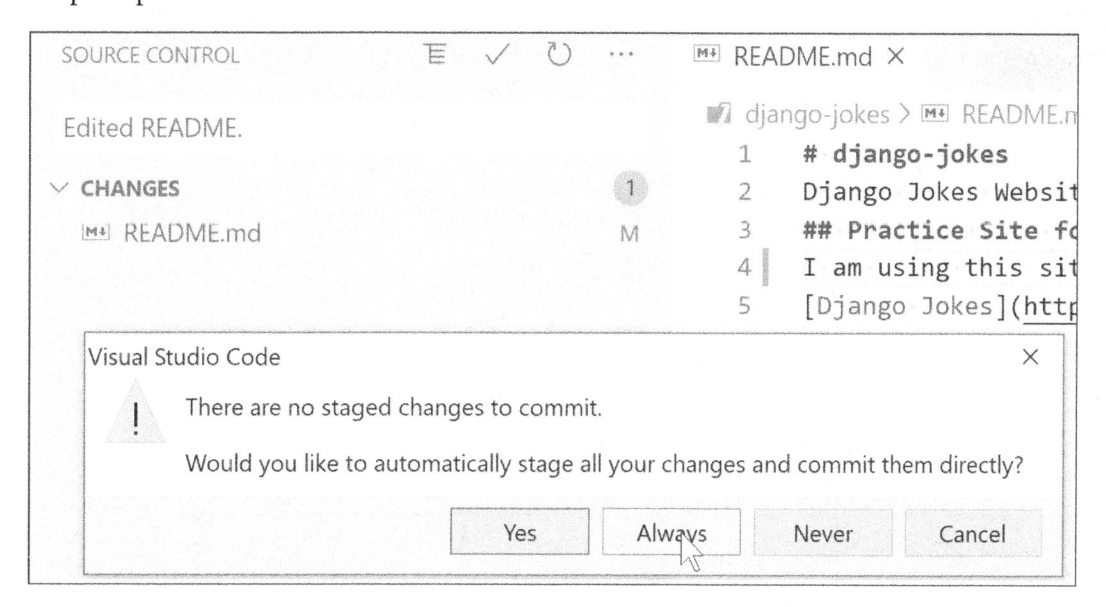

Click **Always** to always auto-stage your changes.

❖ E6.7. Setting Up the Environment

1. In Visual Studio Code, right-click on the `djangojokes.com` folder and select **Open in Terminal.**
2. Create the virtual environment by running the following command:

```
…/projects/djangojokes.com> python -m venv .venv
```

3. You don't want to commit the `.venv` folder to version control. It doesn't contain code you wrote and it's huge! Among other things, it will contain the Python interpreter, all of the Django code, and every other library you install. Open the `.gitignore` file in Visual Studio Code and search it for ".venv". You will find it in a section that contains common virtual environment files and folders. It looks like this:

```
# Environments
.env
.venv
env/
venv/
ENV/
env.bak/
venv.bak/
```

The `.gitignore` file tells Git what to ignore – that is, what to leave out of version control. It is a plain text file with one string or regular expression per line. GitHub created this one for us, but if you were to create your own, you would want to include, at the very least:

```
__pycache__/
.venv
local_settings.py
db.sqlite3
```

4. Set the Python Interpreter for the workspace:
   A. Select **Command Palette** from the **View** menu.
   B. Enter "Python: Select Interpreter" and select **Python: Select Interpreter**:

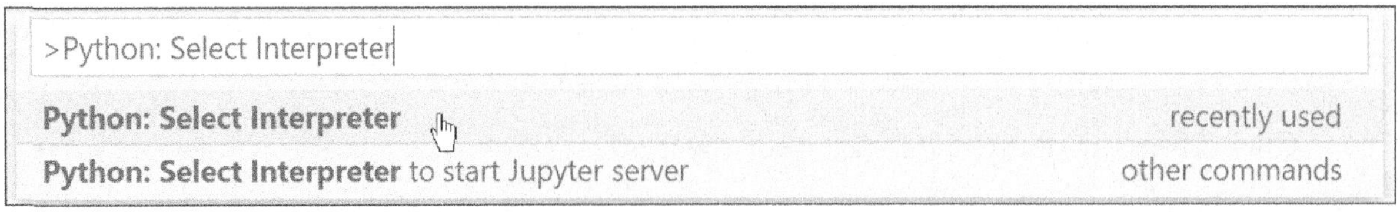

C. Select **Entire workspace**:

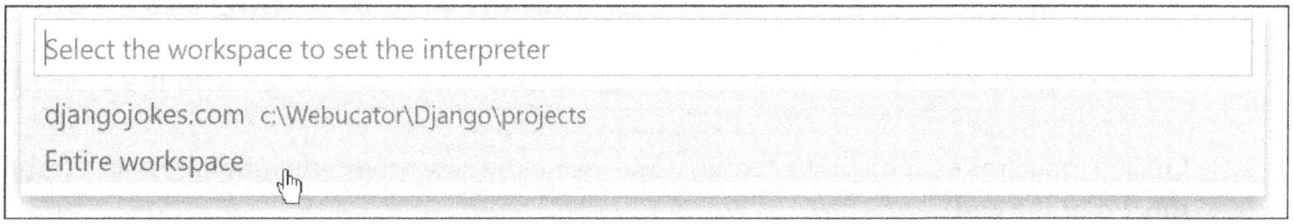

Select the workspace to set the interpreter

djangojokes.com c:\Webucator\Django\projects

Entire workspace

D. Select the Python executable from the virtual directory you just created:

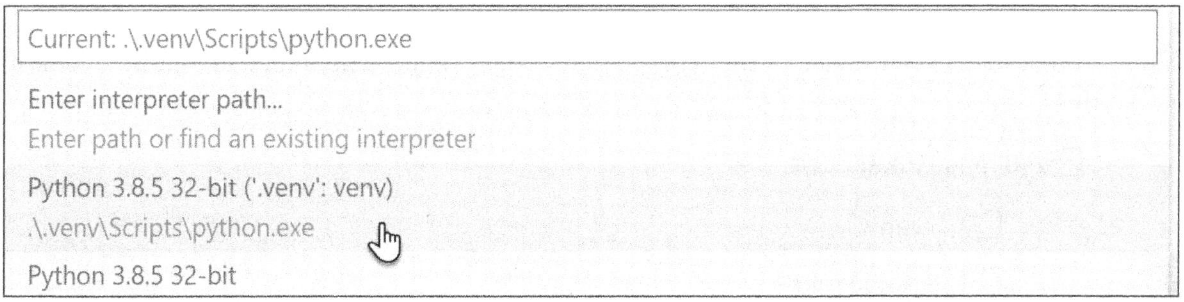

Current: .\.venv\Scripts\python.exe

Enter interpreter path...

Enter path or find an existing interpreter

Python 3.8.5 32-bit ('.venv': venv)

.\.venv\Scripts\python.exe

Python 3.8.5 32-bit

5. Activate the virtual environment:

Windows

```
.venv\Scripts\activate
```

Mac

```
source .venv/bin/activate
```

6. Install Django:

```
pip install django
```

Exercise 7: Creating the Project

15 to 25 minutes

1. Open `djangojokes.com` in the terminal and create the new project by running (**Don't forget the dot at the end**):

```
(.venv) …/projects/djangojokes.com> django-admin startproject djangojokes .
```

2. Add a `templates` folder to the `djangojokes.com` folder. The folder should now look like this:

```
djangojokes.com
    .venv
    djangojokes
    templates
    .gitignore
    LICENSE
    manage.py
    README.md
```

❖ E7.1. Starter Code

We have a lot of code pre-written for you in the `starter-code` folder. We also have the final solutions for each lesson in the `solutions` folder. It will be easier for you to access this code if those folders are in your workspace:

1. Right-click in the **Explorer** area and select **Add Folder to Workspace...**:

2. Select `solutions` and `starter-code` from `Webucator/Django`:

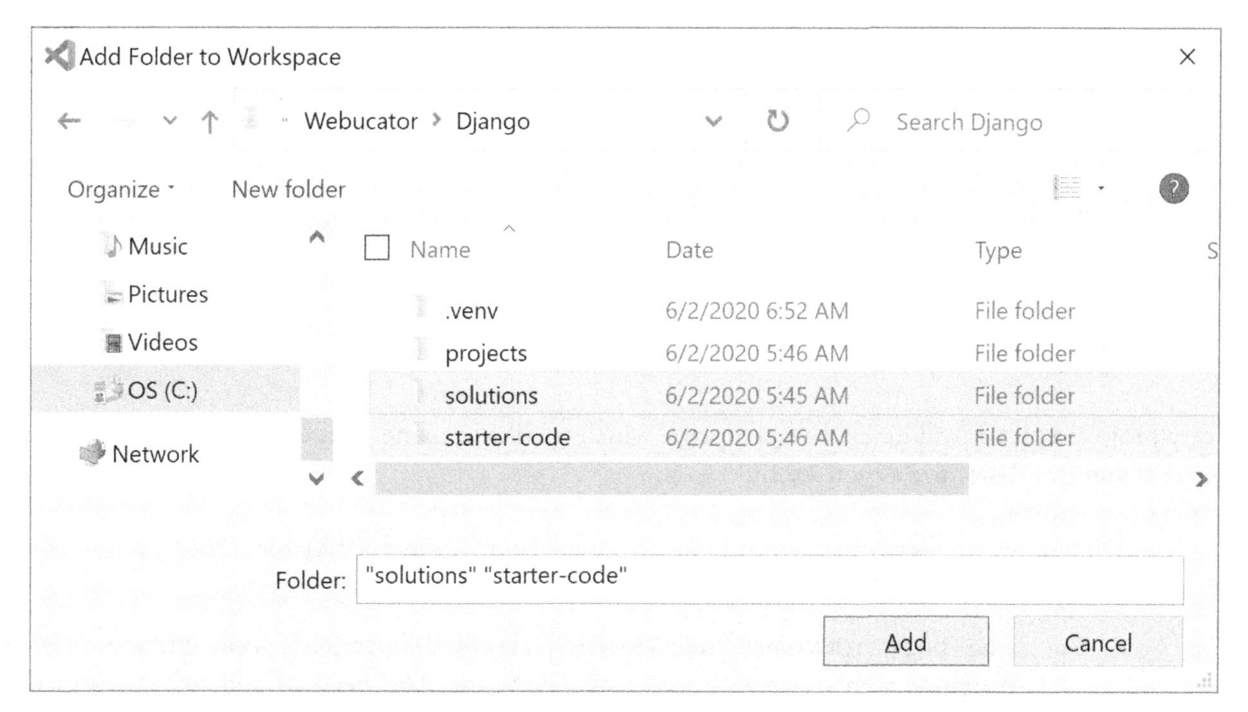

3. You don't want the `solutions` and `starter-code` folders to be in version control. Open `.gitignore` and add a "# MY ADDITIONS" section to the bottom of the file:

```
# MY ADDITIONS
solutions
starter-code
```

Git Commit

1. Click the **Source Control** icon:

The changes should include:

- `.gitignore`
- `manage.py`
- `__init__.py`
- `asgi.py`

- `settings.py`
- `urls.py`
- `wsgi.py`

They should **not include** anything in your `solutions` or `starter-code` folders.

2. Add a short message (e.g., “Initial project”), click the “Commit” check, click the ellipsis, and select **Push**.

❖ E7.2. Adding a Base Template

Every project typically will have a base template, which we like to name `_base.html`. We have created one that you can customize as you see fit:

1. Directly in your `starter-code` folder, you will find a `_base.html` file. Open `_base.html` for editing:
   A. The `_base.html` file includes Bootstrap classes. Bootstrap is a popular framework for designing web pages with CSS and JavaScript. You need to add references to the Bootstrap CSS and JavaScript files in `_base.html`:
      i. Visit `https://getbootstrap.com`.
      ii. Click the **Get Started** button.
      iii. Copy the Bootstrap CSS `<link>` tag on that page and paste it over the “ADD BOOTSTRAP CSS” comment in the `head` of `_base.html`.
      iv. Copy the Bootstrap JS `<script>` tags on that page and paste them over the “ADD BOOTSTRAP JS” comment immediately above the closing `</body>` tag at the bottom of `_base.html`.
   B. You will also use some Font Awesome icons. Font Awesome provides a collection of free vector icons that you can use on your websites. You can get access to these icons through a free content delivery network (CDN). To do so, you will need get your own unique `<script>` tag with the latest version of Font Awesome:
      i. Go to `https://fontawesome.com/start`.
      ii. Enter your email address in the form and submit. You will be sent an email asking you to confirm your email address and create an account. After creating

an account, you will be provided with a `<script>` tag that looks something like this:

```
<script src="https://kit.fontawesome.com/yoursecretcode.js"
        crossorigin="anonymous"></script>
```

iii. Paste this tag over the "ADD FONT AWESOME" comment in the `head` of `_base.html`.

2. Close `_base.html`. Then, copy the `_base.html` file (not the text of the file but the file itself) from the `starter-code` folder and paste it into the `djangojokes.com/templates` folder you just created.
3. Open `djangojokes.com/templates/_base.html` for editing.
4. Replace all instances of "SITENAME" in `_base.html` with "Django Jokes".
5. Replace the link text that reads "NavLink" with "Jokes".
6. We need to tell Django to look in this `templates` folder when searching for templates. Open `djangojokes/settings.py` and add the following to the `DIRS` value of the dictionary in `TEMPLATES`:

```
'DIRS': [BASE_DIR / 'templates'],
```

And that's it: the project is created and ready to use.

Git Commit

Whenever you make significant changes, you should commit your code to Git. From here on out, we will remind you to commit (you can commit even more often if you wish), but we will not walk you through the process every time. If you need to, you can refer back to the initial instructions (see page 55). Note that you do not need to push your code every time, but it won't be backed up on GitHub until you do.

Exercise 8: Creating a pages App

25 to 40 minutes

In this exercise, you will create a `pages` app to hold the home page and the about-us page. Remember, the steps for creating a new app are:

1. Create the scaffolding of the app by running:

   ```
   python manage.py startapp app_name
   ```

   where "app_name" is the name of the app.
2. Add the new application to the `INSTALLED_APPS` list.
3. Create one or more views.
4. Configure URLs. Generally, this involves creating a URLConf file in the app and adding a path to the main URLConf file to hand off certain paths to the new app's URLConf file.
5. Create and update any necessary templates. For the `pages` app, you will create two templates:

   `templates/pages/home.html`

   `templates/pages/about_us.html`

   Both templates will extend `_base.html`, and just need minimal HTML in the body (e.g., an `h2` element and a `p` element). You will also want to update the links in the header and footer of `_base.html` to point to the new pages.

Try this on your own before looking at the solution. Test your solution by running the server and visiting the site.

Solution

1. Create the scaffolding:

```
(.venv) …/projects/djangojokes.com> python manage.py startapp pages
```

2. Add the new application to the INSTALLED_APPS list in djangojokes/settings.py:

```
INSTALLED_APPS = [
    # Built-in Django apps
    'django.contrib.admin',
    'django.contrib.auth',
    'django.contrib.contenttypes',
    'django.contrib.sessions',
    'django.contrib.messages',
    'django.contrib.staticfiles',

    # Local apps
    'pages.apps.PagesConfig',
]
```

3. Create the views:

Exercise Code 8.1: pages/views.py

```
1.  from django.views.generic import TemplateView
2.
3.  class HomePageView(TemplateView):
4.      template_name = 'pages/home.html'
5.
6.
7.  class AboutUsView(TemplateView):
8.      template_name = 'pages/about_us.html'
```

4. Configure the main URLConf:

Exercise Code 8.2: djangojokes/urls.py

```
1.  from django.contrib import admin
2.  from django.urls import path, include
3.
4.  urlpatterns = [
5.      path('admin/', admin.site.urls),
6.      path('', include('pages.urls')),
7.  ]
```

You can remove the long comment at the beginning of the file or leave it, whichever you prefer.

5. Create a new `urls.py` file in the `pages` folder:

Exercise Code 8.3: pages/urls.py

```
1.  from django.urls import path
2.
3.  from .views import AboutUsView, HomePageView
4.
5.  app_name = 'pages'
6.  urlpatterns = [
7.      path('', HomePageView.as_view(), name='homepage'),
8.      path('about-us/', AboutUsView.as_view(), name='about-us'),
9.  ]
```

6. Create a `pages` folder in the `templates` folder. Then, create these two templates in that `pages` folder:

Exercise Code 8.4: pages/home.html

```
1.  {% extends "_base.html" %}
2.
3.  {% block title %}Home{% endblock %}
4.  {% block main %}
5.    <h2>Welcome!</h2>
6.    <p>Ready to laugh?</p>
7.  {% endblock %}
```

Exercise Code 8.5: pages/about_us.html

```
1.  {% extends "_base.html" %}
2.
3.  {% block title %}About Us{% endblock %}
4.  {% block main %}
5.    <h2>About Us</h2>
6.    <p>We tell funny jokes.</p>
7.  {% endblock %}
```

7. Update `templates/_base.html`:

   navbar-brand Link in Header

   ```
   <a class="navbar-brand" href="{% url 'pages:homepage' %}">Django Jokes</a>
   ```

   Home Link in Header

   ```
   <li class="nav-item active">
     <a class="nav-link" href="{% url 'pages:homepage' %}">Home
       <span class="sr-only">(current)</span>
     </a>
   </li>
   ```

   About-Us Link in Footer

   ```
   <li class="nav-item">
     <a class="nav-link" href="{% url 'pages:about-us' %}">About</a>
   </li>
   ```

8. With `djangojokes.com` open at the terminal, run:

   ```
   (.venv) …/projects/djangojokes.com> python manage.py runserver
   ```

9. In your browser, navigate to `http://127.0.0.1:8000`. The page should look like this:

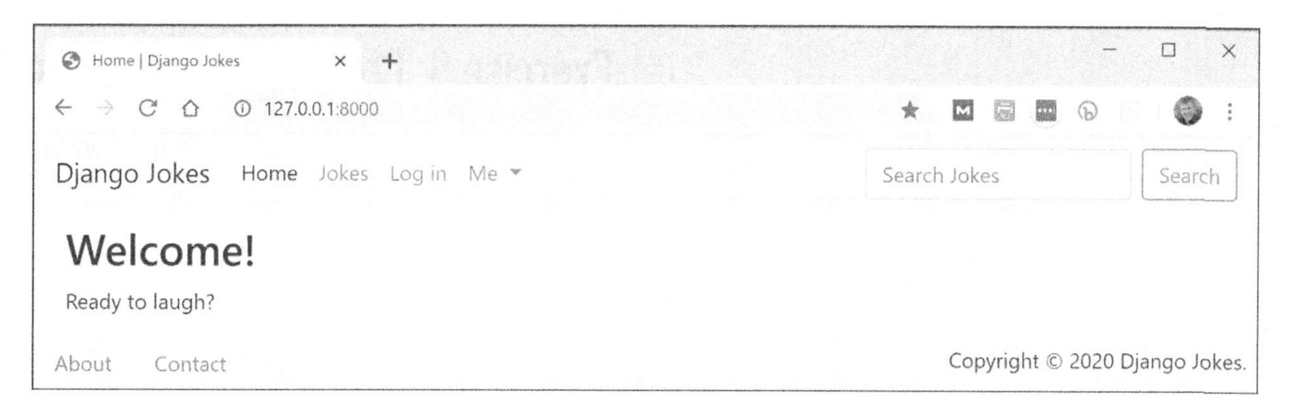

Click on the **About** link in the footer to visit the about-us page.

You can press Ctrl+C at the terminal to stop the server, or leave it running and open a new terminal to continue working on the project.

Git Commit

Commit your code to Git.

Exercise 9: Creating the jokes App

25 to 40 minutes

The website is going to allow visitors to read other users' jokes and write, edit, and delete their own jokes.

So, you will need to create a `jokes` app.

❖ E9.1. Scaffolding

With `djangojokes.com` open in the terminal, run the following command to create the **jokes** app:

```
(.venv) …/projects/djangojokes.com> python manage.py startapp jokes
```

The `djangojokes.com` folder should now look like this:

```
djangojokes.com
    .venv
    djangojokes
    jokes
    pages
    templates
    .gitignore
    db.sqlite3
    LICENSE
    manage.py
    README.md
```

❖ E9.2. Installed Apps

Add the new **jokes** app to `INSTALLED_APPS` in `djangojokes/settings.py`:

```
INSTALLED_APPS = [
    …

    # Local apps
    'jokes.apps.JokesConfig',
    'pages.apps.PagesConfig',
]
```

Tip: All Else Equal, Alphabetize

In some cases, the order in which code runs makes a difference, but when it doesn't, try to organize similar lines of code in alphabetical order. It makes the code easier to navigate. It's with this in mind that we add `'jokes.apps.JokesConfig'` before `'pages.apps.PagesConfig'`.

❖ E9.3. URLs

Next, you need to create a URLConf for the jokes app and let the main URLConf know to hand off some paths to it.

1. Within the `jokes` folder, create a `urls.py` file with the following content:

   Exercise Code 9.1: jokes/urls.py

   ```
   1.  from django.urls import path
   2.
   3.  app_name = 'jokes'
   4.  urlpatterns = []
   ```

   This URLConf has a namespace of "jokes," which is also the name of the app. The `urlpatterns` list is currently empty, but you will be adding paths to it shortly.

2. Now, you need to let the main URLConf know that it should hand off some paths to the jokes URLConf. Open `djangojokes/urls.py` and modify it as follows:

Exercise Code 9.2: djangojokes/urls.py

```
1.  from django.contrib import admin
2.  from django.urls import path, include
3.
4.  urlpatterns = [
5.      path('admin/', admin.site.urls),
6.      path('jokes/', include('jokes.urls')),
7.      path('', include('pages.urls')),
8.  ]
```

Now, all paths that begin with "jokes/" will get handed off to the jokes URLConf.

3.3. Models

Models contains the data fields and behaviors for an app.

❖ 3.3.1. The Database

The data for the data fields is stored in a database. By default, that is a SQLite database; however, for production projects, you should use something more robust. You will use SQLite for now, but later you will switch to PostgreSQL, which is the most common database used with Django.

Open `djangojokes/settings.py` and look for the `DATABASES` constant:

```
DATABASES = {
    'default': {
        'ENGINE': 'django.db.backends.sqlite3',
        'NAME': BASE_DIR / 'db.sqlite3',
    }
}
```

This is where the database is set. Remember that `BASE_DIR` is set at the top of the settings file. Let's use the shell to see where exactly that `db.sqlite3` file is saved:

```
(.venv) …/projects/djangojokes.com> python manage.py shell
>>> from djangojokes.settings import *
>>> DATABASES['default']['NAME']
WindowsPath('C:/Webucator/Django/projects/djangojokes.com/db.sqlite3')
```

This shows that `db.sqlite3` is right in the `djangojokes.com` folder:

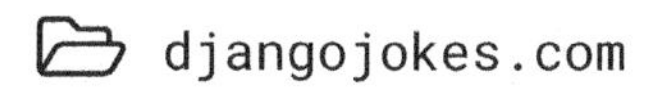
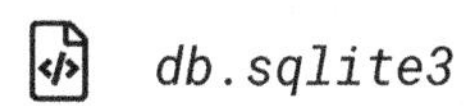

It was created the first time you ran `python manage.py runserver`. SQLite files are not stored in a readable format, so don't bother opening the file in your editor. Just know that this file is holding the data for the project.

Make sure to exit the shell:

```
>>> exit()
(.venv) …/projects/djangojokes.com>
```

Git Commit

Commit your code to Git.

Exercise 10: Migrating

5 to 10 minutes

Remember the apps that are in `INSTALLED_APPS` by default?

```
INSTALLED_APPS = [
    'django.contrib.admin',
    'django.contrib.auth',
    'django.contrib.contenttypes',
    'django.contrib.sessions',
    'django.contrib.messages',
    'django.contrib.staticfiles',
]
```

Several of those have their own models. Although these apps are put in the settings file when new projects are created, they do not automatically get built into the database. You have to do that yourself by running the following:

```
python manage.py migrate
```

Run that now. You should see output similar to this:

```
(.venv) …/projects/djangojokes.com> python manage.py migrate
Operations to perform:
  Apply all migrations: admin, auth, contenttypes, sessions
Running migrations:
  Applying contenttypes.0001_initial... OK
  Applying auth.0001_initial... OK
  Applying admin.0001_initial... OK
  Applying admin.0002_logentry_remove_auto_add... OK
  Applying admin.0003_logentry_add_action_flag_choices... OK
  Applying contenttypes.0002_remove_content_type_name... OK
  Applying auth.0002_alter_permission_name_max_length... OK
  Applying auth.0003_alter_user_email_max_length... OK
  Applying auth.0004_alter_user_username_opts... OK
  Applying auth.0005_alter_user_last_login_null... OK
  Applying auth.0006_require_contenttypes_0002... OK
  Applying auth.0007_alter_validators_add_error_messages... OK
  Applying auth.0008_alter_user_username_max_length... OK
  Applying auth.0009_alter_user_last_name_max_length... OK
  Applying auth.0010_alter_group_name_max_length... OK
  Applying auth.0011_update_proxy_permissions... OK
  Applying auth.0012_alter_user_first_name_max_length... OK
  Applying sessions.0001_initial... OK
```

The initial database has now been set up to use these apps. Next, you will create the model for the `jokes` app.

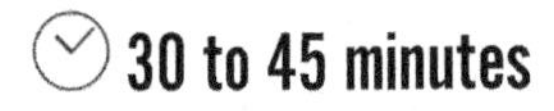

Exercise 11: Creating a Model

30 to 45 minutes

In this exercise, you will create a `Joke` model to store joke data. Before doing that though, look in the `jokes` folder for a folder named `migrations`. The important thing to notice is that it does not contain any Python files other than `__init__.py`. When you change models, you will need to make migration files, which will get stored in this directory. Every time you change the model, you need to make a new migration file. Let's get started…

1. Open `jokes/models.py` and add the highlighted code after the `import` statement:

Exercise Code 11.1: jokes/models.py

```
1.    from django.db import models
2.
3.    class Joke(models.Model):
4.        question = models.TextField(max_length=200)
5.        answer = models.TextField(max_length=100, blank=True)
6.        created = models.DateTimeField(auto_now_add=True)
7.        updated = models.DateTimeField(auto_now=True)
8.
9.        def __str__(self):
10.           return self.question
```

Things to notice about the Joke model:

A. It inherits from `models.Model`. All models will inherit from `models.Model` or from one of its subclasses.

B. It has four fields:

   i. `question` – A `TextField` that can hold up to 200 characters.

   ii. `answer` – A `TextField` that can hold up to 100 characters. Because `blank` is set to `True`, this field can be left empty in forms that are created from this model. This would be for jokes that don't require an answer.

   iii. `created` – A `DateTimeField`. By setting `auto_now_add` to `True`, the field will automatically be assigned the current date and time when the joke is inserted.

   iv. `updated` – A `DateTimeField`. By setting `auto_now` to `True`, the value of the field will be changed to the current date and time when the joke is updated.

C. The `__str__()` method determines what gets output when a `Joke` instance is converted to a string, either explicitly with `str()` or implicitly as occurs when an object is passed to certain functions such as `print()`.

2. As you have changed the model, you need to make new migration files. With `djangojokes.com` open in the terminal, run the following:

```
(.venv) …/projects/djangojokes.com> python manage.py makemigrations
Migrations for 'jokes':
  jokes\migrations\0001_initial.py
    - Create model Joke
```

3. Look again in the `jokes/migrations` folder. You will see that a `0001_initial.py` file has been added.

4. Now that you have created the migration file, you need to run the migration. Run the following:

```
(.venv) …/projects/djangojokes.com> python manage.py migrate
Operations to perform:
  Apply all migrations: admin, auth, contenttypes, jokes, sessions
Running migrations:
  Applying jokes.0001_initial... OK
```

The migration is complete and the `Joke` model has been added to the database.

❖ E11.1. Exploring the Joke Model

Let's play with the new `Joke` model in the shell:

1. Open the shell:

```
(.venv) …/projects/djangojokes.com> python manage.py shell
```

2. Import the Joke class and retrieve all the `Joke` instances by running:

```
>>> from jokes.models import Joke
>>> Joke.objects.all()
<QuerySet []>
```

As you can see, this returns an empty `QuerySet`, which is an iterable containing records returned from a database. It is empty, because you haven't created any jokes yet.

3. Create your first joke:

```
>>> q = 'Why did the chicken cross the road?'
>>> a = 'To get to the other side.'
>>> joke = Joke(question=q, answer=a)
```

4. Now, let's look at the `QuerySet` again:

```
>>> Joke.objects.all()
<QuerySet []>
```

It's still empty. That's because you haven't saved the new joke. Run this:

```
>>> joke.save()
```

Now, check the `QuerySet`:

```
>>> Joke.objects.all()
<QuerySet [<Joke: Why did the chicken cross the road?>]>
```

There is your joke! Notice that it only outputs the question. That comes from the value returned by the `__str__()` function of the `Joke` class. You can get the values of the other fields easily enough:

```
>>> joke.question
'Why did the chicken cross the road?'
>>> joke.answer
'To get to the other side.'
>>> joke.created
datetime.datetime(2020, 8, 4, 21, 27, 53, 277762, tzinfo=<UTC>)
>>> joke.updated
datetime.datetime(2020, 8, 4, 21, 27, 53, 277762, tzinfo=<UTC>)
```

5. In addition to the fields explicitly named in the model, an auto-incrementing `id` field is added to every model as the primary key for the table. It can be referenced as `id` or as `pk` (for **p**rimary **k**ey):

```
>>> joke.id
1
>>> joke.pk
1
```

6. Add another joke:

```
>>> q = 'What kind of music do windmills like?'
>>> a = 'Dude, they\'re big heavy metal fans.'
>>> joke = Joke(question=q, answer=a)
>>> joke.save()
```

7. Now, look at the jokes again, this time using a for loop:

```
>>> for joke in Joke.objects.all():
...     print('Q:', joke.question)
...     print('A:', joke.answer)
...
Q: Why did the chicken cross the road?
A: To get to the other side.
Q: What kind of music do windmills like?
A: Dude, they're big heavy metal fans.
```

8. I think "*huge* heavy metal fans" sounds better than "*big* heavy metal fans." Let's update that. Assign the last joke you entered to a variable:

```
>>> windmill_joke = Joke.objects.last()
```

9. Look at the current answer to that joke:

```
>>> windmill_joke.answer
"Dude, they're big heavy metal fans."
```

10. Change the answer and save:

```
>>> windmill_joke.answer = "Dude, they're huge heavy metal fans!"
>>> windmill_joke.save()
```

11. Now, loop through the jokes again:

```
>>> for joke in Joke.objects.all():
...     print('Q:', joke.question)
...     print('A:', joke.answer)
...
Q: Why did the chicken cross the road?
A: To get to the other side.
Q: What kind of music do windmills like?
A: Dude, they're huge heavy metal fans.
```

12. Let's see how many jokes you have written:

```
>>> Joke.objects.count()
2
```

13. That joke about the chicken crossing the road never was funny. Let's delete it. You could get it using:

```
Joke.objects.first()
```

But let's assume you don't know that it is the first joke you entered and get it using the `get()` method:

```
>>> chicken_joke = Joke.objects.get(question = 'Why did the chicken cross the road?')
```

14. Confirm you have the right joke:

```
>>> chicken_joke
<Joke: Why did the chicken cross the road?>
```

15. Delete it:

```
>>> chicken_joke.delete()
(1, {'jokes.Joke': 1})
```

The `delete()` method returns a tuple. The first element contains the total number of objects that were deleted. The second element contains a dictionary showing the number of deletions per object type. In this case, just one object was deleted: a `jokes.Joke` object.

16. Finally, let's see how many jokes you have left:

    ```
    >>> Joke.objects.count()
    1
    ```

    It looks like the delete worked.

This shows how to create a model and how to create, save, and view instances of that model, but with Django, you really want to do all this using web pages. You will learn how to do that next.

Make sure to exit the shell:

```
>>> exit()
(.venv) …/projects/djangojokes.com>
```

Git Commit

Commit your code to Git.

3.4. Types of Views

You used a `TemplateView` to create the home page. `TemplateView` is a class-based view. Django has *view functions* in addition to *class-based views*, but class-based views make development much easier, so you will (mostly) stick with them. You imported `TemplateView` from `django.views.generic`. There are many other view classes available in that module, including:

- `ListView` – A view for listing objects (records in a queryset).
- `DetailView` – A view for displaying details about an object (one retrieved from a queryset).
- `CreateView` – A view for creating a new object.
- `UpdateView` – A view for updating an object.
- `DeleteView` – A view for deleting an object.

You will work with all of these views in the next exercises to list jokes, show joke details, and create, edit, and delete jokes.

Exercise 12: Creating a ListView

20 to 30 minutes

In this exercise, you will create the page for listing jokes. To do this, you will inherit from `ListView`.

1. Open `jokes/views.py` in your editor and delete the current contents.
2. Import `ListView` from `django.views.generic`:

```
from django.views.generic import ListView
```

3. Import the `Joke` model from `models.py`, which is in the same directory:

```
from .models import Joke
```

4. Create a `JokeListView` view that inherits from `ListView`:

```
class JokeListView(ListView):
    model = Joke
```

   A minimal `ListView` is incredibly simple. It just requires the model to query.

The `jokes/views.py` file should now look like this:

Exercise Code 12.1: jokes/views.py

```
1.  from django.views.generic import ListView
2.
3.  from .models import Joke
4.
5.  class JokeListView(ListView):
6.      model = Joke
```

URLConf

You must now configure a path to the new view.

1. Open `jokes/urls.py` in your editor.

2. Import the JokeListView view from views.py, which is in the same directory:

```
from .views import JokeListView
```

3. Add a new path to urlpatterns to JokeListView.as_view() at '':

```
path('', JokeListView.as_view(), name='list'),
```

Remember that only URL paths that begin with '/jokes/' will be handed off to the URLConf of the jokes app, so '' will actually be '/jokes/'. The second argument of the path() function must be a *view function* (as opposed to a class-based view), which is why you have to pass JokeListView.**as_view()**. The as_view() method of class-based views returns a view function.

The jokes/urls.py file should now look like this:

Exercise Code 12.2: jokes/urls.py

```
1.  from django.urls import path
2.
3.  from .views import JokeListView
4.
5.  app_name = 'jokes'
6.  urlpatterns = [
7.      path('', JokeListView.as_view(), name='list'),
8.  ]
```

Let's try it out.

1. If it's not still running, start up the server:

```
(.venv) …/projects/djangojokes.com> python manage.py runserver
```

2. Point your browser to http://127.0.0.1:8000/jokes/.
3. You should get an error that reads something like:

```
TemplateDoesNotExist at /jokes/
jokes/joke_list.html
```

Oops! We forgot to create a template for JokeListView. But, there is something even more interesting about this error: it tells us where it looked for that template: jokes/joke_list.html.

The Template

Take another look at the JokeListView code:

```
class JokeListView(ListView):
    model = Joke
```

Notice that you do not define a template_name attribute as you did with HomePageView. When no template_name is defined for a ListView, Django infers a template_name as:

```
app_name/model_list.html
```

where app_name is the name of the app (e.g., jokes) and model is the lowercase name of the model. So, for JokeListView, Django is looking for the template at:

```
jokes/joke_list.html
```

Create that template:

Create a jokes folder within the templates folder, and within that, create a joke_list.html file with the following content:

Exercise Code 12.3: templates/jokes/joke_list.html

```
1.   {% extends "_base.html" %}
2.
3.   {% block title %}Jokes{% endblock %}
4.   {% block main %}
5.     <h2>Jokes</h2>
6.     <ul class="list-group list-group-flush mb-3">
7.       {% for joke in joke_list %}
8.         <li class="list-group-item">{{ joke.question }}</li>
9.       {% endfor %}
10.    </ul>
11.  {% endblock %}
```

Things to notice:

1. The template extends `_base.html`:

```
{% extends "_base.html" %}
```

2. You use the `for` template tag, which we will cover in detail later (see page 143), to loop through the queryset, which is stored in an auto-created variable called `joke_list` (created by appending "_list" to the lowercase model name):

```
{% for joke in joke_list %}
<li class="list-group-item">{{ joke.question }}</li>
{% endfor %}
```

The double curly braces hold a template variable (or expression) that should be evaluated. This for loop is the Django template equivalent of:

```
for joke in Joke.objects.all():
print(f'\n    <li class="list-group-item">{joke.question}</li>\n')
```

While you are working on templates, change the **NavLink** link in the header of the `_base.html` template to link to the jokes page using a `url` template tag:

```
<li class="nav-item">
  <a class="nav-link" href="{% url 'jokes:list' %}">Jokes</a>
</li>
```

Try It Out

In your browser, go to `http://127.0.0.1:8000/` and click on the **Jokes** link in the header. It should look like this:

Right now, you only have one joke. You will add more soon, but first, you will create a `DetailView` for jokes.

Git Commit

Commit your code to Git.

Exercise 13: Creating a DetailView

25 to 40 minutes

In this exercise, you will create the page to show information about an individual joke. To do this, you will inherit from `DetailView`.

1. Open `jokes/views.py` in your editor.
2. Import `DetailView` from `django.views.generic`:

```
from django.views.generic import DetailView, ListView
```

3. Create a `JokeDetailView` view that inherits from `DetailView`:

```
class JokeDetailView(DetailView):
    model = Joke
```

   Just like a `ListView`, a minimal `DetailView` only requires the model to query.

The `jokes/views.py` file should now look like this:

Exercise Code 13.1: jokes/views.py

```
1.  from django.views.generic import DetailView, ListView
2.
3.  from .models import Joke
4.
5.  class JokeDetailView(DetailView):
6.      model = Joke
7.
8.
9.  class JokeListView(ListView):
10.     model = Joke
```

URLConf

You must now configure a path to the new view. Because each joke will have its own detail page, you must identify the specific joke to show. For now, you will do this using the `joke` object's primary key.

1. Open `jokes/urls.py` in your editor.

2. Import the JokeDetailView view from views.py, which is in the same directory:

```
from .views import JokeDetailView, JokeListView
```

3. Add a new path to urlpatterns to JokeDetailView.as_view() at 'joke/<int:pk>/':

```
path('joke/<int:pk>/', JokeDetailView.as_view(), name='detail'),
```

   The path is constructed as "joke/<int:pk>/". int:pk indicates that the value entered for this part of the path must be an integer. The view will have access to this value via self.kwargs.get('pk') and will use it to get the specific joke object to use.[12]

The jokes/urls.py file should now look like this:

Exercise Code 13.2: jokes/urls.py

```
1.  from django.urls import path
2.
3.  from .views import JokeDetailView, JokeListView
4.
5.  app_name = 'jokes'
6.  urlpatterns = [
7.      path('joke/<int:pk>/', JokeDetailView.as_view(), name='detail'),
8.      path('', JokeListView.as_view(), name='jokes'),
9.  ]
```

The Template

Can you guess the default name of the template used by the JokeDetailView? If you guessed jokes/joke_detail.html, you're right. Create that template:

Within the templates/jokes folder, add a joke_detail.html file with the following content:[13]

12. Look in .venv\Lib\site-packages\django\views\generic\detail.py at the get_object() method of the SingleObjectMixin class to see how this magic works behind the scenes.

13. **Don't want to type?** Copy from starter-code/app-with-model/joke_detail.html.

Exercise Code 13.3: templates/jokes/joke_detail.html

```
1.    {% extends "_base.html" %}
2.
3.    {% block title %}Joke{% endblock %}
4.    {% block main %}
5.      <div class="card border-primary m-auto mb-3 text-center"
6.        style="max-width: 30rem">
7.        <div class="card-header">{{ joke.question }}</div>
8.        <div class="card-body text-primary">
9.          <h5 class="card-title">{{ joke.answer }}</h5>
10.       </div>
11.       <div class="card-footer">
12.         <small class="text-muted">
13.           Created on: {{ joke.created }}
14.           Last updated: {{ joke.updated }}
15.         </small>
16.       </div>
17.     </div>
18.   {% endblock %}
```

Things to notice:

1. The template extends `_base.html`:

   ```
   {% extends "_base.html" %}
   ```

2. The template has access to an auto-created variable called `joke` (the lowercase model name) containing the `joke` object.

Open `templates/jokes/joke_list.html` and make `joke.question` a link:

Exercise Code 13.4: templates/jokes/joke_list.html

```
      -------Lines 1 through 6 Omitted-------
7.        {% for joke in joke_list %}
8.          <li class="list-group-item">
9.            <a href="{% url 'jokes:detail' joke.pk %}">{{ joke.question }}</a>
10.         </li>
11.       {% endfor %}
      -------Lines 12 through 13 Omitted-------
```

In the `url` tag, `joke.pk` holds the primary key for the joke, which it will use to construct the URL. Think of a tag as a function with each subsequent item being an argument passed to the function. So, the following `url` tag:

```
{% url 'joke' joke.pk %}
```

...becomes:

```
url('joke', joke.pk)
```

The function constructs and returns the URL based on the arguments it receives.

Try It Out

Return to the browser and refresh the **jokes** page. The joke question should now be a link. Click it. The resulting page should look like this:

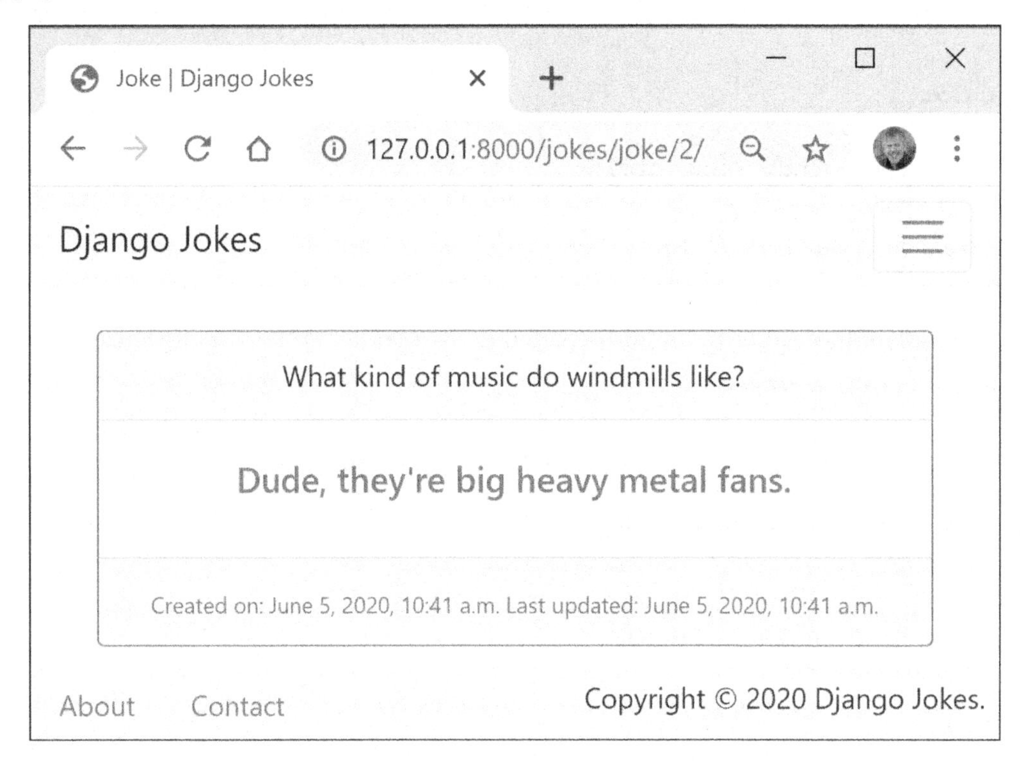

If you have followed along with everything exactly, the URL should read:

```
http://127.0.0.1:8000/jokes/joke/2/
```

However, if you added more jokes, it may show a different primary key.

Avoid Using Primary Keys in URLs

It is not a great idea to use primary keys in URLs. We will show a better way of creating URLs for jokes in a later lesson (see page 207).

get_absolute_url()

An alternative to constructing URLs with the `url` tag as we did in `joke_list.html` is to use the `get_absolute_url()` method, like this:

```
joke.get_absolute_url
```

However, before you do that, you need to add the `get_absolute_url()` method to the model:

1. Open `jokes/models.py` in your editor.
2. Import the `reverse()` function from `django.urls`:

   ```
   from django.urls import reverse
   ```

   The `reverse()` function gets and returns the URL based on the passed-in URL pattern name.
3. Add the `get_absolute_url()` function above the `__str()__` function in the `Joke` model:[14]

   ```
   def get_absolute_url(self):
       return reverse('jokes:detail', args=[str(self.pk)])
   ```

   The arguments passed to the preceding `reverse()` function are:

   A. The URL pattern name preceded by the namespace as defined in the URLConf:

      ```
      app_name = 'jokes'
      urlpatterns = [
          path('joke/<int:pk>/', JokeDetailView.as_view(), name='detail'),…
      ```

14. See `https://docs.djangoproject.com/en/3.1/ref/models/instances/#django.db.models.Model.get_absolute_url` for documentation on `get_absolute_url()`.

B. The arguments required by the URL pattern. In this case, it is just the pk of the joke converted to a string.[15]

The jokes/models.py file should now look like this:

Exercise Code 13.5: jokes/models.py

```
1.   from django.db import models
2.   from django.urls import reverse
3.
4.   class Joke(models.Model):
5.       question = models.TextField(max_length=200)
6.       answer = models.TextField(max_length=100, blank=True)
7.       created = models.DateTimeField(auto_now_add=True)
8.       updated = models.DateTimeField(auto_now=True)
9.
10.      def get_absolute_url(self):
11.          return reverse('jokes:detail', args=[str(self.pk)])
12.
13.      def __str__(self):
14.          return self.question
```

You can now update the template to use get_absolute_url:

Exercise Code 13.6: templates/jokes/joke_list.html

```
     -------Lines 1 through 6 Omitted-------
7.       {% for joke in joke_list %}
8.         <li class="list-group-item">
9.           <a href="{{ joke.get_absolute_url }}">{{ joke.question }}</a>
10.        </li>
11.      {% endfor %}
     -------Lines 12 through 13 Omitted-------
```

A big advantage of using get_absolute_url is that you don't have to change the template if you change the way that URLs are constructed for jokes, which you will eventually do.

15. See https://docs.djangoproject.com/en/3/ref/urlresolvers/#django.urls.reverse for documentation on reverse().

Git Commit

Commit your code to Git.

3.5. GET and POST Requests

The value of a form's `method` attribute determines how the form data will be passed to the server.

get

When using the `get` method, which is the default, form data is sent to the server in the URL as a *query string*. The query string is appended to the website address starting with a question mark (?) and followed by name-value pairs delimited (separated) by an ampersand (&). A URL with a query string might look like this:

```
https://www.example.com?firstname=Nat&lastname=Dunn
```

The `get` method is commonly used by search engines, because it allows the resulting page to be bookmarked. For example, Google uses the `get` method. You can tell by looking at the location bar after doing a search:

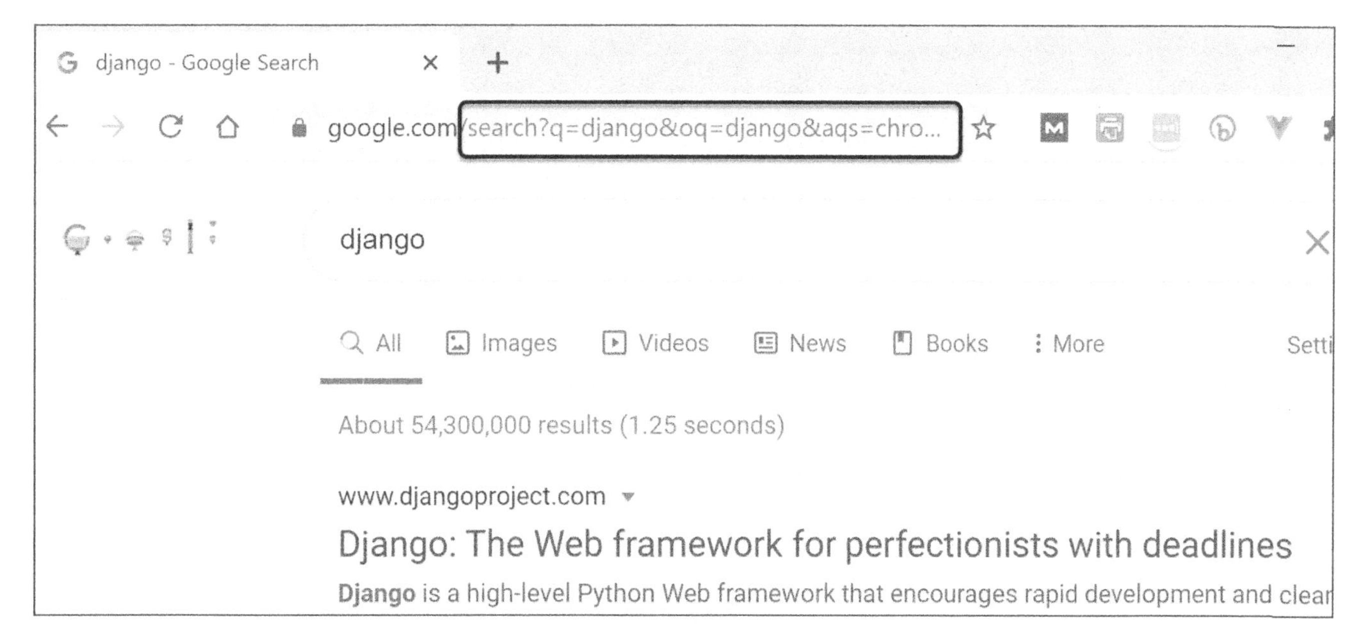

post

When `post` is used, the name-value pairs are not sent as part of the query string. Instead, they are sent behind the scenes. This has the advantage of keeping the values hidden from anyone looking over the user's shoulder. Two other advantages of the `post` method are:

1. It allows for much more data to be submitted (i.e., larger forms).
2. It allows for files to be uploaded to the server.[16]

You should use the `post` method whenever the form submission will (or might) do anything more than request a web page. For example, if the submission will log a user in, modify the database or the file system, or send an email, you should use `post`.

16. Files can be uploaded to the server via the `file` input type. The tag syntax is: `<input type="file" name="filename">`.

Exercise 14: Creating and Updating Jokes

25 to 40 minutes

In this exercise, you will create the views and forms for creating and updating jokes. We will explain just the bare minimum about forms to get the pages working. Later, we will dig much deeper into Django forms (see page 231).

1. Open `jokes/views.py` in your editor.
2. Add `CreateView` and `UpdateView` to the list of imported views from `django.views.generic`:

```
from django.views.generic import CreateView, DetailView, ListView, UpdateView
```

3. Add two new views:

   A. `JokeCreateView`:

```
class JokeCreateView(CreateView):
    model = Joke
    fields = ['question', 'answer']
```

   B. `JokeUpdateView`:

```
class JokeUpdateView(UpdateView):
    model = Joke
    fields = ['question', 'answer']
```

   Notice that each of these views takes the model and the fields you want to include in the form.

The `jokes/views.py` file should now look like this:

Exercise Code 14.1: jokes/views.py

```
1.  from django.views.generic import CreateView, DetailView, ListView, UpdateView
2.
3.  from .models import Joke
4.
5.  class JokeCreateView(CreateView):
6.      model = Joke
7.      fields = ['question', 'answer']
8.
9.
10. class JokeDetailView(DetailView):
11.     model = Joke
12.
13.
14. class JokeListView(ListView):
15.     model = Joke
16.
17.
18. class JokeUpdateView(UpdateView):
19.     model = Joke
20.     fields = ['question', 'answer']
```

URLConf

You must now configure paths to the new views. The `CreateView` view is used to create a *new* object (a joke), so its path will always be the same. But the path for the `UpdateView` view will be unique to each joke. For now, we will continue to use the primary key to identify the joke.

1. Open `jokes/urls.py` in your editor.
2. Add `JokeCreateView` and `JokeUpdateView` to the imported views:

```
from .views import (
    JokeCreateView, JokeDetailView, JokeListView, JokeUpdateView
)
```

Notice that we have wrapped the imported views in parentheses. This is so that we can break the list across lines to limit the length of each line to no longer than 79 characters as per PEP8.[17] We have also listed the imported views in alphabetical order, which makes things easier to find.

17. `https://www.python.org/dev/peps/pep-0008/#maximum-line-length`

3. Add a path for JokeUpdateView constructed as "joke/<int:pk>/update/" and with the name "update". It will resolve to something like "jokes/joke/2/update/":

```
path('joke/<int:pk>/update/', JokeUpdateView.as_view(), name='update'),
```

4. Add a path for JokeCreateView constructed as "joke/create/" and with the name "create":

```
path('joke/create/', JokeCreateView.as_view(), name='create'),
```

Note that "update" and "create" are arbitrary strings in the paths. You could use "edit" and "add" or anything else you like.

The jokes/urls.py file should now look like this:

Exercise Code 14.2: jokes/urls.py

```
1.  from django.urls import path
2.
3.  from .views import (JokeCreateView, JokeDetailView, JokeListView,
4.                      JokeUpdateView)
5.
6.  app_name = 'jokes'
7.  urlpatterns = [
8.      path('joke/<int:pk>/update/', JokeUpdateView.as_view(), name='update'),
9.      path('joke/create/', JokeCreateView.as_view(), name='create'),
10.     path('joke/<int:pk>/', JokeDetailView.as_view(), name='detail'),
11.     path('', JokeListView.as_view(), name='list'),
12. ]
```

The Template

The CreateView and UpdateView views use the same default template_name, which they infer as follows:

```
app_name/model_form.html
```

In this case, that's **jokes/joke**_form.html.

Within the `templates/jokes` folder, add a `joke_form.html` file with the following content:[18]

Exercise Code 14.3: templates/jokes/joke_form.html

```
1.   {% extends "_base.html" %}
2.
3.   {% block title %}Add/Update Joke{% endblock %}
4.   {% block main %}
5.     <div class="card border-primary m-auto mb-3 p-3"
6.       style="max-width: 30rem">
7.       <form method="post">
8.         {% csrf_token %}
9.         {{ form }}
10.        <button class="btn btn-success float-right">Submit</button>
11.      </form>
12.    </div>
13.  {% endblock %}
```

Things to notice:

1. The template must include a `form` element, and the method must be "post".
2. Within the `form` element, you must include:
   A. The `{% csrf_token %}` template tag – This is a security measure that protects against cross site request forgery.[19]
   B. The `form` variable: `{{ form }}` – This will output the form fields and their labels.
   C. A submit button.

Open `templates/jokes/joke_list.html` and add links to the new views. Use Bootstrap to make the links look like buttons:

18. **Don't want to type?** Copy from `starter-code/app-with-model/joke_form.html`.
19. `https://docs.djangoproject.com/en/3.1/ref/csrf/`

Exercise Code 14.4: templates/jokes/joke_list.html

```
1.    {% extends "_base.html" %}
2.
3.    {% block title %}Jokes{% endblock %}
4.    {% block main %}
5.      <a class="btn btn-success btn-sm float-right" href="{% url 'jokes:create' %}">
6.        + New Joke
7.      </a>
8.      <h2>Jokes</h2>
9.      <ul class="list-group list-group-flush mb-3">
10.       {% for joke in joke_list %}
11.         <li class="list-group-item">
12.           <a href="{{ joke.get_absolute_url }}">{{ joke.question }}</a>
13.           <a href="{% url 'jokes:update' joke.pk %}"
14.             class="btn btn-info btn-sm float-right mr-2">Update</a>
15.         </li>
16.       {% endfor %}
17.     </ul>
18.   {% endblock %}
```

Note that you must pass the primary key to the `jokes:update` path so that the resulting page knows which joke to update.

Visit `http://127.0.0.1:8000/jokes/` and click on the **+ New Joke** button. You should see the form, but it won't be very pretty. You can make it look better by using `form.as_table` and nesting the `form` in a `table`:

Exercise Code 14.5: templates/jokes/joke_form.html

```
     -------Lines 1 through 6 Omitted-------
7.        <form method="post">
8.          {% csrf_token %}
9.          <table class="table">
10.           {{ form.as_table }}
11.         </table>
12.         <button class="btn btn-success float-right">Submit</button>
13.       </form>
     -------Lines 14 through 15 Omitted-------
```

Refresh the page with the create-joke form. It should now look like this:

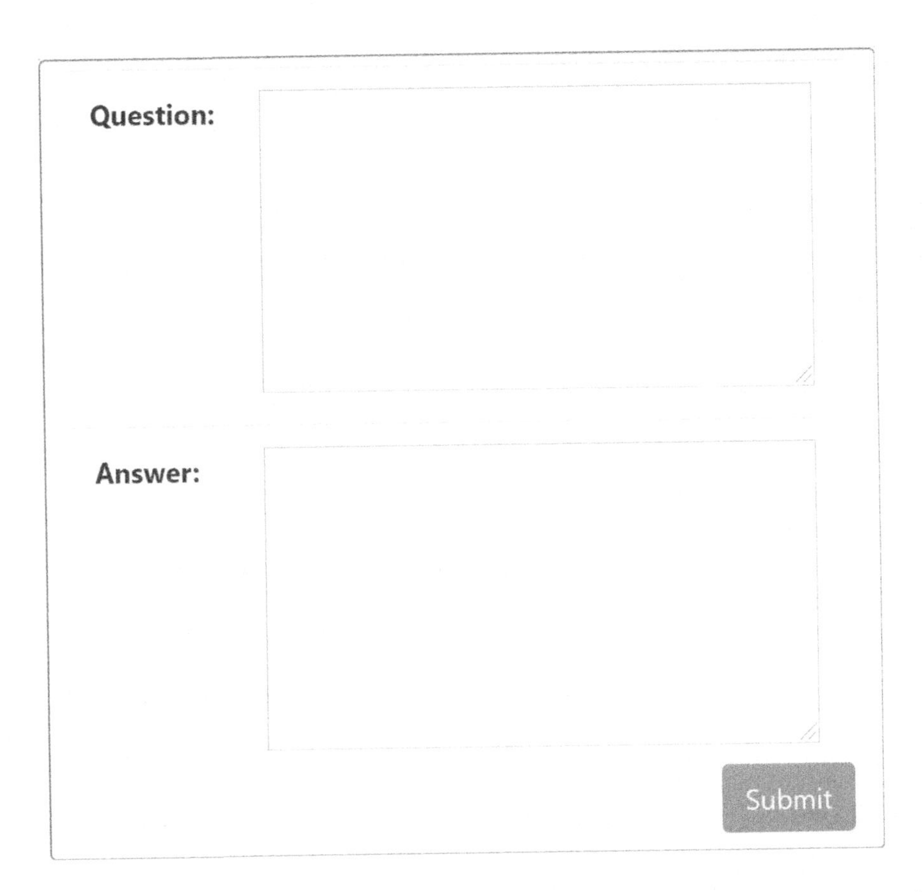

That's better. We'll make additional improvements later. Now, go ahead and submit a joke:

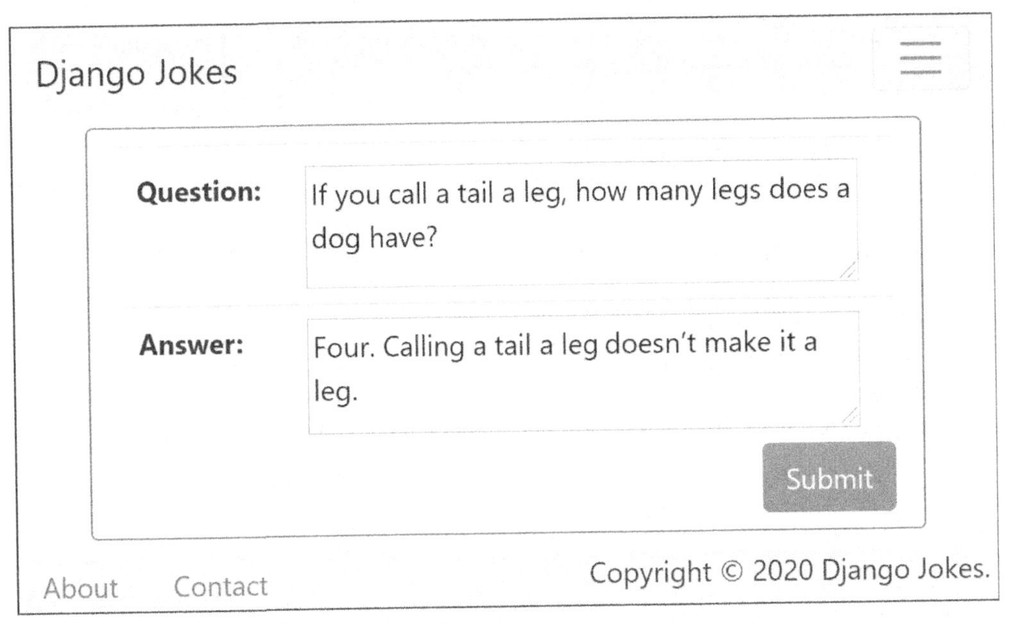

You should be redirected to the detail page for the new joke:

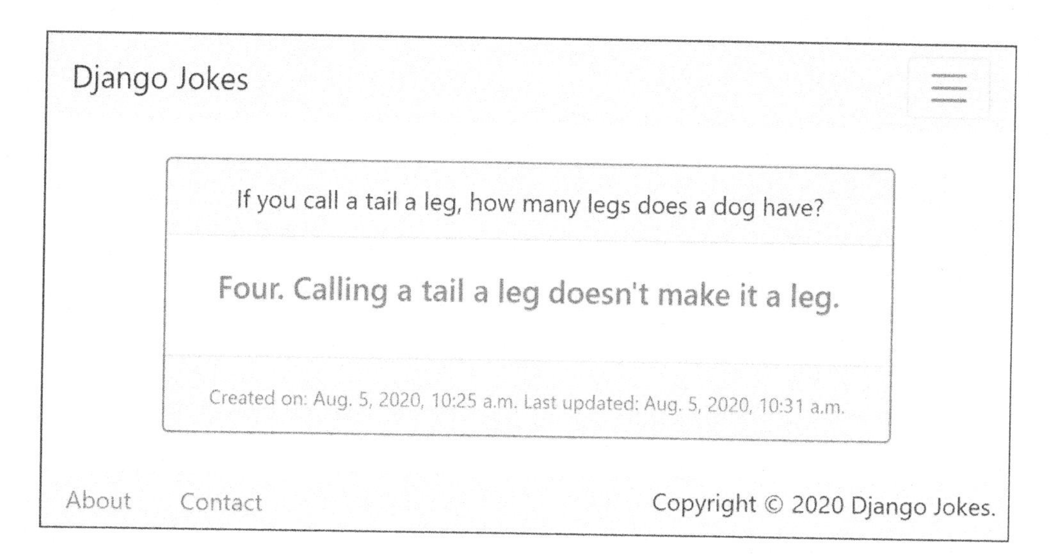

Go to the **Jokes** page. It should show your new joke:

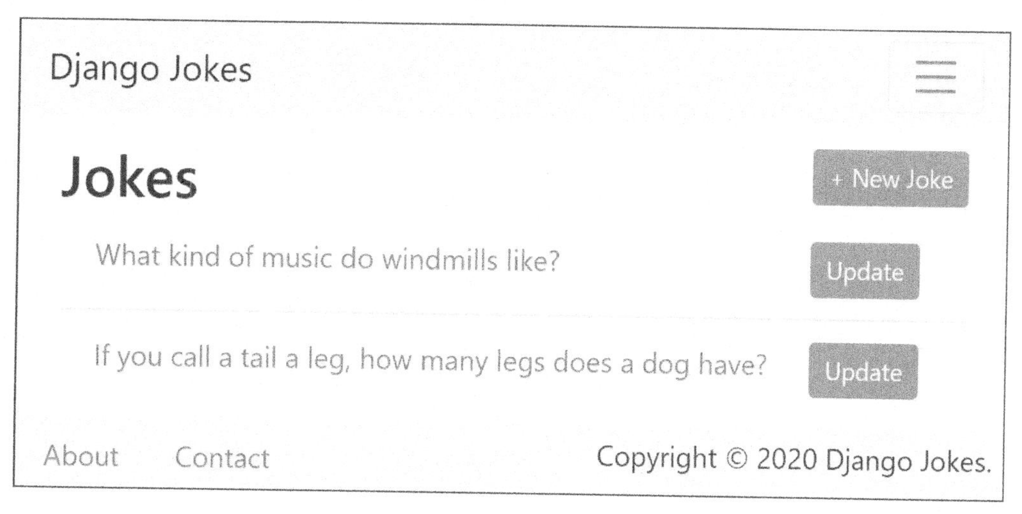

Click on the **Update** button and update the joke:

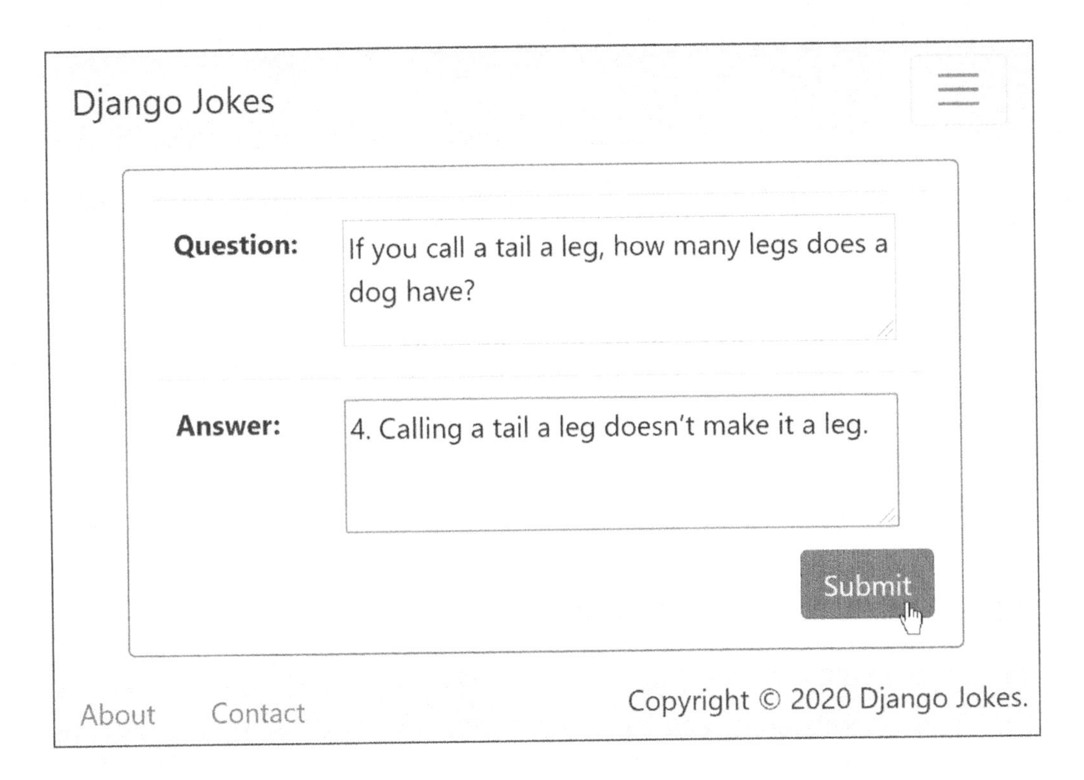

You can now add and update jokes.

Git Commit

Commit your code to Git.

3.6. Deleting Objects

Django's default delete process works like this:

1. The user clicks a **Delete** link or button, resulting in a *get* request to a **Delete Confirmation** page, which contains a simple form with a single submit button.
2. The user submits the form, resulting in a *post* request that deletes the record from the database.
3. The server redirects to a "success url" specified in the view as `success_url`.

Exercise 15: Deleting Jokes

15 to 25 minutes

In this exercise, you will create the view and form for deleting a joke:

1. Open `jokes/views.py` in your editor.
2. At the top of the page, import the `reverse_lazy()` function from `django.urls`:

   ```
   from django.urls import reverse_lazy
   ```

   `reverse_lazy()` works just like `reverse()`: it returns the URL based on the passed-in URL pattern name. But unlike `reverse()`, it waits to get the URL until it is needed. More on this in a moment.

3. Add `DeleteView` to the list of imported views from `django.views.generic`:

   ```
   from django.views.generic import (
       CreateView, DeleteView, DetailView, ListView, UpdateView
   )
   ```

4. Add the view:

   ```
   class JokeDeleteView(DeleteView):
       model = Joke
       success_url = reverse_lazy('jokes:list')
   ```

   Notice that we use `reverse_lazy()` here. The view is created before the URL configuration, so if you try to use `reverse()`, you will likely get an error about a circular import. The issue is that, with `reverse()`, the view needs the URLConf to have already been created, but the URLConf imports the view, so it cannot be created until the view exists.

The complete `jokes/views.py` should now look like this:

Exercise Code 15.1: jokes/views.py

```
1.   from django.urls import reverse_lazy
2.
3.   from django.views.generic import (
4.       CreateView, DeleteView, DetailView, ListView, UpdateView
5.   )
6.
7.   from .models import Joke
8.
9.   class JokeCreateView(CreateView):
10.      model = Joke
11.      fields = ['question', 'answer']
12.
13.
14.  class JokeDeleteView(DeleteView):
15.      model = Joke
16.      success_url = reverse_lazy('jokes:list')
17.
18.
19.  class JokeDetailView(DetailView):
20.      model = Joke
21.
22.
23.  class JokeListView(ListView):
24.      model = Joke
25.
26.
27.  class JokeUpdateView(UpdateView):
28.      model = Joke
29.      fields = ['question', 'answer']
```

URLConf

You must now configure the path to the new view. As you did with `UpdateView`, you will use the primary key to identify the joke to be deleted.

1. Open `jokes/urls.py` in your editor.
2. Add `JokeDeleteView` to the imported views:

    ```
    from .views import (
        JokeCreateView, JokeDeleteView, JokeDetailView, JokeListView, JokeUpdateView
    )
    ```

3. Add a path for `JokeDeleteView` constructed as "`joke/<int:pk>/delete/`" and with the name "delete". It will resolve to something like "`jokes/joke/2/delete/`":

```
path('joke/<int:pk>/delete/', JokeDeleteView.as_view(), name='delete'),
```

"delete" is an arbitrary string. You could use "remove", "destroy" or anything else you like.

Exercise Code 15.2: jokes/urls.py

```
1.  from django.urls import path
2.
3.  from .views import (
4.      JokeCreateView, JokeDeleteView, JokeDetailView, JokeListView, JokeUpdateView
5.  )
6.
7.  app_name = 'jokes'
8.  urlpatterns = [
9.      path('joke/<int:pk>/update/', JokeUpdateView.as_view(), name='update'),
10.     path('joke/<int:pk>/delete/', JokeDeleteView.as_view(), name='delete'),
11.     path('joke/create/', JokeCreateView.as_view(), name='create'),
12.     path('joke/<int:pk>/', JokeDetailView.as_view(), name='detail'),
13.     path('', JokeListView.as_view(), name='list'),
14. ]
```

The Template

The default `template_name` for a `DeleteView` is inferred as follows:

```
app_name/model_confirm_delete.html
```

In this case, that's **`jokes/joke`**`_confirm_delete.html`.

Within the `templates/jokes` folder, add a `joke_confirm_delete.html` file with the following content:[20]

20. **Don't want to type?** Copy from `starter-code/app-with-model/joke_confirm_delete.html`.

Exercise Code 15.3: templates/jokes/joke_confirm_delete.html

```
1.    {% extends "_base.html" %}
2.
3.    {% block title %}Delete Joke{% endblock %}
4.    {% block main %}
5.      <div class="card border-primary m-auto mb-3 text-center"
6.        style="max-width: 30rem">
7.        <form method="post">
8.          {% csrf_token %}
9.          <p><strong>Are you sure you want to delete this joke?</strong></p>
10.         <p>{{ joke.question }}</p>
11.         <button class="btn btn-success form-control">Confirm</button>
12.       </form>
13.     </div>
14.   {% endblock %}
```

Things to notice:

1. The template must include a `form` element, and the method should be "post".
2. Within the `form` element, you must include:
    A. The `{% csrf_token %}` template tag – Again, this is a security measure.
    B. A submit button.

Open `templates/jokes/joke_list.html` and add a delete button link:

Exercise Code 15.4: templates/jokes/joke_list.html

```
      -------Lines 1 through 11 Omitted-------
12.           <a href="{{ joke.get_absolute_url }}">{{ joke.question }}</a>
13.           <a href="{% url 'jokes:update' joke.pk %}"
14.             class="btn btn-info btn-sm float-right mr-2">Update</a>
15.           <a href="{% url 'jokes:delete' joke.pk %}"
16.             class="btn btn-danger btn-sm float-right mr-2">Delete</a>
      -------Lines 17 through 20 Omitted-------
```

Note that you must pass the primary key with to the `delete` path so that the resulting page knows which joke to delete.

Try It Out

1. Visit `http://127.0.0.1:8000/jokes/`.
2. Click on one of the **Delete** buttons. You should see a page like this:

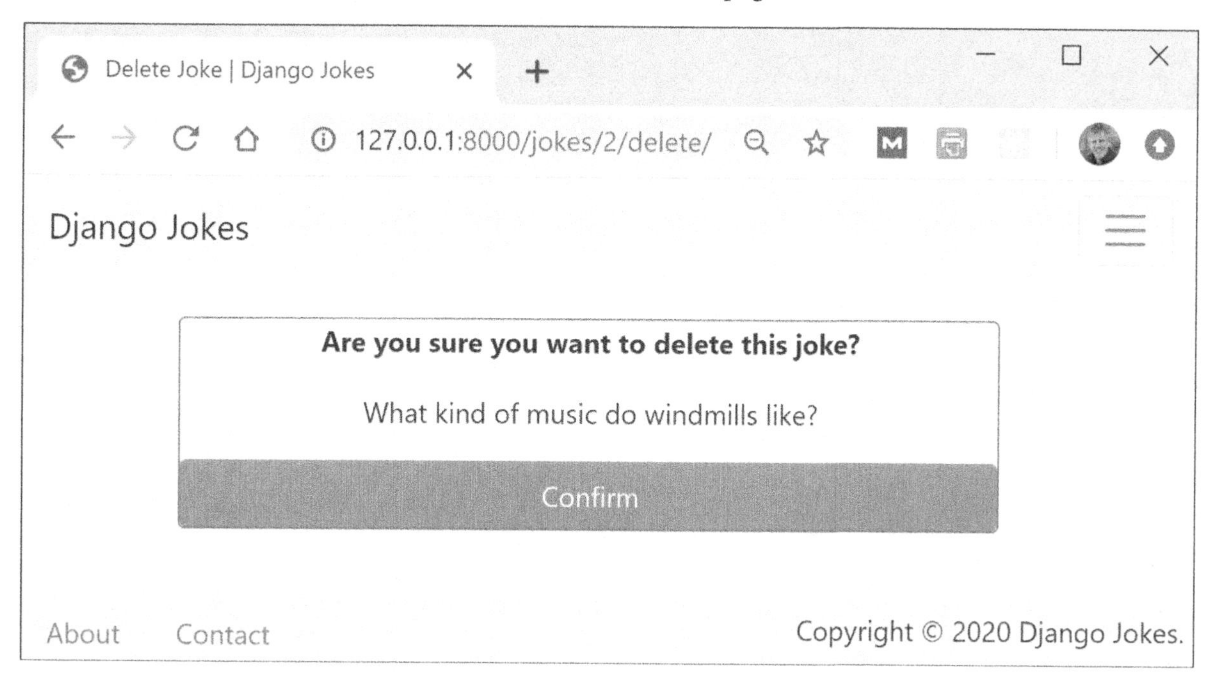

3. Click **Confirm**. It should redirect to the **Jokes** page, and the joke you just deleted should be gone.

Git Commit

Commit your code to Git.

Conclusion

In this lesson, you have learned how models work and how to create a basic Django *CRUDL* (**C**reate, **R**ead, **U**pdate, **D**elete, **L**ist) app. You have also learned to use Git and GitHub for version control.

The completed jokes project for this lesson is available in `solutions/app-with-model/django jokes.com`.

LESSON 4

Template Filters and Tags

Topics Covered

☑ Built-in template filters.

☑ Built-in template tags.

☑ Custom template filters and tags.

> Edna had discovered it accidentally one day when the high-board gate stood ajar. She caught sight of a little green table, blotched with the checkered sunlight that **filter**ed through the quivering leaves overhead.
>
> – *The Awakening, Kate Chopin*

Introduction

The Django template language includes 57 built-in template filters and 25 built-in template tags. In this lesson, we will describe the most useful filters and tags and give a brief overview of the rest of them. We will also teach you how to create *custom* filters and tags.

Exercise 16: Setting Up the Project

30 to 45 minutes

For this lesson, you will create a project that allows you to play with Django's template filters and tags.

1. Open the **webucator-django** workspace in Visual Studio Code.
2. Create a new `templates_proj` directory within the `projects` directory. The `projects` folder will not look like this:

   - projects
     - djangojokes.com
     - hello_proj
     - **template_proj**

3. Open `templates_proj` in the terminal, make sure the virtual environment is activated, and create the new project by running (**Don't forget the dot at the end**):

```
(.venv) …/projects/templates_proj> django-admin startproject templateplay .
```

4. Add a `templates` folder to the `templates_proj` folder. The folder should now look like this:

   - templates_proj
     - templateplay
     - templates
     - manage.py

5. Copy the `_base.html` file[21] from the `starter-code` folder and paste it into the `templates` folder you just created.

   A. Replace all instances of "SITENAME" in `_base.html` with "Template Play".

   B. Replace the link that reads "NavLink" with:

```
<a class="nav-link" href="{% url 'filters' %}">Filters</a>
```

   This will link to the filters practice page.

21. This file should already include Bootstrap and Font Awesome from the changes you made when you first used it (see page 62).

C. Replace the link that reads "Log in" with:

```
<a class="nav-link" href="{% url 'tags' %}">Tags</a>
```

This will link to the tags practice page.

D. Replace the `href` values in the home link and the `Template Play` link with `{% url 'homepage' %}`:

```
<a class="navbar-brand" href="{% url 'homepage' %}">Template Play</a>
```

```
<a class="nav-link" href="{% url 'homepage' %}">Home
  <span class="sr-only">(current)</span>
</a>
```

E. Add the following `style` block to the head right below the `title` tag:

```
<style>
  h2, h3 {
    border-bottom: thin black solid;
    margin: .5em auto;
  }

  h3 {
    font-size: 1.2rem;
  }
</style>
```

This will make your practice pages look a little nicer.

6. You have to let Django know to look for templates in your new `templates` directory. Open `templateplay/settings.py` and add the following to the `DIRS` value of the dictionary in `TEMPLATES`:

```
'DIRS': [BASE_DIR / 'templates'],
```

❖ E16.1. App Scaffolding

This project will just have one app, which you will call `practice`.

With `templates_proj` open in the terminal, run the following command to create the **practice** app:

```
(.venv) …/projects/templates_proj> python manage.py startapp practice
```

The `templates_proj` folder should now look like this:

```
templates_proj
    practice
    templateplay
    templates
    manage.py
```

❖ E16.2. Installed Apps

Add the new **practice** app to the `INSTALLED_APPS` in `templateplay/settings.py`:

```
INSTALLED_APPS = [
    # Built-in Django apps
    'django.contrib.admin',
    'django.contrib.auth',
    'django.contrib.contenttypes',
    'django.contrib.sessions',
    'django.contrib.messages',
    'django.contrib.staticfiles',

    # Local apps
    'practice.apps.PracticeConfig',
]
```

❖ E16.3. Views

This `practice` app will have three views, all of which will inherit from `TemplateView`:

1. HomePageView - for linking to the other two views.[22]
2. FilterView - for playing with filters.
3. TagView - for playing with tags.

Open practice/views.py and change it as shown in the following file:[23]

Exercise Code 16.1: practice/views.py

```
1.  from django.views.generic import TemplateView
2.
3.  class FilterView(TemplateView):
4.      template_name = 'practice/filters.html'
5.
6.
7.  class HomePageView(TemplateView):
8.      template_name = 'home.html'
9.
10.
11. class TagView(TemplateView):
12.     template_name = 'practice/tags.html'
```

❖ E16.4. Templates[24]

1. Create a home.html file within the templates folder with the following content:

Exercise Code 16.2: templates/home.html

```
1.  {% extends "_base.html" %}
2.
3.  {% block title %}Home{% endblock %}
4.  {% block main %}
5.    <h2>Welcome!</h2>
6.    <ul>
7.      <li><a href="{% url 'filters' %}">Filters</a></li>
8.      <li><a href="{% url 'tags' %}">Tags</a></li>
9.    </ul>
10. {% endblock %}
```

---

22. As the project only has one app, you will put the HomePageView in that app. In a multi-app project, you would normally have a separate app for your pages that were general to the project.
23. **Don't want to type?** Copy from starter-code/template-filters-and-tags/views.py.
24. **Don't want to type?** Copy from home.html, filters.html, and tags.html in starter-code/template-filters-and-tags.

2. Add a `practice` folder to the `templates` folder.

3. Within the `templates/practice` folder, add `filters.html` and `tags.html`:

Exercise Code 16.3: templates/practice/filters.html

```
1.  {% extends "_base.html" %}
2.
3.  {% block title %}Filters{% endblock %}
4.  {% block main %}
5.    <h2>Filters</h2>
6.  {% endblock %}
```

Exercise Code 16.4: templates/practice/tags.html

```
1.  {% extends "_base.html" %}
2.
3.  {% block title %}Tags{% endblock %}
4.  {% block main %}
5.    <h2>Tags</h2>
6.  {% endblock %}
```

❖ E16.5. URLs[25]

Create URLConf in New App

Within the `practice` folder (the one in `templates_proj`, not the one in `templates`), create a `urls.py` file with the following content:

Exercise Code 16.5: practice/urls.py

```
1.  from django.urls import path
2.
3.  from .views import FilterView, HomePageView, TagView
4.
5.  urlpatterns = [
6.      path('', HomePageView.as_view(), name='homepage'),
7.      path('filters/', FilterView.as_view(), name='filters'),
8.      path('tags/', TagView.as_view(), name='tags'),
9.  ]
```

25. **Don't want to type?** Copy from `urls.py` and `urls_main.py` in `starter-code/template-filters-and-tags`.

Code Explanation

Notice that you did not set `app_name` to create a namespace for the URLConf as you have done in previous URLConfs. That's because this project just has one app. This is why the `href` values in `_base.html` are written as `{% url 'filters' %}` and `{% url 'tags' %}` instead of `{% url 'practice:filters' %}` and `{% url 'practice:tags' %}`.

Include App URLConf in Main URLConf

Next, you need to let your main URLConf know to hand off some paths to the practice URLConf. Open `templateplay/urls.py` and modify it as follows:

Exercise Code 16.6: templateplay/urls.py

```
1.  from django.contrib import admin
2.  from django.urls import path, include
3.
4.  urlpatterns = [
5.      path('admin/', admin.site.urls),
6.      path('', include('practice.urls')),
7.  ]
```

❖ E16.6. Viewing the Website

Now that you have done the initial setup, you can view your website:

1. If it's not still open, open `templates_proj` at the terminal and run:

   ```
   (.venv) …/projects/templates_proj> python manage.py runserver
   ```

2. In your browser, navigate to `http://127.0.0.1:8000`. The site should look like this:

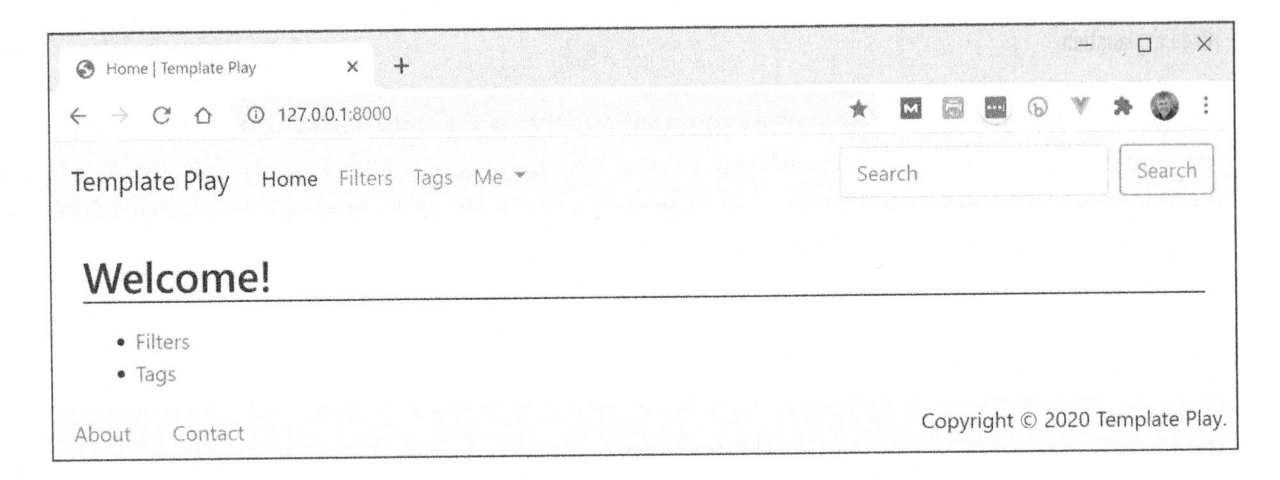

3. Leave this open and running throughout the lesson. If you do shut down the server, just remember to start it back up again to view the site.

4.1. get_context_data()

Class-based views include a get_context_data() method, which returns a dictionary, the keys of which are available as variables in the view's template. This provides a mechanism for providing your template with extra data. For example, you could pull data from various models in the project to include on the home page. The method is written like this:

```
def get_context_data(self, **kwargs):
    # Get context of superclass.
    context = super().get_context_data(**kwargs)

    # Add to context.
    context['featured_book'] = Book.get_featured()
    context['featured_author'] = Author.get_featured()

    Return updated context.
    return context
```

1. The get_context_data() method takes two parameters: self and **kwargs.
2. When you include the get_context_data() method in your view, you are overriding the superclass's get_context_data() method. So that you don't lose data from the superclass, you should assign super().get_context_data(**kwargs) to context, then update the context dictionary, and return the updated context.

In this lesson, you will populate context with arbitrary variables of different types, so that you can use them to experiment with template filters and tags.

Exercise 17: Adding Template Context

15 to 25 minutes

In this exercise, you will add context to the `FilterView` and `TagView` views.

1. Open `practice/views.py` for editing.
2. Add the following `get_context_data()` method to `FilterView`:

```
def get_context_data(self, **kwargs):
    context = super().get_context_data(**kwargs)
    context['company'] = 'Webucator'
    context['url'] = 'https://www.webucator.com'

    return context
```

3. Add the following `get_context_data()` method to `TagView`:

```
def get_context_data(self, **kwargs):
    context = super().get_context_data(**kwargs)
    context['beatles'] = [
        {'firstname': 'Paul', 'lastname': 'McCartney'},
        {'firstname': 'John', 'lastname': 'Lennon'},
        {'firstname': 'George', 'lastname': 'Harrison'},
        {'firstname': 'Ringo', 'lastname': 'Starr'},
    ]

    return context
```

The complete `views.py` should now look like this:

Exercise Code 17.1: practice/views.py

```
1.  from django.views.generic import TemplateView
2.
3.  class FilterView(TemplateView):
4.      template_name = 'practice/filters.html'
5.
6.      def get_context_data(self, **kwargs):
7.          context = super().get_context_data(**kwargs)
8.          context['company'] = 'Webucator'
9.          context['url'] = 'https://www.webucator.com'
10.
11.         return context
12.
13. class HomePageView(TemplateView):
14.     template_name = 'home.html'
15.
16. class TagView(TemplateView):
17.     template_name = 'practice/tags.html'
18.
19.     def get_context_data(self, **kwargs):
20.         context = super().get_context_data(**kwargs)
21.         context['beatles'] = [
22.             {'firstname': 'Paul', 'lastname': 'McCartney'},
23.             {'firstname': 'John', 'lastname': 'Lennon'},
24.             {'firstname': 'George', 'lastname': 'Harrison'},
25.             {'firstname': 'Ringo', 'lastname': 'Starr'},
26.         ]
27.
28.         return context
```

1. Open `templates/practice/filters.html` for editing and add the following code after the `h2` element:

   ```
   <h3>Link</h3>
   <a href="{{ url }}">{{ company }}</a>
   ```

2. Visit `http://127.0.0.1:8000/filters/`. You should see a **Webucator** link:

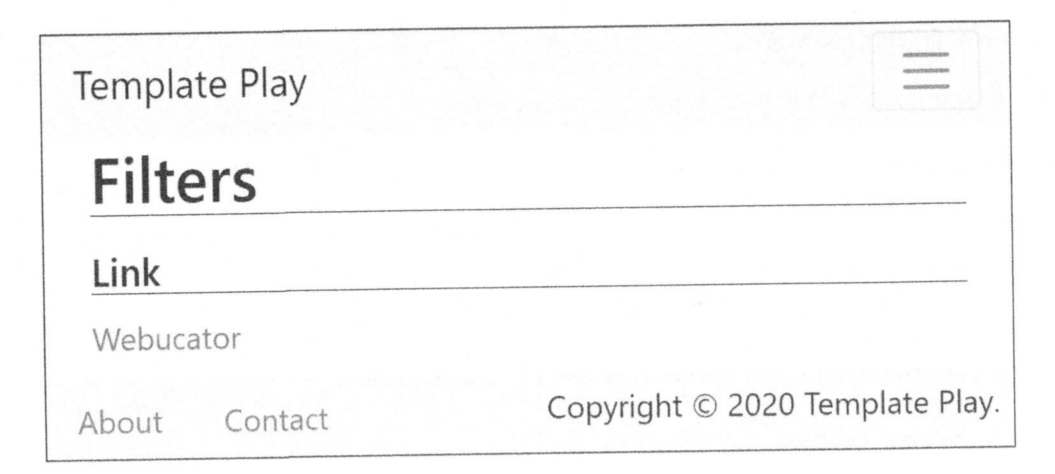

3. Open `templates/practice/tags.html` and add the following code after the `h2` element:

```
<ul>
  {% for beatle in beatles %}
    <li>{{ beatle.firstname }} {{ beatle.lastname }}</li>
  {% endfor %}
</ul>
```

4. Visit `http://127.0.0.1:8000/tags/`. You should see a **Beatles** list:

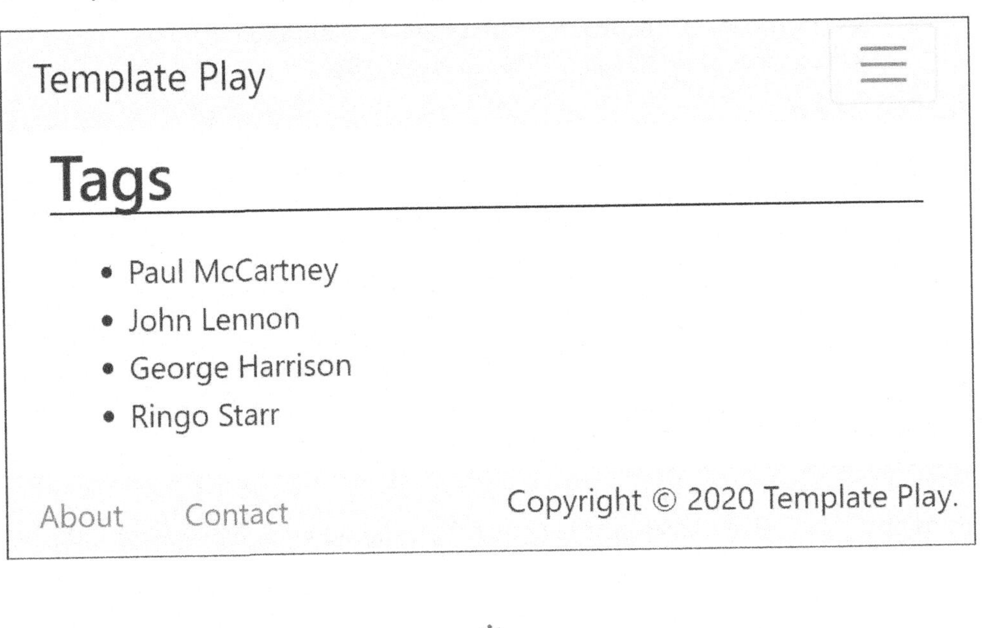

4.2. Template Filter Basics

Template filters are used to modify the display of variables. They are structured as follows:

```
{{ value|filter:arg }}
```

For example, the `add` filter is used to add a number to `value`. If `age` contains `30`, then the following code would output 32:

```
{{ age|add:2 }}
```

Filters are actually functions that could be represented like this:

```
filter(value, arg)
```

Not all filters take an argument, and many of those that do provide a default value for the argument.

Let's look at the actual code used to create the `add` filter:[26]

```
def add(value, arg):
    """Add the arg to the value."""
    try:
        return int(value) + int(arg)
    except (ValueError, TypeError):
        try:
            return value + arg
        except Exception:
            return ''
```

The function first tries to return the sum of the integer values of `value` and `arg`. If that results in a `ValueError` or `TypeError`, it tries to add them without converting them to integers, which could work for strings, lists, and some other data types. If that fails, it returns an empty string.

❖ 4.2.1. Chaining Filters

Filters can be chained using additional pipes:

26. You can find this in the Django source code in `django/template/defaultfilters.py`.

```
{{ value|filter1:arg|filter2:arg }}
```

In this case `filter1` acts on `value` and the result is applied to `filter2`. This could be represented like this:

```
filter2(filter1(value, arg), arg)
```

For example:

```
{{ age|add:2|divisibleby:3 }}
```

The preceding code will return `True` if `age + 2` is divisible by `3`. Otherwise, it will return `False`.

Order Matters

When chaining filters, order matters. Consider the following two lines of code:

```
{{ age|add:2|divisibleby:3 }}
{{ age|divisibleby:3|add:2 }}
```

The first line of code is equivalent to:

```
divisibleby(add(age, 2), 3)
```

It first adds `2` to `age` and then checks if the result is divisible by `3`. If `age` is `9`, then the equation is:

```
(9 + 2) % 3 == 0
```

This will return `False`, because `11` is not divisible by `3`.

The second line of code is equivalent to:

```
add(divisibleby(age, 3), 2)
```

It first checks if the `age` is divisible by `3` and then adds `2` to the result. The equivalent equation is:

```
(age % 3 == 0) + 2
```

This doesn't seem to make much sense, but Python will handle it by converting `(age % 3 == 0)` to an integer:

- `1` if the equation is `True`.
- `0` if the equation is `False`.

If `age` is `9`, then the equation is:

```
(9 % 3 == 0) + 2
```

As `9 % 3` does equal `0`, that evaluates to `1 + 2` or `3`.

The takeaway is that the order in which the filters are applied matters.

❖ 4.2.2. Filters without Arguments

Filters that don't take any arguments are written like this:

```
{{ value|filter }}
```

For example, the following code will output the value of `company` with the first letter capitalized:

```
{{ company|capfirst }}
```

Exercise 18: Adding Filters

10 to 15 minutes

In this exercise, you will add a couple of filters to `templates/practice/filters.html` to see how they work.

1. Open `templates/practice/filters.html` for editing.
2. Add the following code before the `{% endblock %}` line:

```
<h3>First Filters</h3>
{{ company|upper }}:
{{ url|urlize }}
```

3. Visit `http://127.0.0.1:8000/filters/`. You should see "WEBUCATOR" in all uppercase letters followed by the URL converted into a link. View the source of the page and notice that that portion of the code looks like this:

```
WEBUCATOR:
<a href="https://www.webucator.com" rel="nofollow">https://www.webucator.com</a>
```

   The `upper` filter converted "Webucator" to all uppercase letters, and the `urlize` filter converted the URL into an HTML link.

While neither of these filters is particularly useful, they demonstrate how you go about using filters in a template. In the next section, we will take a look at more useful filters.

4.3. Most Useful Template Filters

Django includes many filters that you will rarely, if ever, use, either because they are meant for special cases or because there are alternative ways of accomplishing the same thing. In this section, we list the most useful filters and provide usage examples. You should read this section carefully and then read more quickly through the rest of the filters, so that you know what is available.

Practicing

As you learn about these filters, add to the context in the `FilterView` view and add the filters in the `templates/practice/filters.html` template.

`date:format` and `time:format`

The `date` and `time` filters are used to format the date and time of a `datetime`, `date`, or `time` object.

They take an optional `format` argument:

```
{{ datetime|date:format }}
{{ datetime|time:format }}
```

The `format` argument can be constructed using format strings[27] or (for the `date` filter only) using one of the following predefined formats:

1. `DATE_FORMAT`
2. `DATETIME_FORMAT`
3. `SHORT_DATE_FORMAT`
4. `SHORT_DATETIME_FORMAT`

In `practice/views.py`, import `datetime` and add the following `datetime` object to the context in the `get_context_data()` method of `FilterView`:

27. See `https://docs.djangoproject.com/en/3.1/ref/templates/builtins/#std:templatefilter-date` for documentation.

```python
import datetime

from django.views.generic import TemplateView

class FilterView(TemplateView):
    template_name = 'practice/filters.html'

    def get_context_data(self, **kwargs):
        context = super().get_context_data(**kwargs)
        context['company'] = 'Webucator'
        context['url'] = 'https://www.webucator.com'
        context['moon_landing'] = datetime.datetime(
            year=1969, month=7, day=21,
            hour=2, minute=56, second=15,
            tzinfo=datetime.timezone.utc
        )

        return context
```

Try adding some of these filters in the template:

- `{{ moon_landing }}` – July 21, 1969, 2:56 a.m.
- `{{ moon_landing|date }}` – July 21, 1969
- `{{ moon_landing|date:"DATE_FORMAT" }}` – July 21, 1969
- `{{ moon_landing|date:"DATETIME_FORMAT" }}` – July 21, 1969, 2:56 a.m.
- `{{ moon_landing|date:"SHORT_DATE_FORMAT" }}` – 07/21/1969
- `{{ moon_landing|date:"SHORT_DATETIME_FORMAT" }}` – 07/21/1969 2:56 a.m.
- `{{ moon_landing|date:"Y-m-d H:i" }}` – 1969-07-21 02:56
- `{{ moon_landing|time }}` – 2:56 a.m.
- `{{ moon_landing|time:'G:i:s' }}` – 2:56:15

Note that the predefined formats are based on the current locale.

`timesince:to_date`

The `timesince` filter outputs the amount of time between the value and the `to_date` argument, which defaults to the current time.

Add the following `datetime` object to the `context`:

```
context['launch_date'] = datetime.datetime(
    year=1969, month=7, day=16, hour=13, minute=32, second=0,
    tzinfo=datetime.timezone.utc
)
```

And add these filters in the template:

```
{{ moon_landing|timesince }}<br>
{{ launch_date|timesince:moon_landing }}
```

This will output something like:

```
51 years<br>
4 days, 13 hours
```

- The first time period is the amount of time that has passed since the moon landing (at the time of this writing).
- The second time period is the time between the rocket launch and the moment Neil Armstrong stepped on the moon.

The `timesince` filter is commonly used to output how much time has passed since an article was written (e.g., "Posted 1 year, 2 months ago.").

`timeuntil:from_date`

The `timeuntil` filter outputs the amount of time between the `from_date` argument, which defaults to the current time, and the value.

Add the following `datetime` object to the context:

```
context['century22'] = datetime.datetime(
    year=2100, month=1, day=1, tzinfo=datetime.timezone.utc
)
```

And add this in the template:

```
{{ century22|timeuntil }}<br>
{{ century22|timeuntil:moon_landing }}
```

This will output:

```
79 years, 4 months<br>
130 years, 5 months
```

- The first time period is the time left until January 1, 2100 (at the time of this writing).
- The second time period is the time between the moon landing and January 1, 2100.

The `timeuntil` filter is commonly used to output how much time is remaining before some event takes place (e.g., "Sale ends in 9 hours, 50 minutes.").

default:default

The `default` filter is used to provide a default string when `value` evaluates to `False`.

Add this dictionary to the context:

```
context['inventory'] = {
    'gloves': 0,
    'hats': 51,
    'scarves': 2,
    'socks': 13
}
```

And add this loop in the template:

```
<ol>
  {% for item, remaining in inventory.items %}
    <li>{{ item }}: {{ remaining|default:"out of stock" }}</li>
  {% endfor %}
</ol>
```

The output will be:

```
<ol>
  <li>gloves: out of stock</li>
  <li>hats: 51</li>
  <li>scarves: 2</li>
  <li>socks: 13</li>
</ol>
```

Because the value for `'gloves'` is `0`, which evaluates to `False`, the filter outputs "out of stock" for the remaining gloves. The other values all evaluate to `True`, so the default is not used.

`floatformat:n`

The `floatformat` filter takes an `n` argument for the number of decimal places to round to. Without that argument, it will round to one decimal place unless the decimal value is `0`, in which case it will just output the integer.

Filter \ Value of i:	**1000.0**	**1000.11**	**3.14159**
`{{ i|floatformat }}`	1000	1000.1	3.1
`{{ i|floatformat:2 }}`	1000.00	1000.11	3.14
`{{ i|floatformat:0 }}`	1000	1000	3

`length` and `pluralize:suffix`

The `length` and `pluralize` filters can be used independently, but are often used together.

- `{{ value|length }}` – The `length` filter returns the length of `value`, which can be a string or a sequence.
- `{{ value|pluralize:suffix }}` – If `value` is not 1, '1', or an object of length 1, the `pluralize` filter outputs an "s" or the value of the `suffix` argument if one is used.

Add the following dictionary to the context:

```
context['classes'] = {
    'Python': [
        'Introduction to Python', 'Advanced Python',
        'Data Science', 'Django'
    ],
    'Databases': [
        'Introduction to PostgreSQL', 'Introduction to MySQL',
        'Introduction to SQL Server', 'Introduction to Oracle'
    ],
    'Web': [
        'HTML', 'CSS', 'JavaScript'
    ],
    'XML': [
        'Introduction to XML'
    ]
}
```

And add this loop in the template:

```
<ol>
  {% for category, titles in classes.items %}
    <li>
      {{ category }}: {{ titles|length }}
      class{{ titles|pluralize:"es" }}
    </li>
  {% endfor %}
</ol>
```

The output will be:

```
<ol>
  <li>Python: 4 classes</li>
  <li>Databases: 4 classes</li>
  <li>Web: 3 classes</li>
  <li>XML: 1 class</li>
</ol>
```

`truncatewords_html:n` and `safe`

The `truncatewords_html` filter outputs the first `n` words of a value followed by an ellipsis. It is smart about HTML tags, meaning it does not count them as words and closes any tags that were left open as a result of the truncation.

Add the following blurb to the context:

```
context['blurb'] = '<p>You are <em>pretty</em> smart!</p>'
```

And add this filter in the template:

```
{{ blurb|truncatewords_html:3 }}
```

The output will be:

```
&lt;p&gt;You are &lt;em&gt;pretty …&lt;/em&gt;&lt;/p&gt;
```

That's probably not what you want. As the HTML is escaped, the tags will actually show up in the browser. That's where the `safe` filter comes in to play. Chain the `safe` filter to the `truncatewords_html` filter you just added:

```
{{ blurb|truncatewords_html:3|safe }}
```

The `safe` filter indicates that the value is known to be safe and therefore does not need to be escaped. This will output:

```
<p>You are <em>pretty …</em></p>
```

The output in the browser without and with the `safe` filter is shown in the following image:

truncatewords_html **and** safe

<p>You are <em>pretty ...</em></p> ← w/o the `safe` filter.

You are *pretty* ... ← with the `safe` filter.

yesno:mapping

The yesno filter maps values that evaluate to True, False, and None to "yes", "no", and "maybe" or to alternative strings passed in as a comma-delimited string. Using the inventory dictionary again:

```
context['inventory'] = {
    'gloves': 0,
    'hats': 51,
    'scarves': 2,
    'socks': 13
}
```

Add this loop in the template:

```
<ol>
  {% for item, remaining in inventory.items %}
    <li class="{{ remaining|yesno:'instock,outofstock' }}">
      {{ item }}: {{ remaining }} remaining
      {{ remaining|yesno:',(time to place an order)' }}
    </li>
  {% endfor %}
</ol>
```

Notice how the yesno filter is used once to determine the value of the class attribute and again to determine whether or not to output "(time to place an order)".

The output will be:

```
<ol>
  <li class="outofstock">gloves: 0 remaining (time to place an order)</li>
  <li class="instock">hats: 51 remaining</li>
  <li class="instock">scarves: 2 remaining</li>
  <li class="instock">socks: 13 remaining</li>
</ol>
```

The next few filters are useful in specific situations. You should read through them, but you don't need to write the code (unless you want to):

`slice`

The `slice` filter is useful in combination with CSS and JavaScript for hiding a portion of the results of query (or some other data structure) under a "Show More" button. For example, given the following list of colors in the context:

```
context['colors'] = [
    'Red', 'Green', 'Blue', 'Orange', 'Purple', 'Yellow', 'Pink'
]
```

You can use the `slice` filter to hide all but the first three elements with CSS, and then toggle their visibility with JavaScript:[28]

```
<style>
  .hidden {
    display: none;
  }
</style>
<ol id="color-list">
  {% for color in colors|slice:':3' %}
    <li>{{ color }}</li>
  {% endfor %}
  {% for color in colors|slice:'3:' %}
    <li class="extra hidden">{{ color }}</li>
  {% endfor %}
</ol>
<button class="btn btn-link"
  onclick="for (const li of document.querySelectorAll('#color-list li.extra')) {
  li.classList.toggle('hidden');
}">
  Toggle Extra Colors
</button>
```

`colors|slice:':3'` gets the first three colors and `colors|slice:'3:'` gets the remaining colors.

28. We use inline CSS and JavaScript here for demonstration purposes only. Generally, that code should be in external files.

filesizeformat

The `filesizeformat` filter converts a value in bytes to a friendly file size format. For example, given the following:

```
context['files'] = [
    {
        'filename': 'macOS 64-bit installer',
        'filesize': 29163525
    },
    {
        'filename': 'Windows x86-64 executable installer',
        'filesize': 26797616
    },
    {
        'filename': 'Windows x86-64 web-based installer',
        'filesize': 1348896
    }
]
```

... and this loop in the template:

```
<ol>
  {% for file in files %}
    <li>{{ file.filename }} ({{ file.filesize|filesizeformat }})</li>
  {% endfor %}
</ol>
```

The output would be:

```
<ol>
  <li>macOS 64-bit installer (27.8 MB)</li>
  <li>Windows x86-64 executable installer (25.6 MB)</li>
  <li>Windows x86-64 web-based installer (1.3 MB)</li>
</ol>
```

json_script

The `json_script` filter outputs a Python object as JSON inside of a `script` element.

> **What is JSON**
>
> JSON stands for **J**ava**S**cript **O**bject **N**otation. According to the `https://json.org`, JSON is:
>
> 1. A lightweight data-interchange format.
> 2. Easy for humans to read and write.
> 3. Easy for machines to parse and generate.
>
> Because most modern programming languages have tools for working with JSON, JSON is commonly used for transferring data between applications.

This is the safest way to include data to be used by JavaScript. For example, imagine the `classes` dictionary we saw earlier was dynamically generated from data in a database and then added to the context. Here is the dictionary again:

```
context['classes'] = {
    'Python': [
        'Introduction to Python', 'Advanced Python',
        'Data Science', 'Django'
    ],
    'Databases': [
        'Introduction to PostgreSQL', 'Introduction to MySQL',
        'Introduction to SQL Server', 'Introduction to Oracle'
    ],
    'Web': [
        'HTML', 'CSS', 'JavaScript'
    ],
    'XML': [
        'Introduction to XML'
    ]
}
```

The following line of code will convert the dictionary to JSON and add it to the template inside of a `<script>` tag with an `id` of "classdata":

```
{{ classes|json_script:'classdata' }}
```

The output (with indenting added for readability) would be:

```
<script id="classdata" type="application/json">
  {
    "Python": [
      "Introduction to Python", "Advanced Python", "Data Science", "Django"
    ],
    "Databases": [
      "Introduction to PostgreSQL", "Introduction to MySQL",
      "Introduction to SQL Server", "Introduction to Oracle"
    ],
    "Web": ["HTML", "CSS", "JavaScript"],
    "XML": ["Introduction to XML"]
  }
</script>
```

You can then use another `script` element to consume this content:

```
<ol>
  <script>
    const classes = JSON.parse(document.getElementById('classdata').textContent);
    const pythonClasses = classes['Python'];
    for (let i=0; i < pythonClasses.length; i++) {
      document.write(`<li>${pythonClasses[i]}</li>`);
    }
  </script>
</ol>
```

You could (and probably should) use an external JavaScript file instead of embedded JavaScript.

Summary

These are, in our experience, the most useful of Django's built-in filters.

4.4. Template Filter Quick Reference

Most of the filters not covered in the previous section are rarely used. Here, we break out all the template filters, including the most useful ones previously covered, into the following categories:

1. Formatting Filters
2. String Filters
3. URL Filters
4. Number Filters
5. Date and Time Filters
6. Logic Filters
7. Data Structure Filters
8. Coding Filters

We recommend you read through this section quickly, so that you know what types of filters are available. There is no reason to memorize this list or to dig deep into any of these filters until you find yourself needing to use one.

For More Information...

See `https://www.djangotemplatetagsandfilters.com/filters/` for more detailed information and examples.

❖ 4.4.1. Formatting Filters

Capitalization

1. `capfirst` – Capitalizes the first letter of `value`.
2. `lower` – Lowercases all letters in `value`.
3. `title` – Capitalizes the first letter of each word in `value`.
4. `upper` – Capitalizes all letters in `value`.

Alignment

Alignment filters add whitespace on one or both sides of the value. As whitespace is condensed by default in HTML pages, alignment filters wouldn't affect the output unless the text is within a `pre` element or CSS is used to prevent whitespace from being condensed. However, Django can be used to create non-HTML documents as well. In those, formatting with whitespace might make more sense.

1. `center:n` – Centers `value` within text of `n` characters. For example:

   ```
   "{{ company|center:20 }}"
   ```

   would result in:

   ```
   "     Webucator      "
   ```

2. `ljust:n` – Left justifies `value` within text of `n` characters. For example:

   ```
   "{{ company|ljust:20 }}"
   ```

   would result in:

   ```
   "Webucator           "
   ```

3. `rjust:n` – Right justifies `value` within text of `n` characters. For example:

   ```
   "{{ company|rjust:20 }}"
   ```

   would result in:

   ```
   "           Webucator"
   ```

❖ 4.4.2. String Filters

Truncation

1. `truncatechars:n` – Truncates `value` to `n` characters and appends an ellipsis (…).
2. `truncatechars_html:n` – Like `truncatechars`, but it is smart about HTML tags, meaning it does not count them as words and closes any tags that were left open as a result of the truncation.

3. `truncatewords:n` – Truncates `value` to `n` words and appends an ellipsis (...).
4. `truncatewords_html:n` – Covered in **Most Useful Filters** (see page 131).

Other String Filters

1. `cut:string_to_cut` – Removes all instances of `string_to_cut` from `value`.
2. `linenumbers` – Prepends each line of text with a line number. Useful for plain text, but not typically for HTML.
3. `phone2numeric` – Converts letters to numbers for a phone number (e.g., `877-WEBUCAT` becomes `877-9328228`).
4. `pluralize:suffix` – Covered in **Most Useful Filters** (see page 129).
5. `stringformat:format` – Formats `value` using the old printf-style string formatting.[29]
6. `wordwrap:n` – Implements word wrapping by inserting a newline character every `n` characters. Useful for plain text, but not typically for HTML.

4.4.3. URL Filters

1. `iriencode` – Converts an IRI (Internationalized Resource Identifier) to a string that can be used in a URL.
2. `slugify` – Converts `value` to a slug.[30]
3. `urlencode` – Escapes `value` for use in a URL. This is useful for passing data on the querystring in a link.
4. `urlize` – Converts URLs in `value` to clickable links by wrapping them in an `<a>` tag.
5. `urlizetrunc:n` – Same as `urlize`, but truncates the link text to `n` characters.

4.4.4. Number Filters

1. `add:arg` – Adds `arg` to `value`.
2. `divisibleby:n` – Returns `True` if `value` is divisible by `n`, and `False` otherwise.
3. `filesizeformat` – Covered in **Most Useful Filters** (see page 134).
4. `floatformat` – Covered in **Most Useful Filters** (see page 129).

---

29. `https://docs.python.org/3/library/stdtypes.html#old-string-formatting`
30. We will discuss slugs in detail the URLs and Slugs lesson (see page 207).

5. `get_digit:i` – Returns the digit `i` characters from the right side of `value`. For example, the following will output `9, 8, 7, 6`:

```
{{ 6789|get_digit:1 }}, {{ 6789|get_digit:2 }},
{{ 6789|get_digit:3 }}, {{ 6789|get_digit:4 }}
```

6. `length` – Covered in **Most Useful Filters** (see page 129).
7. `wordcount` – Outputs the number of words in `value`.

❖ 4.4.5. Date and Time Filters

1. `date:format` – Covered in **Most Useful Filters** (see page 125).
2. `time:format` – Covered in **Most Useful Filters** (see page 125).
3. `timesince:to_date` – Covered in **Most Useful Filters** (see page 126).
4. `timeuntil:from_date` – Covered in **Most Useful Filters** (see page 127).

❖ 4.4.6. Logic Filters

1. `default:default` – Covered in **Most Useful Filters** (see page 128).
2. `default_if_none:default` – Outputs `default` if and only if `value` is `None`.
3. `length_is:n` – Returns `True` if the length of `value` is `n`, and `False` otherwise.
4. `yesno` – Covered in **Most Useful Filters** (see page 132).

❖ 4.4.7. Data Structure Filters

1. `dictsort:key` – Sorts a list of dictionaries by `key`.
2. `dictsortreversed:key` – Reverse sorts a list of dictionaries by `key`.
3. `first` – Outputs the first element in a sequence.
4. `join:s` – Joins a list on `s`. Works just like Python's `s.join(value)`.
5. `last` – Outputs the last element in a sequence.
6. `make_list` – Converts `value` to a list of characters.
7. `random` – Outputs a random item from a sequence. Like Python's `random.choice(value)`.

8. `safeseq` – Applies the `safe` filter to each element of a sequence.

9. `slice:slice` –Covered in **Most Useful Filters** (see page 133).

10. `unordered_list` – Creates an unordered HTML list from a Python list that contains other lists, which also may contain lists, etc. You must add the outermost `<ul>` tags. In theory, this is interesting, but it requires an oddly structured Python list to work correctly.

❖ 4.4.8. Coding Filters

1. `addslashes` – Adds backslashes before quotation marks to escape them (e.g., "That's" becomes "That\'s").

2. `escape` – Escapes HTML characters. Only relevant if autoescaping is off (see page 150).

3. `escapejs` – Escapes characters used in JavaScript strings.

4. `force_escape` – Almost identical to `escape`, and you almost definitely want to use `escape` instead.

5. `json_script` – Covered in **Most Useful Filters** (see page 135).

6. `linebreaks` – Adds `<br>` tags between lines of text separated by a single newline character, and wraps lines of text separated by two newline characters in `<p>` tags.

7. `linebreaksbr` – Converts all newline characters in `value` to `<br>` tags.

8. `pprint` – Pretty prints a Python object. Used for debugging.

9. `safe` – Covered in **Most Useful Filters** (see page 131).

10. `striptags` – Strips HTML tags. This can be useful for converting a template HTML email to text when you want to send both HTML and text versions of an email.

4.5. Template Tag Basics

Template tags add logic to the template. They are structured as follows:

```
{% tag arg arg %}
```

Some tags take no arguments, some take a set number of arguments, and some take an arbitrary number of arguments.

Many tags have ending tags, which means that they affect the content between the beginning and ending tags. Ending tags are prefixed with "end". For example:

```
<ul>
  {% for beatle in beatles %}
    <li>{{ beatle.firstname }} {{ beatle.lastname }}</li>
  {% endfor %}
</ul>
```

You added this `for` loop to `templates/practice/tags.html` earlier in the lesson, along with this dictionary in the `get_context_data` method of `TagView`:

```
context['beatles'] = [
    {'firstname': 'Paul', 'lastname': 'McCartney'},
    {'firstname': 'John', 'lastname': 'Lennon'},
    {'firstname': 'George', 'lastname': 'Harrison'},
    {'firstname': 'Ringo', 'lastname': 'Starr'},
]
```

The resulting output is:

```
<ul>
  <li>Paul McCartney</li>
  <li>John Lennon</li>
  <li>George Harrison</li>
  <li>Ringo Starr</li>
</ul>
```

❖ 4.5.1. Filters in Tags

Filters can be used within tags. For example, you can change the order in which the Beatles get output using the `dictsort` filter:

```
{% for beatle in beatles|dictsort:'firstname' %}
```

4.6. Most Useful Template Tags

As with template filters, Django includes many tags that you will rarely, if ever, use. In this section, we list the most useful tags and provide usage examples. You should read this section carefully and then read more quickly through the rest of the tags, so that you know what is available.

Practicing

As you learn about these tags, add to the `context` in the `TagView` view and add the tags in the `templates/practice/tags.html` template.

`{% for obj in sequence %}` and `{% empty %}`

The `for` tag is often used to loop through querysets, but it can be used to loop through any iterable. Some examples:

Looping through a Queryset

```
<ul>
  {% for joke in joke_list %}
    <li>{{ joke.question }}</li>
  {% endfor %}
</ul>
```

Looping through a Dictionary

```
<ol>
  {% for item, remaining in inventory.items %}
    <li>{{ item }}: {{ remaining }}</li>
  {% endfor %}
</ol>
```

Looping through a List

```
<ol>
  {% for fruit in fruits %}
    <li>{{ fruit }}</li>
  {% endfor %}
</ol>
```

To loop through a sequence in reverse order, add `reversed` after the sequence:

Looping through a List in Reverse

```
<ol>
  {% for fruit in fruits reversed %}
    <li>{{ fruit }}</li>
  {% endfor %}
</ol>
```

Empty Iterables

Sometimes, you won't be sure that your iterable contains any values. This is especially true with querysets. In such case, you can use the `empty` tag to output a message indicating that no records were found. For example:

```
<ul>
  {% for joke in joke_list %}
    <li>{{ joke.question }}</li>
  {% empty %}
    <li>Sorry, there are no jokes.</li>
  {% endfor %}
</ul>
```

Variables Available in `for` Loops

The following variables are available within `for` loops:

1. `forloop.counter` – The current iteration starting with `1`.
2. `forloop.counter0` – The current iteration starting with `0`.
3. `forloop.revcounter` – The iteration's position from the end. For the last iteration, this will be `1`.
4. `forloop.revcounter0` – The remaining iterations. For the last iteration, this will be `0`.
5. `forloop.first` – `True` for the first iteration.
6. `forloop.last` – `True` for the last iteration.
7. `forloop.parentloop` – The current loop's parent loop.

{% cycle value1 value2 value3… %}

Given the following list:

```
context['fruits'] = ['Apples', 'Bananas', 'Pears', 'Grapes', 'Oranges']
```

... and this loop in the template:

```
<ol>
  {% for fruit in fruits %}
    <li class="{% cycle 'odd' 'even' %}">{{ fruit }}</li>
  {% endfor %}
</ol>
```

The output would be:

```
<ol>
  <li class="odd">Apples</li>
  <li class="even">Bananas</li>
  <li class="odd">Pears</li>
  <li class="even">Grapes</li>
  <li class="odd">Oranges</li>
</ol>
```

{% if %}, {% elif %}, and {% else %}

Conditionals in Django templates work just like they do in Python. The syntax is:

```
{% if some_conditions %}
    Output this block.
{% elif other_conditions %}
  Output this block.
{% else %}
  Output this block.
{% endif %}
```

All of the Python comparison and logical operators are available:

Comparison Operators

`==`	Equals.
`!=`	Doesn't equal.
`>`	Is greater than.
`<`	Is less than.
`>=`	Is greater than or equal to.
`<=`	Is less than or equal to.
`is`	Is the same object.
`is not`	Is not the same object.

Logical Operators

`and`	`{% if a and b %}`
`or`	`{% if a or b %}`
`not`	`{% if not a %}`

`{% block name %}` and `{% extends template %}`

The `block` tag is used to create named content blocks that can be overridden in *child* templates, which extend the template using the `{% extends %}` tag.

The `{% block %}` and `{% extends %}` tags are covered in Template Inheritance (see page 36).

The `{% include %}` tag is used to include one template in another.

Parent Template

```
{% block main %}
  <p>Content before include</p>
  {% include 'asides/book-ad.html' %}
  <p>Content after include</p>
{% endblock main %}
```

Included Template: `templates/asides/book-ad.html`

```
<aside>
  <p><strong>Read our Python Book!</strong></p>
</aside>
```

Result

```
<p>Content before include</p>
  <aside>
    <p><strong>Read our Python Book!</strong></p>
  </aside>
<p>Content after include</p>
```

The `{% include %}` tag should not be used to include headers and footers. Use Template Inheritance (see page 36) for that kind of thing. Use the `{% include %}` tag to include asides or callouts that show up on some, but not all pages.

`{% comment "comment" %}`

The `comment` tag is used to comment out code to prevent template tags or variables from being interpreted and/or to prevent the content from being delivered to the browser.

```
{% comment "Should we include this?" %}
  <small class="text-muted">
    Created on: {{ joke.created }}
    Last updated: {{ joke.updated }}
  </small>
{% endcomment %}
```

`{% csrf_token %}`

The `csrf_token` tag must be included in all Django forms that post data. It protects against cross site request forgery.[31]

---

31. `https://docs.djangoproject.com/en/3.1/ref/csrf/`

`{% load library1 library2… %}`

The `load` tag is used to load one or more libraries of tags and filters. This could be a library built in to Django, such as `django.contrib.humanize`,[32] a third-party library, or a library you create yourself.

You can only load template tag libraries from apps that are included in `INSTALLED_APPS` in `settings.py`.

`{% url urlname arg1 arg2… %}`

The `url` tag is used to output the path to the view mapping to `urlname` as defined in the URLConf file.

`{% with var1=value1 var2=value2… %}`

The code between an open `with` tag (e.g., `{% with var1=value1 var2=value2… %}`) and close `endwith` tag (e.g., `{% endwidth %}`) has access to the variables defined in the open `with` tag.

The `with` tag is useful for reusing the results of an expensive method. Consider the following:

```
{{ jokes.count }} joke{{ jokes.count|pluralize }} that match your search.
```

In the preceding code, `jokes.count` has to be evaluated twice. The following code assigns `jokes.count` to `joke_count` and then uses the result within the block:

```
{% with joke_count=jokes.count %}
  {{ joke_count }} joke{{ joke_count|pluralize }} that match your search.
{% endwith %}
```

This way, the database is only hit once and the count is stored in a variable, which can be reused as often as necessary.

32. See `https://docs.djangoproject.com/en/3.1/ref/contrib/humanize`.

`widthratio`

The `widthratio` tag is used to create bar charts and the like. The syntax is:

```
{% widthratio this_value max_value max_width %}
```

The value is calculated using this formula:

```
(this_value/max_value) * max_width
```

For example:

```
<div id="barchart">
  <div id="red" style="width:{% widthratio 25 100 300 %}px"></div>
  <div id="blue" style="width:{% widthratio 10 100 300 %}px"></div>
  <div id="green" style="width:{% widthratio 45 100 300 %}px"></div>
</div>
```

Output

```
<div id="barchart">
  <div id="red" style="width:75px"></div>
  <div id="blue" style="width:30px"></div>
  <div id="green" style="width:135px"></div>
</div>
```

With some CSS applied, the resulting output might look like this:

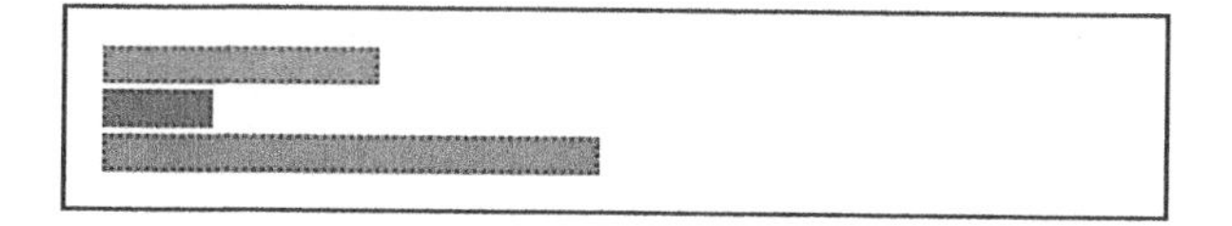

Summary

These are, in our experience, the most useful of Django's built-in tags.

4.7. Template Tag Quick Reference

Most of the tags not covered in the previous section are rarely used. Here, we break out all the template tags, including the most useful ones previously covered, into the following categories:

1. Coding Tags
2. Logic Tags
3. Utility Tags

We recommend you read through this section quickly, so that you know what types of tags are available. There is no reason to memorize this list or to dig deep into any of these tags until you find yourself needing to use one.

> **For More Information…**
>
> See `https://www.djangotemplatetagsandfilters.com/tags/` for more detailed information and examples.

❖ 4.7.1. Coding Tags

1. `autoescape` – Turns autoescaping of HTML on or off. The `autoescape` tag takes one argument, which must be either "on" or "off":

    - `on` (the default) – The HTML in all variables will be escaped using HTML entities.
    - `off` – The HTML will not be escaped.

    As autoescaping is applied by default, you are most likely to use this tag to turn autoescaping off. It can be used to output HTML stored in a database (e.g., for a blog article or a product description). For example, given the following:

    ```
    context['blurb'] = '<p>You are <em>pretty</em> smart!</p>'
    ```

    This would output *escaped* HTML:

    ```
    {{ blurb }}
    ```

    Output

    ```
    <p>You are <em>pretty</em> smart!</p>
    ```

And this would output *unescaped* HTML:

```
{% autoescape off %}
  {{ blurb }}
{% endautoescape %}
```

Output

```
<p>You are <em>pretty</em> smart!</p>
```

An alternative, and often a better/safer approach, is to use the `safe` filter (see page 131) on each variable that you want to output without escaping.

2. `spaceless` – Removes irrelevant whitespace between HTML tags.

```
{% spaceless %}
  <p>
    <small class="text-muted">
      Created on: {{ joke.created }}
      Last updated: {{ joke.updated }}
    </small>
  </p>
{% endspaceless %}
```

Output

```
<p><small class="text-muted">
      Created on: April 12, 2020, 2:54 p.m.
      Last updated: April 15, 2020, 1:11 p.m.
    </small></p>
```

Notice that the whitespace within the `small` element has not been removed. Only whitespace between successive opening tags and successive closing tags is removed.

3. `templatetag` – Outputs special characters used to create template tags (e.g., braces and percentage signs). Unless you're planning to write an online Django tutorial in which you need to output symbols used in Django templates, you're unlikely to need this tag.

```
{% templatetag openblock %} tag {% templatetag closeblock %}
{% templatetag openvariable %} variable {% templatetag closevariable %}
{% templatetag openbrace %} braces {% templatetag closebrace %}
{% templatetag opencomment %} comment {% templatetag closecomment %}
```

Output

```
{% tag %}
{{ variable }}
{ braces }
{# comment #}
```

4. `verbatim` – Template rendering is turned off between open `{% verbatim blockname %}` and closing `{% endverbatim blockname %}`.
5. `widthratio` – Covered in **Most Useful Tags** (see page 149).

❖ 4.7.2. Logic Tags

1. `cycle` – Covered in **Most Useful Tags** (see page 145).
2. `firstof` – Returns the first argument in a list of arguments that evaluates to `True`. For example, given:

```
context['a'] = False
context['b'] = 0
context['c'] = ""
context['d'] = "hello"
```

...the following will output "hello".

```
{% firstof a b c d %}
```

The tag allows for a default string literal:

```
{% firstof a b c d "goodbye" %}
```

3. `for` – Covered in **Most Useful Tags** (see page 143).

4. `for ... empty` – Covered in **Most Useful Tags** (see page 143).

5. `if` – Covered in **Most Useful Tags** (see page 145).

6. `ifchanged` – Used within a loop to output something if one or more values has changed since the last loop iteration. For example, given the following list of dictionaries:

   ```
   context['foods'] = [
       {'name': 'Apple', 'category': 'Fruit'},
       {'name': 'Banana', 'category': 'Fruit'},
       {'name': 'Grape', 'category': 'Fruit'},
       {'name': 'Hamburger', 'category': 'Meat'},
       {'name': 'Pepper', 'category': 'Vegetable'},
       {'name': 'Corn', 'category': 'Vegetable'}
   ]
   ```

   ...and this loop:

   ```
   {% for food in foods %}
     {% ifchanged food.category %}<h4>{{ food.category }}</h4>{% endifchanged %}
     <p>{{ food.name }}</p>
   {% endfor %}
   ```

   The output would be:

   ```
   <h4>Fruit</h4>
   <p>Apple</p>
   <p>Banana</p>
   <p>Grape</p>

   <h4>Meat</h4>
   <p>Hamburger</p>

   <h4>Vegetable</h4>
   <p>Pepper</p>
   <p>Corn</p>
   ```

   Notice that the `h4` elements only get inserted if the category has changed since the previous iteration.

7. `resetcycle` – Used to reset a `cycle`. This is most useful in nested `for` loops.

8. `with` – Covered in **Most Useful Tags** (see page 148).

❖ 4.7.3. Utility Tags

1. `block` – Covered in **Template Inheritance** (see page 36).
2. `comment` – Covered in **Most Useful Tags** (see page 147).
3. `csrf_token` – Covered in **Most Useful Tags** (see page 147).
4. `debug` – Outputs debugging information.
5. `extends` – Covered in **Template Inheritance** (see page 36).
6. `filter` – Applies a pipe-delimited list of filters to the contained content.

```
{% filter upper|linenumbers|linebreaksbr %}Apple
Banana
Grape
Hamburger
Pepper{% endfilter %}
```

Output

```
1. APPLE<br>2. BANANA<br>3. GRAPE<br>4. HAMBURGER<br>5. PEPPER
```

7. `include` – Covered in **Most Useful Tags** (see page 146).
8. `load` – Covered in **Most Useful Tags** (see page 148).
9. `lorem` – Outputs lorem ipsum[33] placeholder text.
   - `{% lorem 2 b %}` - outputs two blocks of lorem ipsum.
   - `{% lorem 2 p %}` - outputs two paragraphs of lorem ipsum.
   - `{% lorem 10 w %}` - outputs ten words of lorem ipsum.
   - `{% lorem 2 b random %}` - outputs two blocks of random words.
10. `now` – Outputs the current date and/or time.
11. `regroup` – Used for outputting lists of dictionaries in different orders and structures.[34]
12. `url` – Covered in **Most Useful Tags** (see page 148).

33. `https://en.wikipedia.org/wiki/Lorem_ipsum`
34. See `https://docs.djangoproject.com/en/3.1/ref/templates/builtins/#regroup` for documentation.

4.8. Custom Filters

Here is the function we saw earlier that creates the built-in `add` filter:

```
def add(value, arg):
    """Add the arg to the value."""
    try:
        return int(value) + int(arg)
    except (ValueError, TypeError):
        try:
            return value + arg
        except Exception:
            return ''
```

You can also create your own custom filter functions, which take one or two parameters:

1. The value to be filtered.
2. An optional argument providing additional information on how the filter should work.

The names usually used for these parameters are `value` and `arg`, but sometimes the second parameter is given a more informative name. For example, here is a custom filter function for repeating a string:

```
def repeat(value, times=2):
    return value * times
```

This can be called with or without an argument:

```
{{ value|repeat:5 }}
{{ value|repeat }}
```

The steps involved in writing a custom filter are:

1. Create or find the Python file in which to write the filter.
2. Write the filter.
3. Register the filter.

To use the filter in a template, you need to load the filter library in the template.

Exercise 19: Creating Custom Filters

20 to 30 minutes

In this exercise, you will go through the steps previously outlined to create a couple of custom filters.

❖ E19.1. Where to Write the Filter

Filters have to be written in a file that exists within a folder named "`templatetags`" in an app directory. If the filter is specific to an app, you can create the `templatetags` folder within that app. However, we find that it is more common that your filters will apply to more than one of your apps in your project, so we generally create a new app, which we like to call **common** that holds functionality used in more than one app in the project. You then create the `templatetags` folder within the `common` app folder, and create a Python file (e.g., `common_filters.py`) within `templatetags`:

```
common
    templatetags
        common_filters.py
    __init__.py
    …
```

Let's get the custom filters file ready:

1. With `templates_proj` open at the terminal, create a new "common" app by running:

```
(.venv) …/projects/templates_proj> python manage.py startapp common
```

2. Add the new app to `INSTALLED_APPS`:

```
INSTALLED_APPS = [
    …
    # Local apps
    'common.apps.CommonConfig',
    'practice.apps.PracticeConfig',
]
```

3. Within the new `template_proj/common` folder, add a `templatetags` folder.

4. Within the new templatetags folder, add common_filters.py file.

You now have the file in which to write your custom filters.

❖ E19.2. Writing and Registering the Filter

Open common_filters.py for editing and add the following code:

Exercise Code 19.1: common/templatetags/common_filters.py

```
1.  from django import template
2.
3.  register = template.Library()
4.
5.  @register.filter
6.  def repeat(value, times=2):
7.      return value * times
```

Things to notice:

1. You must import template from django:

   ```
   from django import template
   ```

2. The function is just a regular function that returns a value:

   ```
   def repeat(value, times=2):
   return value * times
   ```

3. To register the function, you must create an instance of template.Library in a variable named register.

   ```
   register = template.Library()
   ```

   The register variable is used to register the filters. The easiest way to do that is to use a decorator before the filter function:

   ```
   @register.filter
   def …
   ```

Your custom filter is now ready to use.

❖ E19.3. Using the Filter

1. Open `templates/practice/filters.html` for editing.
2. Immediately after the `{% extends %}` tag, add the following tag to load the new `custom_filters` tag library:

   ```
   {% load common_filters %}
   ```

3. At the end of the `main` block, add the following:

   ```
   <p>{{ company|repeat:3 }}</p>
   ```

4. Start up the server. If it's already running, stop and restart it, as tag libraries are registered when the server starts up.
5. In your browser, navigate to `http://127.0.0.1:8000/filters/`. You should see the following towards the bottom of the page:

   ```
   WebucatorWebucatorWebucator
   ```

❖ E19.4. Filters that Act on Strings

Some filters, like the `repeat` filter you just created are meant to act on strings. Such filters can take the `stringfilter` decorator, which will force the value to be converted to a string. To see why this is necessary, add the following code to `templates/practice/filters.html` at the end of the `main` block:

```
<p>{{ 5|repeat:3 }}</p>
```

Return to `http://127.0.0.1:8000/filters/` in your browser and refresh the page. Towards the bottom of the page, you should see the number `15`.

The `repeat` filter is supposed to repeat "`5`" three times, but it is multiplying instead. Because `5` is an integer, `5 * 3` returns `15`.

Modify `common_filters.py` to match the following code, which imports `stringfilter` from `django.template.defaultfilters` and uses it to decorate the `repeat` filter:

Exercise Code 19.2: common/templatetags/common_filters.py

```
1.  from django import template
2.  from django.template.defaultfilters import stringfilter
3.
4.  register = template.Library()
5.
6.  @register.filter
7.  @stringfilter
8.  def repeat(value, times=2):
9.      return value * times
```

Refresh `http://127.0.0.1:8000/filters/` in your browser. Where it showed `15` before, it should now show `555`.

❖ E19.5. Cleaning Cusses

Let's add a filter for cleaning cuss words.

1. Add the following highlighted code to `common_filters.py`:

Exercise Code 19.3: common/templatetags/common_filters.py

```
1.    import random
2.    import re
3.    from django import template
4.    from django.template.defaultfilters import stringfilter
5.
6.    register = template.Library()
7.
8.    @register.filter
9.    @stringfilter
10.   def repeat(value, times=2):
11.       return value * times
12.
13.   @register.filter
14.   def clean(value):
15.       cusses = ['stupid', 'stinky', 'darn', 'shucks', 'crud', 'dirt']
16.       for cuss in cusses:
17.           cuss_re = re.compile(re.escape(cuss), re.IGNORECASE)
18.           chars = ''.join([random.choice('!@#$%^&*') for letter in cuss])
19.           value = cuss_re.sub(chars, value)
20.       return value
```

Things to notice:

A. We have imported the `random` and `re` libraries.

B. The `clean()` function loops through a list of "cuss" words, which you would normally get from a file, a database, or a service,[35] and uses a regular expression to replace any case-insensitive matches of those words with random symbols.

C. The `clean` filter does not take an argument.

2. Add the following to the `context` of the `FilterView` view in `practice/views.py`:

```
context['user_blurb'] = """Shucks! What a cruddy day I\'ve had.
I spent the whole darn day with my dirtiest
friend darning his STINKY socks."""
```

3. At the end of the `main` block of `templates/practice/filters.html`, add the following:

```
<p>{{ user_blurb|clean }}</p>
```

35. It is nearly impossible to create a filter that captures all cuss words.

4. Refresh `http://127.0.0.1:8000/filters/` in your browser. You should see something like this towards the bottom of the page:

```
&&!!&^! What a ^&&#dy day I've had. I spent the whole $@%# day with my #!#@iest
friend $@%#ing his @#@&%% socks.
```

4.9. Custom Tags

Custom tags are a bit more complex than custom filters, but Django provides two decorators that make it easy to create most types of custom tags: `simple_tag` and `inclusion_tag`. A simple custom tag can be very much like a custom filter:

Demo 4.1: common/templatetags/common_tags.py

```
1.  from django import template
2.  from django.template.defaultfilters import stringfilter
3.
4.  register = template.Library()
5.
6.  @register.simple_tag
7.  @stringfilter
8.  def repeat(text, times=2):
9.      return text * times
```

Things to notice:

1. As with custom filters, custom tags must be stored in a file within a `templatetags` directory. In this case, we have named that file `common_tags.py` to indicate that they are common to the project. You will need to restart your server before you can use this new tag library.
2. The `repeat` tag is registered with `@register.simple_tag`.
3. The `repeat` tag takes two arguments, one of which has a default. Unlike filters, which can only take one argument, tags can take any number of arguments.

In the template, you would first need to load the tag library:

```
{% load common_tags %}
```

You could then use the custom tag like this:

```
<p>{% repeat company 3 %}</p>
```

The `inclusion_tag` decorator is more powerful as it allows you to include a custom template. You will create a custom inclusion tag in the next exercise.

Exercise 20: Creating Custom Tags

20 to 30 minutes

In this exercise, you will add a custom tag to the djangojokes.com project. The custom tag will make it easy to put a random joke on any page on the site using this simple template tag:

```
{% random_joke %}
```

1. Open the **djangojokes.com** workspace in Visual Studio Code.
2. With `djangojokes.com` open at the terminal and the virtual environment activated, run:

   ```
   (.venv) …/projects/djangojokes.com> python manage.py startapp common
   ```

3. Add the new app to `INSTALLED_APPS`:

   ```
   INSTALLED_APPS = [
       …

       # Local apps
       'common.apps.CommonConfig',
       'jokes.apps.JokesConfig',
       'pages.apps.PagesConfig',
   ]
   ```

4. Within the `common` folder, create a `templatetags` folder, and create a `common_tags.py` file within that.
5. Add the following code to `common_tags.py`:[36]

36. **Don't want to type?** Copy from `starter-code/template-filters-and-tags/common_tags.py`.

Exercise Code 20.1: common/templatetags/common_tags.py

```
1.  import random
2.  from django import template
3.
4.  from jokes.models import Joke
5.
6.  register = template.Library()
7.
8.  @register.inclusion_tag('common/joke.html')
9.  def random_joke():
10.     count = Joke.objects.count()
11.     if count > 0: # In case we haven't added any jokes yet
12.         i = random.randint(0, count-1)
13.         joke = Joke.objects.all()[i]
14.         return {'joke': joke}
15.     else:
16.         return {
17.             'joke': {
18.                 'question': 'You know what is funny?',
19.                 'answer': 'There are no jokes in the database.'
20.             }
21.         }
```

Things to notice:

A. Just as with custom filters, you need to import `template` from `django` and create the `register` variable.

B. You import `Joke` from `jokes.models`.

C. The template function is decorated with:

```
@register.inclusion_tag('common/joke.html')
```

`inclusion_tag` functions must return a dictionary, which provides context for the associated template (in this case, `common/joke.html`), which Django will search for in the same places it searches for other templates.

D. The function itself gets a random integer between `0` and one less than the number of jokes in the database. It uses that integer to get a random joke, which it returns in the dictionary. If there are no jokes, it returns a default joke.

6. Within the project's `templates` folder, create a new `common` folder, and within that, create a `joke.html` template with the following content:[37]

37. **Don't want to type?** Copy from `starter-code/template-filters-and-tags/joke.html`.

Exercise Code 20.2: templates/common/joke.html

```
1.  <div class="card border-primary m-auto mb-3 text-center"
2.    style="max-width: 30rem">
3.    <div class="card-header">Random Joke</div>
4.    <div class="card-body">
5.      <h5 class="card-title">{{ joke.question }}</h5>
6.      <p class="card-text">{{ joke.answer }}</p>
7.    </div>
8.  </div>
```

This template works like any other template and will be included within the template that uses the custom `{% random_joke %}` tag.

7. Open `templates/pages/home.html`:

   A. Immediately below the `{% extends "_base.html" %}` tag, add:

   ```
   {% load common_tags %}
   ```

   B. Immediately above the final `{% endblock %}`, add:

   ```
   {% random_joke %}
   ```

8. Start up the server:

   ```
   (.venv) …/projects/djangojokes.com> python manage.py runserver
   ```

9. In your browser, navigate to `http://127.0.0.1:8000`. The site should look like this:

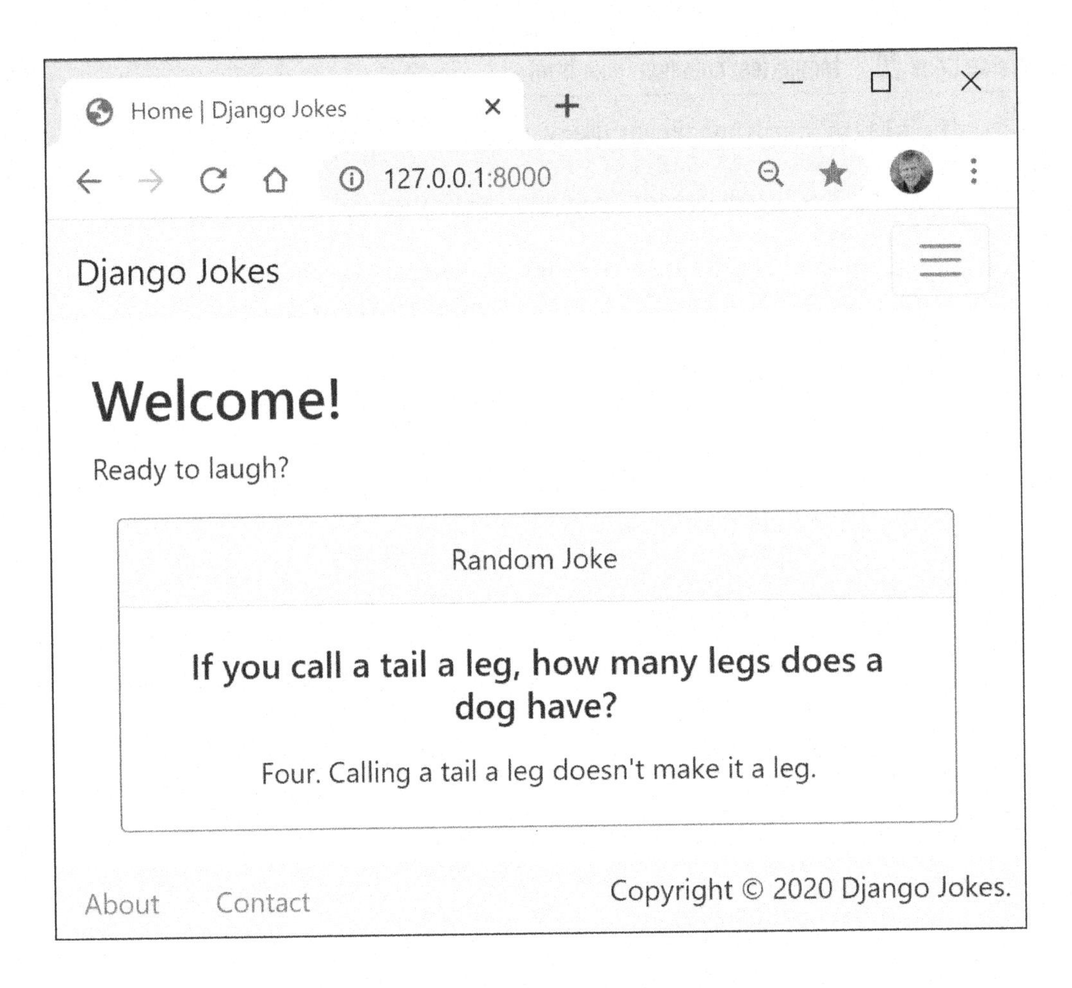

This custom template tag can be used on any page throughout the project.

Git Commit

Commit your code to Git.

Conclusion

In this lesson, you have learned to use Django's built-in template filters and tags to create your own custom filters and tags.

LESSON 5

Static Files

Topics Covered

☑ What is a "static" file?

☑ Managing static files in Django.

> I saw myself then as I see myself now, driven step by step towards that hasty blow, the creature of a sequence of accidents leading inevitably to that. I felt no condemnation; yet the memory, **static**, unprogressive, haunted me.
>
> – *The War of the Worlds, H. G. Wells*

Introduction

In this lesson, you will learn to add static files, such as JavaScript, CSS, and image files, to your site.

5.1. Static File Basics

Static files are files that do not need to be processed on the server before being sent to the browser. Django differentiates between static files created during development and static files that users upload, such as profile pictures. It refers to the latter as *media* files (see page 383). The static files we are concerned with here are files that make up part of the website (e.g., JavaScript, CSS, and image files).

❖ 5.1.1. `settings.py`

The first step to delivering static files is to configure the settings in `settings.py`:

1. `django.contrib.staticfiles` should be in the `INSTALLED_APPS` list. It gets added when you first create a project. Don't remove it.

2. Make sure the settings include this line:

```
STATIC_URL = '/static/'
```

It also gets added to `settings.py` (at the very bottom) when you first create a project. This is the path that Django will use to deliver static files.

3. Add the following setting:

```
STATICFILES_DIRS = [
    BASE_DIR / 'static',
]
```

A good place to put this is right below `STATIC_URL`. It tells Django to look in the project root for a `static` folder. It is a list, because you can set it to look in multiple places. Django will also look in each app for a `static` folder, but for most projects, it makes sense to keep all static files in subfolders of the project-level `static` folder.

❖ 5.1.2. Organizing the `static` Folder

There are different ways to organize the project-level `static` folder. This organization is largely a matter of personal preference. The important thing is that you organize it in a way that makes sense, so developers know where to put and where to find different static files.

Here's one option:

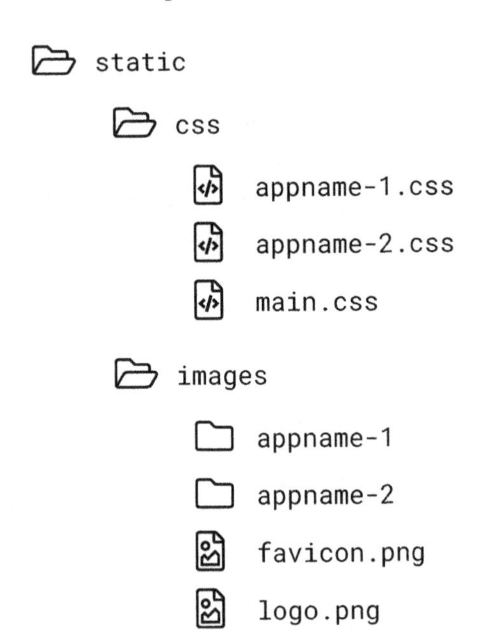

- js
  - appname-1.js
  - appname-2.js
  - main.js

5.1.3. The Templates

To include static files in a template, you must load the `static` template tag:

```
{% load static %}
```

You then reference static files using the `static` tag. For example:

```
<img src="{% static 'images/logo.png' %}" alt="Logo">
```

5.1.4. Deploying Your Site

The `django.contrib.staticfiles` app takes care of delivering static files when the `DEBUG` setting (in `settings.py`) is set to `True`. When it comes time to deploy your site, Django will collect all the static files into a single directory. The way in which this is handled varies by deployment, but always involves these two steps:

1. Setting the location where static files should be stored. The default storage class (`django.contrib.staticfiles.storage.StaticFilesStorage`) uses the value of `STATIC_ROOT` in `settings.py` to set this location. As a rule, if you plan to store static files on the same server your Django application is running, you should set `STATIC_ROOT` to an absolute path on that server. Often, the setting will look like this:

   ```
   STATIC_ROOT = BASE_DIR / 'staticfiles'
   ```

2. Running the following to collect all the static files into the `STATIC_ROOT` directory:

   ```
   python manage.py collectstatic
   ```

   As you will see when you deploy your website to production (see page 529), this step is often baked into the deployment process in such a way that you do not have to manually run it.

Exercise 21: Adding Static Files to Django Jokes

20 to 30 minutes

In this exercise, you will add the following static files to the Django Jokes site:

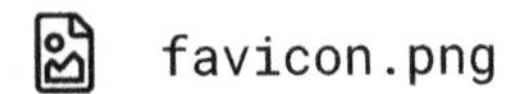

- `favicon.png`
- `logo.png`
- `main.css`

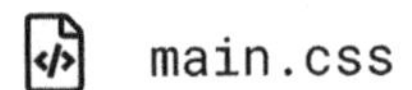

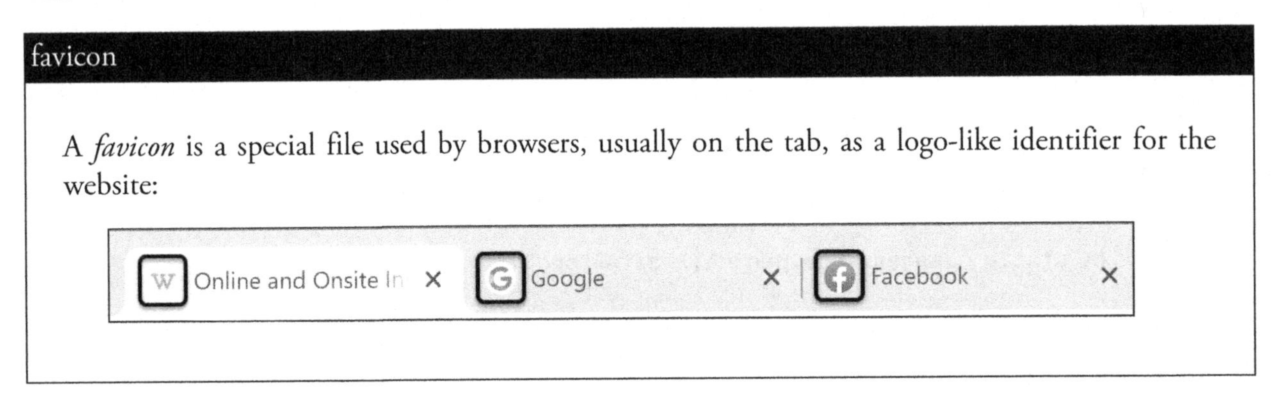

favicon

A *favicon* is a special file used by browsers, usually on the tab, as a logo-like identifier for the website:

❖ E21.1. settings.py

Open `djangojokes.com/djangojokes/settings.py` in your editor. Locate the `STATIC_URL` line at the end of the file and add a `STATICFILES_DIRS` setting below it:

```
STATIC_URL = '/static/'

STATICFILES_DIRS = [
    BASE_DIR / 'static',
]
```

❖ E21.2. Images

1. Create a `static` directory in the `djangojokes.com` folder, and create an `images` directory within that.

2. Add `favicon.png` and `logo.png` images to the `images` directory. You can create your own images or use the ones located in the `starter-code/static-files` folder.[38]
3. Open `templates/_base.html` in your editor.
   A. At the very top of the document, load the `static` tag:

   ```
   {% load static %}
   ```

   B. Add the following `link` element immediately before the `title` element in the `head`:

   ```
   <link rel="shortcut icon" type="image/png"
     href="{% static 'images/favicon.png' %}">
   ```

   C. Replace the "Django Jokes" text within the `navbar-brand` link with an image:

   ```
   <a class="navbar-brand" href="{% url 'homepage' %}">
     <img src="{% static 'images/logo.png' %}" alt="Logo" class="img-fluid"/>
   </a>
   ```

Start the server by opening `djangojokes.com` at the terminal and running:

```
(.venv) …/projects/djangojokes.com> python manage.py runserver
```

Then, point your browser to `http://127.0.0.1:8000/`. The page should look similar to this:

38. The `https://commons.wikimedia.org/wiki/File:Gaim_balloon-free.svg` image is in the public domain (`https://commons.wikimedia.org/wiki/Public_domain`)

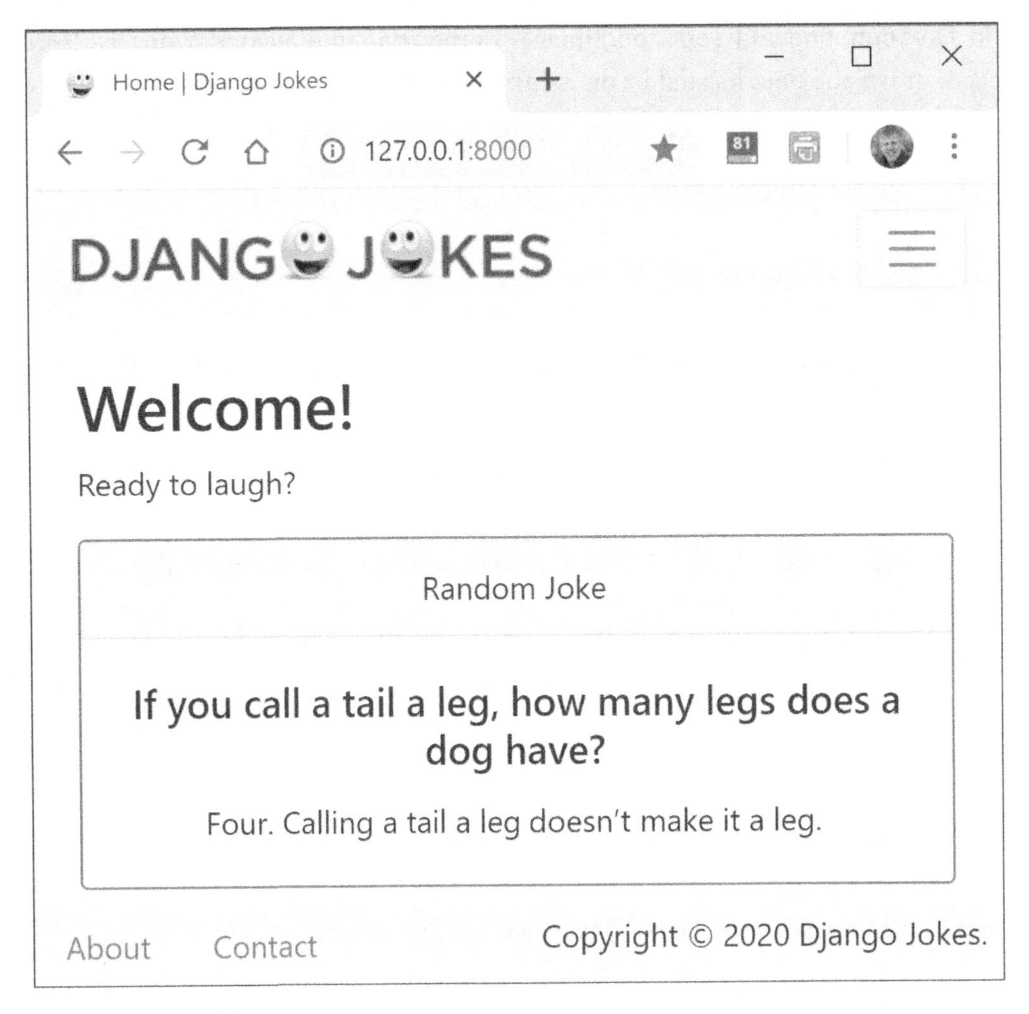

In addition to the logo in the upper left, notice the favicon image on the tab:

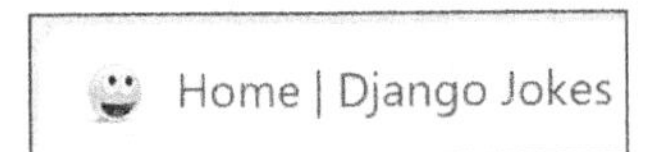

❖ E21.3. CSS File

1. Within the `static` folder, create a `css` folder.
2. Create a `main.css` file within the `css` folder with the following content, which you can copy from `starter-code/static-files/main.css`.

Exercise Code 21.1: static/css/main.css

```
1.   body {
2.     padding-bottom: 50px;
3.   }
4.
5.   footer {
6.     border-top: 1px solid darkgreen;
7.   }
8.
9.   header {
10.    border-bottom: 1px solid darkgreen;
11.  }
12.
13.  h2 {
14.    font-style: italic;
15.  }
```

If you like, you may add some of your own styles.

3. In `templates/_base.html`, add a `<link>` tag below the existing Bootstrap `<link>` tag to include `main.css`:

```
<link rel="stylesheet" href="{% static 'css/main.css' %}">
```

4. Return to the browser and refresh the page to see the new styles you added.

Git Commit

Commit your code to Git.

5.2. Review of the Settings

The settings for static files can be confusing. Let's review the difference between `STATIC_URL` and `STATICFILES_DIRS`.

❖ 5.2.1. STATIC_URL

Remember that `STATIC_URL` is set to `'/static/'`. While this also happens to be the name of the folder that holds static files, there is no connection between the `STATIC_URL` setting and the actual location of static files. Rather, this is the URL pattern that tells Django to look for static files. Let's prove this:

1. With the Django Jokes site running, go to the following URLs in your browser:
   A. http://127.0.0.1:8000/**static/**css/main.css – The CSS page should load.
   B. http://127.0.0.1:8000/**static/**images/logo.png – The logo should load.
   C. http://127.0.0.1:8000/**static/**images/favicon.png – The favicon should load.

2. Return to your editor and modify the `STATIC_URL` setting in `settings.py` as follows:

```
STATIC_URL = '/foo/'
```

3. Back in your browser, visit the following URLs. The files should still load:
   A. http://127.0.0.1:8000/**foo/**css/main.css
   B. http://127.0.0.1:8000/**foo/**images/logo.png
   C. http://127.0.0.1:8000/**foo/**images/favicon.png

4. Visit the home page at `http://127.0.0.1:8000/` and notice that it works just as before.
5. Right-click on the home page, select **View (or Show) page source**, and look for these tags:

```
<link rel="stylesheet" href="/foo/css/main.css">

<link rel="shortcut icon" type="image/png" href="/foo/images/favicon.png">

<img src="/foo/images/logo.png" alt="Logo" class="img-fluid"/>
```

Change `STATIC_URL` back to `'/static/'` as that is the standard practice for Django development:

```
STATIC_URL = '/static/'
```

Again, the `STATIC_URL` setting sets the URL pattern, not the location of static files.

❖ 5.2.2. STATICFILES_DIRS

The STATICFILES_DIRS setting, on the other hand, does have to do with where static files are stored. Again, the easiest way to see this is to make a quick change:

1. Modify the STATICFILES_DIRS setting in settings.py as follows:

    ```
    STATICFILES_DIRS = [
        BASE_DIR / 'bar',
    ]
    ```

2. Point your browser to http://127.0.0.1:8000/ and refresh the page. The logo and favicon images and the styles you added in main.css should disappear. If they don't, try doing a hard refresh by holding the Shift key down and pressing the browser's refresh button.
3. Change the name of the static folder to bar. In Visual Studio Code, you can do this by right-clicking on the folder and selecting **Rename**.
4. Return to your browser and refresh the page (again, you may need to do a hard refresh). The logo and favicon images should now show up and your styles should be back.

This illustrates that the STATICFILES_DIRS setting tells Django where to look for static files.

Change the name of the bar folder back to static and STATICFILES_DIRS back to its original setting:

```
STATICFILES_DIRS = [
    BASE_DIR / 'static',
]
```

Conclusion

In this lesson, you have learned to add static files to your Django web pages.

LESSON 6

Django Admin and the User Model

Topics Covered

☑ The default user model.

☑ Superusers.

☑ Django admin.

> "I'm Mister Noah Claypole," said the charity-boy, "and you're under me. Take down the shutters, yer idle young ruffian!" With this, Mr. Claypole **admin**istered a kick to Oliver, and entered the shop with a dignified air, which did him great credit.
>
> – *Oliver Twist, Charles Dickens*

Introduction

In this lesson, you will switch from SQLite to PostgreSQL, create a superuser, and learn about Django admin – Django's built-in administration interface.

6.1. The Database

Up until this point, you have been using a SQLite database. This works great for practicing, but on production websites, you will want to use something more robust. While you can use any of the major databases, including MySQL, Microsoft SQL Server, and Oracle, the most popular database to use with Django is PostgreSQL. In the following exercise, you will download and install PostgreSQL and create a `jokes` database to use with the Django Jokes project.

Exercise 22: Setting Up PostgreSQL

45 to 60 minutes

In this exercise, you will set up PostgreSQL and set up your Django project to work with it.

E22.1. Installing PostgreSQL

The process for getting PostgreSQL set up depends on your operating system.

Windows

1. Go to `https://www.enterprisedb.com/downloads/postgres-postgresql-downloads` and download the latest version of the installer for Windows.
2. Run through the installer. On the **Select Components** screen, uncheck **Stack Builder**. Leave the other options checked. **Make note of the password you set for the database superuser.**
3. Add PostgreSQL to your path:[39]
   A. Find the path to the `bin` folder where you installed PostgreSQL. It should be something like `C:\Program Files\PostgreSQL\12\bin`.
   B. Enter "environment" in **Windows Search** and select "Edit the system environment variables:"

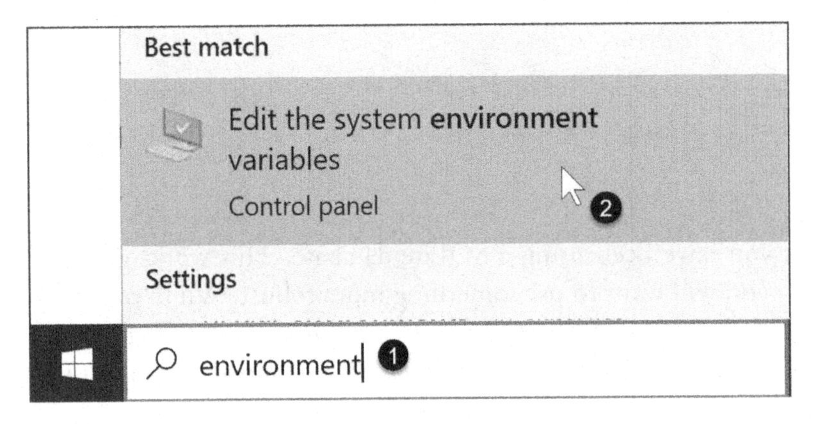

   C. Click the **Environment Variables…** button:

39. The screenshots shown here are for Windows 10.

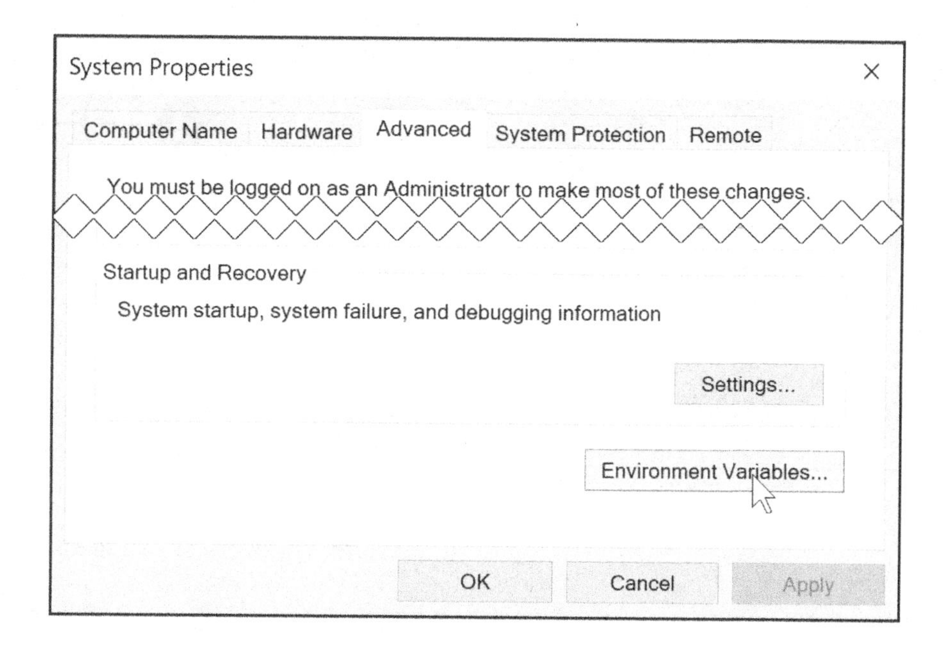

D. Under **System variables**, select **Path** and click the **Edit** button:

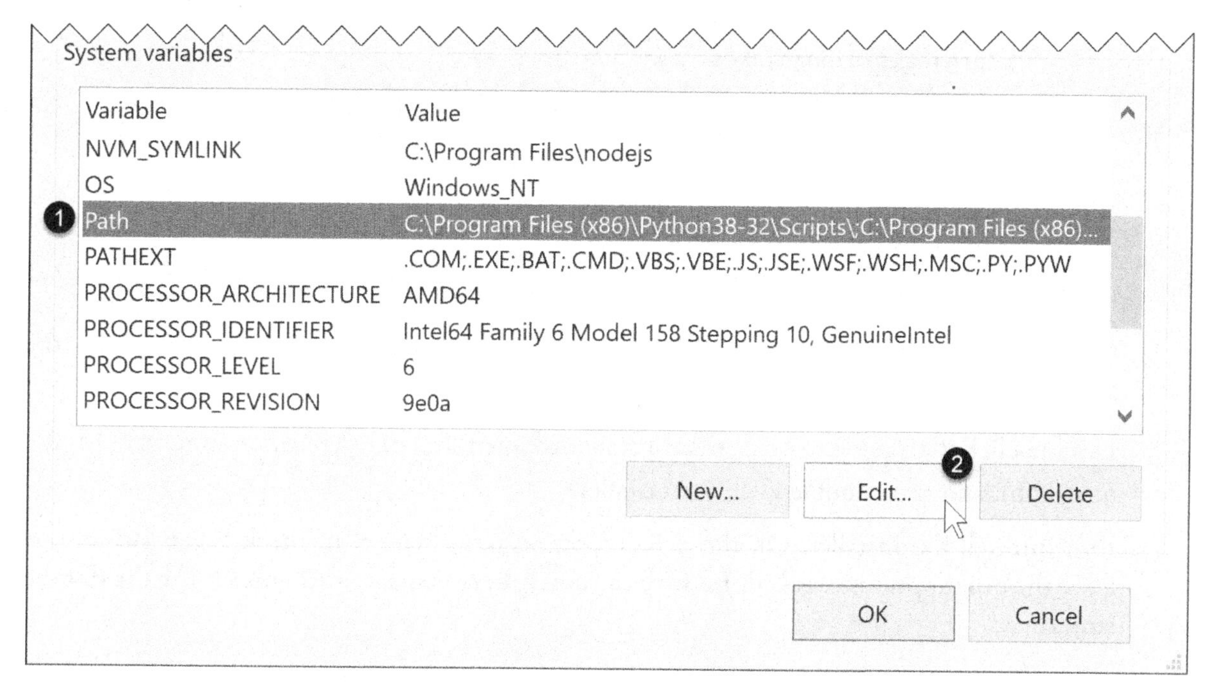

E. Click the **New** button, enter the path you found in step 3-A, and click **OK**:

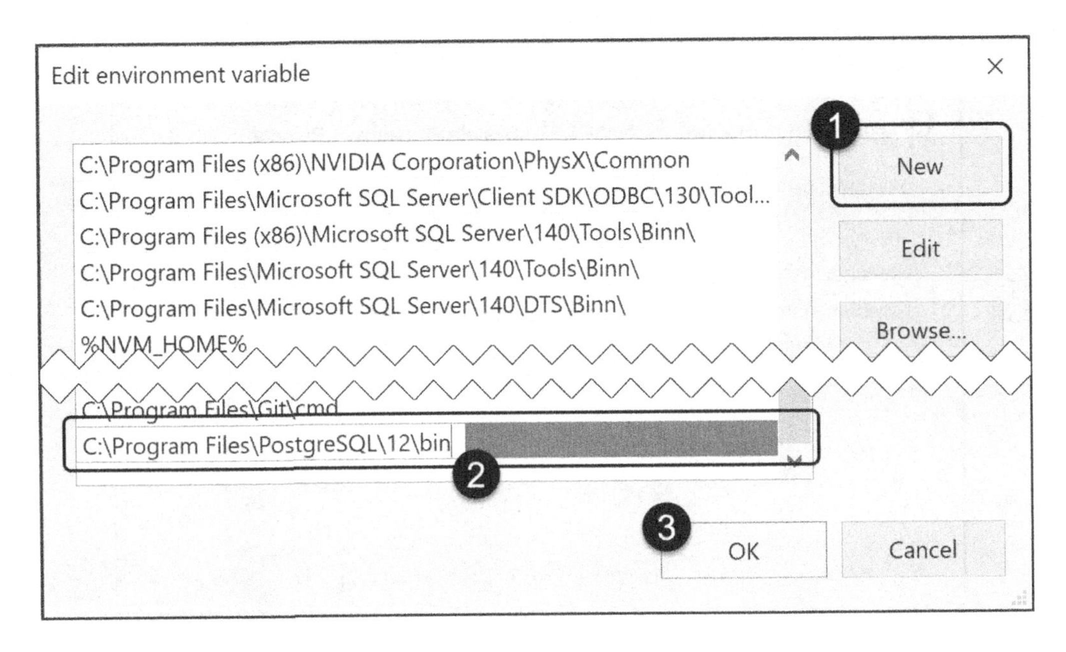

F. To test that the path is set up correctly, open a command prompt and run:

```
…/projects/djangojokes.com> postgres -V
postgres (PostgreSQL) 12.3
```

It should return the version of PostgreSQL that you installed.

Mac

1. Go to `https://www.enterprisedb.com/downloads/postgres-postgresql-downloads` and download the latest version of the installer for Mac.
2. Double-click the zip file to extract the installer (named something like `postgresql-12.3-2-osx.app`), and then double-click the installer.
3. Run through the installer. On the **Select Components** screen, uncheck **Stack Builder**, but leave the other options checked. **Be sure to remember the password you set for the database superuser.**

Linux/Other

Visit `https://www.postgresql.org/download` and follow the appropriate instructions for your operating system. Then download and install the latest version of pgAdmin for your operating system at `https://www.pgadmin.org/download`.

❖ E22.2. pgAdmin

pgAdmin, which you should have installed along with PostgreSQL, is a free front-end browser-based client for PostgreSQL. Although you do not need a PostgreSQL client to work with Django, having it gives you the ability to easily explore the tables Django creates behind the scenes.

1. Open pgAdmin just as you would open any other application on your computer. On Windows, you can type in "pgAdmin" in Windows Search and select **pgAdmin 4**. On a Mac, you can press Cmd+Space, enter "pgAdmin," and select **pgAdmin 4.app**.
2. pgAdmin will open in your browser. The first time it opens, it will prompt you to set a master password. This is different from the password you entered for the database superuser when installing PostgreSQL; however, you can use the same password. **Don't forget it!**

❖ E22.3. Creating a Database

While Django will take care of the database structure and data, you need to create the initial database first. You can use pgAdmin's graphical interface or the command line.

pgAdmin

To create a database using pgAdmin's graphical interface:

1. Expand **Servers**.
2. Right-click on **Databases** and select **Create > Database**:

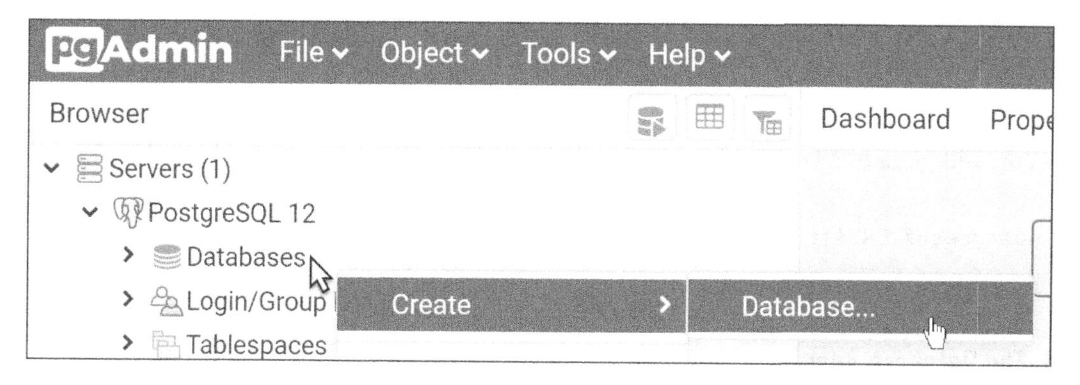

3. In the resulting dialog, enter "jokes" for the **Database** and click **Save**:

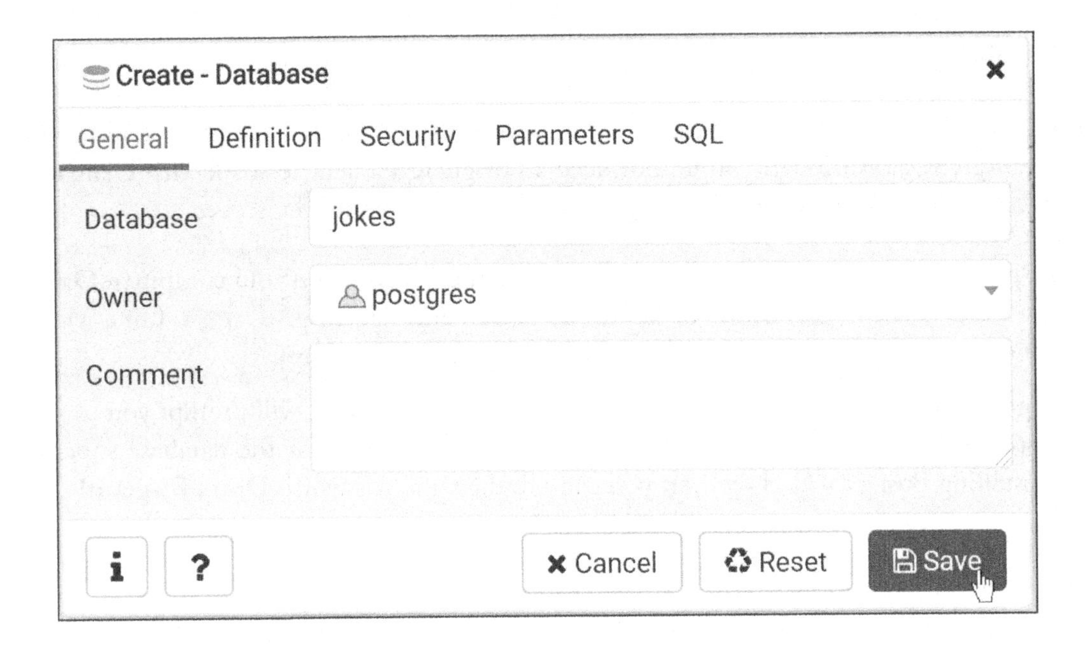

Command Line

If you don't want to go through the trouble of opening up pgAdmin just to create a database, you can use the command line:

1. Open a command prompt.
2. Run the following command to log in to PostgreSQL:

   ```
   psql -U postgres
   ```

   You will be prompted for the superuser password. Enter it and press Enter.
3. You will get a `postgres=#` prompt, at which you can create the database like this:

   ```
   postgres=# CREATE DATABASE jokes;
   ```

❖ E22.4. The Database Adapter

Python requires a database adapter to communicate with a database. The most popular database adapter used with PostgreSQL is `psycopg2`. Install `psycopg2` with `pip` in the virtual environment:

```
(.venv) …/projects/djangojokes.com> pip install psycopg2
```

❖ E22.5. Switching the Django Jokes Project to PostgreSQL

You are now ready to switch from SQLite to PostgreSQL for the Django Jokes project.

1. Open `settings.py` from `djangojokes` for editing.
2. Change the DATABASES setting to:

```
DATABASES = {
    'default': {
        'ENGINE': 'django.db.backends.postgresql',
        'NAME': 'jokes',
        'USER': 'postgres',
        'PASSWORD': 'YOURPASSWORD',
        'HOST': 'localhost',
        'PORT': 5432
    }
}
```

   Be sure to replace **YOURPASSWORD** with the password you created while installing PostgreSQL.

3. Because you have changed the database, all your data will be lost. Luckily, you only had one or two jokes in there, unless you added more on your own. Even more importantly, your database structure will be lost. The new PostgreSQL `jokes` database has no tables yet. You can see that using pgAdmin by clicking on **Tables** under **jokes** > **Schemas (1)** > **public**:

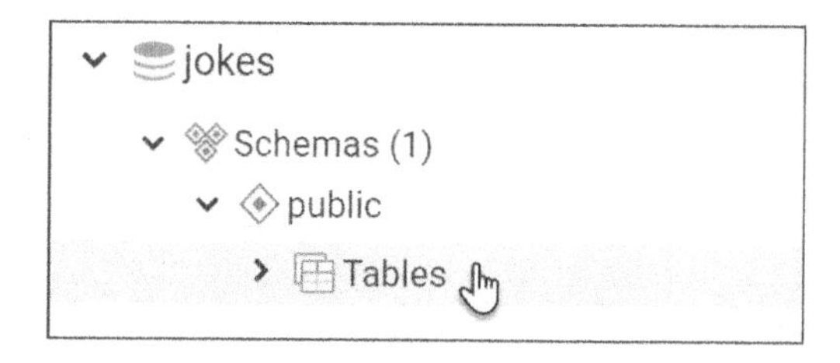

   As you can see, there are no tables in there. While you cannot get your data back,[40] you can get your tables back. You just need to run the migrations again. But before you do that, you need to create a custom user model. You'll learn to do that next.

Git Commit

Commit your code to Git.

40. Well, you could, but in this case, it's not worth the trouble.

6.2. The Default User Model

Before creating a custom user model, let's take a look at the default user model included with `django.contrib.auth`, which is included in the `INSTALLED_APPS` setting of new projects:

```
INSTALLED_APPS = [
    'django.contrib.admin',
    'django.contrib.auth',
    'django.contrib.contenttypes',
    'django.contrib.sessions',
    'django.contrib.messages',
    'django.contrib.staticfiles',
]
```

1. With `djangojokes.com` open at the terminal, run the following to open the shell:

   ```
   (.venv) …/projects/djangojokes.com> python manage.py shell
   ```

2. Import the default user model and inspect it:

   ```
   >>> from django.contrib.auth.models import User
   >>> User
   <class 'django.contrib.auth.models.User'>
   ```

   This indicates that the `User` class is defined in the `django/contrib/auth/models.py` file.

3. Exit out of the Python shell:

   ```
   >>> exit()
   ```

Find the file that contains the `User` class definition. Starting from `.venv/lib/site-packages/django`, look in:

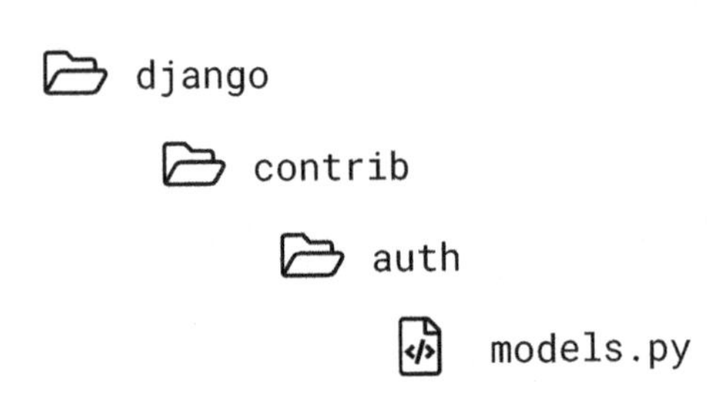

Let's see how the class is defined:

1. Open `models.py` in your editor and search the file for "class User(". You should find this:

   ```
   class User(AbstractUser):
       ...
   ```

   That indicates that `User` inherits from `AbstractUser`.

2. Search the file for "class AbstractUser". You should find a class that looks something like this:

Demo 6.1: AbstractUser

```
1.  class AbstractUser(AbstractBaseUser, PermissionsMixin):
2.      """
3.      An abstract base class implementing a fully featured User model with
4.      admin-compliant permissions.
5.
6.      Username and password are required. Other fields are optional.
7.      """
8.      username_validator = UnicodeUsernameValidator()
9.
10.     username = models.CharField(…)
11.     first_name = models.CharField(_('first name'), max_length=30, blank=True)
12.     last_name = models.CharField(_('last name'), max_length=150, blank=True)
13.     email = models.EmailField(_('email address'), blank=True)
14.     is_staff = models.BooleanField(…)
15.     is_active = models.BooleanField(…)
16.     date_joined = models.DateTimeField(_('date joined'), default=timezone.now)
```

Notice that the `AbstractUser` class contains the following fields:

A. `username`

B. `first_name`

C. `last_name`

D. `email`

E. `is_staff`

F. `is_active`

G. `date_joined`

`AbstractUser` gets additional fields from the two classes it inherits from:

AbstractBaseUser

A. `password`
B. `last_login`

PermissionsMixin

A. `is_superuser`

While the default user model that comes baked in to Django may be fine for your initial plans, there will likely come a time when you will want to make some modifications to it. For example, you might want to add a `date_of_birth` or a `timezone` field. As the `User` model is part of the built-in `django.contrib.auth` app, you won't be able to make changes to the model.[41] As such, you should *always* create a custom user model when starting a new project. This will give you full control over the user model as your project develops. And, as it turns out, it's easy to do.

41. Well, you could, but you shouldn't.

Exercise 23: Creating a Custom User Model

20 to 30 minutes

In this exercise, you will create a new app with a custom user model in the djangojokes project.

1. With djangojokes.com open in the terminal, run the following command to create the **users** app:

```
(.venv) …/projects/djangojokes.com> python manage.py startapp users
```

2. Open users/models.py for editing, and add the following code:

Exercise Code 23.1: users/models.py

```
1.  from django.contrib.auth.models import AbstractUser
2.  from django.db import models
3.
4.  class CustomUser(AbstractUser):
5.      pass
```

Things to notice:

- You import AbstractUser from django.contrib.auth.models.
- The CustomUser class inherits from AbstractUser, but doesn't change it at all. While you haven't made any changes yet, creating this subclass of AbstractUser gives you the option of making changes in the future.

3. Open djangojokes/settings.py for editing:

   A. Add the new **users** app to the INSTALLED_APPS:

```
INSTALLED_APPS = [
    …

    # Local apps
    'common.apps.CommonConfig',
    'jokes.apps.JokesConfig',
    'jokes.apps.PagesConfig',
    'users.apps.UsersConfig',
]
```

B. Immediately below the `AUTH_PASSWORD_VALIDATORS` setting,[42] set `AUTH_USER_MODEL` to `users.CustomUser`:

```
# AUTHENTICATION SETTINGS
AUTH_USER_MODEL = 'users.CustomUser'
```

The `AUTH_USER_MODEL` setting[43] sets the model used to represent a `User` in the project. It defaults to `'auth.User'`. You are overriding that default to set it to the `CustomUser` class you just created.

❖ E23.1. Migrating

Remember that you waited to migrate (see page 183) until you created the custom user model? That is because the initial migration will create the user model. Once that user model is created, you have lost your chance to customize it. So, always *always* **always**, create the custom user model before running the initial migration.

Wait, when do you create the custom user model?

Great question! If you are going to create a custom user model, which you almost definitely should, you must create it *before doing the initial migration.* Always.

But wait again! Didn't I already run the migrations?

Yes, you did run migrations for `djangojokes` already (see page 74). But since you replaced the SQLite database with PostgreSQL, you need to run them again, which gives you a fresh start.

42. It could go anywhere in the settings file, but this is a good place for it.
43. `https://docs.djangoproject.com/en/3.1/ref/settings/#auth-user-model`

1. Run `makemigrations` and `migrate` to make the new migration files for the `CustomUser` model and run all the project's migration files:

```
(.venv) …/projects/djangojokes.com> python manage.py makemigrations
Migrations for 'users':
  users\migrations\0001_initial.py
    - Create model CustomUser
(.venv) …/projects/djangojokes.com> python manage.py migrate
Operations to perform:
  Apply all migrations: admin, auth, contenttypes, jokes, sessions, users
Running migrations:
  Applying contenttypes.0001_initial... OK
  Applying contenttypes.0002_remove_content_type_name... OK
  Applying auth.0001_initial... OK
  Applying auth.0002_alter_permission_name_max_length... OK
  Applying auth.0003_alter_user_email_max_length... OK
  Applying auth.0004_alter_user_username_opts... OK
  Applying auth.0005_alter_user_last_login_null... OK
  Applying auth.0006_require_contenttypes_0002... OK
  Applying auth.0007_alter_validators_add_error_messages... OK
  Applying auth.0008_alter_user_username_max_length... OK
  Applying auth.0009_alter_user_last_name_max_length... OK
  Applying auth.0010_alter_group_name_max_length... OK
  Applying auth.0011_update_proxy_permissions... OK
  Applying auth.0012_alter_user_first_name_max_length... OK
  Applying users.0001_initial... OK
  Applying admin.0001_initial... OK
  Applying admin.0002_logentry_remove_auto_add... OK
  Applying admin.0003_logentry_add_action_flag_choices... OK
  Applying jokes.0001_initial... OK
  Applying sessions.0001_initial... OK
```

2. Open pgAdmin and navigate to **Databases > jokes > Schemas > public > Tables**. Right-click on **Tables** and select **Refresh**:

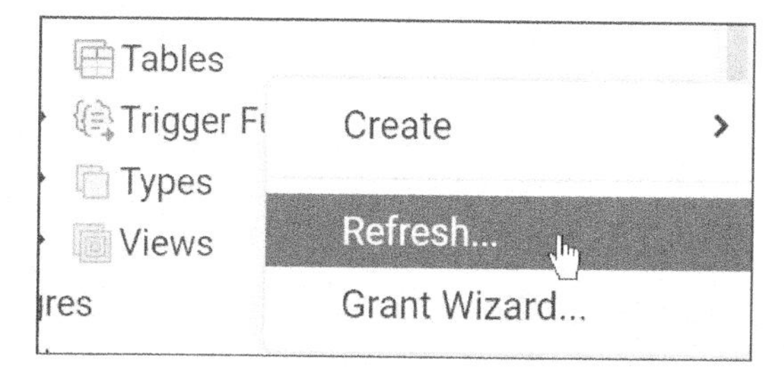

You should see the following tables:

Tables (11)
auth_group
auth_group_permissions
auth_permission
django_admin_log
django_content_type
django_migrations
django_session
jokes_joke
users_customuser
users_customuser_groups
users_customuser_user_permissions

3. Expand **users_customuser** and **Columns**:

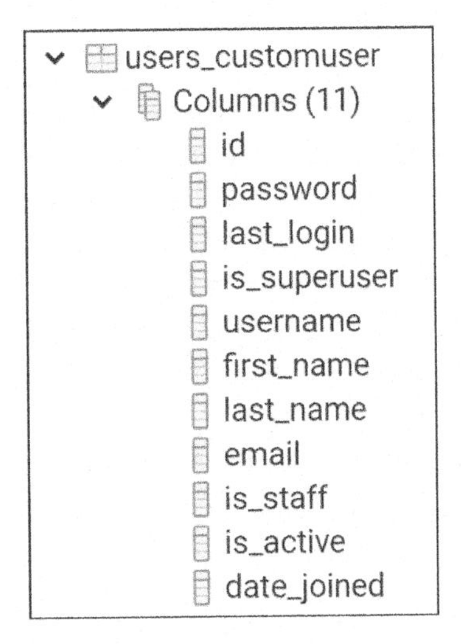

Notice that it contains the same fields as the `AbstractUser` class you looked at earlier (see page 185). In addition, it includes an `id` field. By default, every table created in Django will get an `id` primary key field that is an auto-incrementing integer.

Git Commit

Commit your code to Git.

6.3. Referencing the User Model

There are two commonly used ways of referencing the user model:

1. The `get_user_model()` method from the `django.contrib.auth` app.
2. The `AUTH_USER_MODEL` variable in the project `settings`.

You should use `AUTH_USER_MODEL` when referencing the model as a foreign key to other models. You will see this when you associate users with the jokes they create (see page 357).

In most other cases, you should use `get_user_model()`.

Exercise 24: Getting Started with Django Admin

25 to 40 minutes

Most database-driven websites include an administrative site for managing users and other data. Often, these sites simply provide CRUD (**C**reate, **R**ead, **U**pdate, **D**elete) functionality. Django projects include a built-in administrative site known as *Django admin*.

As you have seen, new Django projects have a default user model baked in. Only superusers (`is_superuser == True`) and staff (`is_staff == True`) have access to Django admin. After creating a user model and making any necessary migrations, the first thing you usually do is create a superuser. But before you do that, let's demonstrate that there are currently no users in the database:

1. In pgAdmin, with the **jokes** database selected on the left, click **Tools > Query Tool**:

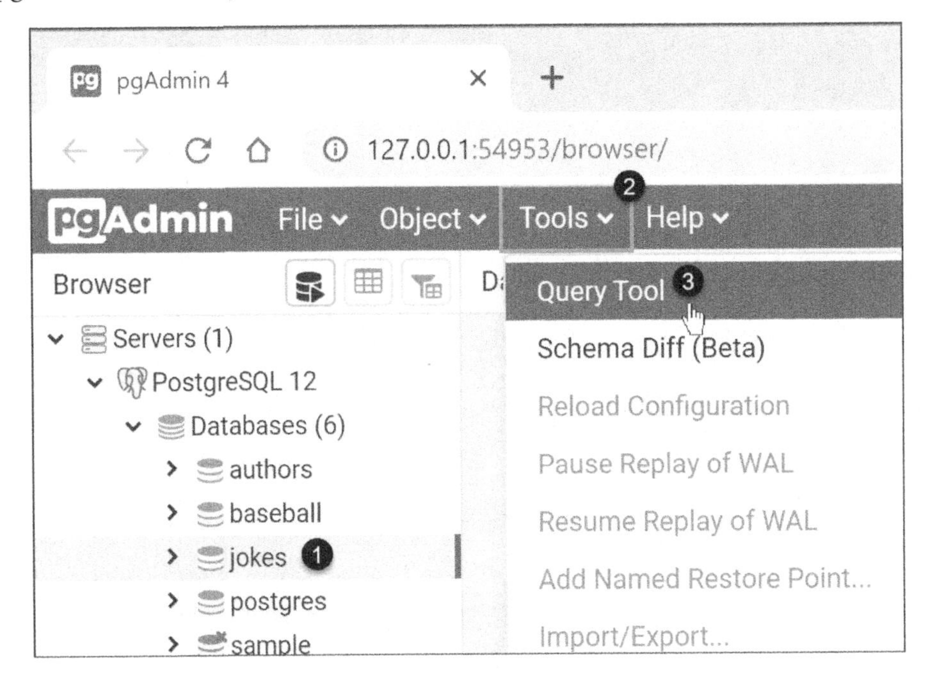

2. Enter the following query and click the black triangle to run it:

```
SELECT id, email, password, username FROM users_customuser;
```

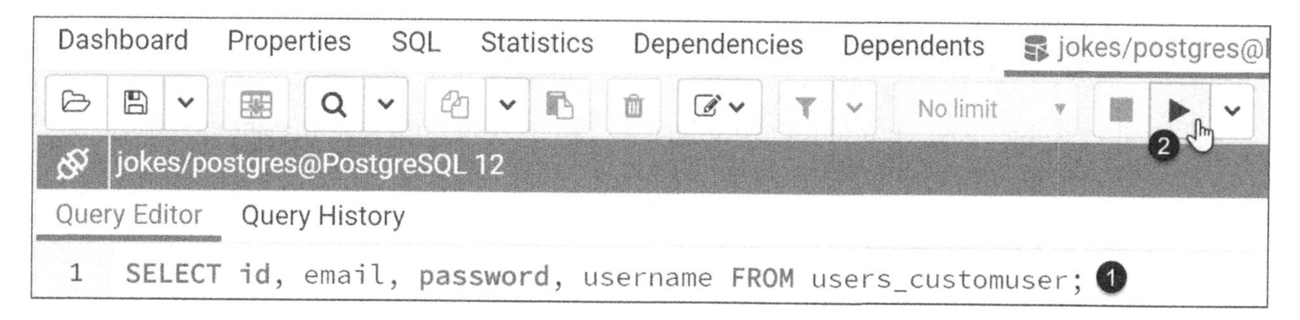

In the bottom right of pgAdmin, you'll get a message indicating that there are no users:

Successfully run. Total query runtime: 73 msec. 0 rows affected.

Now, go ahead and create a superuser:

1. At the terminal, run:

```
(.venv) …/projects/djangojokes.com> python manage.py createsuperuser
Username: ndunn
Email address: me@example.com
Password:
Password (again):
Superuser created successfully
```

   A. **Username**: Enter whatever username you like or accept the default.
   B. **Email address**: Use an email address at which you can receive emails.
   C. **Password**: Enter a secure password (and remember it).
   D. **Password (again)**: Repeat the password.

Now, go back to pgAdmin and run the same SQL query again. This time, you will get a result:

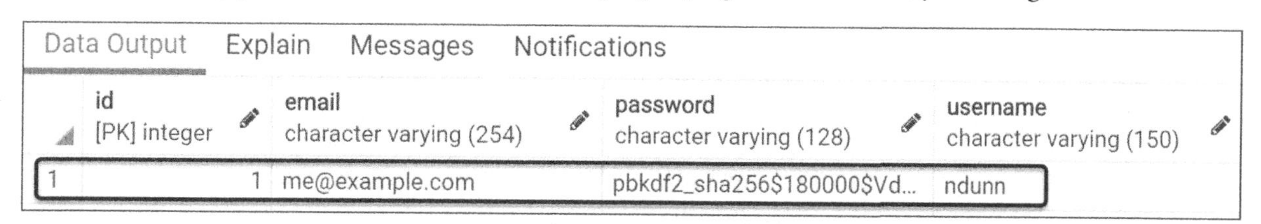

pgAdmin in Django Development

In normal Django development, you do not need to use pgAdmin to inspect the database, but it can be helpful from time to time, especially when you are learning Django.

❖ E24.1. Registering the Custom User

You need to register your custom user with Django admin. You do this in the `users/admin.py` file. Open that file up and add the following content:[44]

Exercise Code 24.1: users/admin.py

```
1.  from django.contrib import admin
2.  from django.contrib.auth import get_user_model
3.  from django.contrib.auth.admin import UserAdmin
4.
5.  CustomUser = get_user_model()
6.
7.  @admin.register(CustomUser)
8.  class CustomUserAdmin(UserAdmin):
9.      model = CustomUser
10.
11.     add_fieldsets = UserAdmin.add_fieldsets + (
12.         ('Optional Fields', {
13.             'classes': ('wide',),
14.             'fields': ('email', 'first_name', 'last_name'),
15.         }),
16.     )
```

Things to notice:

1. On the first line, you import `admin` from `django.contrib`. This is one of the apps included in `INSTALLED_APPS`.
2. You import `get_user_model()` from `django.contrib.auth`:

   ```
   from django.contrib.auth import get_user_model
   ```

3. As you have overridden the default user model, you need to override the default `UserAdmin` class as well:

   A. You import `django.contrib.auth.admin`'s `UserAdmin` class, which is the class used for managing the default user model:

   ```
   from django.contrib.auth.admin import UserAdmin
   ```

44. **Don't want to type?** Copy from `starter-code/django-admin/users_admin.py`.

B. You create a `CustomUserAdmin` class by inheriting from `UserAdmin` and set `model` to `CustomUser`:

```
class CustomUserAdmin(UserAdmin):
model = CustomUser
```

4. You append to the `add_fieldsets` attribute of the `UserAdmin` class. More on this in a moment.
5. You must register `CustomUserAdmin`. You do this using the `@admin.register` decorator:

```
@admin.register(CustomUser)
```

Another way of registering a `ModelAdmin` class is to use the `register()` method:

```
admin.site.register(CustomUser, CustomUserAdmin)
```

But the decorator is more convenient.

`fieldsets` and `add_fieldsets`

The `fieldsets` and `add_fieldsets` properties hold the fieldsets that show up in Django admin's forms:

- `fieldsets` – These are the fieldsets used for updating existing records. Generally, you want this to contain all the fields that can be modified.
- `add_fieldsets` – These are the fieldsets used for creating new records. This only needs to contain the required fields; however, it can contain additional fields that you generally want to have data for in new records.

`fieldsets` and `add_fieldsets` each holds a tuple, which itself contains one or more 2-element tuples:

1. The first element is the fieldset name (or `None` if the fieldset is unnamed).
2. The second element is a dictionary containing the CSS classes and the fields in the fieldset.

The `add_fieldsets` attribute of the built-in `UserAdmin` class looks like this:

```
add_fieldsets = (
    (None, {
        'classes': ('wide',),
        'fields': ('username', 'password1', 'password2'),
    }),
)
```

It contains only one tuple, meaning there is only one fieldset. The `None` value indicates that the fieldset has no name. It has one class: "wide" and three fields: "username," "password1," and "password2". The resulting **Add User** form looks like this:

Add user

First, enter a username and password. Then, you'll be able to edit more user options.

Username:

Required. 150 characters or fewer. Letters, digits and @/./+/-/_ only.

Password:

Your password can't be too similar to your other personal information.

Your password must contain at least 8 characters.

Your password can't be a commonly used password.

Your password can't be entirely numeric.

Password confirmation:

Enter the same password as before, for verification.

Save and add another | Save and continue editing | SAVE

In your `CustomUserAdmin` class, you append[45] another tuple to `UserAdmin`'s `add_fieldsets`:

```
add_fieldsets = UserAdmin.add_fieldsets + (
    ('Optional Fields', {
        'classes': ('wide',),
        'fields': ('email', 'first_name', 'last_name'),
    }),
)
```

You've named the new fieldset "Optional Fields," which also will have the "wide" class, and will have three additional fields: "email," "first_name," and "last_name."

These fields will now be added to Django admin's **Add user** form:

45. You cannot really **append** to a tuple, as tuples are immutable. What you are actually doing is overwriting the `add_fieldsets` property with a new value: its previous value plus the new tuple.

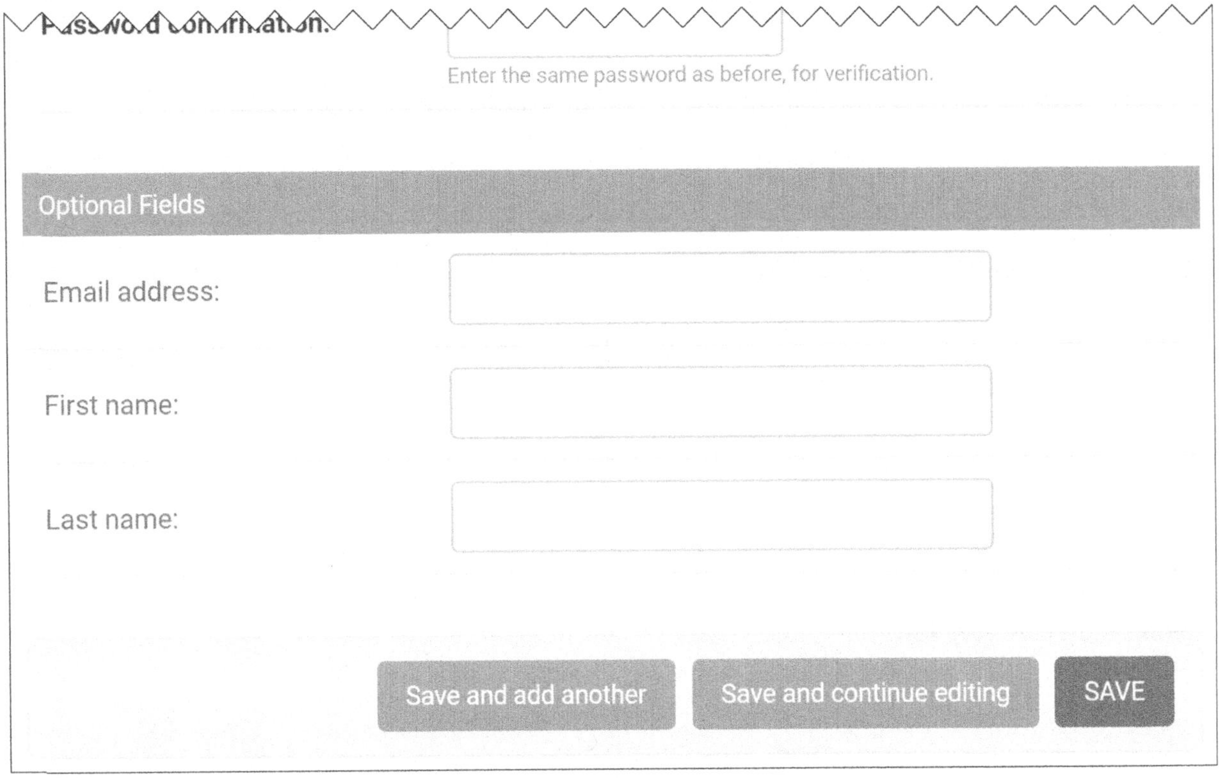

Notice the “Optional Fields” header. That comes from this:

```
add_fieldsets = UserAdmin.add_fieldsets + (
    ('Optional Fields', …
)
```

You will be able to use this same technique to customize other forms in Django admin as you add models to your project.

❖ E24.2. Django admin

It is time to check out Django admin:

1. Open `djangojokes/urls.py` in your editor. Notice the first URL pattern:

   ```
   urlpatterns = [
       path('admin/', admin.site.urls),
       ...
   ]
   ```

   This shows the path to Django admin is `admin/`.

2. Start up the server:

   ```
   (.venv) …/projects/djangojokes.com> python manage.py runserver
   ```

3. Point your browser to `http://127.0.0.1:8000/admin/`. You should see a login screen. Enter the username and password you used when creating the superuser:

   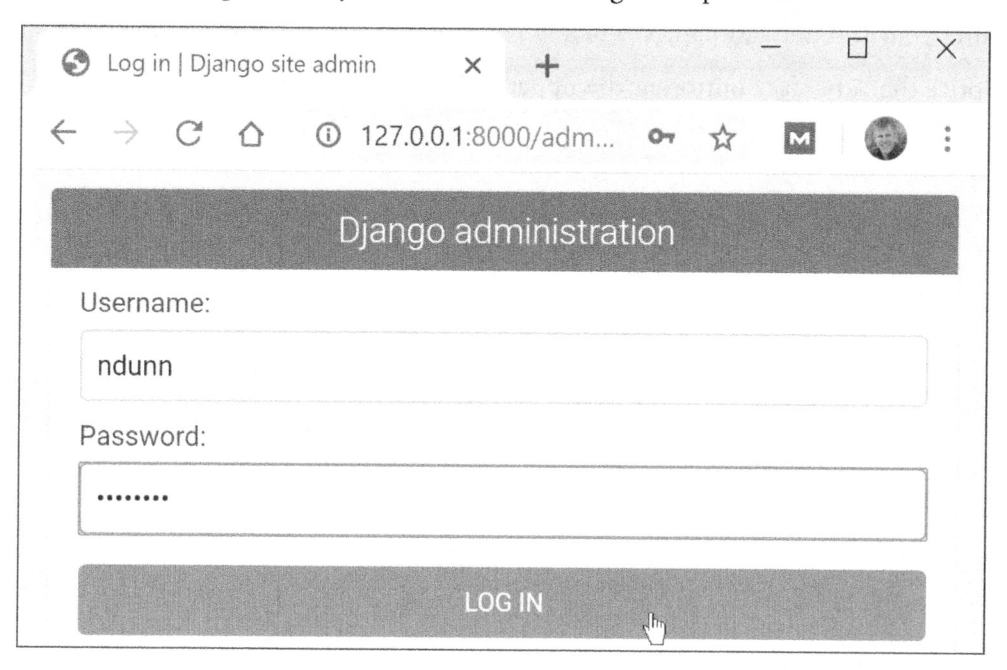

4. You should see a page like this one:

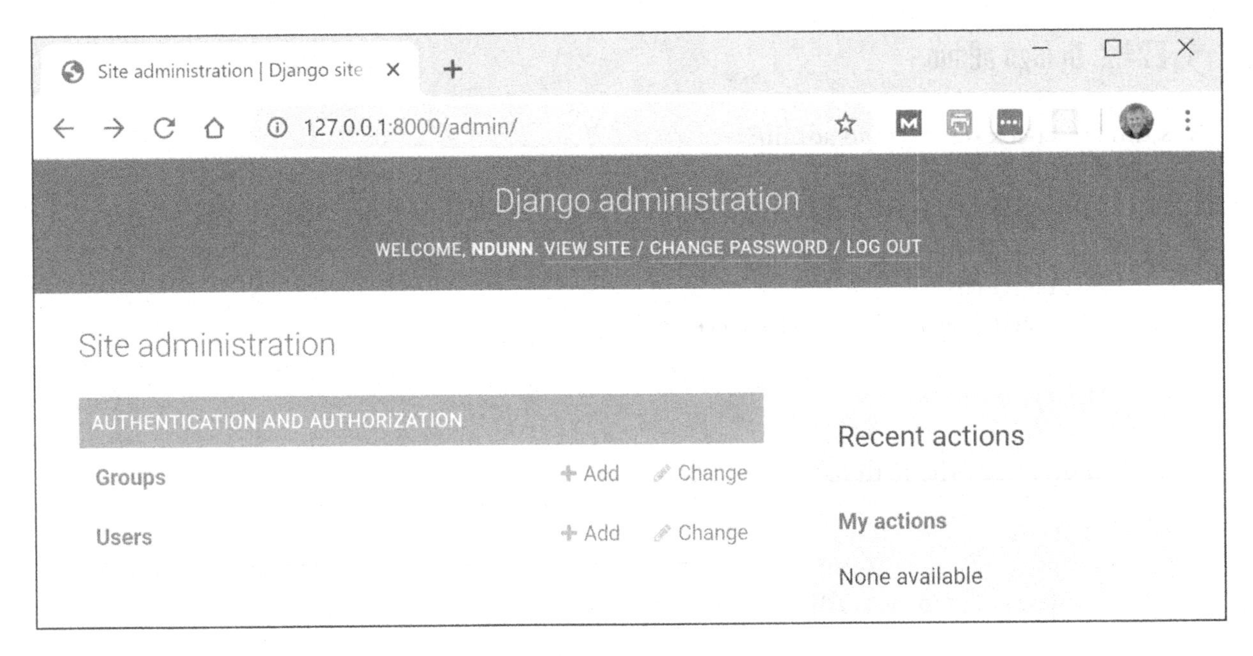

You will see two models: **Groups**[46] and **Users**.

5. Click on **Users** and then click on your username.
6. Enter your first and last names. Then, scroll down to the bottom and click **Save**.
7. Notice the **Add User** button in the upper right. Click that, fill out the form with a new user, and click **Save**:

46. The **Groups** model allows you to categorize users into generic groups. This is particularly useful for applying permissions.

Add user

First, enter a username and password. Then, you'll be able to edit more user options.

Username: jangoldman

Required. 150 characters or fewer. Letters, digits and @/./+/-/_ only.

Password: ••••••••

Your password can't be too similar to your other personal information.

Your password must contain at least 8 characters.

Your password can't be a commonly used password.

Your password can't be entirely numeric.

Password confirmation: ••••••••

Enter the same password as before, for verification.

Optional Fields

Email address: jgoldman@example.com

First name: Jan

Last name: Goldman

Save and add another | Save and continue editing | SAVE

8. Click on **Users** to go back to the list of users and notice the following:

   A. You are marked as staff, but the new user is not.
   B. The **Action** menu allows you to delete selected users.

9. With the new user checked, select **Delete selected users** from the **Action** menu, and click the **Go** button. This will take you to confirmation screen:

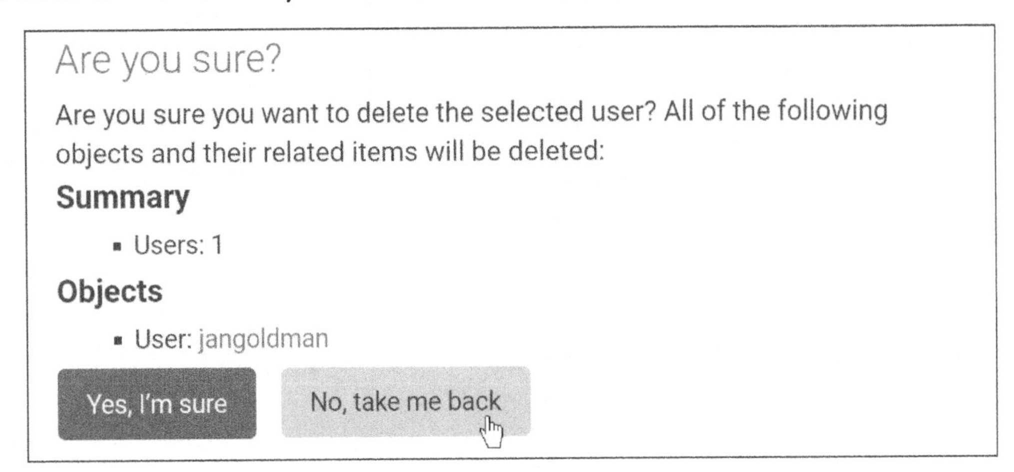

   Click **No, take me back.**

What we have shown here is known as *CRUD* (for **C**reate, **R**ead, **U**pdate, **D**elete) functionality.

Git Commit

Commit your code to Git.

 Exercise 25: Adding the jokes Table to Django Admin

10 to 15 minutes

Every new model you create can be managed in Django admin in the same way that users can be managed. You just need to create and register a `ModelAdmin` class for the model.

Open `jokes/admin.py` for editing and write the following code:[47]

Exercise Code 25.1: jokes/admin.py

```
1.  from django.contrib import admin
2.
3.  from .models import Joke
4.
5.  @admin.register(Joke)
6.  class JokeAdmin(admin.ModelAdmin):
7.      model = Joke
8.      list_display = ['question', 'created', 'updated']
9.
10.     def get_readonly_fields(self, request, obj=None):
11.         if obj: # editing an existing object
12.             return ('created', 'updated')
13.
14.         return ()
```

Things to notice:

1. After importing `admin` from `django.contrib`, you import the `Joke` model, which you then use in the `JokeAdmin` class to set the model being managed in this class.
2. You set `list_display` to specify the fields that should show up in the jokes listing:

	QUESTION	CREATED	UPDATED
☐	Why did the chicken cross the road?	Aug. 6, 2020, 4:10 p.m.	Aug. 6, 2020, 4:10 p.m.

   The `list_display` attribute is not required. If you don't set it, there will only be one column in the table with the value returned by the model's `__str__()` displayed.

47. **Don't want to type?** Copy from `starter-code/django-admin/jokes_admin.py`.

3. `readonly_fields` holds fields that you want to be able to read but not edit. You could have set this attribute like this:

   ```
   readonly_fields = ('created', 'updated')
   ```

   But if you do that, the fields will show up in the form for adding new jokes as well as the form for editing existing jokes. It doesn't make sense that the form for adding new jokes would have readonly fields as those fields will always be empty until the joke is actually added. So, you use the getter function to check if `obj` exists:

   ```
   def get_readonly_fields(self, request, obj=None):
   if obj: # editing an existing object
       return ('created', 'updated')

   return ()
   ```

   This will tell you if you are editing an existing `obj` or creating a new one. If you're editing an existing object, you return `('created', 'updated')`. If you're creating a new one, you return an empty tuple, indicating that there are no readonly fields.

Open Django admin and add some jokes. Then, go to the site, which you can get to by clicking the **VIEW SITE** link at the top of Django admin:

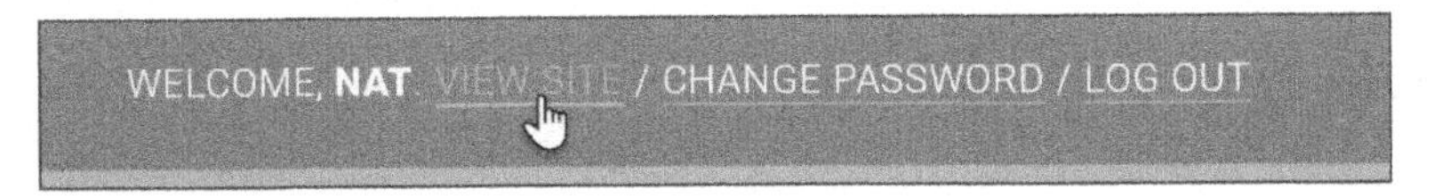

You should see the jokes you added.

Git Commit

Commit your code to Git.

 Exercise 26: Installing the Django Admin Documentation Generator

10 to 15 minutes

The Django admin documentation generator (admindocs) autogenerates documentation for Django admin.

1. Add `django.contrib.admindocs` to `INSTALLED_APPS` in `djangojokes/settings.py`:

```
INSTALLED_APPS = [
    # Built-in Django apps
    'django.contrib.admin',
    'django.contrib.admindocs',
    …
]
```

2. Add `path('admin/doc/', include('django.contrib.admindocs.urls'))` to the `urlpatterns` in `djangojokes/urls.py`. You must add it before the `'admin/'` pattern:

```
urlpatterns = [
    path('admin/doc/', include('django.contrib.admindocs.urls')),
    path('admin/', admin.site.urls),
    path('', include('jokes.urls')),
]
```

3. Install `docutils` with `pip` in the virtual environment:

```
(.venv) …/projects/djangojokes.com> pip install docutils
```

That's it. Stop and restart the server and then return to `http://127.0.0.1:8000/admin/`. You will see a new **DOCUMENTATION** link in the header navigation:

WELCOME, **NAT**. VIEW SITE / DOCUMENTATION / CHANGE PASSWORD / LOG OUT

The documentation is most useful for models. To see the documentation on the `Joke` model:

1. Click **DOCUMENTATION**.
2. Click **Models**.
3. Click **Joke** under the **Jokes (jokes)** heading.

The documentation should look like this:

jokes.Joke

Joke(id, question, answer, created, updated)

Fields

FIELD	TYPE	DESCRIPTION
answer	Text	answer
created	Date (with time)	created
get_absolute_url		
id	Integer	ID
question	Text	question
updated	Date (with time)	updated

Your models are currently quite simple, so the documentation doesn't add much, but as the project gets bigger and the models get more complex, this documentation can be helpful.

Git Commit

Commit your code to Git.

Conclusion

In this lesson, you have installed and switched to PostgreSQL, created a superuser, and learned the basics of Django admin.

LESSON 7
URLs and Slugs

Topics Covered

☑ Slugs.

☑ Utility functions.

☑ Overriding `models.Model.save()`.

Why prat'st thou to thyself, and answer'st not?

Dromio, thou drone, thou snail, thou **slug**, thou sot!

– *Comedy of Errors, William Shakespeare*

Introduction

In this lesson, you will learn to create slugs, rather than primary keys, to use in URLs. In doing so, you will learn to organize and write your own utility functions and to override the model's `save()` method.

7.1. Slugs

A *slug* is a string used in a URL to uniquely identify a web page. For example, instead of:

```
http://127.0.0.1:8000/jokes/joke/1/
```

...the URL to the page with the joke about the chicken crossing the road could be:

```
http://127.0.0.1:8000/jokes/joke/why-did-the-chicken-cross-the-road/
```

This provides several benefits over the primary-key approach:

1. Primary keys shouldn't be exposed as hackers can use that data to try to mess with the database.
2. When you use primary keys as part of the URL, if a joke's primary key changes, which can happen if a joke is deleted and then re-added, the URL of the joke will also change. This means that existing links to that joke from other pages will get broken. If you use slugs, changes in the primary key will not affect changes in the URL (as long as you keep the slug the same).
3. Some search engines use the URL string to learn what the page is about. "why-did-the-chicken-cross-the-road" is much more meaningful than "1".

❖ 7.1.1. `SlugField`

Django models include a `SlugField` field type, which allows for strings that contain letters, numbers, underscores, and hyphens. By default, the maximum length of the string is 50, but that can be changed with the `max_length` argument.

❖ 7.1.2. Implementing Slugs

The steps involved for implementing slugs are:

1. Create a function that automatically generates a unique slug for a model.
2. Add a `slug` field to the model.
3. Use the function created above to auto-populate the `slug` field when a record is saved.
4. Modify the URL pattern to use the slug.

If you had started with this approach, that would be it, but as you already have data in a **jokes** table, you need to do a couple of additional things. Normally, you won't allow `null` values for slugs. However, records that already exist in the table won't have a value for the new `slug` field. In some cases, when you need to add a new required field to a model, you can set a default value for the field. All existing records will get that default value. However, if the field must be unique, as is the case with slugs, setting a default value won't work.

The solution is as follows:

1. Allow for `null` values when first adding the field.
2. Create unique slugs for all existing records.
3. Change the model to disallow `null` values.

You will do all of this in the following exercises.

Exercise 27: Creating a Slug-generating Function

15 to 20 minutes

As you are likely to use slugs in more than one app, it makes sense to create the slug-generating function in the `common` app. Functions like this are called `utility` functions, and as your project may end up having a lot of them, it is important to organize them well:

1. Within the `djangojokes.com/common` folder, create a `utils` folder. This will be the home for all your project's general utility functions.
2. Within the new `utils` folder, create a file called `text.py` for utilities that work with text and add the following content:[48]

Exercise Code 27.1: common/utils/text.py

```
1.  import random
2.  import string
3.
4.  from django.utils.text import slugify
5.
6.  def unique_slug(s, model, num_chars=50):
7.      """
8.      Return slug of num_chars length unique to model
9.
10.     `s` is the string to turn into a slug
11.     `model` is the model we need to use to check for uniqueness
12.     """
13.     slug = slugify(s)
14.     slug = slug[:num_chars].strip('-')
15.     while True:
16.         dup = model.objects.filter(slug=slug)
17.         if not dup:
18.             return slug
19.
20.         slug = slug[:39] + '-' + random_string(10)
21.
22.
23. def random_string(num_chars=10):
24.     letters = string.ascii_lowercase
25.     return ''.join(random.choice(letters) for i in range(num_chars))
```

48. **Don't want to type?** Copy from `starter-code/urls-and-slugs/text.py`.

Code Explanation

Read through this code to make sure it makes sense to you. **Some things to notice:**

1. You import `slugify` from Django's own text utility functions at `django.utils.text`. The `slugify()` function does the following:
    A. Converts to ASCII.
    B. Converts spaces to hyphens.
    C. Removes characters that aren't alphanumerics, underscores, or hyphens.
    D. Converts to lowercase.
    E. Strips leading and trailing whitespace.

2. In the `unique_slug()` function, you first slugify, slice (to make sure the string isn't too long), and strip off any hyphens (so the slug doesn't end with a hyphen). Then, you make sure the slug is unique for the passed-in model:

```
while True:
    dup = model.objects.filter(slug=slug)
    if not dup:
        return slug

    slug = slug[:39] + '-' + random_string(10)
```

    `model.objects.filter(slug=slug)` returns any existing records with that slug.[49]

    A. If it doesn't find any records with the generated slug, it will return it.
    B. If it does find a record with the generated slug, it will create a new slug using the first 39 characters of the slug followed by a hyphen and a random string of ten lowercase ASCII characters generated by the `random_string()` function. It will repeat that process until it comes up with a unique slug at which point it will return the slug.

Git Commit

Commit your code to Git.

49. We will cover querying models in detail in the Making Queries, Ajax, and View Functions lesson (see page 423).

Exercise 28: Changing Jokes to Use Slugs

30 to 45 minutes

In this exercise, you will change the `jokes` app to use slugs instead of ids in URLs.

❖ E28.1. The Model

1. Open `jokes/models.py` in your editor:

   A. Import `unique_slug` from `common.utils.text`:

   ```
   from common.utils.text import unique_slug
   ```

   B. Add a `slug` field to the model:

   ```
   slug = models.SlugField(
       max_length=50, unique=True, null=True, editable=False
   )
   ```

   `editable` is set to `False` because you don't want this field to be editable in Django admin (or anywhere else).[50] Also, remember that you are just temporarily allowing `null` values.

2. You now need to override the model's `save()` method. Remember when you did the following at the Django shell to save a joke object:

   ```
   >>> from jokes.models import Joke
   >>> q = 'Why did the chicken cross the road?'
   >>> a = 'To get to the other side.'
   >>> joke = Joke(question=q, answer=a)
   >>> joke.save()
   ```

50. You may actually want slugs to be editable in Django admin. It depends whether you want admins to be able to modify the URL of a page. If you do, remove `editable=False`.

Before the object's `save()` method is called, you need to set the value of `slug`. To do that, you need to override the `save()` method in the `Joke` model, like this:

```
def save(self, *args, **kwargs):
    if not self.slug:
        value = str(self)
        self.slug = unique_slug(value, type(self))

    super().save(*args, **kwargs)
```

Let's look at this line by line:

A. Only create the slug if the record doesn't already have one:

```
if not self.slug:
```

This will be the case for *all new records* and for jokes that were added before you changed the model.

B. Set `value` to the value returned by the `__str__()` method:

```
    value = str(self)
```

You could set this explicitly to `self.question`, but doing it this way makes the method reusable *as is* in other models.

C. Assign the unique slug to the object:

```
    self.slug = unique_slug(value, type(self))
```

`type(self)` gets the class of this object. You could explicitly use `Joke` here, but doing it this way makes the method reusable *as is* in other models.

D. Call `super().save()` to do whatever the `save()` method of `models.Model` does[51] to save the object:

```
super().save(*args, **kwargs)
```

If you don't do this, the object won't get saved.

51. To see what the `save()` method of `models.Model` does, open `db/models/base.py` from the `django` library and search for "def save". It does quite a lot!

3. Finally, you need to fix the `get_absolute_url()` function to use `slug` instead of `id`:

```
def get_absolute_url(self):
    return reverse('joke', args=[self.slug])
```

The complete code looks like this:

Exercise Code 28.1: jokes/models.py

```
1.  from django.db import models
2.  from django.urls import reverse
3.
4.  from common.utils.text import unique_slug
5.
6.  class Joke(models.Model):
7.      question = models.TextField(max_length=200)
8.      answer = models.TextField(max_length=100, blank=True)
9.      slug = models.SlugField(
10.         max_length=50, unique=True, null=True, editable=False
11.     )
12.     created = models.DateTimeField(auto_now_add=True)
13.     updated = models.DateTimeField(auto_now=True)
14.
15.     def get_absolute_url(self):
16.         return reverse('jokes:detail', args=[self.slug])
17.
18.     def save(self, *args, **kwargs):
19.         if not self.slug:
20.             value = str(self)
21.             self.slug = unique_slug(value, type(self))
22.
23.         super().save(*args, **kwargs)
24.
25.     def __str__(self):
26.         return self.question
```

❖ E28.2. Migrating

As you have changed the model, you need to make and run migrations:

```
(.venv) …/projects/djangojokes.com> python manage.py makemigrations
(.venv) …/projects/djangojokes.com> python manage.py migrate
```

❖ E28.3. Django admin

Because you set `editable` to `False` for the `slug` field, `slug` won't show up in Django admin. To see the `slug` value when editing a joke, add `slug` to the returned read-only fields in `jokes/admin.py`:

```
if obj: # editing an existing object
    return ('slug', 'created', 'updated')
```

❖ E28.4. Reconfiguring the URLs

You need to make the URL patterns for joke pages use the slug. The current URLConf looks like this:

Exercise Code 28.2: jokes/urls.py

```
1.  from django.urls import path
2.
3.  from .views import (
4.      JokeCreateView, JokeDeleteView, JokeDetailView, JokeListView,
5.      JokeUpdateView
6.  )
7.
8.  app_name = 'jokes'
9.  urlpatterns = [
10.     path('joke/<int:pk>/update/', JokeUpdateView.as_view(), name='update'),
11.     path('joke/<int:pk>/delete/', JokeDeleteView.as_view(), name='delete'),
12.     path('joke/create/', JokeCreateView.as_view(), name='create'),
13.     path('joke/<int:pk>/', JokeDetailView.as_view(), name='detail'),
14.     path('', JokeListView.as_view(), name='list'),
15. ]
```

Replace every instance of `<int:pk>` with `<slug>`:

Exercise Code 28.3: jokes/urls.py

```
    -------Lines 1 through 8 Omitted-------
9.  urlpatterns = [
10.     path('joke/<slug>/update/', JokeUpdateView.as_view(), name='update'),
11.     path('joke/<slug>/delete/', JokeDeleteView.as_view(), name='delete'),
12.     path('joke/create/', JokeCreateView.as_view(), name='create'),
13.     path('joke/<slug>/', JokeDetailView.as_view(), name='detail'),
14.     path('', JokeListView.as_view(), name='list'),
15. ]
```

Notice that you do not need to preface `slug` with `str:` as you do with `<int:pk>`. All values coming in over the URL are already strings.

The view will have access to the slug value via `self.kwargs.get('slug')` and will use it to get the joke object to use.

❖ E28.5. Viewing Jokes

1. Start up the server:

```
(.venv) …/projects/djangojokes.com> python manage.py runserver
```

2. Visit the site, click on the **Jokes** link in the header, and then on one of the jokes. You should get a 404 error:

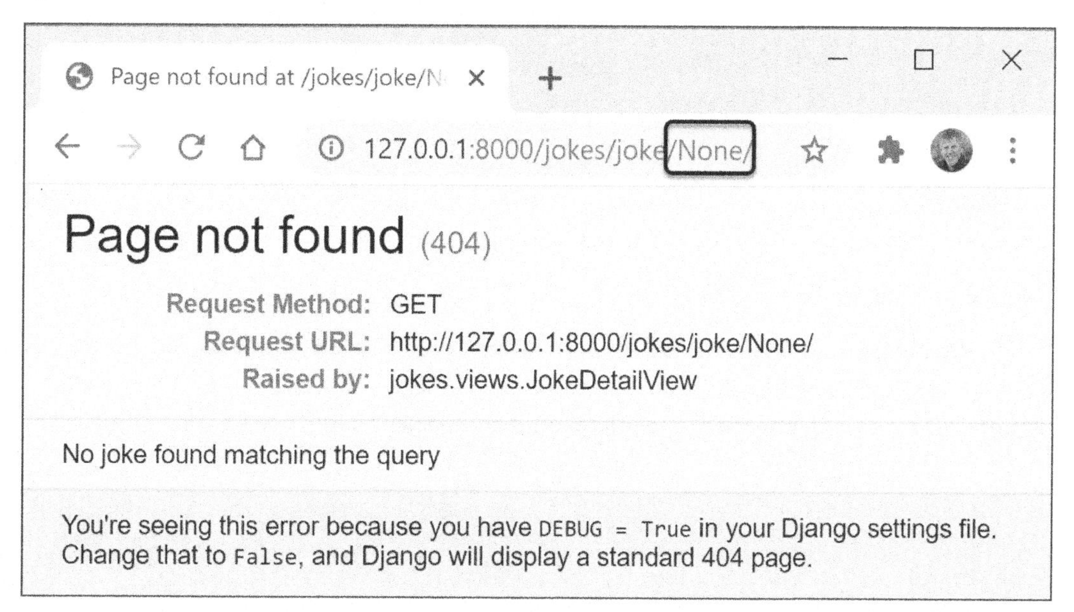

This is because existing jokes don't have slugs yet. You need to add them.

3. In Django admin (`http://127.0.0.1:8000/admin/`), open up a joke:

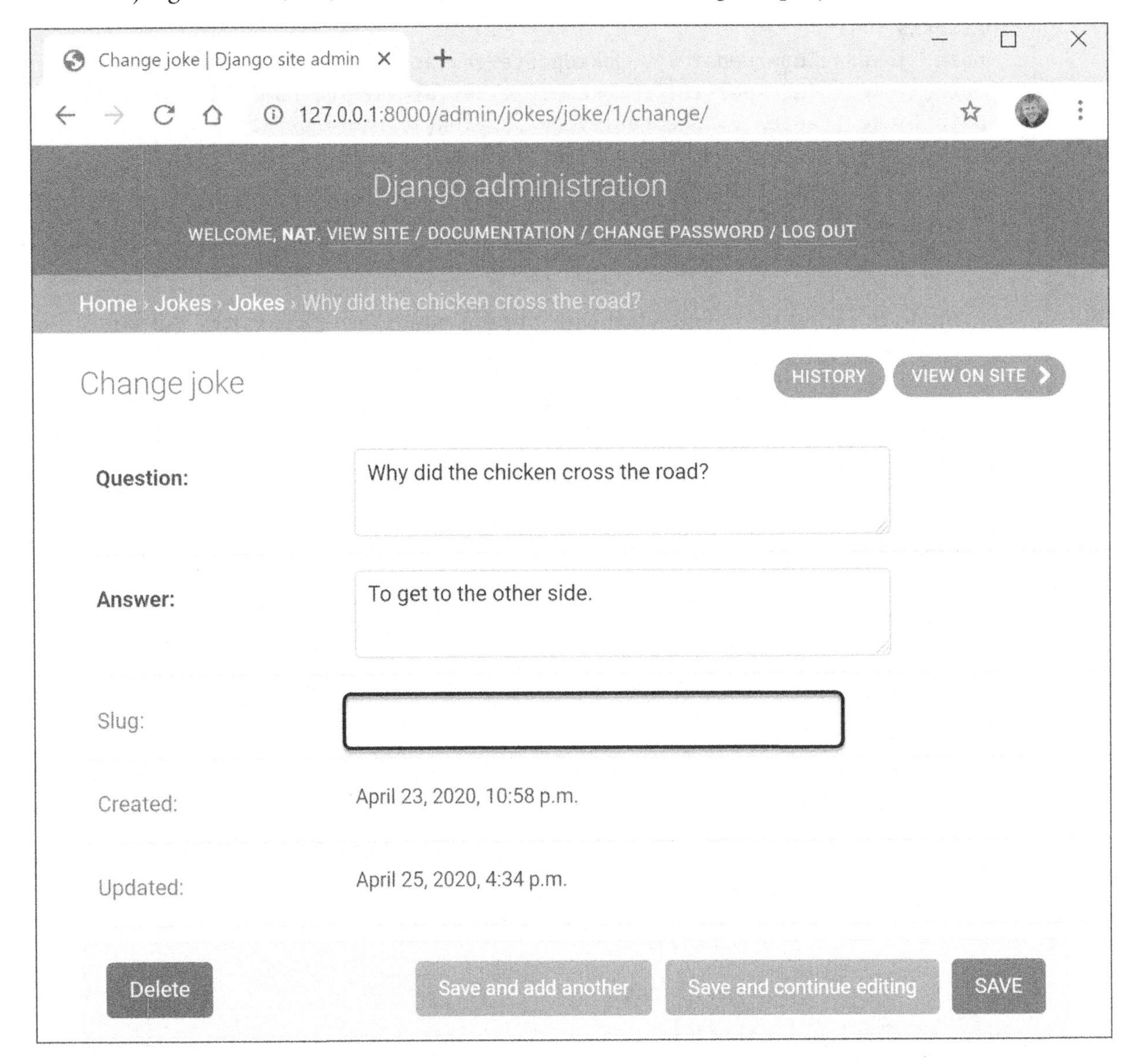

Notice the slug field is empty.

4. Click the **Save and continue editing** button. The slug should now show up as something like:

```
Slug:           why-did-the-chicken-cross-the-road
```

❖ E28.6. Saving All Existing Jokes

You could open and save each joke individually in Django admin, which would be easy in this case, because you don't have many jokes yet. However, if you did have a lot of jokes, you would want to do this at the shell, so let's learn to do it that way:

1. Open the shell:

```
(.venv) …/projects/djangojokes.com> python manage.py shell
```

2. Import the Joke model:

```
>>> from jokes.models import Joke
```

3. Loop through all the jokes, saving each one and then exit the shell:

```
>>> for joke in Joke.objects.all():
...     joke.save()
...
>>> exit()
```

4. Restart the server if necessary:

```
(.venv) …/projects/djangojokes.com> python manage.py runserver
```

5. Return to the site, click on the **Jokes** link in the header, and then on one of the jokes. The page should now come up and the URL should be something like:

```
http://127.0.0.1:8000/jokes/joke/why-did-the-chicken-cross-the-road/
```

❖ E28.7. Setting `null` to `False` for the `SlugField`

Now that you have updated all the `slug` values, change the value of `null` to `False` for `slug`:

```
slug = models.SlugField(
    max_length=50, unique=True, null=False, editable=False
)
```

As you have changed the model, you will need to make and run migrations:

```
(.venv) …/projects/djangojokes.com> python manage.py makemigrations
```

When you run this you will get a warning and a message with various options. The warning will say something like "You are trying to change the nullable field 'slug' on joke to non-nullable without a default; we can't do that." Django doesn't appear to know that you've already dealt with all the `null` values. Since you have, you can safely precede, but you will have to choose one of the options. Enter 1 to provide a one-off default and then enter `'foo'` (in quotes) or any random string for the default:

```
Select an option: 1
Please enter the default value now, as valid Python
The datetime and django.utils.timezone modules are available, so you can do e.g. time ↵
zone.now
Type 'exit' to exit this prompt
>>> 'foo'
Migrations for 'jokes':
  jokes\migrations\0004_auto_20200425_2147.py
    - Alter field slug on joke
```

You have made the migrations script. Now, you can run migrations:

```
(.venv) …/projects/djangojokes.com> python manage.py migrate
```

❖ E28.8. Update Joke List Template

The joke list template (`templates/jokes/joke_list.html`), currently still uses `joke.pk` for the links to **Update** and **Delete**:

```
<a href="{% url 'jokes:update' joke.pk %}"
    class="btn btn-info btn-sm float-right mr-2">Update</a>
<a href="{% url 'jokes:delete' joke.pk %}"
  class="btn btn-danger btn-sm float-right mr-2">Delete</a>
```

Change those both to `joke.slug`.

❖ E28.9. Add a New Joke

1. Go to the Jokes listing and click on the **+ New Joke** button.

2. Add a new joke and notice that the URL that you're redirected to for the new joke uses the joke's slug.
3. Add this joke (be sure to include spaces before and after the plus sign):
    - Question: What is 1 + 1?
    - Answer: 11

   Notice that the slug is `what-is-1-1`.
4. Now, add this joke:
    - Question: What is 1 - 1?
    - Answer: H

   Notice that the slug ends with a random string of characters (e.g., `what-is-1-1-jemfemkhxx`).

While neither of these last two jokes is funny, they do demonstrate how the `unique_slug()` function prevents duplicate slugs by adding a random string.

Play around with the site some by adding, updating, and deleting jokes.

Git Commit

Commit your code to Git.

Conclusion

In this lesson, you have learned to create slugs and to override the `save()` method in your models, so that you can autogenerate slugs when a new record is created. You have also learned how to make changes to an existing model.

LESSON 8
Sending Email with SendGrid

Topics Covered

☑ Development settings.

☑ SendGrid.

☑ Sending email.

> The Dover **mail** was in its usual genial position that the guard suspected the passengers, the passengers suspected one another and the guard, they all suspected everybody else, and the coachman was sure of nothing but the horses; as to which cattle he could with a clear conscience have taken his oath on the two Testaments that they were not fit for the journey.
>
> – *Tale of Two Cities, Charles Dickens*

Introduction

In this lesson, you will learn to send email with SendGrid. You will also create a utility function for sending email that you can use throughout your apps.

8.1. Transactional Email Services

A *transactional email* is an automated email triggered by some event, such as:

- A new site registration.
- A password-reset-form submission.
- A contact-form submission.
- An online purchase.

There are many transactional email services that include Python libraries you can install with `pip`. These include:

- SendGrid (`https://pypi.org/project/sendgrid`).
- Amazon Simple Email Service (SES) (`https://pypi.org/project/django-amazon-ses/`).
- Mailgun (`https://pypi.org/project/mailgun2/`).

All three of these services include free tiers. You will be using SendGrid.

Things Change!

Companies often change their registration and setup processes. SendGrid is no exception. If the instructions here do not work, please visit `https://www.webucator.com/books/errata.cfm` to see if we have posted any updates. If we haven't posted any updates that help, please email us at actionable@webucator.com.

Exercise 29: Getting a SendGrid Account

45 to 60 minutes

SendGrid is an email service that provides a simple-to-use API for sending emails.

❖ E29.1. Getting Ready

You're about to sign up for a SendGrid account and get an API key. On production you will store that API key in an environment variable. You could do the same thing on development, but we're going to take a different approach. You will create a `local_settings.py` file to hold settings specific to development.

1. Open `djangojokes.com/djangojokes/settings.py`.
2. At the top of the file, above the line importing `Path`, import `os`:

    ```
    import os
    from pathlib import Path
    ```

3. At the very bottom of the file, add this:

    ```
    # BOTTOM OF settings.py
    if os.environ.get('ENVIRONMENT') != 'production':
        from .local_settings import *
    # DON'T PUT ANYTHING BELOW THIS
    ```

4. Create a new file called `local_settings.py` in `djangojokes`. This file will host settings that you only want to use on development. You will not put this file on your production server.
5. Add the following line to `local_settings.py`:

    Exercise Code 29.1: djangojokes/local_settings.py

    ```
    1.    SENDGRID_API_KEY = 'sendgridapikey'
    ```

    You will soon paste a real SendGrid API key over `sendgridapikey`.

❖ E29.2. Getting the API Key

1. Go to `https://signup.sendgrid.com/` and register for an account.

2. After registering, go to `https://app.sendgrid.com/guide/integrate/langs/python`. This is SendGrid's Python Web API integration guide.

3. Skip to step 2 of the integration guide. This is the only step you need to do. Enter a name for your API key. This can be any name you want. You will not use the name in your code. Then, click **Create Key**:

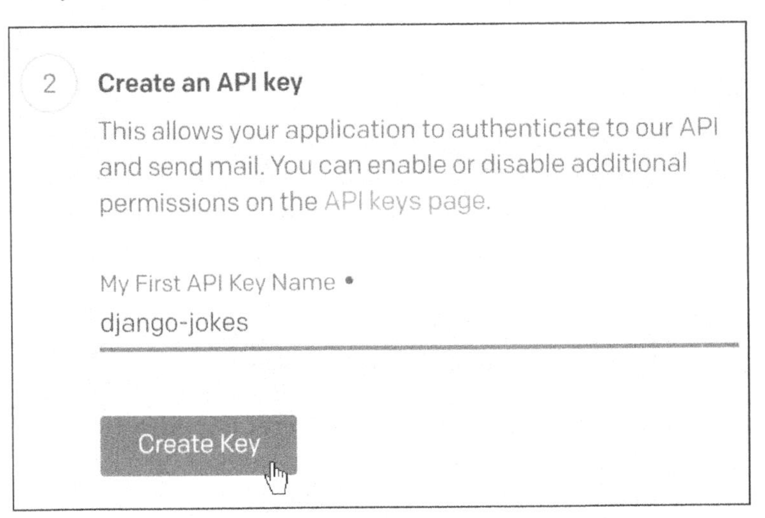

4. Copy the generated API key:

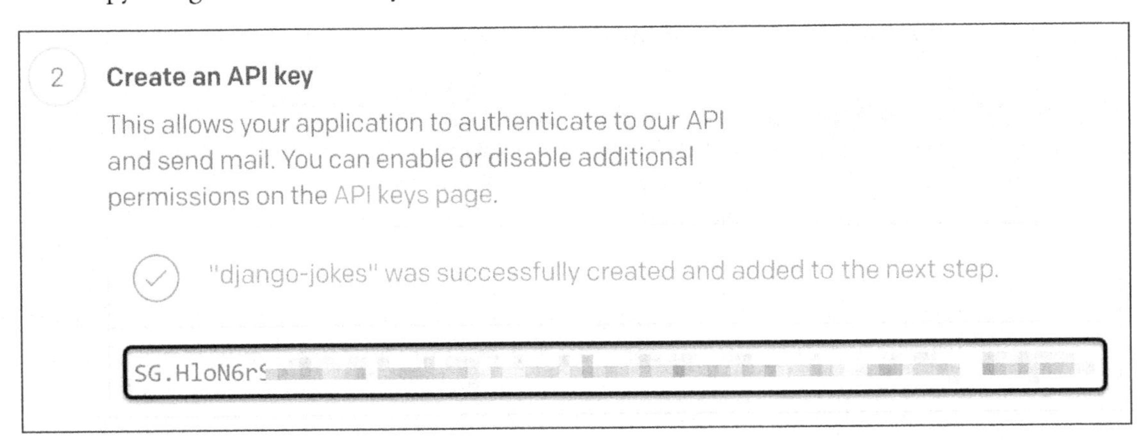

5. Paste the key in `local_settings.py` as the value for `SENDGRID_API_KEY`. This will look something like:

```
SENDGRID_API_KEY = 'SG.HloN6rASKCjX6yDkk1GyQ…'
```

❖ E29.3. Create Sender Identity

You will now need to create a sender identity.

1. Go to `https://app.sendgrid.com/guide`.
2. You should see a **Create a Single Sender** button:

Create a sender identity

Before sending email, you'll need to create a sender identity. There are two ways to do this, but we recommend creating a Single Sender to get set up quickly and test your email integration.

Create a Single Sender   Authenticate a domain instead

   Click the button.

3. Fill out the form to create your sender identity. If you use a free email address (like gmail.com), you may get a warning telling you that using a free email address domain is not recommended. For our purposes, it is fine, as you are just learning to use SendGrid, but if you are going to use it in practice, you are better off emailing from a custom domain as transactional emails from free domains are often filtered as spam.
4. Check your email. You should receive an email asking you to verify the email you used. Click the button to verify the email address. This should take you to a **Sender Verified** page:

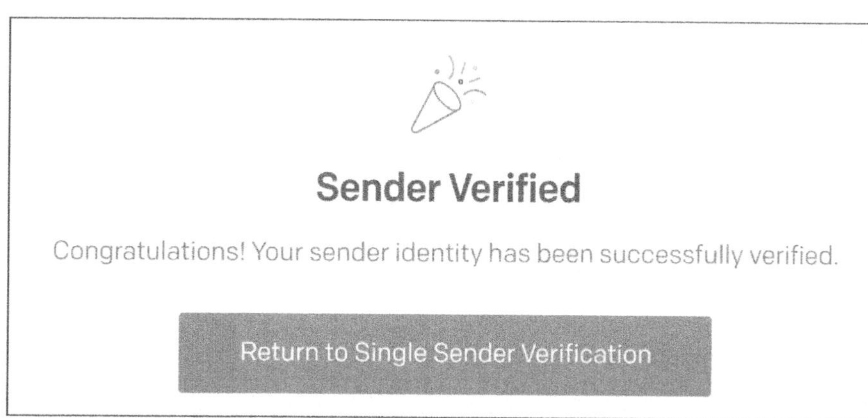

❖ E29.4. Install SendGrid

Install SendGrid with pip:

```
(.venv) …/projects/djangojokes.com> pip install sendgrid
```

❖ E29.5. Try It Out

1. With `djangojokes.com` open at the terminal, run the following to open the shell:

    ```
    (.venv) …/projects/djangojokes.com> python manage.py shell
    ```

2. Import `sendgrid`, its `To` and `Mail` helpers, and `settings`:

    ```
    >>> import sendgrid
    >>> from sendgrid.helpers.mail import To, Mail
    >>> from django.conf import settings
    ```

3. Create your variables. Replace both instances of `'you@example.com'` with the email you verified with SendGrid:

    ```
    >>> from_email = 'you@example.com'
    >>> to_emails = 'you@example.com'
    >>> subject = 'SendGrid Test'
    >>> html_content = '<h1>Hello, from SendGrid!</h1>'
    ```

4. Prepare and send the email:

    ```
    >>> mail = Mail(
    ...     from_email=from_email,
    ...     to_emails=to_emails,
    ...     subject=subject,
    ...     html_content=html_content
    ... )
    >>> sg = sendgrid.SendGridAPIClient(settings.SENDGRID_API_KEY)
    >>> sg.send(mail)
    ```

    You should get a response similar to this:

    ```
    <python_http_client.client.Response object at 0x012A51A8>
    ```

5. Check your email. You should receive an email similar to this one:

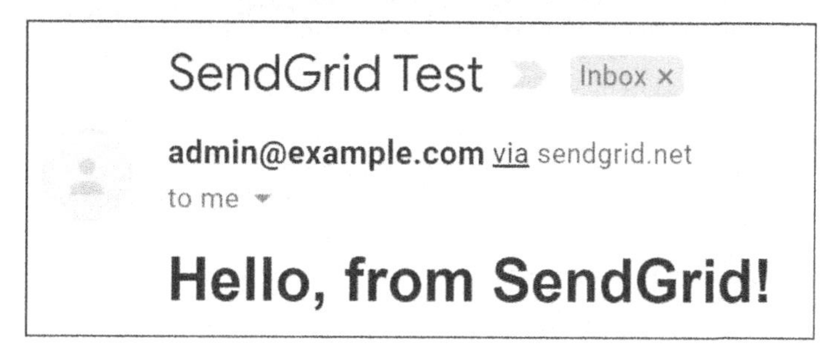

Git Commit

Commit your code to Git.

Exercise 30: Creating an Email Utility Function

10 to 15 minutes

As you may create many apps that make use of email, it makes sense to create a `send_email()` utility function in the common app.

Create a new `email.py` file within `common/utils` with the following content:[52]

Exercise Code 30.1: common/utils/email.py

```
1.  import sendgrid
2.  from sendgrid.helpers.mail import Mail
3.
4.  from django.conf import settings
5.
6.
7.  def send_email(to, subject, content, sender='admin@example.com'):
8.      sg = sendgrid.SendGridAPIClient(settings.SENDGRID_API_KEY)
9.      mail = Mail(
10.         from_email=sender,
11.         to_emails=to,
12.         subject=subject,
13.         html_content=content
14.     )
15.     return sg.send(mail)
```

Code Explanation

This encapsulates everything you did at the Django shell into a function. The `to`, `subject`, and `content` arguments are all required, and `sender` defaults to `'admin@example.com'`.

❖ E30.1. Try It Out

1. With `djangojokes.com` open at the terminal, run the following to open the shell:

```
(.venv) …/projects/djangojokes.com> python manage.py shell
```

52. **Don't want to type?** Copy from `starter-code/sendgrid/email.py`.

2. Create your variables (don't forget to replace `'you@example.com'`) and send the email:

```
>>> from common.utils import email
>>> to = 'you@example.com'
>>> subject = 'SendGrid Test 2'
>>> content = '<h1>It worked!</h1><p>So cool!</p>'
>>> email.send_email(to, subject, content)
```

3. Check your email. If you received an email with the subject "SendGrid Test 2," you are all set.

Git Commit

1. Open the `.gitignore` file.
2. Confirm that it contains `local_settings.py`. You don't want that file in source control as it contains sensitive data.
3. Commit your code to Git.

Conclusion

In this lesson, you have set up Django to use SendGrid to send email. You are now ready to create forms that autogenerate emails.

LESSON 9

Forms and Widgets

Topics Covered

☑ Form processing.

☑ Form fields.

☑ Widgets.

☑ Validators.

☑ Crispy Forms.

> Heathcliff bore his degradation pretty well at first, because Cathy taught him what she learnt, and worked or played with him in the **fields**.
>
> – *Wuthering Heights, Emily Bronte*

Introduction

In this lesson, you will create a job application for the Django Jokes website. In doing so, you will learn to work with Django forms and a third-party library for styling forms.

*

9.1. Form Processing

In Django, form processing usually works like this:

1. User visits page with form. This is a `GET` request.
2. User fills out and submits form. This is a `POST` request.
3. If there are any errors, the form is returned with the form fields still filled in with one or more error messages showing.

4. When the form submission passes validation, the data is processed, and the user is redirected to a success page.

❖ 9.1.1. `ProcessFormView`

Most Django form views (e.g., `FormView`, `CreateView`, `UpdateView`) inherit from `django.views.generic.ProcessFormView`, which includes `get()` and `post()` methods:

- The `get()` method handles the `GET` request, which outputs the form to submit.
- The `post()` method handles the `POST` request, which takes care of processing the form data. Part of that involves checking if the form is valid. When the form is deemed valid, the `form_valid()` method is called. By default, it just redirects to the success page; however, as you shall soon see, it can be overridden to perform additional tasks (e.g., sending an email or saving data to a database) before redirecting to the success page.

9.2. Understanding Form Fields

The term "field" can be confusing in Django development as it can mean several different things:

1. Model Fields (`django.db.models.fields`) – These fields make up a model:

Demo 9.1: jokes/models.py

```
    -------Lines 1 through 5 Omitted-------
6.  class Joke(models.Model):
7.      question = models.TextField(max_length=200)
8.      answer = models.TextField(max_length=100, blank=True)
9.      slug = models.SlugField(
10.         max_length=50, unique=True, null=False, editable=False
11.     )
12.     created = models.DateTimeField(auto_now_add=True)
13.     updated = models.DateTimeField(auto_now=True)
    -------Lines 14 through 25 Omitted-------
```

We will dig into model fields in the ModelForms lesson (see page 275).

2. Form Fields (`django.forms.fields`) – These fields make up a form. We will cover them in detail in this lesson.

3. HTML Form Fields – These are the HTML form controls that make up an HTML form. In the Django documentation, these are referred to as *HTML input elements*, but that's a little misleading, as not all HTML form controls are `input` elements (e.g., `textarea`, `select`, `button`, etc.). We will use the term *form control* when referring to HTML form fields.

❖ 9.2.1. Default Widgets

Every type of form field has a default *widget*, which determines the HTML form control used for the field. Except where noted, form field data is validated on the browser and on the server.

Simple Fields

- `forms.BooleanField()`
  - Default Widget: `CheckboxInput`
  - Resulting HTML: `<input type="checkbox" … >`
- `forms.CharField()`
  - Default Widget: `TextInput`
  - Resulting HTML: `<input type="text" … >`
- `forms.DateField()`
  - Default Widget: `DateInput`
  - Resulting HTML: `<input type="text" … >`
  - Format validation is only done on the server.
- `forms.DateTimeField()`
  - Default Widget: `DateTimeInput`
  - Resulting HTML: `<input type="text" … >`
  - Format validation is only done on the server.
- `forms.DecimalField()`
  - Default Widget: `NumberInput` (`TextInput` if `localize` is `True`)
  - Resulting HTML: `<input type="number" … >`
- `forms.DurationField()`
  - Default Widget: `TextInput`

- Resulting HTML: `<input type="text" … >`
- The expected input format is `DD HH:MM:SS.uuuuuu`.[53]

- `forms.EmailField()`
  - Default Widget: `EmailInput`
  - Resulting HTML: `<input type="email" … >`
- `forms.FloatField()`
  - Default Widget: `NumberInput` (`TextInput` if `localize` is `True`)
  - Resulting HTML: `<input type="number" … >`
- `forms.IntegerField()`
  - Default Widget: `NumberInput` (`TextInput` if `localize` is `True`)
  - Resulting HTML: `<input type="number" … >`
- `forms.JSONField()`[54]
  - Default Widget: `Textarea`
  - Resulting HTML: `<textarea … ></textarea>`
- `forms.RegexField()`
  - Default Widget: `TextInput`
  - Resulting HTML: `<input type="text" … >`
  - Format validation is only done on the server.
- `forms.TimeField()`
  - Default Widget: `TimeInput`
  - Resulting HTML: `<input type="text" … >`
  - Format validation is only done on the server.
- `forms.URLField()`
  - Default Widget: `URLInput`
  - Resulting HTML: `<input type="url" … >`

53. As of Django 3.1, a comma can also be used as the separator for decimal fractions (`DD HH:MM:SS,uuuuuu`).
54. New in Django 3.1.

Date and Time Field Widgets

> It may seem odd that the date and time widgets use `text` instead of HTML's `date` and `time` form controls. This is because not all browsers have the same level of support for those controls.

Choice Fields

1. `forms.ChoiceField`
2. `forms.MultipleChoiceField`
3. `forms.NullBooleanField`
4. `forms.TypedChoiceField`
5. `forms.TypedMultipleChoiceField`

All of these fields except for `forms.NullBooleanField` take a `choices` argument, which must be an iterable of 2-item tuples or a function that returns such an iterable. A common practice is to create a variable holding the choices and then assign that variable to the `choices` argument. For example:

```
BIRDS = (
    (None, '----------'),
    ('cardinal', 'Cardinal'),
    ('chicken', 'Chicken'),
    ('eagle', 'Eagle')
)
```

Notice that the `BIRDS` variable includes an empty option, which you typically will include for fields that only allow the user to make one selection:

- `forms.ChoiceField(choices=BIRDS)`
    - Default Widget: `Select`

- Resulting HTML:

```
<select name="…" id="id_…">
  <option value="" selected>----------</option>
  <option value="cardinal">Cardinal</option>
  <option value="chicken">Chicken</option>
  <option value="eagle">Eagle</option>
</select>
```

The resulting unstyled HTML widget looks like this:

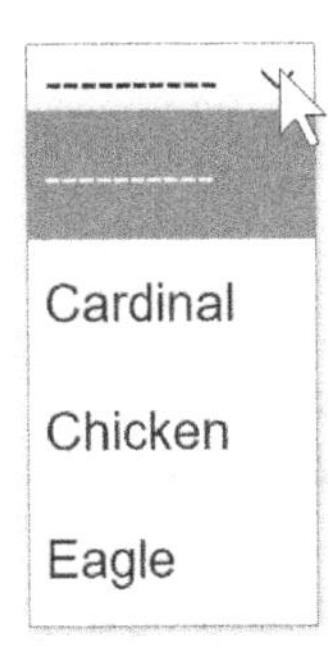

If the field is required and has a default value then you shouldn't include an empty option:

```
FISH = (
    ('barracuda', 'Barracuda'),
    ('bass', 'Bass'),
    ('perch', 'Perch'),
    ('trout', 'Trout')
)

forms.ChoiceField(choices=FISH, default='barracuda', required=True)
```

For fields that allow the user to make multiple selections, you would also typically not include an empty option:

- `forms.MultipleChoiceField(choices=FISH)`
    - Default Widget: `SelectMultiple`

- Resulting HTML:

```
<select name="..." required id="id_..." multiple>
  <option value="barracuda">Barracuda</option>
  <option value="bass">Bass</option>
  <option value="perch">Perch</option>
  <option value="trout">Trout</option>
</select>
```

The resulting unstyled HTML widget looks like this:

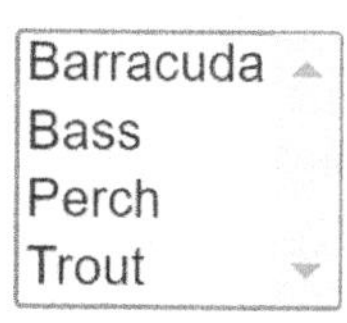

The `NullBooleanField` also presents the user with choices, but it doesn't take a `choices` argument. The preset choices are "Unknown," "Yes," and "No".

- `forms.NullBooleanField()`
  - Default Widget: `NullBooleanSelect`
  - Resulting HTML:

```
<select name="..." id="id_...">
  <option value="unknown" selected>Unknown</option>
  <option value="true">Yes</option>
  <option value="false">No</option>
</select>
```

- `forms.TypedChoiceField()` – Like `ChoiceField` except the string values in the form are coerced (see page 253) into the specified type.
- `forms.TypedMultipleChoiceField()` – Like `MultipleChoiceField` except the string values in the form are coerced (see page 253) into the specified type.

File Fields

- `forms.FileField()`
    - Default Widget: `ClearableFileInput`
    - Resulting HTML (after a file is uploaded):

```
Currently:
<a href="/media/private/resumes/ndunn.pdf">resumes/ndunn.pdf</a>
<span class="clearable-file-input">
  <input type="checkbox" name="resume-clear" id="resume-clear_id">
  <label for="resume-clear_id">Clear</label>
</span><br>
Change: <input type="file" name="resume" id="id_resume">
```

The resulting unstyled HTML widget looks like this:

- `forms.ImageField()` – Like `FileField`, but the uploaded file is validated with Pillow.[55]
- `forms.FilePathField()`
    - Default Widget: `Select`
    - Outputs a `select` component listing the contents of the directory specified by the required `path` argument.

We will cover uploading files and images in the Media Files lesson (see page 383).

Additional Rarely Used Form Fields

- `forms.GenericIPAddressField()`
- `forms.SlugField()`
- `forms.UUIDField()`

55. `https://pypi.org/project/Pillow/`

Exercise 31: Creating a Job Application Form

45 to 60 minutes

In this exercise, you will create a job application form for a joke writer. When an applicant submits the form, Django will send an email to your email address with the data from the form.

1. Create the scaffolding:

```
(.venv) …/projects/djangojokes.com> python manage.py startapp jobs
```

2. Add the new application to the `INSTALLED_APPS` list in `djangojokes/settings.py`:

```
INSTALLED_APPS = [
    …

    # Local apps
    'common.apps.CommonConfig',
    'jobs.apps.JobsConfig',
    …
]
```

E31.1. The Form

Create a new `forms.py` file within the `jobs` folder and add the following content:

Exercise Code 31.1: jobs/forms.py

```
1.  from django import forms
2.
3.  class JobApplicationForm(forms.Form):
4.      first_name = forms.CharField()
5.      last_name = forms.CharField()
6.      email = forms.EmailField()
```

Things to notice:

1. `forms` is imported from `django`.
2. `JobApplicationForm` inherits from `forms.Form`.

3. The form includes two `CharField` fields and one `EmailField` field.

❖ E31.2. The Views

You will need two views: one for the application form (a `FormView`) and one for the success page (a `TemplateView`). You are already familiar with `TemplateView` views. `FormView` (`django.views.generic.edit.FormView`) is a generic editing view for creating a form that is not based on a model.

1. Open `jobs/views.py` for editing.
2. Remove the line importing `render` and add the following lines importing `reverse_lazy` and `FormView` and `TemplateView`:

```
from django.urls import reverse_lazy
from django.views.generic import FormView, TemplateView
```

3. Import `JobApplicationForm` from the `forms.py` file you created in the same directory:

```
from .forms import JobApplicationForm
```

4. Create a new `JobAppView` that inherits from `FormView` using the following code:

```
class JobAppView(FormView):
    template_name = 'jobs/joke_writer.html'
    form_class = JobApplicationForm
    success_url = reverse_lazy('jobs:thanks')
```

   A. `template_name` identifies the template used to render the form.
   B. `form_class` identifies the `Form` class, which contains the form fields.
   C. `success_url` points to the URL to open when the form is successfully processed.

   This is all you need in the view to get the form to display and submit. The view context will contain a `form` object with the three fields specified in the `JobApplicationForm` class.

5. When the user submits the form with no errors, Django will redirect to the page identified by `success_url`. That page needs a view too. Below `JobAppView`, add this simple view:

```
class JobAppThanksView(TemplateView):
    template_name = 'jobs/thanks.html'
```

6. Your `views.py` file should now look like this:

Exercise Code 31.2: jobs/views.py

```
1.  from django.urls import reverse_lazy
2.  from django.views.generic import FormView, TemplateView
3.
4.  from .forms import JobApplicationForm
5.
6.  class JobAppView(FormView):
7.      template_name = 'jobs/joke_writer.html'
8.      form_class = JobApplicationForm
9.      success_url = reverse_lazy('jobs:thanks')
10.
11. class JobAppThanksView(TemplateView):
12.     template_name = 'jobs/thanks.html'
```

❖ E31.3. The Templates

Create a new `jobs` folder within the `templates` folder and add these two files:[56]

Exercise Code 31.3: templates/jobs/joke_writer.html

```
1.  {% extends "_base.html" %}
2.
3.  {% block title %}Job Application: Joke Writer{% endblock %}
4.  {% block main %}
5.    <h2 class="text-center">Joke Writer Application</h2>
6.    <div class="card border-primary m-auto mb-3 p-3" style="max-width: 40rem">
7.        <form method="post">
8.          {% csrf_token %}
9.          {{ form.as_p }}
10.         <button class="btn btn-success float-right">Apply</button>
11.       </form>
12.   </div>
13. {% endblock %}
```

56. **Don't want to type?** Copy from `starter-code/forms-and-widgets/joke_writer.html` and `starter-code/forms-and-widgets/thanks.html`.

Exercise Code 31.4: templates/jobs/thanks.html

```
1.  {% extends "_base.html" %}
2.
3.  {% block title %}Job Application Submitted{% endblock %}
4.  {% block main %}
5.    <div class="card border-primary m-auto mb-3 p-3 text-center"
6.      style="max-width: 50rem">
7.      <p>Thanks! We will get back to you soon!</p>
8.    </div>
9.  {% endblock %}
```

Add a link to the job application in the `pages/about_us.html` template:

Exercise Code 31.5: templates/pages/about_us.html

```
1.  {% extends "_base.html" %}
2.
3.  {% block title %}About Us{% endblock %}
4.  {% block main %}
5.    <h2>About Us</h2>
6.    <p>We tell funny jokes.</p>
7.    <p><a href="{% url 'jobs:app' %}">Work for us.</a></p>
8.  {% endblock %}
```

❖ E31.4. Configure URLs

Update the root `urls.py` file to hand off paths that begin with "/jobs" to the `jobs` app, and create a URLConf file for the `jobs` app with paths for `JobAppView` and `JobAppThanksView`:

Exercise Code 31.6: djangojokes/urls.py

```
    -------Lines 1 through 3 Omitted-------
4.  urlpatterns = [
5.      path('admin/doc/', include('django.contrib.admindocs.urls')),
6.      path('admin/', admin.site.urls),
7.      path('jobs/', include('jobs.urls')),
8.      path('jokes/', include('jokes.urls')),
9.      path('', include('pages.urls')),
10. ]
```

Exercise Code 31.7: jobs/urls.py

```
1.  from django.urls import path
2.
3.  from .views import JobAppView, JobAppThanksView
4.
5.  app_name = 'jobs'
6.  urlpatterns = [
7.      path('job-app/', JobAppView.as_view(), name='app'),
8.      path('job-app/thanks/', JobAppThanksView.as_view(), name='thanks'),
9.  ]
```

❖ E31.5. Try It Out

1. With `djangojokes.com` open at the terminal, run:

   ```
   (.venv) …/projects/djangojokes.com> python manage.py runserver
   ```

2. In your browser, navigate to `http://127.0.0.1:8000/jobs/job-app/`. The page should look like this:

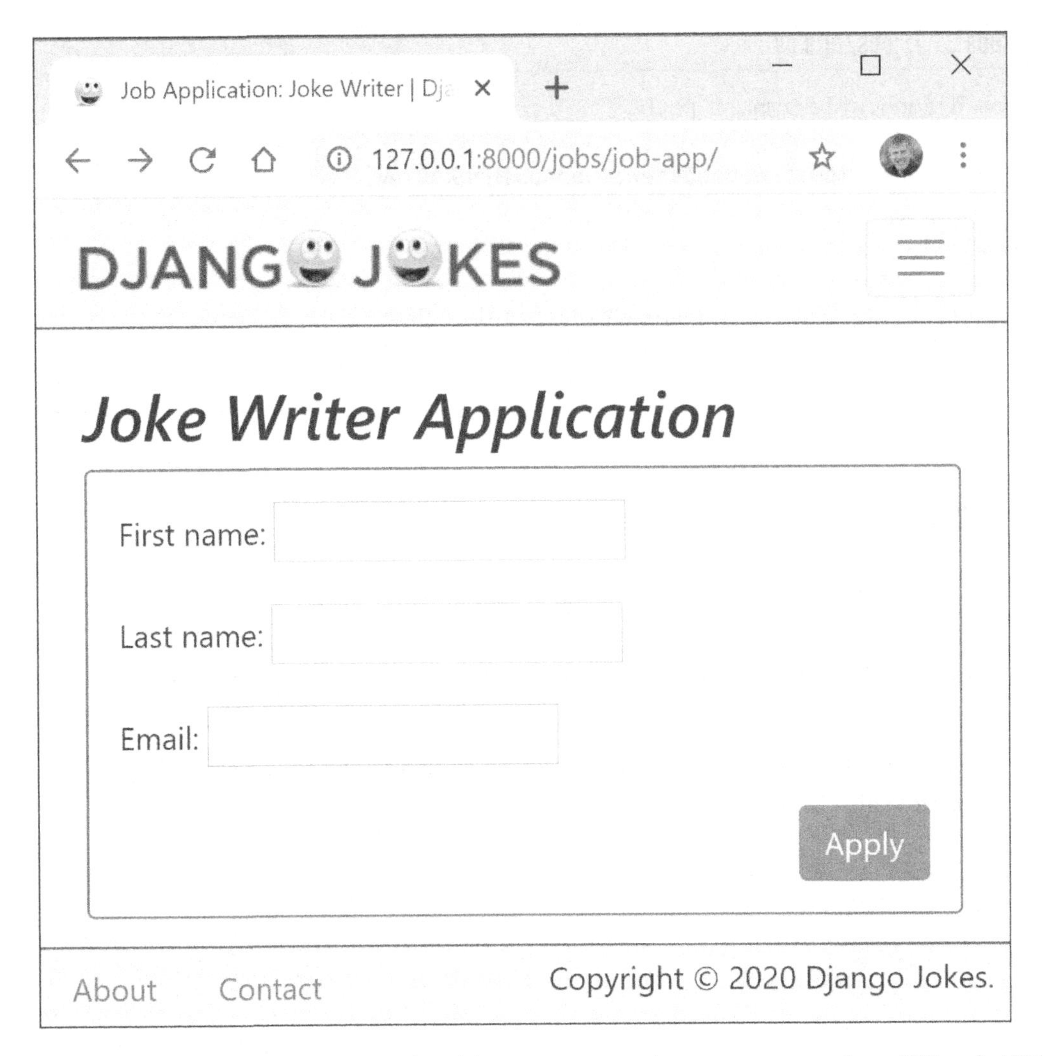

Fill out and submit the form. You should get a page with a message reading "Thanks! We will get back to you soon!".

Don't worry about the form design.

You will soon learn to make the form prettier.

At this point, there is no way you will be able to get back to applicants soon, because you haven't collected any of their information.

❖ E31.6. Emailing the Application

Add the following highlighted code to `jobs/views.py` (replace `'you@example.com'` with your email):

Exercise Code 31.8: jobs/views.py

```
1.   import html
2.   from django.urls import reverse_lazy
3.   from django.views.generic import FormView, TemplateView
4.
5.   from common.utils.email import send_email
6.   from .forms import JobApplicationForm
7.
8.   class JobAppView(FormView):
9.       template_name = 'jobs/joke_writer.html'
10.      form_class = JobApplicationForm
11.      success_url = reverse_lazy('jobs:thanks')
12.
13.      def form_valid(self, form):
14.          data = form.cleaned_data
15.          to = 'you@example.com'
16.          subject = 'Application for Joke Writer'
17.          content = f'''<p>Hey HR Manager!</p>
18.              <p>Job application received:</p>
19.              <ol>'''
20.          for key, value in data.items():
21.              label = key.replace('_', ' ').title()
22.              entry = html.escape(str(value), quote=False)
23.              content += f'<li>{label}: {entry}</li>'
24.
25.          content += '</ol>'
26.
27.          send_email(to, subject, content)
28.          return super().form_valid(form)
     -------Lines 29 through 31 Omitted-------
```

Things to notice:

1. The `send_email()` utility function you wrote is imported from `common.utils.email`.
2. The `form_valid()` function is executed when the form passes validation. `form.cleaned_data` will contain all the data submitted in the form. Depending on how the form fields are implemented, some of the data may have been "cleaned," which is why the variable is called `cleaned_data`. We had you immediately assign `cleaned_data` to `data`, both to have a simpler variable name and to make it clear that you have access to this data.
3. You set values for `to`, `subject`, and `content` and pass those variables to `send_email()`. To create the `content` variable, you loop through all the items in the cleaned data, outputting key-value pairs in an HTML list.

- Notice that you use `html.escape` to escape the values entered by the user. That's to protect against malicious HTML.

4. Finally, you return `super().form_valid(form)`, which will take care of redirecting the page to the "jobs:thanks" named URL pattern (as per `success_url`).

❖ E31.7. Try It Out Again

python manage.py runserver

From here on out, when we say "start up the server" or "run the server," you should run:

```
python manage.py runserver
```

1. With `djangojokes.com` open at the terminal, start up the server.
2. In your browser, navigate to `http://127.0.0.1:8000/jobs/job-app/`, fill out and submit the form. Then, check your email. You should have received something like this:

Application for Joke Writer Inbox ×

admin@example.com via sendgrid.net 5:17 PM (0 minutes ago)

to me

Hey HR Manager!

Job application received:

1. First Name: Nat
2. Last Name: Dunn
3. Email: ndunn@example.com

Git Commit

Commit your code to Git.

*

9.3. Core Field Arguments

The form field's arguments control how the HTML form control is displayed and how the form field is validated. The different field types all take the following core arguments:

1. `required` – Whether the user must provide an answer. The default is `True`.
2. `label` – A friendly label for the HTML form control. By default, the label will be generated from the field name.
3. `label_suffix` – The string that separates the label from the HTML form control. In English, the default is a colon (":").
4. `initial` – An initial value for the HTML form control. For example:

    ```
    website = forms.URLField(initial='https://')
    ```

5. `widget` – Used to override the default widget (see page 253).
6. `help_text` – Help text to show up next to the HTML form control. For example:

    ```
    first_name = forms.CharField(help_text='Your first name please.')
    ```

    The result will be:

7. `error_messages` – Used to override default error messages (see page 261).
8. `validators` – Used to add or override validators (see page 261).
9. `localize` – Enables localization.[57]
10. `disabled` – Indicates whether the field is disabled. The default is `False`.

Some field types take additional arguments. For example, `ChoiceField` requires a `choices` argument.

57. https://docs.djangoproject.com/en/3.1/topics/i18n/formatting/#locale-aware-input-in-forms

 Exercise 32: Building out the Application

45 to 60 minutes

In this exercise, you will build out the job application by adding the following form fields:

1. `website` – A field for entering a valid URL. This field should be optional.
2. `employment_type` – A field for choosing an employment type. Options should be "Full-time," "Part-time," and "Contract work" and the applicant should only be able to choose one option.
3. `start_date` – The date the applicant can start. Provide the following help text: "The earliest date you can start working."
4. `available_days` – The days of the week the applicant can work. Options should be "MON," "TUE," "WED," "THU," and "FRI". Provide the following help text: "Select all days that you can work."
5. `desired_hourly_wage` – A field for entering a decimal.
6. `cover_letter` – A field for entering a cover letter. Note that there are no good default options for this one. Use a `CharField` and you will improve it later.
7. `confirmation` – A required checkbox. Change the label to "I certify that the information I have provided is true."

Try this on your own before looking at the solution. Test your solution by running the server, visiting `http://127.0.0.1:8000/jobs/job-app/`, and filling out and submitting the form, which should look like this:

First name:

Last name:

Email:

Website:

Employment type: --Please choose-- ▾

Start date: The earliest date you can start working.

Available days: MON TUE WED THU Select all days that you can work.

Desired hourly wage:

Cover letter:

I certify that the information I have provided is true.

Apply

Then, check your email. You should receive something like this:

Application for Joke Writer Inbox x 

admin@example.com via sendgrid.net 6:52 AM (8 minutes ago)  
to me

Hey HR Manager!

Job application received:

1. First Name: Jane
2. Last Name: Goldman
3. Email: janego@example.com
4. Website: https://www.example.com
5. Employment Type: ft
6. Start Date: 2021-11-11
7. Available Days: ['1', '2', '3', '4', '5']
8. Desired Hourly Wage: 42.42
9. Cover Letter: Dear HR Director, Question: How many HR directors does it take to screw in a light bulb? Answer: I'll tell at my job interview. Jane Go
10. Confirmation: True

Skipping HTML Validation

Because the form is validated by the browser before it is validated on the server, you often do not get to see the server-side validation errors. When testing, you can turn off client-side validation by adding the `novalidate` attribute to the `form` element in the template:

```
<form method="post" novalidate>
```

Try this out. Just don't forget to remove `novalidate` before you push your code to production.

Solution: jobs/forms.py

```
1.  from django import forms
2.
3.  class JobApplicationForm(forms.Form):
4.      EMPLOYMENT_TYPES = (
5.          (None, '--Please choose--'),
6.          ('ft', 'Full-time'),
7.          ('pt', 'Part-time'),
8.          ('contract', 'Contract work')
9.      )
10.
11.     DAYS = (
12.         (1, 'MON'),
13.         (2, 'TUE'),
14.         (3, 'WED'),
15.         (4, 'THU'),
16.         (5, 'FRI')
17.     )
18.
19.     first_name = forms.CharField()
20.     last_name = forms.CharField()
21.     email = forms.EmailField()
22.     website = forms.URLField(required=False)
23.     employment_type = forms.ChoiceField(choices=EMPLOYMENT_TYPES)
24.     start_date = forms.DateField(
25.         help_text='The earliest date you can start working.'
26.     )
27.     available_days = forms.MultipleChoiceField(
28.         choices=DAYS,
29.         help_text='Select all days that you can work.'
30.     )
31.     desired_hourly_wage = forms.DecimalField()
32.     cover_letter = forms.CharField()
33.     confirmation = forms.BooleanField(
34.         label='I certify that the information I have provided is true.'
35.     )
```

Git Commit

Commit your code to Git.

9.4. Typed Choice Fields

All values sent to the server via HTML forms are strings. Consider the following code:

```
DAYS = (
    (1, 'MON'),
    (2, 'TUE'),
    (3, 'WED'),
    (4, 'THU'),
    (5, 'FRI')
)

available_days = forms.MultipleChoiceField(
    choices=DAYS
)
```

If the user selects `TUE` and `THU` in the HTML form, Django will treat the response as a list of strings: `['2', '4']`.

You can use the *typed choice* fields (`TypedChoiceField` and `TypedMultipleChoiceField`) to tell Django to convert the items selected to integers. For example:

```
available_days = forms.TypedMultipleChoiceField(
    choices=DAYS, coerce=int
)
```

Given the same submission as before, Django will coerce the results into a list of integers: `[2, 4]`.

The `coerce` argument takes a function, which can be a built-in function (in this case, `int`) or a custom function that takes a string and returns the appropriate type.

9.5. Changing Widgets

Sometimes, the default widget used by a form field is not the ideal for your form. You can change it using the `widget` argument.

All widgets can take the `attrs` argument, which takes a dictionary and is used to assign attributes to the HTML form control. For example, the form control for `URLInput` is often too narrow:

Website: https://www.webucator.c

You can increase its width by adding a `size` attribute:

```
website = forms.URLField(
    widget=forms.URLInput(attrs={'size': '50'})
)
```

The resulting HTML form control will have a `size` attribute:

```
<input type="url" name="website" size="50" required id="id_website">
```

This will make it wider:

Website: https://www.webucator.com

You can use the `attrs` argument to provide any valid HTML attributes. For example:

```
website = forms.URLField(
    widget=forms.URLInput(
        attrs={
            'class': 'form-control',
            'placeholder': 'https://www.example.com',
            'autofocus': True
        }
    )
)
```

This will create the following HTML form control:

```
<input type="url" name="website" class="form-control"
  placeholder="https://www.example.com" autofocus required id="id_website">
```

The default widget for a `URLField` is `URLInput`. This example doesn't change that; it just adds attributes to the widget. As you will soon see, you can also change the actual widget.

Three of the most useful widgets are `Textarea`, `CheckboxSelectMultiple`, and `SelectDateWidget`.

❖ 9.5.1. Textarea

The default widget for `forms.CharField` is `TextInput`, but the `Textarea` widget is more appropriate for longer text entries:

```
comments = forms.CharField(
    widget=forms.Textarea(attrs={'cols': '100', 'rows': '5'})
)
```

This will create the following HTML form control:

```
<textarea name="comments" cols="100" rows="5" required id="id_comments"></textarea>
```

❖ 9.5.2. CheckboxSelectMultiple

The default widget for `MultipleChoiceField` and `TypedMultipleChoiceField` is `SelectMultiple`, which results in an expanded `select` menu, in which the user can select multiple options by holding down the Ctrl key and clicking with the mouse:

Often, a better option is to use the `CheckboxSelectMultiple` widget to create a series of checkboxes:

```
days = forms.MultipleChoiceField(
    choices=DAYS,
    widget=forms.CheckboxSelectMultiple
)
```

The unstyled result in the browser will be:

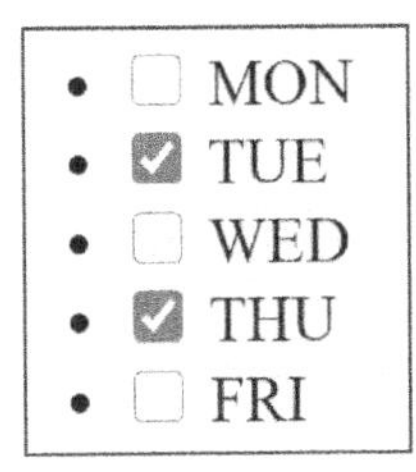

And the generated HTML is:

```
<ul id="id_days">
  <li>
    <label for="id_days_0">
      <input type="checkbox" name="days" value="1" id="id_days_0">
      MON
    </label>
  </li>
  <li>
    <label for="id_days_1">
      <input type="checkbox" name="days" value="2" id="id_days_1">
      TUE
    </label>
  </li>
  …
</ul>
```

❖ 9.5.3. SelectDateWidget

The default widget for `forms.DateField` is `TextInput`. Users are then expected to enter a correctly formatted date. A better option is to use the `SelectDateWidget`:

```
YEARS = range(1900, datetime.now().year+1)
birth_date = forms.DateField(
    required=False,
    widget=forms.SelectDateWidget(
        years=YEARS,
        empty_label=("Choose Year", "Choose Month", "Choose Day")
    )
)
```

The unstyled result in the browser will be:

Birth date: Choose Month ˅ Choose Day ˅ Choose Year ˅

And the generated HTML will include the following form controls:

```
<select name="birth_date_month" id="id_birth_date_month">
  <option value="" selected>Choose Month</option>
  <option value="1">January</option>
  …
  <option value="12">December</option>
</select>
<select name="birth_date_day" id="id_birth_date_day">
  <option value="" selected>Choose Day</option>
  <option value="1">1</option>
  …
  <option value="31">31</option>
</select><select name="birth_date_year" id="id_birth_date_year">
  <option value="" selected>Choose Year</option>
  <option value="1900">1900</option>
  …
  <option value="2020">2020</option>
</select>
```

The `SelectDateWidget` takes three optional arguments:

1. `years` – A sequence of years to include. The default is the next ten years, starting with the current year.
2. `months` – A dictionary of month values. The keys are `1` through `12` and the default values are full month names.
3. `empty_label` – A tuple containing values for the first field in the `select` menus. This is only used if the field is not required.

Exercise 33: Improving the Job Application Form

45 to 60 minutes

Make the following improvements to the job application form:

1. Autofocus on the `first_name` field.
2. Add an "https://www.example.com" placeholder to the `website` field and add a `size` attribute with a value of `50`.
3. Change the `start_date` field to use a `SelectDateWidget` widget with only this year and next year as options. You can either hard code the years or calculate them using `datetime`.
4. Change the `available_days` field to use a `CheckboxSelectMultiple` widget. See if you can figure out how to have all days checked by default.
5. Add the following attributes to the `number` HTML form control produced by `desired_hourly_wage`:
    A. `'min': '10.00'`
    B. `'max': '100.00'`
    C. `'step': '.25'`
6. Change the `cover_letter` field to use a `Textarea` widget. The resulting `textarea` should have `cols` set to `75` and `rows` set to `5`.

Try this on your own before looking at the solution.

Solution: jobs/forms.py

```
1.    from datetime import datetime
2.    from django import forms
3.
4.    class JobApplicationForm(forms.Form):
      -------Lines 5 through 19 Omitted-------
20.       YEARS = range(datetime.now().year, datetime.now().year+2)
21.
22.       first_name = forms.CharField(
23.           widget=forms.TextInput(attrs={'autofocus': True})
24.       )
25.       last_name = forms.CharField()
26.       email = forms.EmailField()
27.       website = forms.URLField(
28.           required=False,
29.           widget=forms.URLInput(
30.               attrs={'placeholder':'https://www.example.com', 'size':'50'}
31.           )
32.       )
33.       employment_type = forms.ChoiceField(choices=EMPLOYMENT_TYPES)
34.       start_date = forms.DateField(
35.           help_text='The earliest date you can start working.',
36.           widget=forms.SelectDateWidget(
37.               years=YEARS,
38.           )
39.       )
40.       available_days = forms.TypedMultipleChoiceField(
41.           choices=DAYS,
42.           coerce=int,
43.           help_text='Check all days that you can work.',
44.           widget=forms.CheckboxSelectMultiple(
45.               attrs={'checked':True}
46.           )
47.       )
48.       desired_hourly_wage = forms.DecimalField(
49.           widget=forms.NumberInput(
50.               attrs={'min':'10.00', 'max':'100.00', 'step':'.25'}
51.           )
52.       )
53.       cover_letter = forms.CharField(
54.           widget=forms.Textarea(attrs={'cols': '75', 'rows': '5'})
55.       )
56.       confirmation = forms.BooleanField(
57.           label='I certify that the information I have provided is true.'
58.       )
```

To make all days checked by default, you use the `checked` attribute:

```
available_days = forms.TypedMultipleChoiceField(
  choices=DAYS,
  coerce=int,
  help_text='Check all days that you can work.',
  widget=forms.CheckboxSelectMultiple(
      attrs={'checked':True}
  )
)
```

Git Commit

Commit your code to Git.

9.6. Validators

Django includes built-in validators, which many of the form field types use. For example, the `URLField` class definition starts like this:[58]

```
class URLField(CharField):
    widget = URLInput
    default_error_messages = {
        'invalid': _('Enter a valid URL.'),
    }
    default_validators = [validators.URLValidator()]
```

Notice that it inherits from `CharField` and includes one default validator: `URLValidator`. `URLValidator` inherits from `RegexValidator` and uses a complex regular expression to validate the URL. `URLValidator()` takes a `schemes` argument to set the allowed protocols. The default list is:

```
['http', 'https', 'ftp', 'ftps']
```

In your job application, you may want to require that the website field uses either "http" or "https":

58. The `_()` function is a special Django function for internationalization. See `https://docs.djangoproject.com/en/3.1/topics/i18n/translation/#internationalization-in-python-code`.

```
website = forms.CharField(
    validators=[URLValidator(schemes=['http', 'https'])]
)
```

Notice that you used a `CharField` instead of a `URLField`. This is because the `validators` get *added to* the `default_validators` of the superclass. If you had used a `URLField`, the field would have two `URLValidators` and if both failed, it would give two error messages.[59]

9.6.1. Custom Validator Functions

You can create your own validators using `django.core.exceptions.ValidationError`. For example, the following code creates a validator function that raises an error if the passed-in date is in the past:

```
from datetime import datetime
from django.core.exceptions import ValidationError

def validate_future_date(value):
    if value < datetime.now().date():
        raise ValidationError(message=f'{value} is in the past.', code='past_date')
```

You can now use this function as a validator:

```
start_date = forms.DateField(
    help_text='The earliest date you can start working.',
    widget=forms.SelectDateWidget(years=YEARS),
    validators=[validate_future_date]
    error_messages={'past_date': 'Please enter a future date.'}
)
```

When the user submits the form with a date that has already passed, they will get the following error message: "Please enter a future date."

The following code sample shows how to integrate these validators into the job application form:

59. See `https://docs.djangoproject.com/en/3.1/ref/validators/#built-in-validators` for a list of built-in validators.

Demo 9.2: jobs/forms.py

```
1.    from datetime import datetime
2.    from django import forms
3.    from django.core.exceptions import ValidationError
4.    from django.core.validators import URLValidator
5.
6.    def validate_future_date(value):
7.        if value < datetime.now().date():
8.            raise ValidationError(
9.                message=f'{value} is in the past.', code='past_date'
10.           )
11.
12.
13.   class JobApplicationForm(forms.Form):
      -------Lines 14 through 36 Omitted-------
37.           required=False,
38.           widget=forms.TextInput(
39.               attrs={'placeholder':'https://www.example.com', 'size':'50'}
40.           ),
41.           validators=[URLValidator(schemes=['http', 'https'])]
42.       )
43.       employment_type = forms.ChoiceField(choices=EMPLOYMENT_TYPES)
44.       start_date = forms.DateField(
45.           help_text='The earliest date you can start working.',
46.           widget=forms.SelectDateWidget(
47.               years=YEARS,
48.           ),
49.           validators=[validate_future_date],
50.           error_messages = {'past_date': 'Please enter a future date.'}
51.       )
      -------Lines 52 through 70 Omitted-------
```

You can copy the preceding code from `starter-code/forms-and-widgets/forms.py` and paste it over your existing code in `jobs/forms.py`. Then, return to the job application form, enter "ftp://www.example.com" for the website and a past date for the start date.

You should get errors like these:

- Enter a valid URL.

Website: ftp://www.example.com

- This field is required.

Employment type: --Please choose-- ▼

- Please enter a future date.

Start date: August ▼ 1 ▼ 2020 ▼

Exercise 34: Crispy Forms

20 to 30 minutes

Time to make the form look good! You can write your own custom CSS to design the forms any way you like, but you can save a lot of time by using `django-crispy-forms` with Bootstrap.

1. Install `django-crispy-forms`:

```
(.venv) …/projects/djangojokes.com> pip install django-crispy-forms
```

2. Add `crispy_forms` to `INSTALLED_APPS` and immediately below `INSTALLED_APPS` add `CRISPY_TEMPLATE_PACK = 'bootstrap4'`:

```
INSTALLED_APPS = [
    # Built-in Django apps
    …

    # Third-party
    'crispy_forms',

    # Local apps
    …
]

CRISPY_TEMPLATE_PACK = 'bootstrap4'
```

3. Open `templates/jobs/joke_writer.html` for editing.

   A. Immediately below the `{% extends %}` tag, load `crispy_form_tags`:

   ```
   {% load crispy_forms_tags %}
   ```

   B. Change the form from using `form.as_p` to using the `crispy` filter:

   ```
   <form method="post">
     {% csrf_token %}
     {{ form|crispy }}
     <button class="btn btn-success float-right">Apply</button>
   </form>
   ```

4. Run the server and navigate to `http://127.0.0.1:8000/jobs/job-app/`:

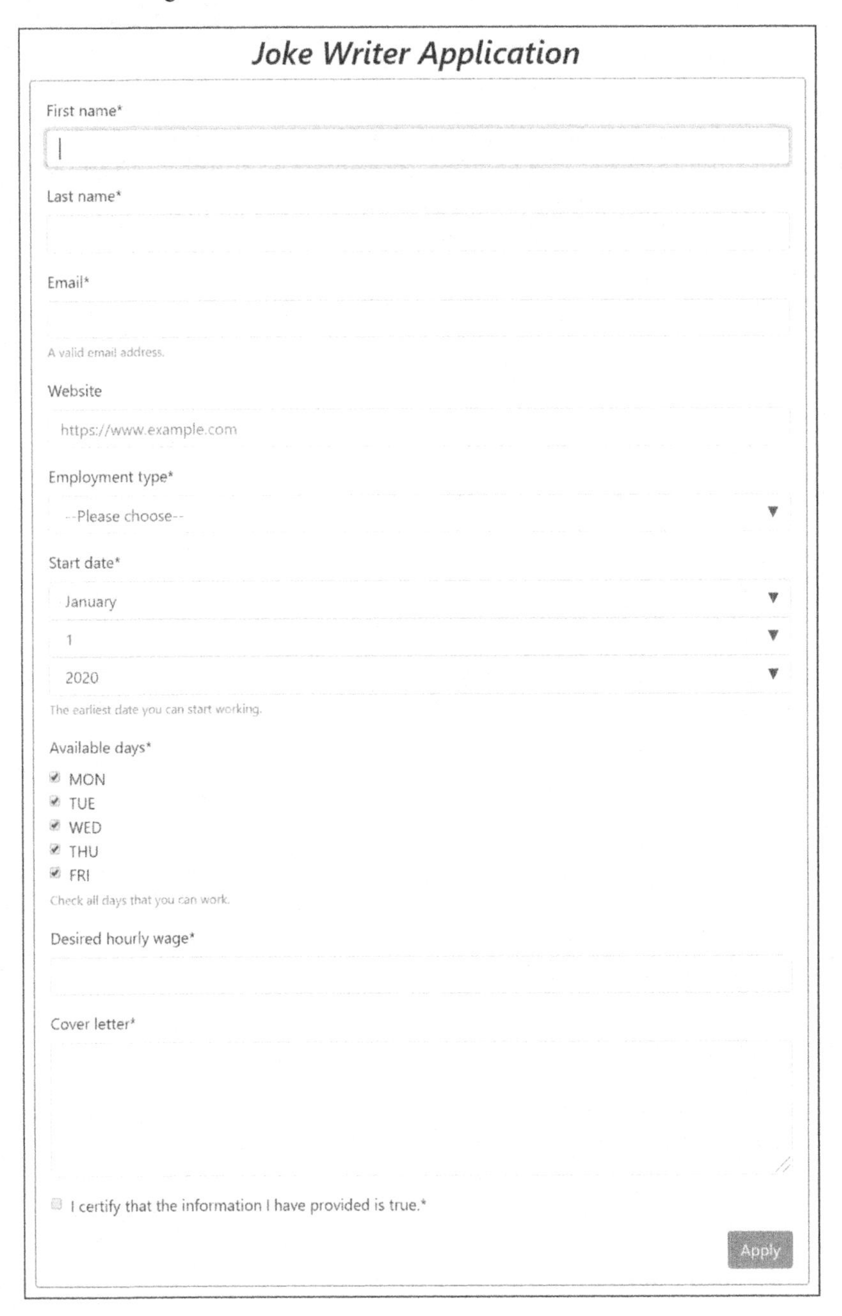

Just this simple change improves the form a lot. With a little more work, you can make it look even better.

5. Open `jobs/forms.py` for editing and add `attrs` to style the widget of `start_date`:

```
start_date = forms.DateField(
    help_text='The earliest date you can start working.',
    widget=forms.SelectDateWidget(
        years=YEARS,
        attrs={'style': 'width: 31%; display: inline-block; margin: 0 1%'}
    ),
    validators=[validate_future_date],
    error_messages={'past_date': 'Please enter a future date.'}
)
```

This will make the three date-part `selects` each only take up one-third of the available width:

Start date*

January ▾ 1 ▾ 2020 ▾

The earliest date you can start working.

6. Open `static/css/main.css` and add these two rules:

```
/* FORM STYLES */
label {
  font-variant: small-caps;
}

.form-check {
  display: inline-block;
  font-weight: normal;
  margin: 0 1rem;
}
```

The first rule makes the labels use small caps. The second rule aligns the checkboxes horizontally instead of vertically:

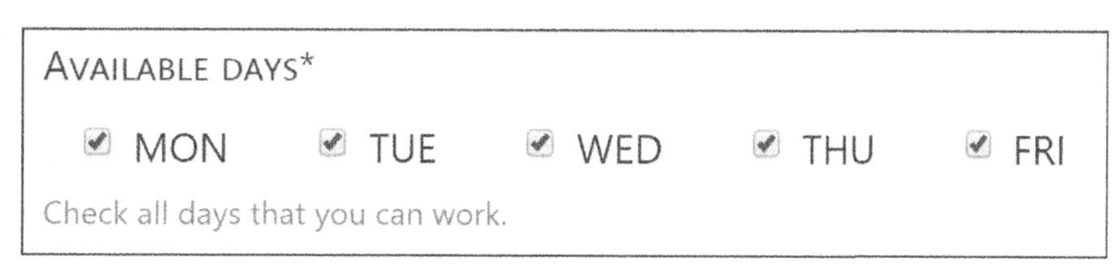

Refresh the job application again. You may need to do a hard refresh to get your new CSS to load. Much better, right?

❖ E34.1. The `as_crispy_field` Filter

If you need more control over the layout of the form, you can use the `as_crispy_field` filter on each form element instead of using the `crispy` filter on the complete form. This does, of course, create more work. Here is a completed template taking this approach:

Exercise Code 34.1: templates/jobs/joke_writer.html

```
-------Lines 1 through 9 Omitted-------
10.       <div class="form-row">
11.         <div class="form-group col-md-6 mb-0">
12.           {{ form.first_name|as_crispy_field }}
13.         </div>
14.         <div class="form-group col-md-6 mb-0">
15.           {{ form.last_name|as_crispy_field }}
16.         </div>
17.       </div>
18.       <div class="form-row">
19.         <div class="form-group col-md-6 mb-0">
20.           {{ form.email|as_crispy_field }}
21.         </div>
22.         <div class="form-group col-md-6 mb-0">
23.           {{ form.website|as_crispy_field }}
24.         </div>
25.       </div>
26.       <div class="form-row">
27.         <div class="form-group col-md-6 mb-0">
28.           {{ form.employment_type|as_crispy_field }}
29.         </div>
30.         <div class="form-group col-md-6 mb-0">
31.           {{ form.start_date|as_crispy_field }}
32.         </div>
33.       </div>
34.       <div class="form-row">
35.         <div class="form-group col-md-8 mb-0">
36.           {{ form.available_days|as_crispy_field  }}
37.         </div>
38.         <div class="form-group col-md-4 mb-0">
39.           {{ form.desired_hourly_wage|as_crispy_field }}
40.         </div>
41.       </div>
42.       {{ form.cover_letter|as_crispy_field }}
43.       {{ form.confirmation|as_crispy_field }}
-------Lines 44 through 47 Omitted-------
```

If you don't want to type all this out, you can copy this code from `starter-code/forms-and-widgets/joke_writer_crispy_final.html` and paste it over your current code in `templates/jobs/joke_writer.html`.

This template includes the `novalidate` attribute of the <form> tag so that you can skip client-side validation to test the server-side validation. If you want to use client-side validation as well, you should remove the `novalidate` attribute.

The resulting form looks like this:

FIRST NAME*

LAST NAME*

EMAIL*

A valid email address.

WEBSITE

https://www.example.com

EMPLOYMENT TYPE*

--Please choose--

START DATE*

January 1 2020

The earliest date you can start working.

AVAILABLE DAYS*

MON TUE WED THU FRI

Check all days that you can work.

DESIRED HOURLY WAGE*

COVER LETTER*

I CERTIFY THAT THE INFORMATION I HAVE PROVIDED IS TRUE.*

Apply

And here is the result of an invalid form submission:

FIRST NAME*

This field is required.

LAST NAME*

This field is required.

EMAIL*

This field is required.

A valid email address.

WEBSITE

http

Enter a valid URL.

EMPLOYMENT TYPE*

--Please choose--

This field is required.

START DATE*

Janua 1 2020

Please enter a future date.

The earliest date you can start working.

AVAILABLE DAYS*

MON TUE WED THU FRI

Check all days that you can work.

DESIRED HOURLY WAGE*

This field is required.

COVER LETTER*

This field is required.

I CERTIFY THAT THE INFORMATION I HAVE PROVIDED IS TRUE.*

This field is required.

Apply

All of that nice validation styling comes with `django-crispy-forms`.

Git Commit

Commit your code to Git.

Exercise 35: Making the Joke Form Crispy

5 to 10 minutes

Open `templates/jokes/joke_form.html` and modify it to use `django-crispy-forms`. You only need to add one line of code, change another, and delete the opening and closing `<table>` tags.

Test your solution by visiting `http://127.0.0.1:8000/jokes/` and clicking on the buttons to create a new joke. Or you can update an existing joke. The create and update views use the same form.

Solution: templates/jokes/joke_form.html

```
1.  {% extends "_base.html" %}
2.  {% load crispy_forms_tags %}
3.
4.  {% block title %}Add/Update Joke{% endblock %}
5.  {% block main %}
6.    <div class="card border-primary m-auto mb-3 p-3"
7.      style="max-width: 30rem">
8.        <form method="post">
9.          {% csrf_token %}
10.         {{ form|crispy }}
11.         <button class="btn btn-success float-right">Submit</button>
12.       </form>
13.   </div>
14. {% endblock %}
```

Git Commit

Commit your code to Git.

Conclusion

In this lesson, you have learned to build, process, validate, and style Django forms.

LESSON 10

ModelForms

Topics Covered

☑ Models revisited.

☑ Model fields.

☑ Model field arguments.

☑ `ModelForms`.

☑ Many-to-one relationships.

☑ Many-to-many relationships.

> Most disquieting reflection of all, was it not bad **form** to think about good **form**? His vitals were tortured by this problem. It was a claw within him sharper than the iron one; and as it tore him, the perspiration dripped down his tallow countenance.
>
> *– James Matthew Barrie, Peter and Wendy*

Introduction

In this lesson, you will learn to create relationships between models and to use `ModelForms` to manage those relationships.

*

10.1. Models

A model, according to the documentation, is "the single, definitive source of information about your data."[60]

60. `https://docs.djangoproject.com/en/3.1/topics/db/models/`

Some basics:

1. A model maps to a table in a database.
2. Each attribute in the model maps to a field within the table.
3. By default, models are given a primary key `id` field, which is an auto-incrementing integer. While this can be overridden, there is generally no reason to do so.
4. Models have methods for saving, deleting, validating, and getting information about instances. You can override these methods and you can add your own custom methods.
5. Models have a *manager* attribute, which by default is named `objects`. The manager is used to create, update, delete, and get instances of the Model.

10.2. Model Fields

Attributes of models are assigned field types from `django.db.models`. As previously mentioned (see page 232), the term "field" can be confusing because it can refer to a model field (`django.db.models.fields`), a form field (`django.forms.fields`), or an HTML form field (i.e., an HTML form control). Every *model field type* has a default *form field type*, which often uses the same name. For example, the default form field for `models.CharField` is `forms.CharField`. But there are exceptions. For example, the default form field for `models.TextField` is also `forms.CharField`,[61] but it is modified to use a `forms.Textarea` widget.

It is important to know the default widget each model field will use. The following tables map model fields to default form fields and default widgets:

61. There is no `forms.TextField` field type.

Text-based Model Fields

Model Field	Form Field	Default Widget
CharField[62]	CharField	TextInput
TextField	CharField	Textarea
URLField	URLField	URLInput
EmailField	EmailField	EmailInput
GenericIPAddressField	GenericIPAddressField	TextInput
JSONField	JSONField	Textarea

Numeric Model Fields

Model Field	Form Field	Default Widget
DecimalField	DecimalField	NumberInput
FloatField	FloatField	NumberInput
IntegerField	IntegerField	NumberInput
BigIntegerField	IntegerField	NumberInput
PositiveIntegerField	IntegerField	NumberInput
PositiveSmallIntegerField	IntegerField	NumberInput
SmallIntegerField	IntegerField	NumberInput

Date and Time Model Fields

Model Field	Form Field	Default Widget
DateField	DateField	DateInput
DateTimeField	DateTimeField	DateTimeInput
DurationField	DurationField	TextInput
TimeField	TimeField	TimeInput

Boolean Model Fields

Model Field	Form Field	Default Widget
BooleanField	BooleanField	CheckboxInput[63]

62. `models.CharField` requires the `max_length` argument.
63. If `null=True`, `BooleanField` gets a `NullBooleanSelect` widget.

File-related Model Fields

Model Field	Form Field	Default Widget
FileField	FileField	ClearableFileInput
ImageField	ImageField	ClearableFileInput
FilePathField	CharField	Select

The following additional model fields would rarely if ever show up in a form:

- `BinaryField` – A field for holding binary data. The Django documentation[64] recommends against storing files as binary data in the database in most cases.
- `SlugField` – A field for holding slugs. Slugs are usually generated rather than added via a form.
- `UUIDField` – A field that is sometimes used in addition to or in place of the default auto-incrementing integer primary key to uniquely identify a record. A UUID would usually be generated rather than added in a form.

10.3. Model Field Arguments

All field types can take the following arguments:[65]

- `default` – The default value to use for the field.
- `blank` (boolean) – If set to `True`, the field can be left blank. The default is `False`.
- `unique` (boolean) – If set to `True`, no two records in the table may have the same value for this field. The default is `False`.
- `null` (boolean) – If set to `True`, `null` values are allowed in the database and empty fields will be stored as `null`. The default is `False`.
- `help_text` – Help text to be displayed with the form widget and in documentation. You can include HTML as it will not be escaped.
- `verbose_name` – A friendly name for the field. If this isn't provided, Django will create it by replacing underscores in the attribute name with spaces. For example, `first_name` will become "first name". If this is the first argument passed to the field type, it can be passed as a positional argument (i.e., without using `verbose_name="..."`).

64. `https://docs.djangoproject.com/en/3.1/ref/models/fields/#binaryfield`
65. There are additional arguments that all field types can take; however, the ones listed here are the most useful.

- `choices` – A sequence of 2-item tuples to be used as options within a select list.

Again, all field types can take the preceding arguments, but some can take additional arguments.

10.4. ModelForms

Let's take another look at the `Joke` model you have been working with:

Demo 10.1: jokes/models.py

```
-------Lines 1 through 5 Omitted-------
6.  class Joke(models.Model):
7.      question = models.TextField(max_length=200)
8.      answer = models.TextField(max_length=100, blank=True)
9.      slug = models.SlugField(
10.         max_length=50, unique=True, null=False, editable=False
11.     )
12.     created = models.DateTimeField(auto_now_add=True)
13.     updated = models.DateTimeField(auto_now=True)
-------Lines 14 through 25 Omitted-------
```

The `Joke` model has five attributes: two `TextFields`, a `SlugField`, and two `DateTimeFields`.

The view for creating new jokes is super simple: you inherit from `CreateView` and specify the model you want to use and the fields you want in the form:

```
class JokeCreateView(CreateView):
    model = Joke
    fields = ['question', 'answer']
```

The view for updating jokes is equally simple:

```
class JokeUpdateView(UpdateView):
    model = Joke
    fields = ['question', 'answer']
```

A great thing about CreateView and UpdateView views is that the ModelForm is autogenerated from the model and the fields attributes. However, if you want to make changes to the form fields (e.g., modifying the default widgets), you need to explicitly create the ModelForm.

A ModelForm is similar to a regular Form, like the job-application form you created earlier. The major difference is that a ModelForm automatically creates form fields based on the model. You can control certain aspects of those form fields using the ModelForm's Meta inner class, which takes the following attributes:

1. model (required) – The model the form is based on.
2. fields (required) – A list or tuple containing the fields you want in the form.
3. widgets – A dictionary with keys for each field whose widget you want to modify.
4. help_texts – A dictionary with keys for each field whose help_text you want to modify.
5. labels – A dictionary with keys for each field whose label you want to modify.
6. error_messages – A dictionary with keys for each field whose error_message you want to modify.

A ModelForm is constructed like this:

```
class MyModelForm(ModelForm):
    class Meta:
        model = MyModel
        fields = ('field_name1', 'field_name2', 'field_name3')
        widgets = {
          'field_name1': TextInput(
              attrs={'size': '80', 'autofocus': True}
          ),
          'field_name3': Textarea(
              attrs={'cols': '80', 'rows': '5', 'class': 'some-class'}
          ),
        }
        help_texts = {'field_name2': 'Some helpful tip.'}
        labels = {'field_name1': 'Field Name One'}
        error_messages = {'field_name3': 'That is just plain wrong!'}
```

Note that the dictionaries only need to contain keys for the fields that you want to change.

While you could create the custom model form within the models.py file itself, we recommend writing your form classes in a forms.py file within the app folder. You'll do this in the upcoming exercise.

Exercise 36: Creating a ModelForm

20 to 30 minutes

In this exercise, you will build a `ModelForm` so that you can customize the form for adding and updating jokes. In the `jokes` folder, create a new `forms.py` file with the following content:[66]

Exercise Code 36.1: jokes/forms.py

```
1.  from django.forms import ModelForm, Textarea
2.
3.  from .models import Joke
4.
5.  class JokeForm(ModelForm):
6.      class Meta:
7.          model = Joke
8.          fields = ['question', 'answer']
9.          widgets = {
10.             'question': Textarea(
11.                 attrs={'cols': 80, 'rows': 3, 'autofocus': True}
12.             ),
13.             'answer': Textarea(
14.                 attrs={'cols': 80, 'rows': 2, 'placeholder': 'Make it funny!'}
15.             )
16.         }
17.         help_texts = {
18.             'question': 'No dirty jokes please.'
19.         }
```

Things to notice:

1. You import `ModelForm` from `django.forms` and inherit from it to create your `JokeForm` class:

```
from django.forms import ModelForm, Textarea
…

class JokeForm(ModelForm):
```

66. **Don't want to type?** Copy from `starter-code/modelforms/jokes_forms.py`.

2. You import the `Joke` model from the `models.py` file in the same directory:

```
from .models import Joke
```

3. You create the `Meta` inner class and set `model`, `fields`, `widgets`, and `help_texts`:

   A. You set `model` to `Joke` and specify the fields you want in the form:

   ```
   model = Joke
   fields = ('question', 'answer')
   ```

   You must include all the fields you want in the form. This will take the place of the views' `fields` attributes, which you will soon remove.

   B. You specify the `widgets` you want to override. This is the main reason for creating `JokeForm` in the first place: you want to override the widgets used by the default `ModelForm` implementation, which bases them on the model fields. Specifically, you want to change some attributes on the HTML `textarea` produced by the `Textarea` widget. To do so, you need to import `Textarea` from `django.forms`, which you did on line 1:

   ```
   from django.forms import ModelForm, Textarea
   ```

   The `widgets` attribute takes a dictionary with keys for each field whose widget you want to modify. In this case, you want to make the following changes:

      i. Make both `question` and `answer` use shorter `textareas` (i.e., fewer rows).

      ii. Use the `autofocus` attribute to put focus on the question `textarea` as soon as the page loads.

      iii. Add a "Make it funny!" placeholder to the answer `textarea`.

   ```
   widgets = {
       'question': Textarea(
           attrs={'cols': 80, 'rows': 3, 'autofocus': True}
       ),
       'answer': Textarea(
           attrs={'cols': 80, 'rows': 2, 'placeholder': 'Make it funny!'}
       )
   }
   ```

C. You specify the `help_texts` you want to override (just one actually):

```
help_texts = {
    'question': 'No dirty jokes please.'
}
```

Note that you could have set `help_text` in the model, but if you do that, the help text will show up in Django admin as well. This way, it will only show up in this form.

❖ E36.1. The Views

1. Open `jokes/views.py` for editing.
2. Import `JokeForm` from the `forms.py` file you just created in the same directory:

```
from .forms import JokeForm
```

3. In both `CreateView` and `UpdateView`:

   A. Remove the `fields` attribute.

   B. Add the `form_class` attribute.

```
class JokeCreateView(CreateView):
  model = Joke
  fields = ['question', 'answer']
  form_class = JokeForm

class JokeUpdateView(UpdateView):
  model = Joke
  fields = ['question', 'answer']
  form_class = JokeForm
```

Note that a view cannot have both the `form_class` and the `fields` attributes. When `form_class` is present, the `fields` will be managed in the form specified in `form_class`.

❖ E36.2. Try It Out

Start up the server and go to the new-joke form. The form should look like this:

QUESTION*

No dirty jokes please.

ANSWER

Submit

Notice the resized textareas and the help text below the question `textarea`. Also notice that joke field gets focus when the page loads.

Git Commit

Commit your code to Git.

10.5. Many-to-One Relationships

Many-to-One relationships are created with `ForeignKey` fields, like this:

```
class Author(models.Model):
    ...

class Book(models.Model):
    author = models.ForeignKey(Author, on_delete=models.CASCADE)
```

The `on_delete` argument is required. If it is set to `models.CASCADE` then all the objects of a class (e.g., `Book`) will be deleted when the object referenced by the foreign key (e.g., an `Author`) is deleted. If you want to prevent users from deleting in such cases (e.g., prevent authors who have books in the database from being deleted), set `on_delete` to `models.PROTECT`. In that case, the user would have to delete all of the author's book before deleting the author.

Exercise 37: Adding Joke Categories

30 to 45 minutes

1. Open `jokes/models.py` and add this `Category` model at the bottom:[67]

Exercise Code 37.1: jokes/models.py

```
-------Lines 1 through 28 Omitted-------
29. class Category(models.Model):
30.     category = models.CharField(max_length=50)
31.     slug = models.SlugField(
32.         max_length=50, unique=True, null=False, editable=False
33.     )
34.     created = models.DateTimeField(auto_now_add=True)
35.     updated = models.DateTimeField(auto_now=True)
36.
37.     def get_absolute_url(self):
38.         return reverse('jokes:category', args=[self.slug])
39.
40.     def save(self, *args, **kwargs):
41.         if not self.slug:
42.             value = str(self)
43.             self.slug = unique_slug(value, type(self))
44.         super().save(*args, **kwargs)
45.
46.     def __str__(self):
47.         return self.category
```

   Make sure you understand the code used to make this model. It is similar to the `Joke` model.

2. In the `Joke` model, below the `answer` field, add a foreign key to the new `Category` model:

```
category = models.ForeignKey(Category, on_delete=models.PROTECT)
```

   You use `models.PROTECT`, because you don't want to let users delete categories that have jokes in them.

3. If your server isn't running, start it up. You should see an error like this one in the terminal:

```
NameError: name 'Category' is not defined
```

67. **Don't want to type?** Copy from `starter-code/modelforms/jokes_models.py`.

The problem is Category is referenced in the Joke model, which is defined before the Category model. There are two ways to fix this:

A. Move the Category class definition above the Joke class definition.

B. Use the string 'Category' instead of the object Category:

```
category = models.ForeignKey('Category', on_delete=models.PROTECT)
```

This is called a "lazy" reference, meaning that Django sees the reference, and says "I'll do that later, after I find the Category model."

Do one or the other. When you save after making that change, the error at the terminal should go away.

4. Because you have changed the model, you need to make and run migrations, but before you do, you need to make one more quick change: Add null=True to the category field in the Joke model:

```
category = models.ForeignKey(
    'Category', on_delete=models.PROTECT, null=True
)
```

Take a moment to think about this: why do you need to allow null values here? Have you taken a moment? I'm about to tell you... You need to allow for null values because there are already jokes in the database that don't have a category assigned to them. If you try to run migrations without allowing for null values, you will get an error.

5. Now, make and run the migrations:

```
(.venv) …/projects/djangojokes.com> python manage.py makemigrations
(.venv) …/projects/djangojokes.com> python manage.py migrate
```

The Database Relationship

The following diagram shows the database relationship between jokes and categories:

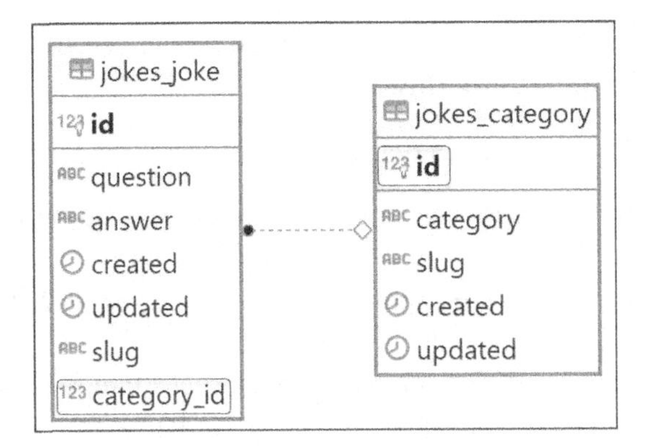

❖ E37.1. Registering the Category Model

You need to register the `Category` model, so that you can manage it in Django admin. Open `jokes/admin.py` in your editor and edit it as follows:[68]

Exercise Code 37.2: jokes/admin.py

```
-------Lines 1 through 2 Omitted-------
3.  from .models import Category, Joke
4.
5.  @admin.register(Category)
6.  class CategoryAdmin(admin.ModelAdmin):
7.      model = Category
8.      list_display = ['category', 'created', 'updated']
9.
10.     def get_readonly_fields(self, request, obj=None):
11.         if obj: # editing an existing object
12.             return ('slug', 'created', 'updated')
13.         return ()
-------Lines 14 through 23 Omitted-------
```

❖ E37.2. Django Admin

Start up the server and open Django admin (`http://127.0.0.1:8000/admin/`). There should be a new **Categorys** link under the **Jokes** heading:

68. **Don't want to type?** Copy from `starter-code/modelforms/jokes_admin.py`.

But that's not how you pluralize "Category!"

The default plural form of a model name is just the name followed by an "s." This can be changed in the model's `Meta` inner class. Open `jokes/models.py` in your editor and add the following at the bottom of the `Category` class definition:

```
class Meta:
    verbose_name_plural = 'Categories'
```

Back in the browser, refresh the Django admin site. "Categories" should now be spelled correctly. Click the link and add a few categories (e.g., Funny, Play on Words, Brain Teaser).

❖ E37.3. Making Categories Required

Now that you have some categories, remove `null=True` from the `category` field in the `Joke` model:

```
category = models.ForeignKey(
    'Category', on_delete=models.PROTECT, null=True
)
```

As you have changed the model again, you will need to make and run migrations:

```
(.venv) …/projects/djangojokes.com> python manage.py makemigrations
```

When you run this you will get a warning and a message with various options. The warning will say something like "You are trying to change the nullable field 'category' on joke to non-nullable without a default; we can't do that." Enter `1` to provide a one-off default and then enter `1` for the default to assign the first category you entered to all existing jokes. Then, you can run migrations:

```
(.venv) …/projects/djangojokes.com> python manage.py migrate
```

❖ E37.4. The `ModelForm`

You now need to add the `category` field to the `fields` attribute in `JokeForm`. Open `jokes/forms.py` and add `'category'` to `fields`:

```
fields = ['question', 'answer', 'category']
```

Visit `http://127.0.0.1:8000/jokes/joke/create/` and notice that the form now includes a **Category** field:

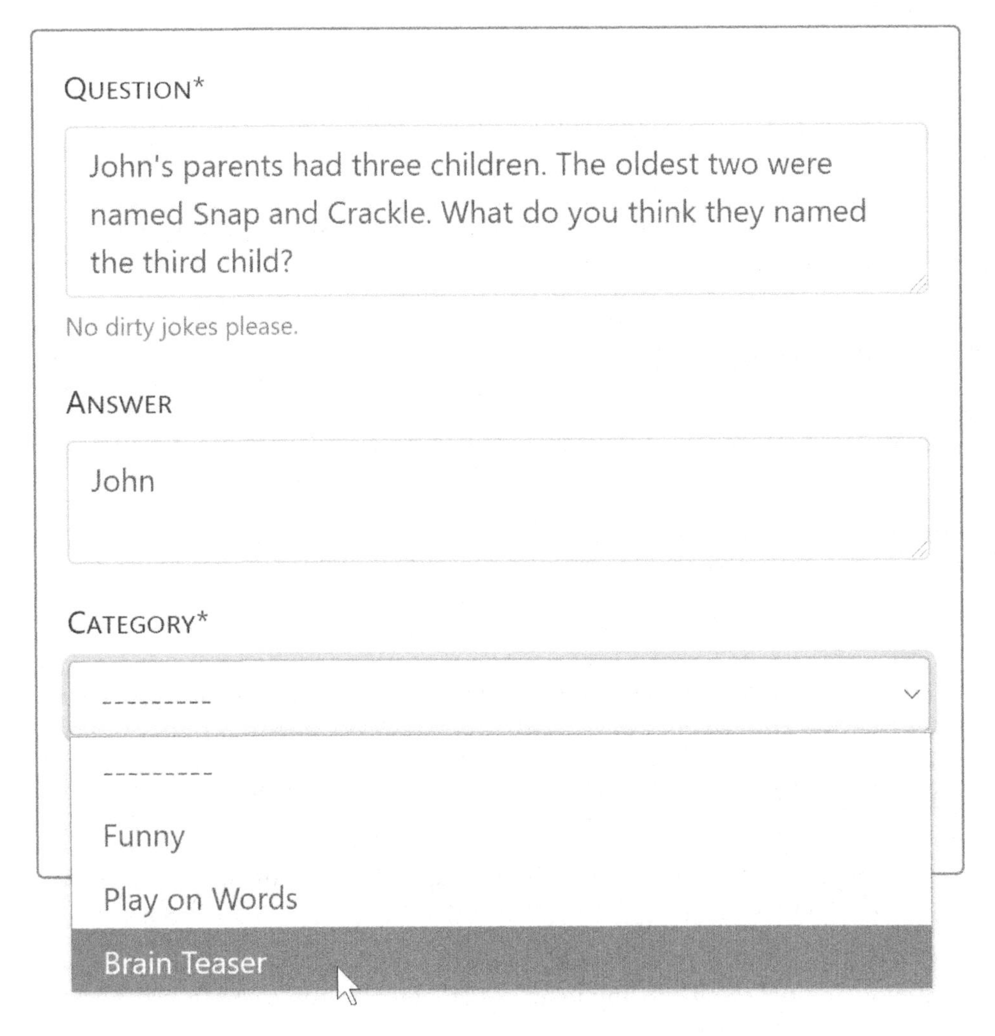

Notice that Django automatically creates a `Select` widget for `ForeignKey` fields.

Git Commit

Commit your code to Git.

10.6. Many-to-Many Relationships

Many-to-Many relationships are created with `ManyToManyField` fields, like this:

```
class Book(models.Model):
    ...

class Library(models.Model):
    books = models.ManyToManyField(Book)
```

A book can be kept in many libraries and a library can keep many books.

You could create this same relationship like this:

```
class Library(models.Model):
    ...

class Book(models.Model):
    libraries = models.ManyToManyField(Library)
```

Which is better? Let your gut guide you. Does it feel more natural for books to contain libraries or for libraries to contain books? I think it feels more natural for libraries to contain books, so I would choose to include `books` in the `Library` model.

Naming ManyToManyField Fields

`ManyToManyField` fields generally get plural names (e.g., `books`).

10.6.1. Lazy Referencing

As with `ForeignKey` fields, the model class you reference in a `ManyToManyField` has to have been defined already unless you use its name in quotes in place of the object itself. For example:

```
books = models.ManyToManyField('Book')
```

10.6.2. The Database

In the database, many-to-many relationships are created using an intermediary join table. The simplified SQL for creating this relationship is shown in the following code:

```
CREATE TABLE books_book (
  id    serial PRIMARY KEY,
  book  varchar(50) NOT NULL
);

CREATE TABLE books_library (
  id         serial PRIMARY KEY,
  library    varchar(50) NOT NULL
);

CREATE TABLE books_library_books (
  id          serial PRIMARY KEY,
  book_id     int REFERENCES book (id) ON UPDATE NO ACTION ON DELETE NO ACTION,
  library_id int REFERENCES library (id) ON UPDATE NO ACTION ON DELETE NO ACTION
);
```

The `books_library_books` table is the intermediary join table that Django would create behind the scenes to hold the relationship data.

Exercise 38: Adding Joke Tags

20 to 30 minutes

1. Open `jokes/models.py` and add this `Tag` model at the bottom. Note that this is almost identical to the `Category` model, so you can start by copying and pasting that and then updating it. The differences are highlighted:

```
class Tag(models.Model):
    tag = models.CharField(max_length=50)
    slug = models.SlugField(
        max_length=50, unique=True, null=False, editable=False
    )
    created = models.DateTimeField(auto_now_add=True)
    updated = models.DateTimeField(auto_now=True)

    def get_absolute_url(self):
        return reverse('jokes:tag', args=[self.slug])

    def save(self, *args, **kwargs):
        if not self.slug:
            value = str(self)
            self.slug = unique_slug(value, type(self))
        super().save(*args, **kwargs)

    def __str__(self):
        return self.tag
```

2. In the `Joke` model, below the `category` field, add a `ManyToManyField` field referencing the new `Tag` model:

```
tags = models.ManyToManyField('Tag')
```

3. Because you have changed the model, you need to make and run migrations:

```
(.venv) …/projects/djangojokes.com> python manage.py makemigrations
(.venv) …/projects/djangojokes.com> python manage.py migrate
```

The Database Relationship

The database relationship between `jokes` and `tags` is as follows:

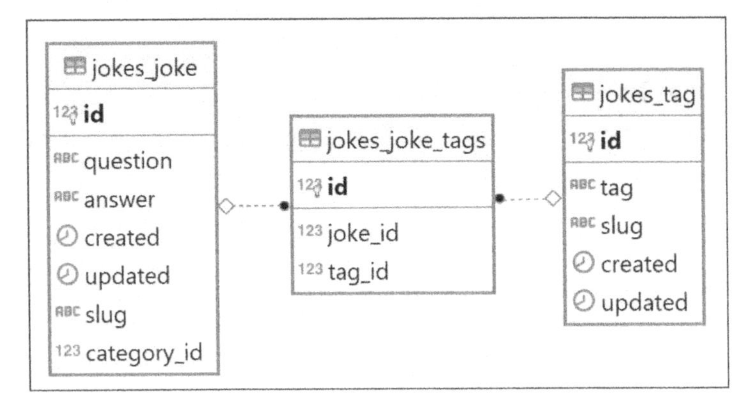

Notice the intermediary `jokes_joke_tags` table.

❖ E38.1. Registering the `Tag` Model

You need to register the `Tag` model, so that you can manage it in Django admin. Open `jokes/admin.py` in your editor and import and register `Tag`:

Exercise Code 38.1: jokes/admin.py

```
1.    from django.contrib import admin
2.
3.    from .models import Category, Joke, Tag
      -------Lines 4 through 26 Omitted-------
27.   @admin.register(Tag)
28.   class TagAdmin(admin.ModelAdmin):
29.       model = Tag
30.       list_display = ['tag', 'created', 'updated']
31.
32.       def get_readonly_fields(self, request, obj=None):
33.           if obj: # editing an existing object
34.               return ('slug', 'created', 'updated')
35.           return ()
```

❖ E38.2. Django Admin

Start up the server and open Django admin (`http://127.0.0.1:8000/admin/`). There should be a new **Tags** link under the **Jokes** heading. Click the link and add a few tags (e.g., Pun, Bar, Birthday, Sports, Animal, Grandparents).

❖ E38.3. The `ModelForm`

You now need to add the `tags` field to the `fields` attribute in `JokeForm`. Open `jokes/forms.py` and add `'tags'` to `fields`:

```
fields = ['question', 'answer', 'category', 'tags']
```

The default widget for a `ManyToManyField` field is a `SelectMultiple`, which some users might not know how to use, so add some help text for the `tags` field:

```
help_texts = {
    'question': 'No dirty jokes please.',
    'tags': 'Use Ctrl-click to select multiple tags.'
}
```

Another option would be to change the widget to a `CheckboxSelectMultiple`, but if you create a lot of tags, that could end up taking up a lot of screen real estate.

Visit `http://127.0.0.1:8000/jokes/joke/create/`. The form should now include a **Tags** field:

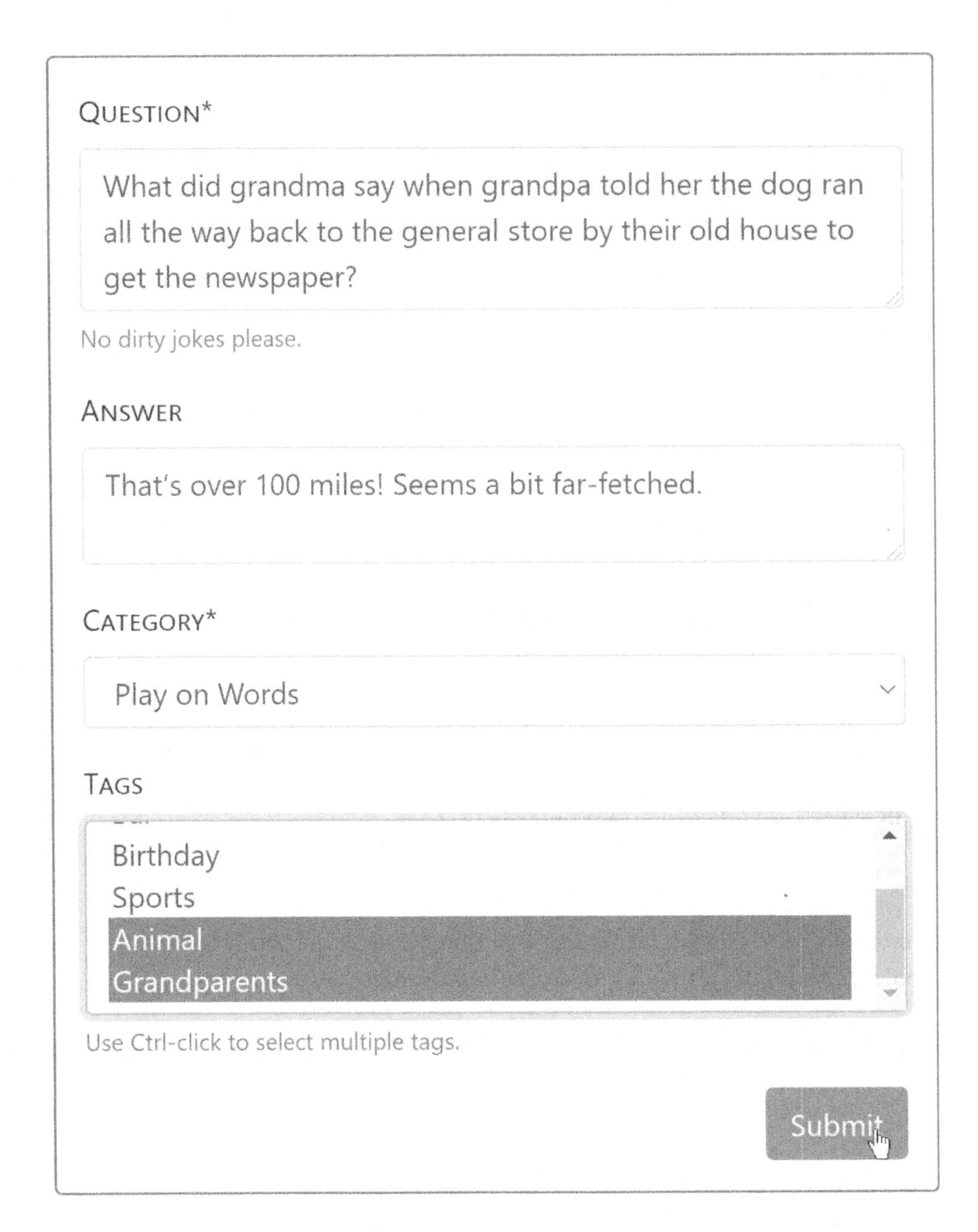

Try to update an existing joke without adding any tags. You will get an error indicating that you need to select a tag. By default, `ManyToManyField` fields will be required in forms. You can make it optional by adding `blank=True` to the field in the model:

```
tags = models.ManyToManyField('Tag', blank=True)
```

❖ E38.4. Ordering `ManyToManyField` Fields

The order of the tags in the `select` field may appear random. The default ordering for a model can be set in the `Meta` inner class. Open `jokes/models.py` in your editor and add the following at the bottom of the `Tag` class definition:

```
class Meta:
    ordering = ['tag']
```

Now return to a page with a joke form and refresh. The tags should be in alphabetical order:

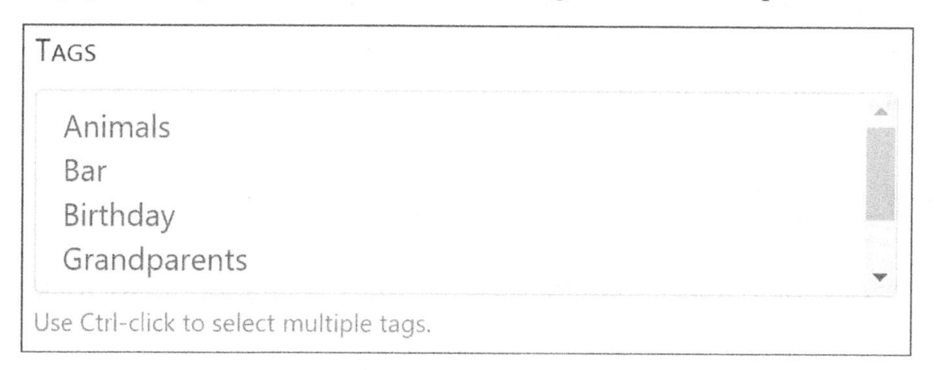

You can order the categories in the **Category** dropdown in the same way:

```
class Meta:
    verbose_name_plural = 'Categories'
    ordering = ['category']
```

Git Commit

Commit your code to Git.

Exercise 39: Updating the Joke Templates

15 to 25 minutes

In this exercise, you will update the `joke_detail.html` and `joke_list.html` templates.

Add the following joke:

- **Question:** What did grandma say when grandpa told her the dog ran all the way back to the general store by their old house to get the newspaper?
- **Answer:** That's over 100 miles! Seems a bit far-fetched.
- **Category:** Play on Words
- **Tags:** Animal, Grandparents

❖ E39.1. `joke_detail.html`

Open `templates/jokes/joke_detail.html` for editing and add the following highlighted content:[69]

69. **Don't want to type?** Copy from `starter-code/modelforms/joke_detail.html`.

Exercise Code 39.1: templates/jokes/joke_detail.html

```
1.   {% extends "_base.html" %}
     -------Lines 2 through 10 Omitted-------
11.      <div class="card-footer">
12.        <div class="border-bottom border-faded pb-2">
13.          <strong>Category:</strong> {{ joke.category }}<br>
14.          {% for tag in joke.tags.all %}
15.            <span class="badge badge-pill badge-secondary">{{ tag }}</span>
16.          {% endfor %}
17.        </div>
18.        <div class="border-bottom border-faded m-2 pb-2">
19.          <a href="{% url 'jokes:update' joke.slug %}"
20.            class="btn btn-info btn-sm mr-2">Update</a>
21.          <a href="{% url 'jokes:delete' joke.slug %}"
22.            class="btn btn-danger btn-sm mr-2">Delete</a>
23.        </div>
24.        <small class="text-muted">
25.          Created on: {{ joke.created }}
26.          Last updated: {{ joke.updated }}
27.        </small>
28.      </div>
     -------Lines 29 through 30 Omitted-------
```

Open a joke page on the site. It should look something like this:

What did grandma say when grandpa told her the dog ran all the way back to the general store by their old house to get the newspaper?

That's over 100 miles! Seems a bit far-fetched.

Category: Play on Words

Animal Grandparents

Update Delete

Created on: Aug. 7, 2020, 4:55 p.m. Last updated: Aug. 7, 2020, 4:55 p.m.

Things to notice:

1. Adding the category to the template is straightforward. That's just an attribute of the `joke` object:

   ```
   {{ joke.category }}
   ```

   However, there's something going on here behind the scenes that may not be immediately obvious. The `category` attribute of `joke` holds the `category` object, not the `category` field of that object. When an object is output in the template, it is converted to a string using the class's `__str__()` method. For the `Category` class, that returns the `category` field:

   ```
   def __str__(self):
       return self.category
   ```

   If someone changes the value that the `__str__()` method returns, the template would reflect that change. So, to be safe, you might want to be more explicit in the template and use:

   ```
   {{ joke.category.category }}
   ```

2. To output the tags associated with a joke, you loop through `joke.tags.all`, which returns a `QuerySet` containing all the `Tag` objects associated with the `joke` object through the many-to-many relationship. Just as with `joke.category`, `tag` will output the value returned by the `__str__()` method of the `Tag` class. To be safe, you should change that to `tag.tag` to explicitly output the value of the `tag` field:

   ```
   {% for tag in joke.tags.all %}
     <span class="badge badge-pill badge-secondary">{{ tag.tag }}</span>
   {% endfor %}
   ```

3. You have also added **Update** and **Delete** buttons so that the joke can be edited from the joke-detail page.

❖ E39.2. `joke_list.html`

For `joke_list.html` let's display the jokes in a table instead of a list. While you're at it, let's change the **Update** and **Delete** buttons to use font-awesome icons:

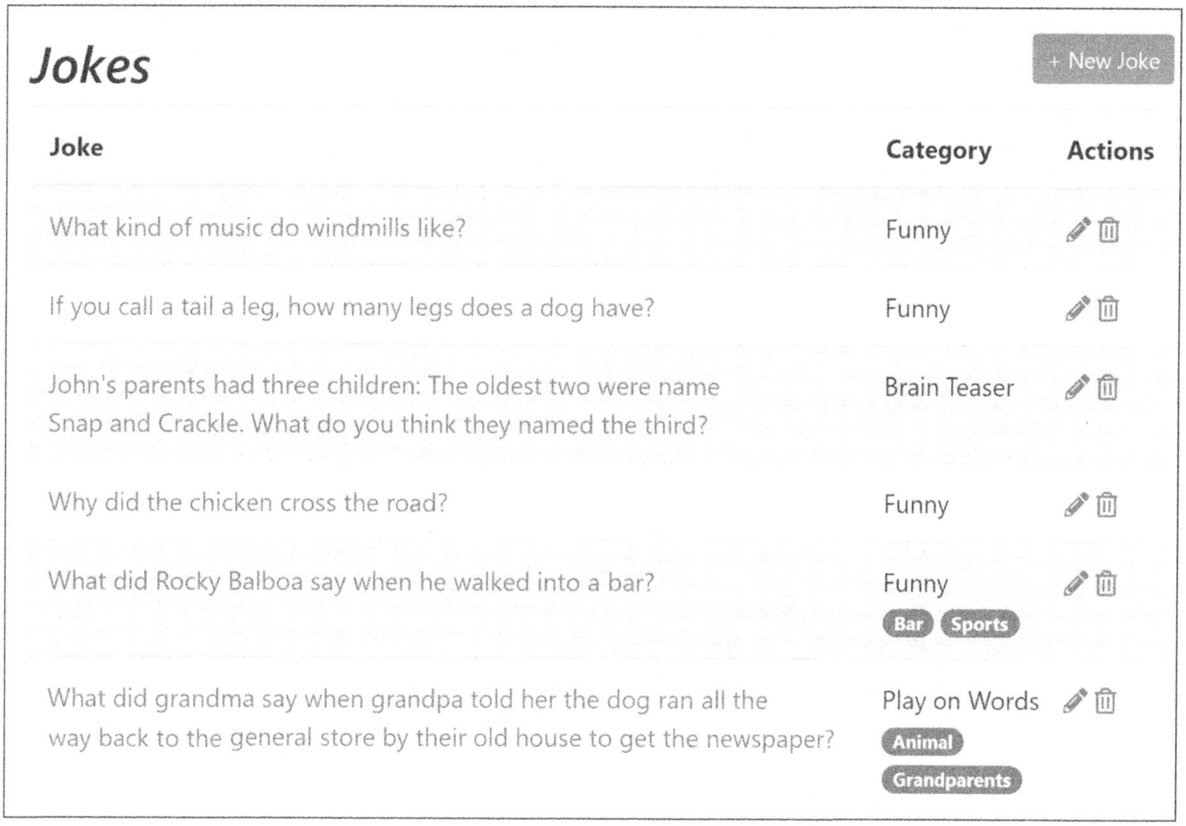

Jokes

+ New Joke

Joke	Category	Actions
What kind of music do windmills like?	Funny	
If you call a tail a leg, how many legs does a dog have?	Funny	
John's parents had three children: The oldest two were name Snap and Crackle. What do you think they named the third?	Brain Teaser	
Why did the chicken cross the road?	Funny	
What did Rocky Balboa say when he walked into a bar?	Funny Bar Sports	
What did grandma say when grandpa told her the dog ran all the way back to the general store by their old house to get the newspaper?	Play on Words Animal Grandparents	

Open `templates/jokes/joke_list.html` for editing and replace the unordered list with the following table. Then visit `http://127.0.0.1:8000/jokes/` to see the new layout:[70]

70. **Don't want to type?** Copy from `starter-code/modelforms/joke_list.html`.

Exercise Code 39.2: templates/jokes/joke_list.html

```
-------Lines 1 through 8 Omitted-------
9.      <div class="table-responsive">
10.       <table class="table table-striped" style="min-width: 500px">
11.         <thead>
12.           <tr>
13.             <th>Joke</th><th>Category</th><th>Actions</th>
14.           </tr>
15.         </thead>
16.         <tbody>
17.           {% for joke in joke_list %}
18.             <tr>
19.               <td>
20.                 <a href="{{ joke.get_absolute_url }}">{{ joke.question }}</a>
21.               </td>
22.               <td>
23.                 {{ joke.category.category }}<br>
24.                 {% for tag in joke.tags.all %}
25.                   <span class="badge badge-pill badge-secondary">
26.                     {{ tag.tag }}
27.                   </span>
28.                 {% endfor %}
29.               </td>
30.               <td>
31.                 <a href="{% url 'jokes:update' joke.slug %}">
32.                   <i class="fas fa-pencil-alt"></i>
33.                 </a>
34.                 <a href="{% url 'jokes:delete' joke.slug %}">
35.                   <i class="far fa-trash-alt"></i>
36.                 </a>
37.               </td>
38.             </tr>
39.           {% endfor %}
40.         </tbody>
41.       </table>
42.     </div>
-------Line 43 Omitted-------
```

Git Commit

Commit your code to Git.

 Exercise 40: Tying Job Applications to Models

90 to 120 minutes

In this exercise, you will convert the job application to use a `ModelForm`. This involves modifying the jobs app as follows:

E40.1. The Models

Create models for `Job` and `Applicant`:

1. `Job` fields:
    A. `title` – `CharField` with `max_length` set to `200`.
    B. `created` – `DateTimeField` with `auto_now_add` set to `True`.
    C. `updated` – `DateTimeField` with `auto_now` set to `True`.

    The `__str__()` method should return the job title.
2. `Applicant` fields:
    A. All the fields that are currently in the `JobApplicationForm` class:
        i. `first_name` – `CharField`.
        ii. `last_name` – `CharField`.
        iii. `email` – `EmailField`.
        iv. `website` – `URLField` with `URLValidator`, which you will need to import from `django.core.validators`.
        v. `employment_type` – `CharField` with `choices`.
        vi. `start_date` – `DateField`.
        vii. `available_days` – `CharField` with `choices`, but because applicants can select multiple choices, this needs to be handled in the form, so for the model, it's just a `CharField`.
        viii. `desired_hourly_wage` – `DecimalField` with five total digits, two of which come after the decimal point.
        ix. `cover_letter` – `TextField`.
        x. `confirmation` – `BooleanField`.

Hint: Move all the `help_text` and `validators` (including the necessary imports) into the model.

B. `job` – A `ForeignKey` field.

C. `created` – `DateTimeField` with `auto_now_add` set to `True`.

D. `updated` – `DateTimeField` with `auto_now` set to `True`.

The `__str__()` method should return the name of the applicant and the job they are applying for.

3. Do not forget to run migrations after creating the models.

❖ E40.2. The View

Change `JobAppView` to inherit from `CreateView`. Be sure to set the model. Remember that `CreateView` views infer the template name from the model name. In this case, the inferred name will be `applicant_form.html`. Rename the `joke_writer.html` template in `templates/jobs/` to `applicant_form.html`.

❖ E40.3. The Form

Rewrite `JobApplicationForm` to inherit from `forms.ModelForm`. Here is some starting code, which you can copy from `starter-code/modelforms/jobs_forms_start.py`:

Exercise Code 40.1: jobs/forms.py

```
1.  from datetime import datetime
2.  from django import forms
3.  from django.core.exceptions import ValidationError
4.
5.  from .models import Applicant
6.
7.  def validate_checked(value):
8.      if not value:
9.          raise ValidationError("Required.")
10.
11. class JobApplicationForm(forms.ModelForm):
12.
13.     DAYS = (
-------Lines 14 through 18 Omitted-------
19.     )
20.
21.     available_days = forms.TypedMultipleChoiceField(
22.         choices=DAYS,
23.         coerce=int,
24.         help_text = 'Check all days that you can work.',
25.         widget = forms.CheckboxSelectMultiple(
26.             attrs = {'checked':True}
27.         )
28.     )
29.
30.     confirmation = forms.BooleanField(
31.         label = 'I certify that the information I have provided is true.',
32.         validators=[validate_checked]
33.     )
34.
35.     class Meta:
36.         model = Applicant
37.         fields = (
38.             'first_name', 'last_name', 'email', 'website', 'employment_type',
39.             'start_date', 'available_days', 'desired_hourly_wage',
40.             'cover_letter', 'confirmation', 'job')
41.         widgets = {
42.             # Fill this out
43.         }
44.         error_messages = {
45.             # Fill this out
46.         }
```

Notice that the `available_days` and the `confirmation` form fields are completely redefined in the body of the `JobApplicationForm` class (before the `Meta` inner class). That's because you override them:

- You override `available_days` to use a `TypedMultipleChoiceField` field type in place of `CharField` as defined in the model.
- You override `confirmation`, so that you can set `validators` to use `validate_checked`, which raises an error if the checkbox isn't checked.

For all other fields, you are using the same form types that the model types use by default as shown in the field-mapping tables earlier in this lesson (see page 276); you are only modifying some of their attributes, which can be done using the dictionaries in the `META` class.

❖ E40.4. The Template

- If the template uses `{{ form|crispy }}`, you don't need to do anything to the template as all the `ModelForm` fields will be included.
- If the template uses `as_crispy_field` (see page 268) filters, you need to add a field for `job`.

❖ E40.5. Admin

Create and register `ModelAdmin` classes in `jobs/admin.py`.

Log into Django admin and add a **Joke Writer** job to the `Jobs` model.

❖ E40.6. Try It Out

Start up the server, visit `http://127.0.0.1:8000/jobs/job-app/`, and notice that the application now includes a Job dropdown:

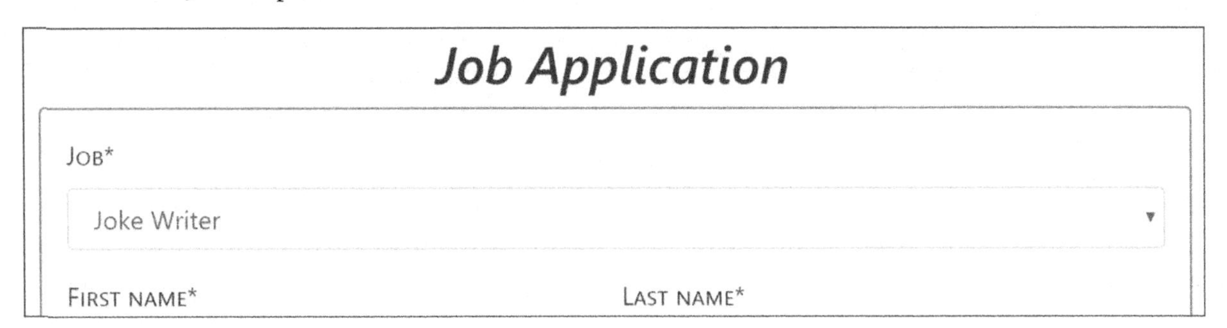

Submit the application. You should get an email (now with a list item for the Job):

And the new applicant should show up in the **Applicants** model in Django admin:

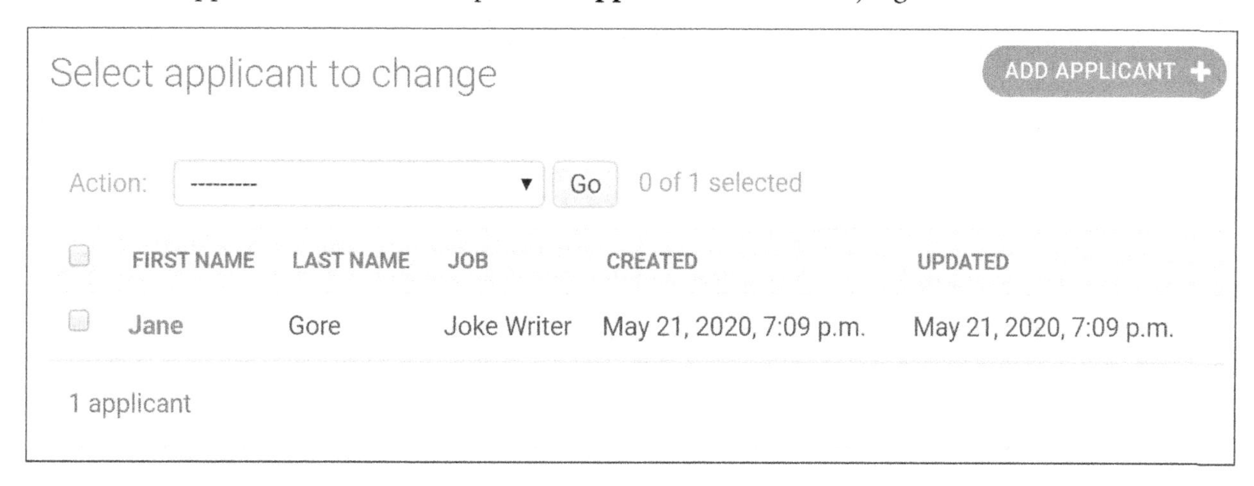

Solutions

The solutions that follow are available to copy from:

- `solutions/modelforms/djangojokes.com/jobs/models.py`
- `solutions/modelforms/djangojokes.com/jobs/views.py`
- `solutions/modelforms/djangojokes.com/jobs/forms.py`
- `solutions/modelforms/djangojokes.com/templates/jobs/applicant_form.html`
- `solutions/modelforms/djangojokes.com/jobs/admin.py`

Solution: jobs/models.py

```
1.  from datetime import datetime
2.
3.  from django.core.exceptions import ValidationError
4.  from django.core.validators import URLValidator
5.  from django.db import models
6.
7.  def validate_future_date(value):
8.      if value < datetime.now().date():
9.          raise ValidationError(
10.             message=f'{value} is in the past.', code='past_date'
11.         )
12.
13. class Job(models.Model):
14.     title = models.CharField(max_length=200)
15.     created = models.DateTimeField(auto_now_add=True)
16.     updated = models.DateTimeField(auto_now=True)
17.
18.     def __str__(self):
19.         return self.title
20.
21.
22. class Applicant(models.Model):
23.     EMPLOYMENT_TYPES = (
24.         (None, '--Please choose--'),
25.         ('ft', 'Full-time'),
26.         ('pt', 'Part-time'),
27.         ('contract', 'Contract work')
28.     )
29.
30.     first_name = models.CharField(max_length=50)
31.     last_name = models.CharField(max_length=50)
32.     email = models.EmailField(help_text='A valid email address.')
33.     website = models.URLField(
34.         blank=True, validators=[URLValidator(schemes=['http', 'https'])]
35.     )
36.     employment_type = models.CharField(max_length=10, choices=EMPLOYMENT_TYPES)
37.     start_date = models.DateField(
38.         help_text = 'The earliest date you can start working.',
39.         validators=[validate_future_date]
40.     )
41.     available_days = models.CharField(max_length=20)
42.     desired_hourly_wage = models.DecimalField(max_digits=5, decimal_places=2)
43.     cover_letter = models.TextField()
44.     confirmation = models.BooleanField()
```

```
45.     job = models.ForeignKey(Job, on_delete=models.CASCADE)
46.     created = models.DateTimeField(auto_now_add=True)
47.     updated = models.DateTimeField(auto_now=True)
48.
49.     def __str__(self):
50.         return f'{self.first_name} {self.last_name} ({self.job})'
```

Solution: jobs/views.py

```
1.  import html
2.  from django.urls import reverse_lazy
3.  from django.views.generic import CreateView, TemplateView
4.
5.  from common.utils.email import send_email
6.
7.  from .models import Applicant
8.  from .forms import JobApplicationForm
9.
10. class JobAppView(CreateView):
11.     model = Applicant
12.     form_class = JobApplicationForm
13.     success_url = reverse_lazy('jobs:thanks')
    -------Lines 14 through 34 Omitted-------
```

Solution: jobs/forms.py

```
-------Lines 1 through 34 Omitted-------
35.     class Meta:
36.         model = Applicant
37.         fields = (
38.             'first_name', 'last_name', 'email', 'website', 'employment_type',
39.             'start_date', 'available_days', 'desired_hourly_wage',
40.             'cover_letter', 'confirmation', 'job')
41.         widgets = {
42.             'first_name': forms.TextInput(attrs={'autofocus': True}),
43.             'website': forms.TextInput(
44.                 attrs = {'placeholder':'https://www.example.com'}
45.             ),
46.             'start_date': forms.SelectDateWidget(
47.                 attrs = {
48.                     'style': 'width: 31%; display: inline-block; margin: 0 1%'
49.                 },
50.                 years = range(datetime.now().year, datetime.now().year+2)
51.             ),
52.             'desired_hourly_wage': forms.NumberInput(
53.                 attrs = {'min':'10.00', 'max':'100.00', 'step':'.25'}
54.             ),
55.             'cover_letter': forms.Textarea(attrs={'cols': '100', 'rows': '5'})
56.         }
57.         error_messages = {
58.             'start_date': {
59.                 'past_date': 'Please enter a future date.'
60.             }
61.         }
```

Solution: templates/jobs/applicant_form.html

```
-------Lines 1 through 7 Omitted-------
8.    <form method="post" novalidate>
9.      {% csrf_token %}
10.     {{ form.job|as_crispy_field }}
11.     <div class="form-row">
-------Lines 12 through 48 Omitted-------
```

Solution: jobs/admin.py

```
1.   from django.contrib import admin
2.
3.   from .models import Applicant, Job
4.
5.   @admin.register(Job)
6.   class JobAdmin(admin.ModelAdmin):
7.       model = Job
8.       list_display = ['title', 'created', 'updated']
9.
10.      def get_readonly_fields(self, request, obj=None):
11.          if obj: # editing an existing object
12.              return ('created', 'updated')
13.          return ()
14.
15.  @admin.register(Applicant)
16.  class ApplicantAdmin(admin.ModelAdmin):
17.      model = Applicant
18.      list_display = ['first_name', 'last_name', 'job', 'created', 'updated']
19.
20.      def get_readonly_fields(self, request, obj=None):
21.          if obj: # editing an existing object
22.              return ('created', 'updated')
23.          return ()
```

Git Commit

Commit your code to Git.

Conclusion

In this lesson, you have learned to create relationships between models and to build `ModelForms` to manage those relationships. You have also learned to loop through and output fields from a many-to-many relationship in a template.

LESSON 11
User Registration

Topics Covered

- ☑ Registering.
- ☑ Logging in and out.
- ☑ Email.
- ☑ Account management.
- ☑ Resetting passwords.

> I had seen the man, dined with him, indeed, the night before; and I could imagine nothing in our intercourse that should justify formality of **registration**.
>
> – *The Strange Case Of Dr. Jekyll And Mr. Hyde, Robert Louis Stevenson*

Introduction

Now that you have the site working pretty well, it is time to let others in on the game. In this lesson, you will learn how to create user registration and login pages.

11.1. The User-Registration Process

The user-registration process generally works something like this:

1. User registers by filling out sign-up form.
2. System sends user email to confirm that they really want to register.
3. User clicks link in email confirming their registration.
4. Database is updated and user is redirected to a login page.
5. User logs in and is redirected to the home page, a profile page, or some other page.

But that's not all there is to user authentication. Additional features include:

- Account management.
- Password resetting.
- Managing failed login attempts.
- Remember-me checkbox, so user doesn't have to log in every time.

Additionally, it's common for websites today to allow users to authenticate using Google, Facebook, LinkedIn, or some other social account they already have.

As you can imagine, building all this on your own would require a lot of work. Luckily, there is a free library called `django-allauth`[71] that makes adding user authentication to your website much easier.

In this lesson, through a series of exercises, you will add many features of the user authentication process to the Django Jokes website.

71. `https://github.com/pennersr/django-allauth`

Exercise 41: Getting Started with django-allauth

60 to 90 minutes

1. Install django-allauth:

```
(.venv) …/projects/djangojokes.com> pip install django-allauth
```

2. In djangojokes/settings.py:

   A. Add the following highlighted apps to INSTALLED_APPS:

```
INSTALLED_APPS = [
    # Built-in Django apps
    …
    'django.contrib.messages',
    'django.contrib.sites',
    'django.contrib.staticfiles',

    # Third-party
    'crispy_forms',
    'allauth',
    'allauth.account',
    'allauth.socialaccount',

    # Local apps
    …
]
```

   B. Set SITE_ID to 1 immediately below INSTALLED_APPS:[72]

```
SITE_ID = 1
```

72. See https://github.com/pennersr/django-allauth/issues/57 if you're curious why django-allauth requires django.contrib.sites.

C. Set AUTHENTICATION_BACKENDS:

```
AUTHENTICATION_BACKENDS = (
    # Needed to login by username in Django admin, even w/o `allauth`
    'django.contrib.auth.backends.ModelBackend',

    # `allauth`-specific auth methods, such as login by e-mail
    'allauth.account.auth_backends.AuthenticationBackend',
)
```

To keep authentication settings grouped together, a good place to set this is right above the AUTH_PASSWORD_VALIDATORS setting.

3. Open djangojokes/urls.py for editing. Remember that this is the project's root URLConf file. It references other URLConf files using include() from django.urls. Add this URL pattern to include the allauth URLConf:

```
path('account/', include('allauth.urls'))
```

Add some comments to categorize the URL patterns. The file should now look like this:

Exercise Code 41.1: djangojokes/urls.py

```
1.  from django.contrib import admin
2.  from django.urls import path, include
3.  
4.  urlpatterns = [
5.      # Admin
6.      path('admin/doc/', include('django.contrib.admindocs.urls')),
7.      path('admin/', admin.site.urls),
8.  
9.      # User Management
10.     path('account/', include('allauth.urls')),
11. 
12.     # Local Apps
13.     path('jobs/', include('jobs.urls')),
14.     path('jokes/', include('jokes.urls')),
15.     path('', include('pages.urls')),
16. ]
```

4. The django-allauth apps include models, so you need to migrate. As the migrations files are already created and included when you install django-allauth, you do not need to run

makemigrations, but you do need to run migrate. Run it now. You should see the following output:

```
(.venv) …/projects/djangojokes.com> python manage.py migrate
Operations to perform:
  Apply all migrations: account, admin, auth, contenttypes, jokes, sessions, sites,
 socialaccount, users
Running migrations:
  Applying account.0001_initial... OK
  Applying account.0002_email_max_length... OK
  Applying sites.0001_initial... OK
  Applying sites.0002_alter_domain_unique... OK
  Applying socialaccount.0001_initial... OK
  Applying socialaccount.0002_token_max_lengths... OK
  Applying socialaccount.0003_extra_data_default_dict... OK
```

❖ E41.1. Email

django-allauth needs to know how to send emails. It gets this information from the settings in settings.py. Add the following below the DATABASES setting:

```
# EMAIL
SENDGRID_API_KEY = os.environ.get('SENDGRID_API_KEY')
EMAIL_HOST = 'smtp.sendgrid.net'
EMAIL_PORT = 587
EMAIL_USE_TLS = True
EMAIL_HOST_USER = 'apikey'
EMAIL_HOST_PASSWORD = SENDGRID_API_KEY
DEFAULT_FROM_EMAIL = 'admin@example.com'
```

Notice that EMAIL_HOST_PASSWORD is set to SENDGRID_API_KEY, which is set to the value of the SENDGRID_API_KEY environment variable. That will work on production, but we had you take a different approach in development. (see page 223) Instead of creating an environment variable on your local machine, you created a local_settings.py file to hold your local settings. Open that file now and add the following on the line below your SENDGRID_API_KEY setting:

```
EMAIL_HOST_PASSWORD = SENDGRID_API_KEY
```

Now, your email password is set and django-allauth can get the information it needs to send emails.

❖ E41.2. Authentication Settings

In `settings.py`, add the following settings below the setting for `AUTH_USER_MODEL`:[73]

```
# AUTHENTICATION SETTINGS
AUTH_USER_MODEL = 'users.CustomUser'
LOGIN_URL = 'account_login'
LOGIN_REDIRECT_URL = 'pages:homepage'
```

And below that, add the following `django-allauth`-specific settings:[74]

```
## django-allauth settings
ACCOUNT_AUTHENTICATION_METHOD = 'email' # Default: 'username'
ACCOUNT_EMAIL_CONFIRMATION_EXPIRE_DAYS = 1 # Default: 3
ACCOUNT_EMAIL_REQUIRED = True # Default: False
ACCOUNT_EMAIL_VERIFICATION = 'mandatory' # Default: 'optional'
ACCOUNT_LOGIN_ATTEMPTS_LIMIT = 5 # Default: 5
ACCOUNT_LOGIN_ATTEMPTS_TIMEOUT = 300 # Default 300
ACCOUNT_LOGOUT_REDIRECT_URL = 'account_login' # Default: '/'
ACCOUNT_USERNAME_REQUIRED = False # Default: True
```

By default, `django-allauth` will require a username, but not an email address, and users will log in using a username/password combination. The settings you have set change this, so that an email address is required, but a username is not, and users will log in using an email/password combination.

Here is what each of these settings does:

1. `LOGIN_URL` – The URL or named URL pattern that Django redirects to when a a user must be logged in to access a page. Django's default value is `'/accounts/login/'` (a URL), but `django-allauth` includes a named URL pattern ("account_login") referencing its login path (`'/account/login/'` without the `'s'`).
2. `LOGIN_REDIRECT_URL` – The default URL or named URL pattern to redirect to after a successful login. You have set it to `'pages:homepage'` – the named URL pattern for the home page.
3. `ACCOUNT_AUTHENTICATION_METHOD` – Specifies how the user logs in: `'email'`, `'username'` (the default), or `'username_email'`. You have set it to `'email'`.

73. These settings are not specific to `django-allauth`, but it does make use of them.
74. See `https://django-allauth.readthedocs.io/en/latest/configuration.html` for documentation on all `django-allauth` settings.

4. ACCOUNT_EMAIL_CONFIRMATION_EXPIRE_DAYS – When a user registers, they will be sent an email with a confirmation link. This setting determines how many days that link will be valid. you have set it to 1.

5. ACCOUNT_EMAIL_REQUIRED – Indicates whether an email address is required at registration. The default is False. You have changed this to True.

6. ACCOUNT_EMAIL_VERIFICATION – Indicates whether the user is required to verify their email address. Possible values are:

   A. 'optional' (the default) – The user is sent a verification email, but is not required to verify.

   B. 'mandatory' – The user is sent a verification email and cannot log in until they have clicked the link. ACCOUNT_EMAIL_REQUIRED must be True.

   C. 'none' – The user is not sent a verification email.

   You have set it to 'mandatory'.

7. ACCOUNT_LOGIN_ATTEMPTS_LIMIT (default: 5) and ACCOUNT_LOGIN_ATTEMPTS_TIMEOUT (default: 300) – A user has ACCOUNT_LOGIN_ATTEMPTS_LIMIT tries to log in before their account is locked for ACCOUNT_LOGIN_ATTEMPTS_TIMEOUT seconds. You have used the defaults.

8. ACCOUNT_LOGOUT_REDIRECT_URL – The URL (or named URL pattern) to redirect to when the user logs out. The default is '/'. You have changed it to 'account_login', which is the named URL pattern used by django-allauth for the login view.

9. ACCOUNT_USERNAME_REQUIRED – Whether a username is required at sign up. The default is True. When set to False, the username will be derived from the email address or the first_name field if it's not empty. You have set it to False.

❖ E41.3. Default django-allauth Pages

The default registration and login URLs for django-allauth are:

- Registration: http://127.0.0.1:8000/account/signup/
- Login: http://127.0.0.1:8000/account/login/

These pages aren't pretty, but don't worry, you'll fix that. First, let's give them a try:

1. Start up the server.
2. Log in to Django admin at http://127.0.0.1:8000/admin/.

3. Notice the new **ACCOUNTS** section. Click on **Email addresses**. This is the model used by `django-allauth` to keep a record of verified email addresses. Since no emails have yet been verified, there are no records.
4. Log out of Django admin:

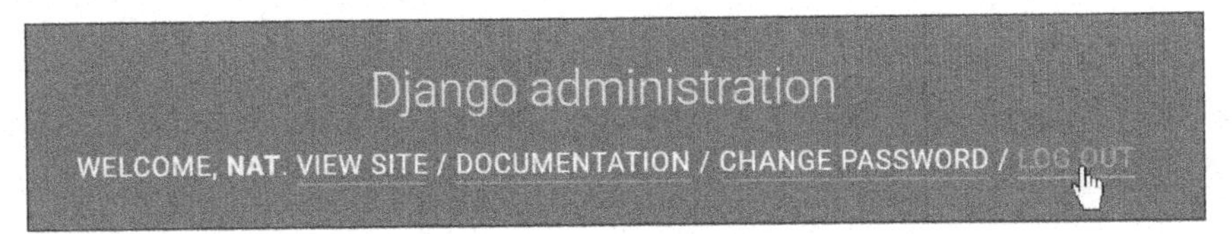

Don't click on the **Log in again** link, as it will take you to Django admin's login form, which is not what you want.

5. Visit `http://127.0.0.1:8000/account/login/` and sign in with your superuser account:

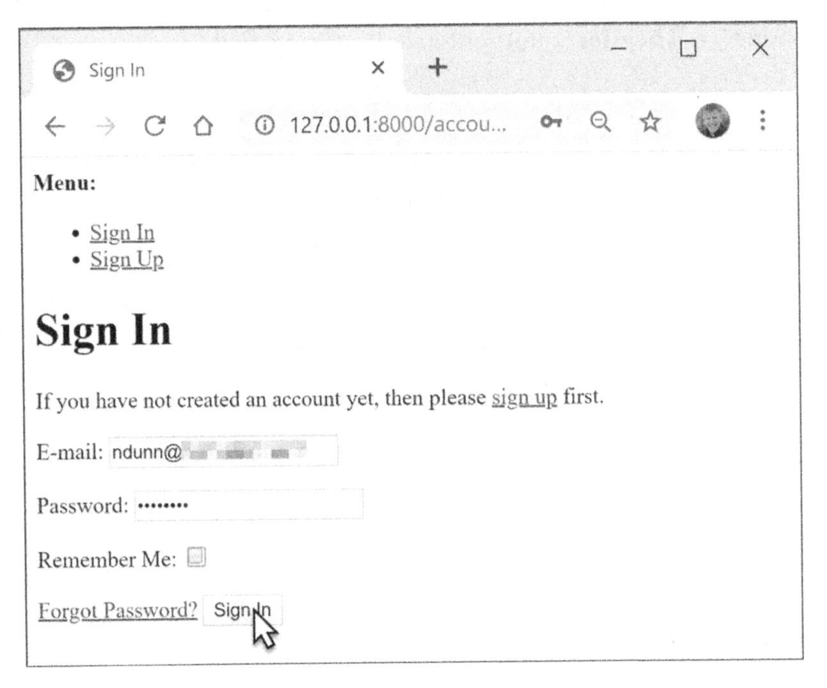

6. Because `django-allauth` has not had a chance to verify your account, you will get a page like this one:

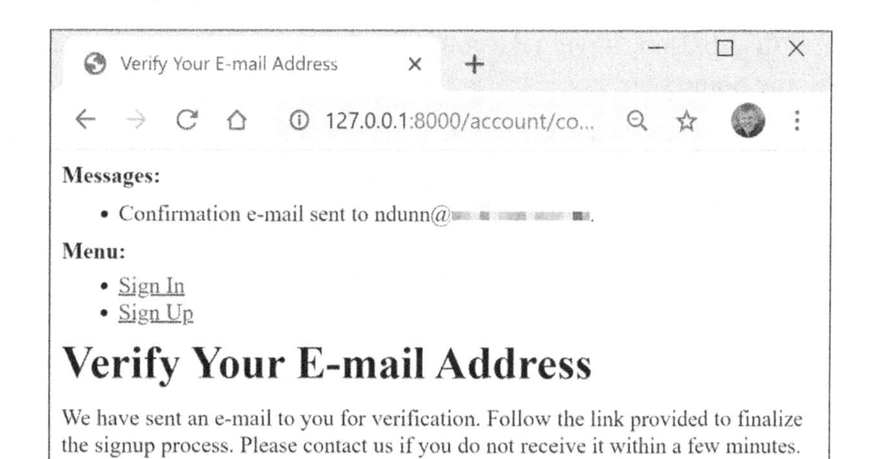

Check your email. You should have received an email like this one:

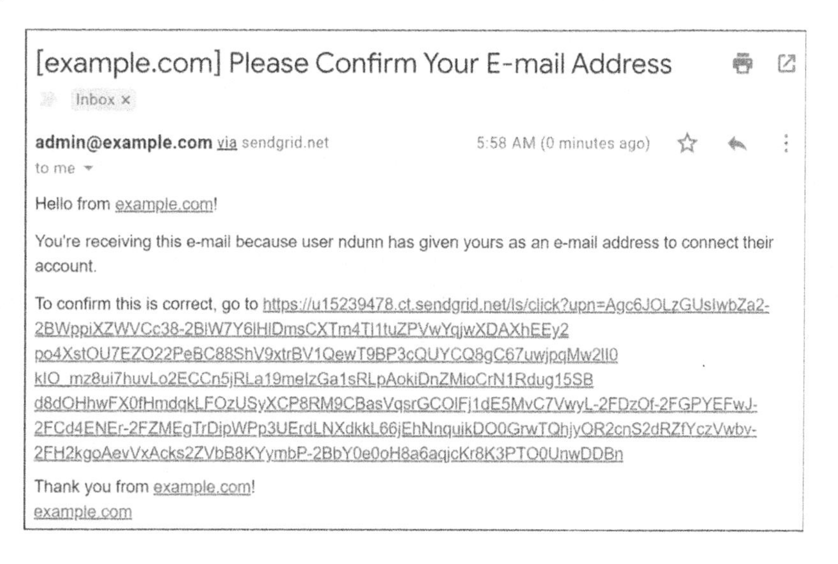

7. Click the link. It will take you to a page like this one:

8. Click the **Confirm** button. It will take you to the login page. Log in. This time you should be redirected to the home page.
9. Let's see how `django-allauth` knows that the email has been verified. Go back to Django admin and click on **Email Addresses**:

Notice that your email address has been verified:

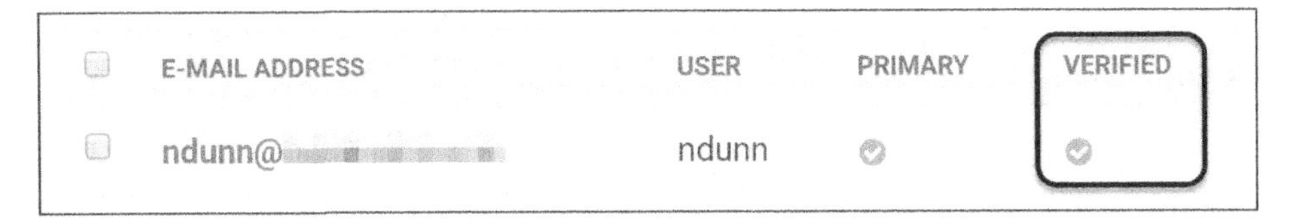

Register a New User

Register a new user. If you have a second browser, open that up so that you can stay logged in as a superuser in your main browser. For example, in Google Chrome, stay logged in to Django admin as a superuser while going through this part of the exercise using Safari, Edge, or Firefox.

1. **As the new user**: Visit `http://127.0.0.1:8000/account/signup/` and fill out the registration form:

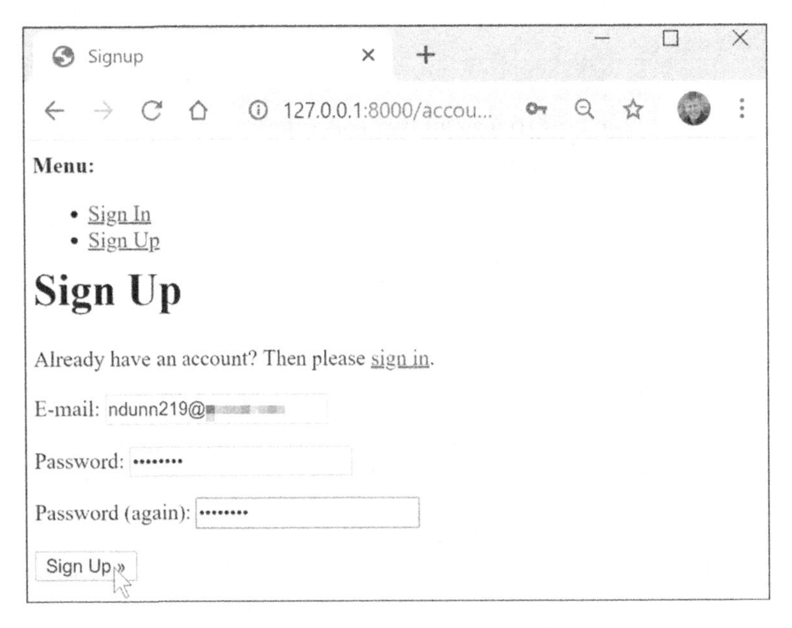

You will get the page asking you to verify your email address. Wait! Don't verify it yet.

2. **As the superuser in Django admin**: Click the **Users** link in the sidebar and notice how the new user's username is derived from the email address:

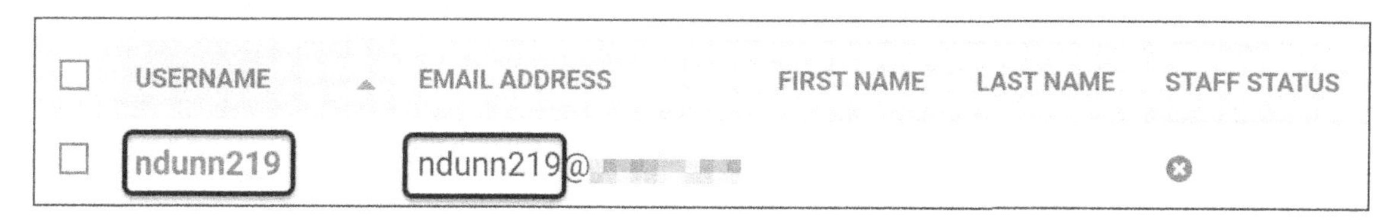

Click on the **Email Addresses** link in the sidebar. Notice that the new user's email address is there, but it has not been verified:

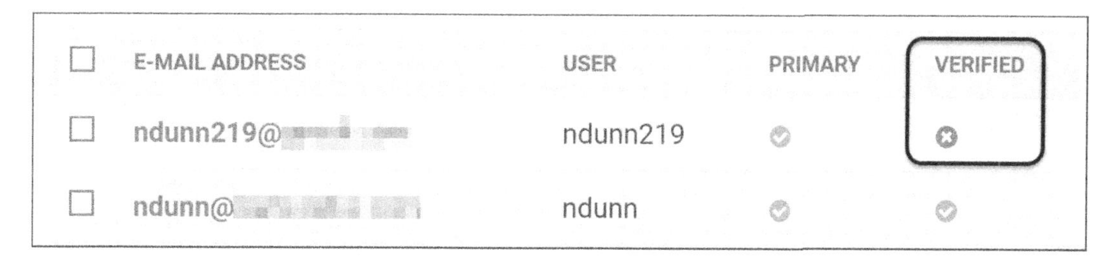

3. **As the new user**: Check your email and click the link to verify your email address. Click the **Confirm** button on the resulting page.

4. **As the superuser in Django admin**: Refresh the **Email Addresses** page. Notice that the new user's email has now been verified:

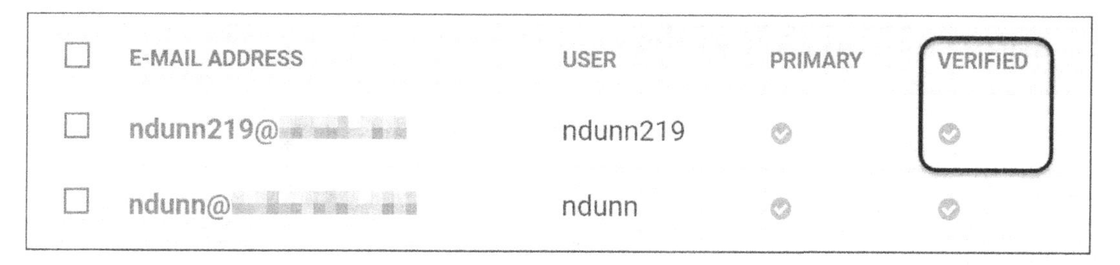

If you ever wanted to force a user to re-verify their email, you could click on their email address, uncheck **Verified**, and save:

Git Commit

Commit your code to Git.

11.2. `django-allauth` Templates

`django-allauth` includes default templates for all of its web pages and for all of the emails it sends. You can override all of these.

❖ 11.2.1. Web Page Templates

The most commonly used `django-allauth` web page templates are:

1. `account/signup.html` – The registration form.
2. `account/verification_sent.html` – The message shown after the user registers letting them know that they have been sent an email.
3. `account/email_confirm.html` – The page that shows up when the user clicks the link in the verification email. This page contains a form to submit to verify that the user really wants to register.
4. `account/login.html` – The login form.

5. `account/password_reset.html` – The password-reset form. This is for non-authenticated users who cannot remember their password.
6. `account/password_reset_done.html` – The message shown after a user submits the password-reset form.
7. `account/password_reset_key.html` – The password-change form a user gets after clicking the link in their email confirming they want to reset their password.
8. `account/password_reset_key_done.html` – The message shown after a user submits the password-change form.

All of the aforementioned templates are for non-authenticated users. The following template is for authenticated users who want to change their password:

9. `account/password_change.html`

❖ 11.2.2. The `user` Object

Django templates have access to the `user` object, which holds the authenticated user when there is one, and `AnonymousUser` when there is not. You can display `user` properties (e.g., the user's `username`) and you can also use `user` properties to decide what parts of the template to display.

Some of the `user` properties include:

1. `email`
2. `first_name`
3. `last_name`
4. `username`
5. `is_active`
6. `is_staff`
7. `is_superuser`
8. `is_authenticated` – `True` for authenticated users. `False` for `AnonymousUsers`.
9. `is_anonymous` – `True` for `AnonymousUsers`. `False` for authenticated users.

 Exercise 42: Making the Authentication Pages Crispy

20 to 30 minutes

Because you have set up Bootstrap and `django-crispy-forms` already, it won't take much effort to make each individual registration page look good; however, there are quite a few to create. So, let's get going.

1. Create an `account` folder within the `templates` folder.
2. Create all of the following templates within the `account` folder. You may copy these templates from `starter-code/user-registration/templates/account/`. Just be sure to review the code:

Exercise Code 42.1: templates/account/signup.html

```
1.  {% extends '_base.html' %}
2.  {% load crispy_forms_tags %}
3.
4.  {% block title %}Register{% endblock %}
5.
6.  {% block main %}
7.  <div class="card border-primary m-auto mb-3" style="max-width: 30rem">
8.    <div class="card-header text-center">Register</div>
9.    <div class="card-body">
10.     <form method="post" class="m-auto mb-2">
11.       {% csrf_token %}
12.       {{ form|crispy }}
13.       <button class="form-control btn btn-primary">REGISTER</button>
14.     </form>
15.   </div>
16.   <div class="card-footer">
17.     Already have an account? <a href="{% url 'account_login' %}">Log in</a>
18.   </div>
19. </div>
20. {% endblock %}
```

Exercise Code 42.2: templates/account/verification_sent.html

```
1.   {% extends '_base.html' %}
2.   {% load crispy_forms_tags %}
3.
4.   {% block title %}Verify Your Email Address{% endblock %}
5.
6.   {% block main %}
7.   <div class="card border-primary m-auto mb-3" style="max-width: 30rem">
8.     <div class="card-header text-center">Verify Your Email Address</div>
9.     <div class="card-body">
10.      <p class="card-text">We have sent an email to you for verification.
11.        Follow the link provided to finalize the registration process.</p>
12.    </div>
13.  </div>
14.  {% endblock %}
```

Exercise Code 42.3: templates/account/email_confirm.html

```
1.   {% extends '_base.html' %}
2.   {% load crispy_forms_tags %}
3.
4.   {% block title %}Confirm Registration{% endblock %}
5.
6.   {% block main %}
7.   <div class="card border-primary m-auto mb-3" style="max-width: 30rem">
8.     <div class="card-header text-center">Confirm Registration</div>
9.     <div class="card-body">
10.      {% if confirmation %}
11.        <p class="card-text text-center">Please confirm your registration.</p>
12.        <form method="post"
13.          action="{% url 'account_confirm_email' confirmation.key %}">
14.          {% csrf_token %}
15.          <button class="form-control btn btn-primary">CONFIRM</button>
16.        </form>
17.      {% else %}
18.        <p class="card-text">
19.          This confirmation link has expired or is invalid. Please try
20.          <a href="{% url 'account_email' %}">logging in again</a>.
21.          You will be sent a new confirmation link.
22.        </p>
23.      {% endif %}
24.    </div>
25.  </div>
26.  {% endblock %}
```

Exercise Code 42.4: templates/account/login.html

```
1.   {% extends '_base.html' %}
2.   {% load crispy_forms_tags %}
3.
4.   {% block title %}Log in{% endblock %}
5.
6.   {% block main %}
7.   <div class="card border-primary m-auto mb-3" style="max-width: 30rem">
8.     <div class="card-header text-center">Log in</div>
9.     <div class="card-body">
10.      <form method="post" class="m-auto">
11.        {% csrf_token %}
12.        {{ form|crispy }}
13.        <button class="form-control btn btn-primary">LOG IN</button>
14.      </form>
15.    </div>
16.    <div class="card-footer">
17.      <p>
18.        Need an account?
19.        <a href="{% url 'account_signup' %}">Register</a>.<br>
20.        Lost your password?
21.        <a href="{% url 'account_reset_password' %}">Reset it</a>.
22.      </p>
23.    </div>
24.  </div>
25.  {% endblock %}
```

Exercise Code 42.5: templates/account/password_reset.html

```
1.   {% extends '_base.html' %}
2.   {% load crispy_forms_tags %}
3.
4.   {% block title %}Reset Password{% endblock %}
5.
6.   {% block main %}
7.   <div class="card border-primary m-auto mb-3" style="max-width: 30rem">
8.     <div class="card-header text-center">Reset Password</div>
9.     <div class="card-body">
10.      <form method="post" class="m-auto">
11.        {% csrf_token %}
12.        {{ form|crispy }}
13.        <button class="form-control btn btn-primary">RESET PASSWORD</button>
14.      </form>
15.    </div>
16.  </div>
17.  {% endblock %}
```

Exercise Code 42.6: templates/account/password_reset_done.html

```
1.   {% extends '_base.html' %}
2.   {% load crispy_forms_tags %}
3.
4.   {% block title %}Check Your Email{% endblock %}
5.
6.   {% block main %}
7.   <div class="card border-primary m-auto mb-3" style="max-width: 30rem">
8.     <div class="card-header text-center">Check Your Email</div>
9.     <div class="card-body">
10.      <p class="card-text text-center">
11.        Check your email for instructions on resetting your password.
12.      </p>
13.    </div>
14.  </div>
15.  {% endblock %}
```

Exercise Code 42.7: templates/account/password_reset_from_key.html

```
1.   {% extends '_base.html' %}
2.   {% load crispy_forms_tags %}
3.
4.   {% block title %}
5.     {% if token_fail %}
6.       Bad Token
7.     {% else %}
8.       Change Password
9.     {% endif %}
10.  {% endblock %}
11.
12.  {% block main %}
13.  <div class="card border-primary m-auto mb-3" style="max-width: 30rem">
14.    <div class="card-header text-center">
15.      {% if token_fail %}
16.        Bad Token
17.      {% else %}
18.        Change Password
19.      {% endif %}
20.    </div>
21.    <div class="card-body">
22.      {% if token_fail %}
23.        <p class="card-text">
24.          The password reset link was invalid, possibly because
25.          it has already been used. Please request a
26.          <a href="{% url 'account_reset_password' %}">new password reset</a>.
27.        </p>
28.      {% else %}
29.        <form method="post" class="m-auto">
30.          {% csrf_token %}
31.          {{ form|crispy }}
32.          <button class="form-control btn btn-primary">CHANGE PASSWORD</button>
33.        </form>
34.      {% endif %}
35.    </div>
36.  </div>
37.  {% endblock %}
```

Exercise Code 42.8: templates/account/password_reset_from_key_done.html

```
1.  {% extends '_base.html' %}
2.  {% load crispy_forms_tags %}
3.
4.  {% block title %}Password Changed{% endblock %}
5.
6.  {% block main %}
7.  <div class="card border-primary m-auto mb-3" style="max-width: 30rem">
8.    <div class="card-header text-center">Password Changed</div>
9.    <div class="card-body">
10.     <p class="card-text text-center">
11.       Your password has been changed.
12.       <a href="{% url 'account_login' %}">Log in</a>.
13.     </p>
14.   </div>
15. </div>
16. {% endblock %}
```

Notice that some of the templates have links to each other:

In `signup.html` and `password_reset_from_key_done.html`

```
<a href="{% url 'account_login' %}">Log in</a>
```

In `login.html`

```
<a href="{% url 'account_signup' %}">Register</a>
```

```
<a href="{% url 'account_reset_password' %}">Reset it</a>
```

These links use named URL patterns from `django-allauth`'s defined URL patterns.[75]

❖ E42.1. Try it Out

1. Log out by visiting `http://127.0.0.1:8000/account/logout/` and clicking the **Sign Out** button. Don't worry about how the sign-out form looks. You're going to build a different way of logging out soon.

75. `https://github.com/pennersr/django-allauth/blob/master/allauth/account/urls.py`

2. You should see a nice login form. Click on the **Register** link at the bottom of it. You should see a form like this one:

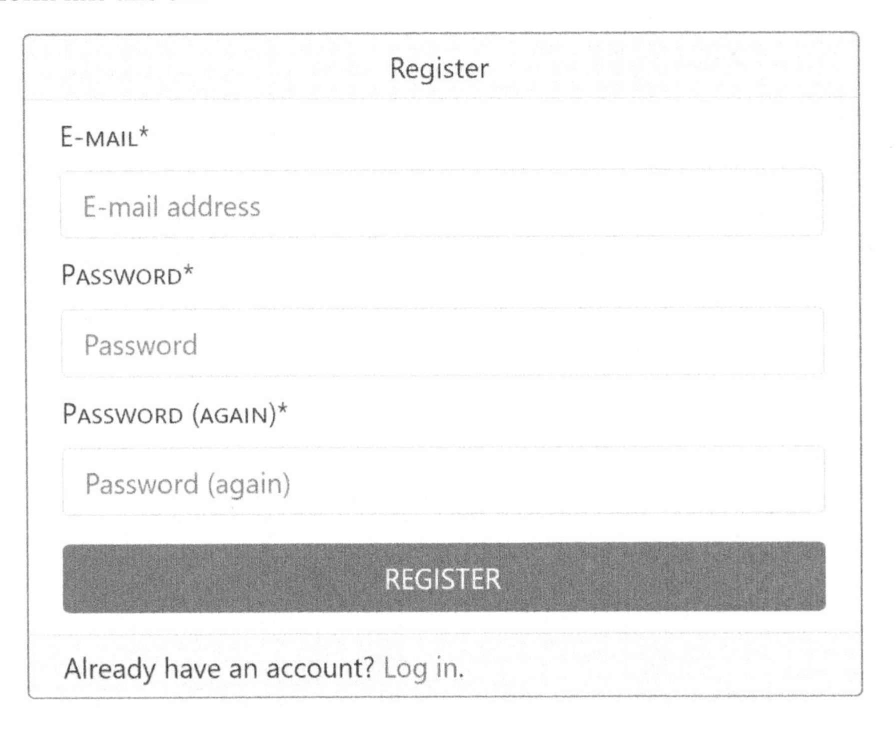

3. Fill out and submit the registration form. The resulting page lets you know to check your email:

Verify Your E-mail Address

We have sent an e-mail to you for verification. Follow the link provided to finalize the registration process.

4. Check your email and click the link in the email you received. You should get a message asking you to confirm your email:

5. Click on the **Confirm** button. That should take you back to the crispy login form:

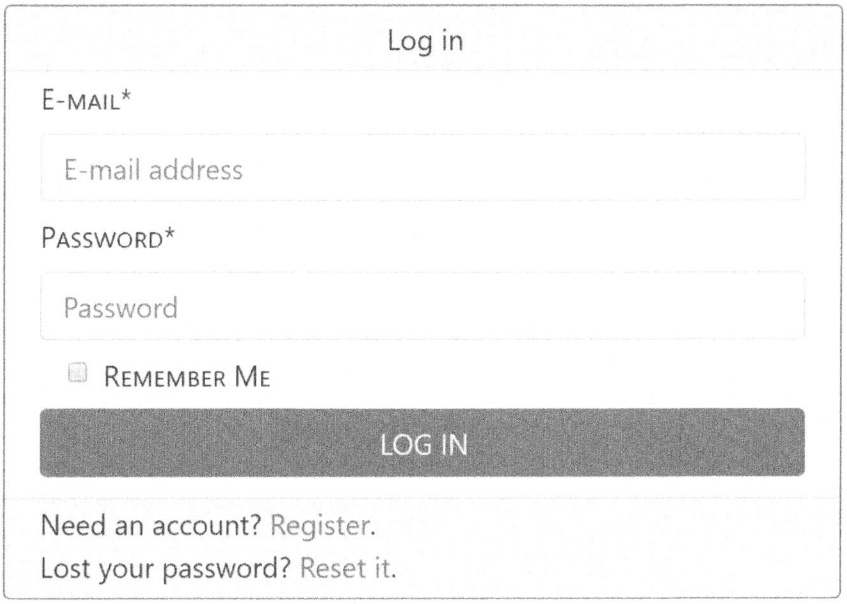

Log in

E-MAIL*

E-mail address

PASSWORD*

Password

REMEMBER ME

LOG IN

Need an account? Register.

Lost your password? Reset it.

6. Click on the **Reset it** link to reset your password. This takes you to the password-reset form:

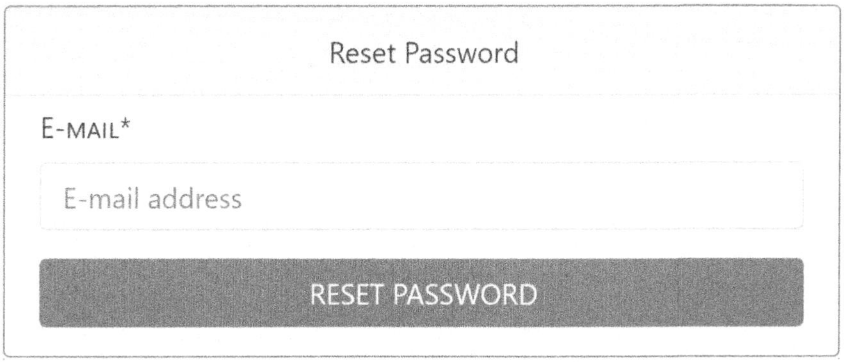

Reset Password

E-MAIL*

E-mail address

RESET PASSWORD

7. Enter your email and submit. This takes you to the password-reset-done page:

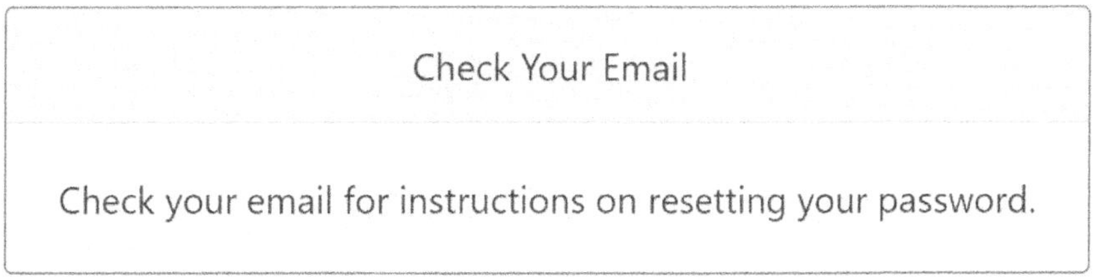

Check Your Email

Check your email for instructions on resetting your password.

8. You should receive an email similar to this one:

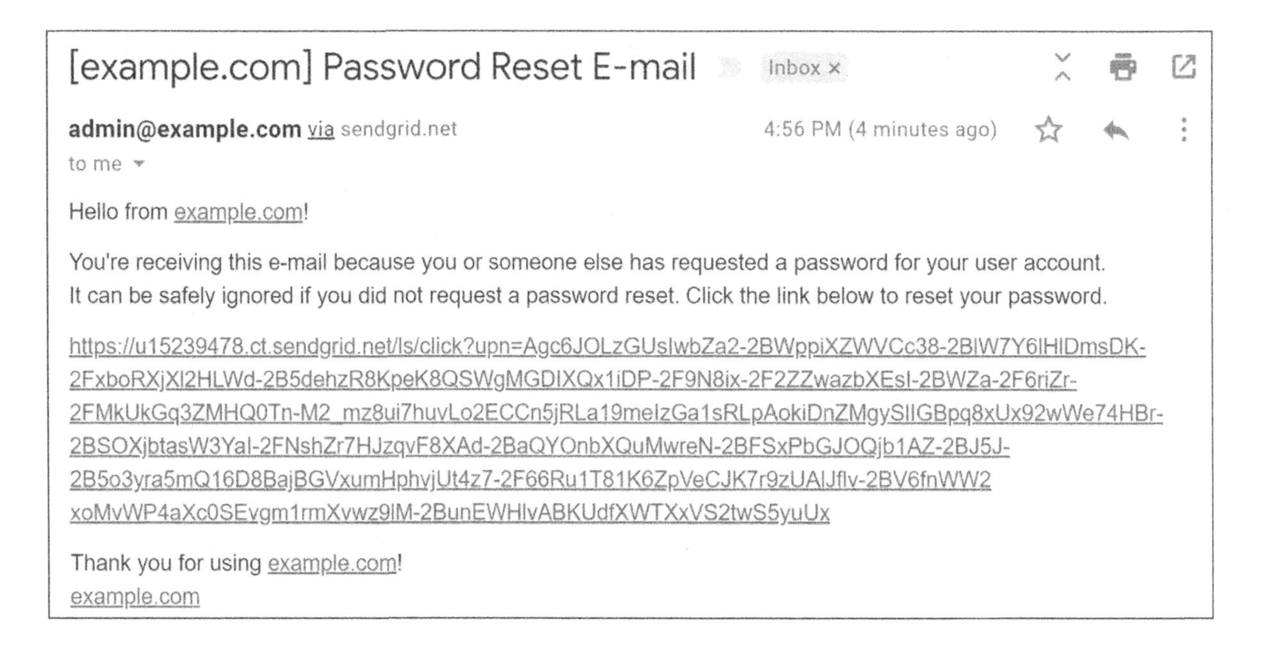

9. Click the link in the email. It should take you to a page with a form like this one:

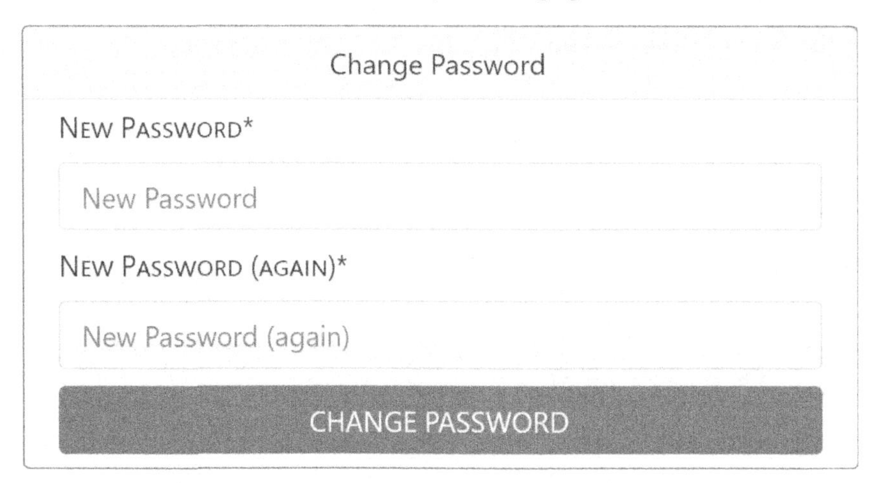

10. Enter your new password twice and submit. You should get a message like this one:

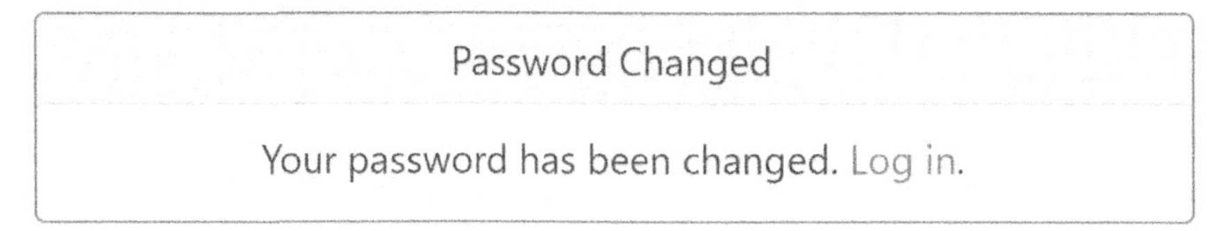

You can now click on the **Log in** link and log in with your new password.

11. The reset-password link sent by email will only work once. If you return to your email and click on the link again, it will take you to a page with this message:

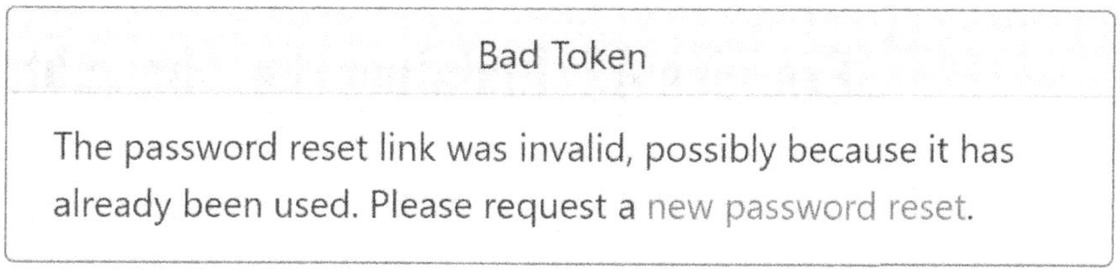

Bad Token

The password reset link was invalid, possibly because it has already been used. Please request a new password reset.

Git Commit

Commit your code to Git.

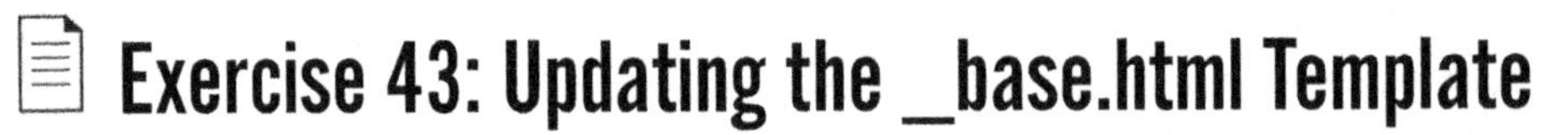

Exercise 43: Updating the _base.html Template

30 to 45 minutes

Time to make some updates to the `_base.html` template. See if you can do the following on your own before checking the solution:

1. Make the **Log in** link work. The named URL pattern is “account_login”.
2. Add a **Sign up** nav item that links to the registration page. The named URL pattern is “account_signup”.
3. Change the **Log out** link to a form. **Why?** `GET` requests should not change the state of the application. As logging out does change the state, it should be done using a `POST` request, which requires a form. Change the link from:

   ```
   <a class="dropdown-item" href="#">Log out</a>
   ```

   … to a form using the following code:

   ```
   <form method="post" action="{% url 'account_logout' %}">
     {% csrf_token %}
     <button class="btn dropdown-item">Log out</button>
   </form>
   ```

4. Use an if-else condition (see page 145) to show the **Log in** and **Sign up** nav items if the user **is not** logged in and show the nav item with the dropdown if the user **is** logged in. You should base this on the value of `user.is_authenticated`, which is `True` if the user is logged in and `False` otherwise.
5. Change the **Contact** link in the footer to an **Admin** link that leads to Django admin (`/admin/`). Make it so this link only shows up if `user.is_staff` is `True`.

❖ E43.1. Try it Out

1. Log into the site with your superuser account. The page should have a header with a dropdown navigation:

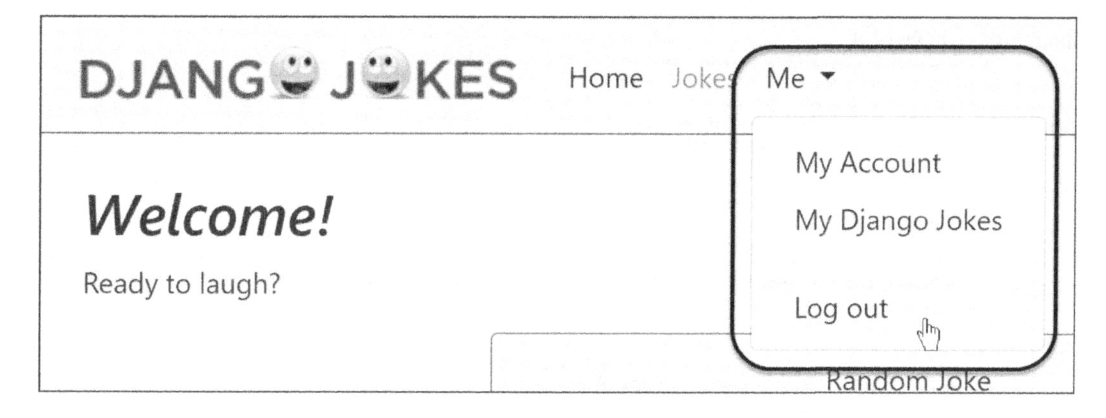

...and a footer with an `Admin` link:

2. Click on the **Admin** link to make sure it takes you to Django admin.
3. Return to the home page and click on **Log out**. It should take you to the Login page, which should include **Log in** and **Sign up** links in the header:

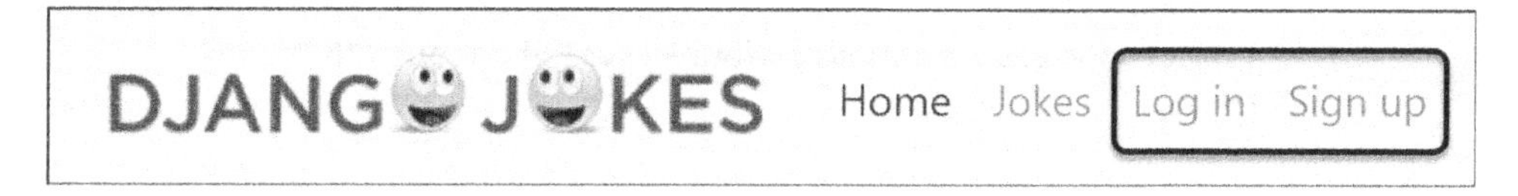

And the `Admin` link **should not** appear in the footer:

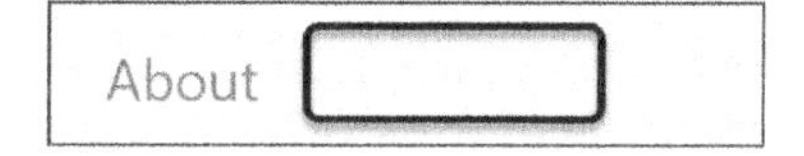

4. Log in as an account that is not staff. The dropdown navigation should show up in the header, but the `Admin` link **should not** show up in the footer.

Our solution follows:

Solution: templates/_base.html

```
-------Lines 1 through 36 Omitted-------
37.         <li class="nav-item">
38.           <a class="nav-link" href="{% url 'account_login' %}">Log in</a>
39.         </li>
40.         <li class="nav-item">
41.           <a class="nav-link" href="{% url 'account_signup' %}">Sign up</a>
42.         </li>
43.       {% else %}
44.         <li class="nav-item dropdown">
45.           <a class="nav-link dropdown-toggle" href="#" id="navbarDropdown"
46.             role="button" data-toggle="dropdown" aria-haspopup="true"
47.             aria-expanded="false">
48.             Me
49.           </a>
50.           <div class="dropdown-menu" aria-labelledby="navbarDropdown">
51.             <a class="dropdown-item" href="#">My Account</a>
52.             <a class="dropdown-item" href="#">My Django Jokes</a>
53.             <div class="dropdown-divider"></div>
54.             <form method="post" action="{% url 'account_logout' %}">
55.               {% csrf_token %}
56.               <button class="btn dropdown-item">Log out</button>
57.             </form>
58.           </div>
59.         </li>
60.       {% endif %}
-------Lines 61 through 79 Omitted-------
80.         <li class="nav-item">
81.           <a class="nav-link" href="{% url 'pages:about-us' %} ">About</a>
82.         </li>
83.         {% if user.is_staff %}
84.           <li class="nav-item">
85.             <a class="nav-link" href="/admin/">Admin</a>
86.           </li>
87.         {% endif %}
-------Lines 88 through 97 Omitted-------
```

Git Commit

Commit your code to Git.

11.3. Email Templates

As you have seen, `django-allauth` sends transactional emails when users register or reset their password. Just as you have overridden the page templates, you can override the email templates by creating your own. Following is a list of the registration confirmation and password reset email templates:

Registration Confirmation Emails

1. `templates/account/email/email_confirmation_signup_subject.txt` – The subject of the email.
2. `templates/account/email/email_confirmation_signup_message.txt` – The body of the text version of the email.
3. `templates/account/email/email_confirmation_signup_message.html` – The body of the HTML version of the email.

Password Reset Emails

1. `templates/account/email/password_reset_key_subject.txt` – The subject of the email.
2. `templates/account/email/password_reset_key_message.txt` – The body of the text version of the email.
3. `templates/account/email/password_reset_key_message.html` – The body of the HTML version of the email.

By default, `django-allauth` will only send a text version of the email, which all email clients will be able to read. If you include an HTML template as well, both the text and HTML versions will be sent. Almost all email clients today will choose to display the HTML version.

Here are some basic email templates that you can use as is or as starting points. You may copy these templates from `starter-code/user-registration/templates/account/`. Just be sure to review the content:

Demo 11.1: account/email/email_confirmation_signup_subject.txt

```
1.    Please Confirm Your Email Address
```

Demo 11.2: account/email/email_confirmation_signup_message.txt

```
1.    Hello!
2.
3.    You are receiving this email because someone (hopefully you) has registered you
              for {{ current_site.name }} using this email address.
4.
5.    To confirm this is correct, go to {{ activate_url }}
6.
7.    Thank you!
```

Demo 11.3: account/email/email_confirmation_signup_subject.html

```
1.    <p>Hello!</p>
2.    <p>You are receiving this email because someone (hopefully you) has registered
3.      you for {{ current_site.name }} using this email address.</p>
4.    <p><a href="{{ activate_url }}">Click here</a> to confirm this is correct.</p>
5.    <p>Thank you!</p>
```

Demo 11.4: account/email/password_reset_key_subject.txt

```
1.    Password Reset Email
```

Demo 11.5: account/email/password_reset_key_message.txt

```
1.    Hello,
2.
3.    Someone (hopefully you) requested a password reset for your {{ current_site.name
              }} account.
4.
5.    If you do not want to reset your password, you can safely ignore this email.
6.
7.    Click the link below to reset your password:
8.
9.    {{ password_reset_url }}
10.
11.   Thank you for using {{ current_site.name }}!
```

Demo 11.6: account/email/password_reset_key_message.html

```
1.    <p>Hello,</p>
2.    <p>Someone (hopefully you) requested a password reset for your
3.      {{ current_site.name }} account.</p>
4.    <p>If you do not want to reset your password, you can safely ignore
5.      this email.</p>
6.    <p><a href="{{ password_reset_url }}">Click here</a> to reset your password:</p>
7.    <p>Thank you for using {{ current_site.name }}!</p>
```

Internationalization

`django-allauth` page and email templates take advantage of Django's internationalization features. The templates we have provided in this lesson do not.

See `https://docs.djangoproject.com/en/3.1/topics/i18n/` to learn more about internationalization.

Exercise 44: Custom User Registration

10 to 15 minutes

If you need to collect additional information in the registration form (e.g., the user's first and last name), you can create a custom `SignupForm` class.

1. In the `users` folder, create a `forms.py` file with the following code:

Exercise Code 44.1: users/forms.py

```
1.   from django import forms
2.
3.   class SignupForm(forms.Form):
4.       first_name = forms.CharField(max_length=50, required=False)
5.       last_name = forms.CharField(max_length=50, required=False)
6.
7.       def signup(self, request, user):
8.           user.first_name = self.cleaned_data['first_name']
9.           user.last_name = self.cleaned_data['last_name']
10.          user.save()
```

2. You now have to let `django-allauth` know to use this custom form. You do that by adding the following setting in `djangojokes/settings.py`:

```
ACCOUNT_SIGNUP_FORM_CLASS = 'users.forms.SignupForm'
```

You should add that directly below the other `django-allauth` settings.

❖ E44.1. Try it Out

If you are logged in, log out of the Django Jokes site, and then click the **Sign up** link in the header. Your form should now include fields for first and last name:

Register

E-MAIL*

E-mail address

FIRST NAME

LAST NAME

PASSWORD*

Password

PASSWORD (AGAIN)*

Password (again)

REGISTER

Already have an account? Log in

Git Commit

Commit your code to Git.

Exercise 45: Creating a My Account Page

30 to 45 minutes

In this exercise, you will create a My Account page and password-change page. You'll start with the password-change page.

❖ E45.1. Password Change Page

Password-change pages are managed by `django-auth`. All you need to do is override the template.

1. Create a new `password_change.html` file in the `templates` folder with the following content:[76]

Exercise Code 45.1: templates/account/password_change.html

```
1.  {% extends '_base.html' %}
2.  {% load crispy_forms_tags %}
3.
4.  {% block title %}Change Password{% endblock title %}
5.
6.  {% block main %}
7.  <div class="card border-primary m-auto mb-3" style="max-width: 30rem">
8.    <div class="card-header text-center">Change Password</div>
9.    <div class="card-body">
10.     <form method="post" action="{% url 'account_change_password' %}">
11.       {% csrf_token %}
12.       {{ form|crispy }}
13.       <button class="form-control btn btn-primary">CHANGE PASSWORD</button>
14.     </form>
15.   </div>
16. </div>
17.
18. {% endblock %}
```

Code Explanation

Log in to the site if you are not logged in already. Then, visit `http://127.0.0.1:8000/account/password/change/` to check out the form. It should look like this:

76. **Don't want to type?** Copy from `starter-code/user-registration/templates/account/password_change.html`.

Change Password

CURRENT PASSWORD*

Current Password

NEW PASSWORD*

New Password

NEW PASSWORD (AGAIN)*

New Password (again)

CHANGE PASSWORD

If you visit that page when you're not logged in, you will be redirected to `http://127.0.0.1:8000/account/login/`**`?next=/account/password/change/`**. Notice the `next` parameter on the querystring. That makes it so that as soon as you log in, you will be directed to `/account/password/change/`.

Fill out the form and submit. It should submit without errors. If it does, it worked, but it won't give you any notification that your password was changed. You'll fix that soon.

❖ E45.2. My Account Page

My Account pages (often called *profile pages*) are not managed by `django-allauth`. So, you'll have to create the form, view, and URLConf yourself. You are also going to add a dob (**d**ate **o**f **b**irth) field to the model.

The Model

1. Open `users/models.py` and add the following highlighted changes:[77]

Exercise Code 45.2: users/models.py

```
1.  from django.contrib.auth.models import AbstractUser
2.  from django.db import models
3.  from django.urls import reverse
4.
5.  class CustomUser(AbstractUser):
6.      dob = models.DateField(
7.          verbose_name="Date of Birth", null=True, blank=True
8.      )
9.
10.     def get_absolute_url(self):
11.         return reverse('my-account')
```

Things to notice:

A. You have added an optional `dob` field.

B. You have imported `reverse` from `django.urls` and used it in the `get_absolute_url()` method to return the page to redirect to after a user is updated.

2. Because the model has changed, you need to make and run the migrations:

```
(.venv) …/projects/djangojokes.com> python manage.py makemigrations
(.venv) …/projects/djangojokes.com> python manage.py migrate
```

The Form

`django.contrib.auth.forms` includes a `UserChangeForm` class that is used to modify `user` objects from the user model.

77. **Don't want to type?** Copy from `starter-code/user-registration/users_models.py`.

Open users/forms.py and add the following highlighted changes:[78]

Exercise Code 45.3: users/forms.py

```
1.  from datetime import datetime
2.
3.  from django import forms
4.  from django.contrib.auth import get_user_model
5.  from django.contrib.auth.forms import UserChangeForm
6.
7.
8.  BIRTH_YEAR_CHOICES = range(1915, datetime.now().year)
9.
10. class SignupForm(forms.Form):
11.     first_name = forms.CharField(max_length=50, required=False)
12.     last_name = forms.CharField(max_length=50, required=False)
13.
14.     def signup(self, request, user):
15.         user.first_name = self.cleaned_data['first_name']
16.         user.last_name = self.cleaned_data['last_name']
17.         user.save()
18.
19. class CustomUserChangeForm(UserChangeForm):
20.     password = None
21.
22.     class Meta:
23.         model = get_user_model()
24.         fields = ('email', 'username', 'first_name', 'last_name', 'dob')
25.         widgets = {
26.             'dob': forms.SelectDateWidget(
27.                 attrs={
28.                     'style': 'width: 31%; display: inline-block; margin: 0 1%'
29.                 },
30.                 years = BIRTH_YEAR_CHOICES
31.             )
32.         }
```

Things to notice:

1. You inherit from UserChangeForm to create your CustomUserChangeForm class. Note that UserChangeForm is imported towards the top of the file.

78. **Don't want to type?** Copy from starter-code/user-registration/users_forms_2.py.

2. You set password to None, because passwords are stored in an encrypted format. That's why you created a separate change-password form.

3. In the Meta inner class:

    A. You use get_user_model() as the model. Note that get_user_model is imported towards the top of the file.

    B. You set the fields that you want in the form.

    C. You specify that you want to use SelectDateWidget for the dob field. Note that before the class definition, BIRTH_YEAR_CHOICES is set to hold a range of years. You assign BIRTH_YEAR_CHOICES to years in the SelectDateWidget.

The View

Open users/views.py and replace the existing content with the following code:[79]

Exercise Code 45.4: users/views.py

```
1.  from django.contrib.auth import get_user_model
2.  from django.views.generic import UpdateView
3.
4.  from .forms import CustomUserChangeForm
5.
6.  class MyAccountPageView(UpdateView):
7.      model = get_user_model()
8.      form_class = CustomUserChangeForm
9.      template_name = 'account/my_account.html'
10.
11.     def get_object(self):
12.         return self.request.user
```

Things to notice:

1. The MyAccountPageView inherits from UpdateView.

2. You set model to get_user_model().

3. You set form_class to CustomUserChangeForm, which you just created.

4. You set template_name to 'account/my_account.html', which you will create shortly.

79. **Don't want to type?** Copy from starter-code/user-registration/users_views.py.

5. You override the superclass's `get_object()` method:

```
def get_object(self):
return self.request.user
```

Why do you need to override the superclass's `get_object()` method? Consider for a moment the view you use to update jokes:

```
class JokeUpdateView(UpdateView):
model = Joke
form_class = JokeForm
```

How does this view know which joke to update? It gets it from the URL pattern in the URLConf:

```
path('<slug>/update/', JokeUpdateView.as_view(), name='update')
```

Class views for single objects (e.g., `DetailView`, `UpdateView`, `DeleteView`) get their object using `self.kwargs.get('pk')` or `self.kwargs.get('slug')`. If neither "pk" nor "slug" is found and the `queryset` attribute is not set explicitly, an exception will be raised. Here is a simplified version of the `get_object()` method used by these views:[80]

80. See `django/views/generic/detail.py` for the full `get_object()` method.

```
def get_object(self):

    # Try looking up by primary key.
    pk = self.kwargs.get('pk')
    if pk is not None:
        queryset = queryset.filter(pk=pk)

    # Next, try looking up by slug.
    slug = self.kwargs.get('slug')
    if slug is not None:
        queryset = queryset.filter(slug=slug)

    # If none of those are defined, it's an error.
    if pk is None and slug is None:
        raise AttributeError("Missing pk or slug.")

    try:
        # Get the single item from the filtered queryset
        obj = queryset.get()
    except queryset.model.DoesNotExist:
        raise Http404("No object found matching the query")
    return obj
```

`MyAccountPageView` inherits from `UpdateView`, but you are not going to pass `pk` or `slug` on the URL, because the view will be used to update the user who is currently logged in, and that user is held in `self.request.user`. That is why you override `get_object()` to immediately return `self.request.user`.

The URLConf

Create a new `urls.py` file in the `users` folder, and enter the following code:

Exercise Code 45.5: users/urls.py

```
1.  from django.urls import path
2.
3.  from .views import MyAccountPageView
4.
5.  urlpatterns = [
6.      path('my-account/', MyAccountPageView.as_view(), name='my-account'),
7.  ]
```

Include App URLConf in Main URLConf

Next, you need to let your main URLConf know to hand off some paths to the users URLConf. Open `djangojokes/urls.py`. Immediately above `path('account/', include('allauth.urls')),`, add the following path:

```
path('account/', include('users.urls')),
```

Now, for paths that begin with `/account/`, Django will first check `users.urls` for matching paths. If it doesn't find a match there, it will check `allauth.urls`.

The Template

Create a new `my_account.html` file in `templates/account`, and enter the following code:[81]

Exercise Code 45.6: templates/account/my_account.html

```
1.   {% extends '_base.html' %}
2.   {% load crispy_forms_tags %}
3.
4.   {% block title %}My Account{% endblock title %}
5.
6.   {% block main %}
7.   <div class="card border-primary m-auto mb-3" style="max-width: 30rem">
8.     <div class="card-header text-center">My Account</div>
9.     <div class="card-body">
10.      <form method="post" class="m-auto">
11.        {% csrf_token %}
12.        {{ form|crispy }}
13.        <button class="form-control btn btn-primary">UPDATE</button>
14.      </form>
15.    </div>
16.    <div class="card-footer text-center">
17.      <p><a href="{% url 'account_change_password' %}">Change Password</a></p>
18.    </div>
19.  </div>
20.  {% endblock %}
```

The Base Template

Open `templates/_base.html` and change the **My Account** link as follows:

```
<a class="dropdown-item" href="{% url 'my-account' %}">
  My Account
</a>
```

❖ E45.3. Try It Out

1. Start up the server if it's not already running.
2. Make sure you are logged in to the site.

81. **Don't want to type?** Copy from `starter-code/user-registration/templates/account/my_account.html`.

3. From the **Me** dropdown menu, select **My Account**. It should lead to a page with a form like this one:

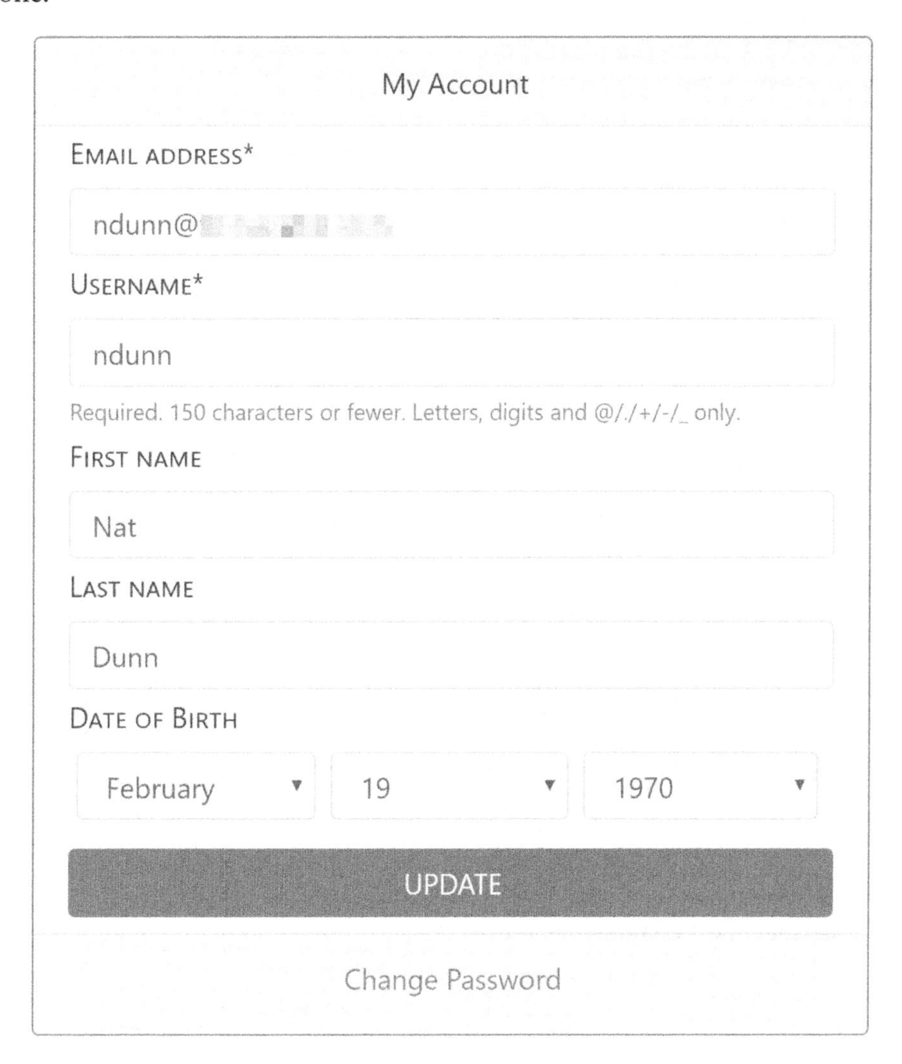

4. Add your date of birth and submit.
5. Click the **Change Password** link. It should take you to the page with the change-password form.

❖ E45.4. Password Change Page Revisited

Remember that the password-change form works, but it just gives you the form right back. It would be better if it redirected to the My Account page. To do this, you need to create your own `CustomPasswordChangeView` that inherits from `django.allauth`'s `PasswordChangeView`. The only thing you need to override is the `success_url` attribute. Open `users/views.py` and add the following highlighted code:

Exercise Code 45.7: users/views.py

```
1.  from django.contrib.auth import get_user_model
2.  from django.urls import reverse_lazy
3.  from django.views.generic import UpdateView
4.
5.  from allauth.account.views import PasswordChangeView
6.
7.  from .forms import CustomUserChangeForm
8.
9.  class CustomPasswordChangeView(PasswordChangeView):
10.     success_url = reverse_lazy('my-account')
    -------Lines 11 through 18 Omitted-------
```

Then, you have to add a path to the users URLConf, so that your custom view is used instead of `django.allauth`'s `PasswordChangeView`. Open `users/urls.py` and add the following highlighted code:

Exercise Code 45.8: users/urls.py

```
1.  from django.urls import path
2.
3.  from .views import CustomPasswordChangeView, MyAccountPageView
4.
5.  urlpatterns = [
6.      path(
7.          "password/change/", CustomPasswordChangeView.as_view(),
8.          name="account_change_password"
9.      ),
10.     path('my-account/', MyAccountPageView.as_view(), name='my-account'),
11. ]
```

Now, try updating your password again. This time it should redirect to the My Account page.

Git Commit

Commit your code to Git.

Exercise 46: Associating Users with Jokes

20 to 30 minutes

In this exercise, you will:

1. Add a `user` field to the `Joke` model.
2. Modify `CreateView` so that when jokes are created, the logged-in user is automatically assigned to `joke.user`.
3. Update the `joke-detail.html` template to show which user created the joke.

❖ E46.1. The Model

1. Open `jokes/models.py` in your editor.
2. Import `settings` from `django.conf`:

```
from django.conf import settings
```

3. Add a `user` field to the model:

```
user = models.ForeignKey(
    settings.AUTH_USER_MODEL, on_delete=models.PROTECT
)
```

   You use `models.PROTECT` for `on_delete` so that you can only delete users who haven't created any jokes. If you were to use `models.CASCADE`, when a user was deleted, all their jokes would also be deleted.

These changes are highlighted in the following code:

```
from django.conf import settings
from django.db import models
from django.urls import reverse

from common.utils.text import unique_slug

class Joke(models.Model):
    question = models.TextField(max_length=200)
    answer = models.TextField(max_length=100)
    user = models.ForeignKey(
        settings.AUTH_USER_MODEL, on_delete=models.PROTECT
    )
    …
```

1. You've changed the model, so create migrations:

   ```
   (.venv) …/projects/djangojokes.com> python manage.py makemigrations
   ```

   You will have to decide what to do with existing jokes that don't have a user associated with them: Select `1` to provide a one-off default and use `1` as the default. That will make the first user you entered the user for all the existing jokes.

   If user_id isn't 1

   On the off chance that you have no user with the `user_id` of `1`, you can use the shell to find out the user_id of your first user like this:

   ```
   (.venv) …/projects/djangojokes.com> python manage.py shell
   >>> from django.contrib.auth import get_user_model
   >>> user = get_user_model()
   >>> first_user = user.objects.first()
   >>> first_user.id
   1
   ```

   Then, make migrations again using that number as your default value.

2. Run migrations:

   ```
   (.venv) …/projects/djangojokes.com> python manage.py migrate
   ```

❖ E46.2. The View

When you created the Job Application form view (see page 244), you needed to override the `form_valid()` method of `FormView` to send an email when the form is submitted. Here, you need to override `form_valid()` of `CreateView` to set the `user` value of the `joke` object.

Open `jokes/views.py` in your editor and add the `form_valid()` method to the `JokeCreateView`:

```
class JokeCreateView(CreateView):
    model = Joke
    form_class = JokeForm

    def form_valid(self, form):
        form.instance.user = self.request.user
        return super().form_valid(form)
```

Notice that `form_valid()` takes a `form` parameter, which has an `instance` property. That holds the data in the `form` object. You are adding another attribute, `user`, to that object before saving. After making that change, you call and return `form_valid()` on the superclass, which takes care of saving the form and redirecting to the success URL.

❖ E46.3. The Template

Open `templates/jokes/joke_detail.html` and make the following highlighted change:

```
<small class="text-muted">
  Created on: {{ joke.created }} by {{ joke.user.username }}<br>
  Last updated: {{ joke.updated }}
</small>
```

❖ E46.4. Try It Out

1. Start up the server if it's not already running.
2. Make sure you are logged in to the site.
3. Click on **Jokes** in the header nav.
4. Click on the **New Joke** button.
5. Add a new joke.

The joke will get added just as before, but now your username will appear in the small text:

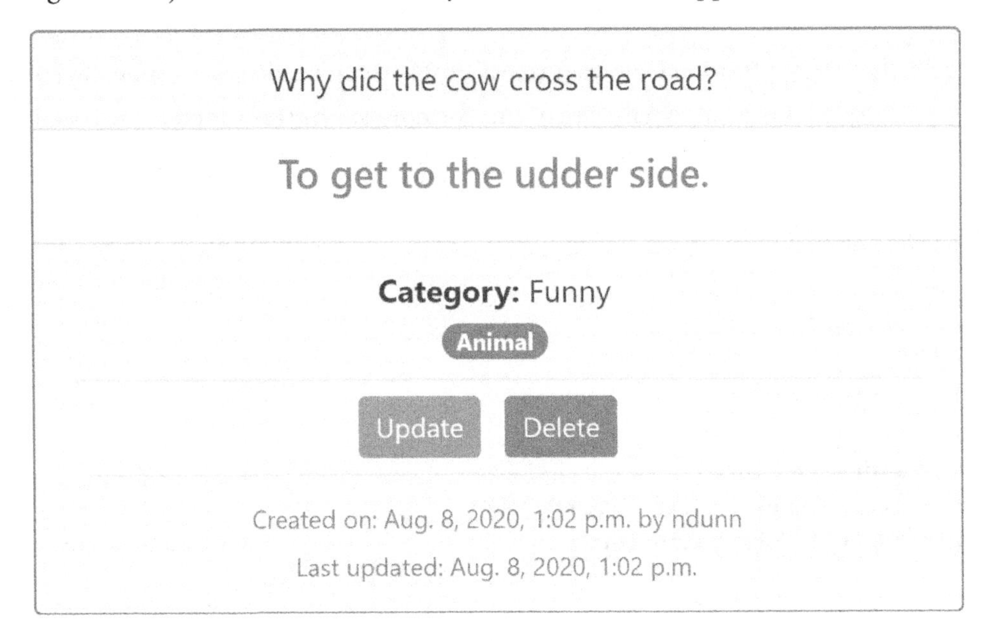

Git Commit

Commit your code to Git.

11.4. Mixins

Mixins are classes used to add features to other classes. The steps to adding a mixin to a class are:

1. Import the mixin.
2. Inherit from the mixin.
3. Implement the mixin's features (if necessary).

The best way to get a feel for how this works is to implement a mixin. You'll do that in the next exercise.

Exercise 47: Restricting Joke Creating and Updating

30 to 45 minutes

Only logged-in users should be able to create jokes and view the profile page. Also, users should only be able to update and delete their own jokes.

❖ E47.1. LoginRequiredMixin

1. Open `jokes/views.py` for editing.
2. Import `LoginRequiredMixin` from `django.contrib.auth.mixins`.

    ```
    from django.contrib.auth.mixins import LoginRequiredMixin
    ```

3. Make `JokeCreateView` inherit `LoginRequiredMixin`:

    ```
    class JokeCreateView(LoginRequiredMixin, CreateView):
    ```

That's all that is required to make use of the `LoginRequiredMixin`. Now, unauthenticated users who try to create a joke will be redirected to the login page. Give it a try. Log out, and then go to `http://127.0.0.1:8000/jokes/joke/create/`.

Now, do the same for the `CustomPasswordChangeView` and `MyAccountPageView` views in `users/views.py`:

Exercise Code 47.1: users/views.py

```
1.  from django.contrib.auth import get_user_model
2.  from django.contrib.auth.mixins import LoginRequiredMixin
    -------Lines 3 through 9 Omitted-------
10. class CustomPasswordChangeView(LoginRequiredMixin, PasswordChangeView):
11.     success_url = reverse_lazy('my-account')
12.
13. class MyAccountPageView(LoginRequiredMixin, UpdateView):
    -------Lines 14 through 19 Omitted-------
```

Try to visit `http://127.0.0.1:8000/account/my-account/` when you're not logged in. You should be redirected to the login page.

❖ E47.2. UserPassesTestMixin

Next, you are going to only allow users who created a joke to update or delete that joke. To do this, you will use UserPassesTestMixin.

1. Open jokes/views.py for editing.
2. Import UserPassesTestMixin:

```
from django.contrib.auth.mixins import LoginRequiredMixin, UserPassesTestMixin
```

3. Make JokeDeleteView inherit UserPassesTestMixin:

```
class JokeDeleteView(UserPassesTestMixin, DeleteView):
```

4. UserPassesTestMixin requires a test_func() method, which returns True if the user passes the test and False otherwise. Add the highlighted test to JokeDeleteView:

```
class JokeDeleteView(UserPassesTestMixin, DeleteView):
    model = Joke
    success_url = reverse_lazy('jokes')

    def test_func(self):
        obj = self.get_object()
        return self.request.user == obj.user
```

   This returns True if and only if the logged-in user is the user who created the joke.

5. Add the mixin and test_func() to JokeUpdateView as well:

```
class JokeUpdateView(UserPassesTestMixin, UpdateView):
    model = Joke
    form_class = JokeForm

    def test_func(self):
        obj = self.get_object()
        return self.request.user == obj.user
```

❖ E47.3. Try It Out

Start up the server and log in to the site as a user. Click on the **Update** button of a joke that the logged-in user did not write. If the same user wrote all the jokes, then log out, and log back in as a different user. Then, try to update a joke. You should see a page with a big "403 Forbidden" message on it.

Go back to the site and try to delete a joke that the logged-in user didn't write. You should get the big "403 Forbidden" message again.

❖ E47.4. Making the 403 Message Prettier

Directly in the `templates` folder, create a new file named `403.html` with the following content:[82]

Exercise Code 47.2: templates/403.html

```
1.  {% extends "_base.html" %}
2.
3.  {% block title %}403: Permission Denied{% endblock %}
4.  {% block main %}
5.    <div class="card border-primary m-auto mb-3 text-center"
6.      style="max-width: 30rem">
7.      <div class="card-header">What are you trying to do?</div>
8.      <div class="card-body text-primary">
9.        <h5 class="card-title">That's not funny.</h5>
10.     </div>
11.     <div class="card-footer">
12.       <small class="text-muted">403: Permission Denied</small>
13.     </div>
14.   </div>
15. {% endblock %}
```

Now, return to the page with the big "403 Forbidden" message and refresh. You should now get a pretty error page like this one:

82. **Don't want to type?** Copy from `starter-code/user-registration/templates/403.html`.

What are you trying to do?

That's not funny.

403: Permission Denied

You can create other error templates (e.g., `templates/404.html` for 404 Page Not Found pages), but some of them only work if `DEBUG` is set to `False` in `settings.py`.

❖ E47.5. Cleaning Up the Templates

It doesn't make sense to provide buttons or links that go to forbidden pages. Remember that Django templates have access to the `user` object. You can use the following if condition to check if the logged-in user is the same user that created the joke:

```
{% if user == joke.user %}
```

Before looking at the solution, try the following:

1. Update `templates/jokes/joke_list.html` so that:
   A. If the logged-in user created the joke, the buttons show up.
   B. For all other users, the username of the joke creator shows up (e.g., "by jangoldman").

   Also, change the header for that column from "Actions" to "Creator".
2. Update `templates/jokes/joke_detail.html` so that the buttons only show up for the user who created the joke.
3. Check your work:
   A. Visit the joke-list page. In the last column, buttons should only show up for jokes the logged-in user created. For all other users, the username of the joke creator should show up.
   B. Visit a joke-detail page for a joke the logged-in user **did not** create. The buttons **should not** show up.
   C. Visit a joke-detail page for a joke the logged-in user **did** create. The buttons **should** show up.

Solution: templates/jokes/joke_list.html

```
-------Lines 1 through 31 Omitted-------
32.           <td>
33.             {% if request.user == joke.user %}
34.               <a href="{% url 'jokes:update' joke.slug %}">
35.                 <i class="fas fa-pencil-alt"></i>
36.               </a>
37.               <a href="{% url 'jokes:delete' joke.slug %}">
38.                 <i class="far fa-trash-alt"></i>
39.               </a>
40.             {% else %}
41.               <small>by {{ joke.user.username }}</small>
42.             {% endif %}
43.           </td>
-------Lines 44 through 49 Omitted-------
```

Solution: templates/jokes/joke_detail.html

```
1.  {% extends "_base.html" %}
-------Lines 2 through 10 Omitted-------
11.     <div class="card-footer">
12.       <div class="border-bottom border-faded pb-2">
13.         <strong>Category:</strong> {{ joke.category.category }}<br>
14.         {% for tag in joke.tags.all %}
15.           <span class="badge badge-pill badge-secondary">{{ tag.tag }}</span>
16.         {% endfor %}
17.       </div>
18.       {% if joke.user == user %}
19.         <div class="border-bottom border-faded m-2 pb-2">
20.           <a href="{% url 'jokes:update' joke.slug %}"
21.             class="btn btn-info btn-sm mr-2">Update</a>
22.           <a href="{% url 'jokes:delete' joke.slug %}"
23.             class="btn btn-danger btn-sm mr-2">Delete</a>
24.         </div>
25.       {% endif %}
26.       <small class="text-muted">
27.         Created on: {{ joke.created }} by {{ joke.user.username }}<br>
28.         Last updated: {{ joke.updated }}
29.       </small>
30.     </div>
-------Lines 31 through 32 Omitted-------
```

Git Commit

Commit your code to Git.

Conclusion

In this lesson, you have learned to use `django-allauth` to register new users, to use mixins, and to customize templates to display different content for different users.

LESSON 12

Messages Framework

Topics Covered

☑ Adding messages to pages.

"Ah!" He looked away and said carelessly, "How were they all?"

"They sent all sorts of sympathetic **messages** to you, and all that sort of thing."

– *The Red House Mystery, A. A. Milne*

Introduction

In this lesson, you will learn to use Django's built-in messages framework.

✻

12.1. Message Framework

Django includes a built-in messages framework to output different types of messages in the templates. While the framework is customizable, the "out-of-the-box" functionality will be enough for most websites.

Every message has a `level` attribute, which is an integer. The framework provides the following constants for the built-in message levels:

1. `DEBUG` (`10`)
2. `INFO` (`20`)
3. `SUCCESS` (`25`)
4. `WARNING` (`30`)
5. `ERROR` (`40`)

The built-in messages each have a `tags` attribute that holds the level in all lowercase letters (e.g., "debug", "info", etc.).

The steps for using the message framework are:

1. In your views file, import `messages` from `django.contrib`:

   ```
   from django.contrib import messages
   ```

2. Within a view, add a message using any one of the following methods:

   ```
   messages.debug(request, 'Debug message.')
   messages.info(request, 'Info message.')
   messages.success(request, 'Success message.')
   messages.warning(request, 'Warning message.')
   messages.error(request, 'Error message.')
   ```

   This must be done within a method that has access to the `request` object.

3. Update a template to output messages.

Message Level in Settings

The default minimum message level is `INFO`. That means that messages added using `messages.debug()` won't show up in the templates. This can be changed by adding the following to your settings:

```
MESSAGE_LEVEL = 10  # DEBUG
```

You do not want to set `MESSAGE_LEVEL` to `10` in your production settings (i.e., `settings.py`). Even if *you don't* explicitly use `DEBUG` messages in the code you write, apps that you import *may use them*, and you don't want `DEBUG` messages showing up on your live site.

Messages in Django Admin

Django admin uses the messages framework. See the success message in the following screenshot that shows up after adding a tag:

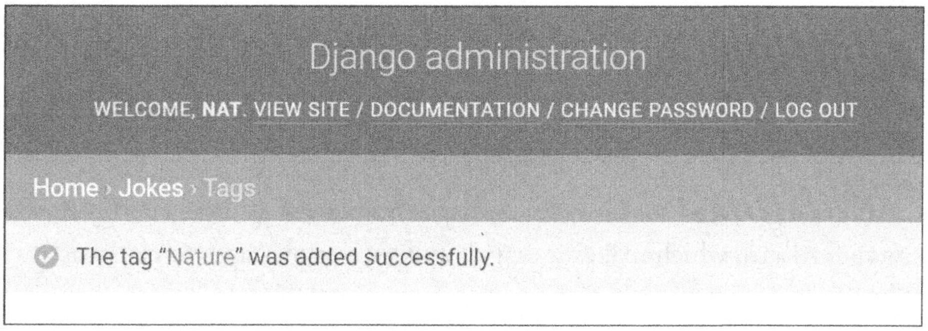

Iterating through Messages

Messages are specific to a session (a single user's visit to the site). They are held in an iterable and removed after they have been displayed. When adding messages to a template, you should first check if there are any messages and then iterate through the messages with a `for` loop. The code below shows how this is done in Django admin:

```
{% if messages %}
  <ul class="messagelist">
    {% for message in messages %}
      <li{% if message.tags %} class="{{ message.tags }}"{% endif %}>
        {{ message|capfirst }}
      </li>
    {% endfor %}
  </ul>
{% endif %}
```

Exercise 48: Adding Messages

20 to 30 minutes

In this exercise, you will get a feel for how the messages framework works. Then, you will learn to use the `SuccessMessageMixin`, which makes it easy to add success messages to class-based views.

❖ E48.1. Outputting Messages

Open `templates/_base.html` in your editor and add the following code right before the “main” template block within the `<main>` tag:

Exercise Code 48.1: templates/_base.html

```
-------Lines 1 through 72 Omitted-------
73.  <main class="m-4 pb-5">
74.    {% if messages %}
75.      <ul>
76.        {% for message in messages %}
77.       <div class="alert message{{ message.tags }} alert-dismissible" role="alert">
78.            <strong>{{message}}</strong>
79.            <button type="button" class="close" data-dismiss="alert"
80.              aria-label="Close">
81.              <i class="fas fa-window-close"></i>
82.            </button>
83.          </div>
84.        {% endfor %}
85.      </ul>
86.    {% endif %}
87.    {% block main %}<h2>Welcome!</h2>{% endblock %}
88.  </main>
-------Lines 89 through 111 Omitted-------
```

Things to notice:

1. You put this code in the base template, so that messages will appear on all pages that extend `_base.html`.
2. You use an `if` condition so that the list is only output if there are any messages to show:

   ```
   {% if messages %}
   ```

3. You use Bootstrap classes for most of the styling, but you also add your own `message...` classes using class names derived from the message's `tags` attribute:

```
<div class="alert message{{ message.tags }} alert-dismissible" role="alert">
```

CSS Rules for the Message Classes

Add the following rules to `main.css` to style the message levels:[83]

Exercise Code 48.2: static/css/main.css

```
    -------Lines 1 through 27 Omitted-------
28. /* MESSAGE STYLES */
29. .message {
30.   background-color: palegoldenrod;
31.   color: black;
32. }
33.
34. .messagedebug {
35.   background-color: slategray;
36.   color: white;
37. }
38. .messageinfo {
39.   background-color: azure;
40.   color: darkblue;
41. }
42.
43. .messagesuccess {
44.   background-color: lightgreen;
45.   color: darkgreen;
46. }
47.
48. .messagewarning {
49.   background-color: lightgoldenrodyellow;
50.   color: darkgoldenrod;
51. }
52.
53. .messageerror {
54.   background-color: pink;
55.   color: darkred;
56. }
```

83. **Don't want to type?** Copy from `starter-code/messages-framework/main.css`.

❖ E48.2. Adding Messages

Rather than creating a new view, you'll use the `AboutUsView` view to show how to add messages:

1. Open `pages/views.py` in your editor.
2. At the top of the page, import the `messages` framework:

```
from django.contrib import messages
```

3. Add the following `get()` method to `AboutUsView`:

```
def get(self, request, *args, **kwargs):
    messages.debug(request, 'Debug message.')
    messages.info(request, 'Info message.')
    messages.success(request, 'Success message.')
    messages.warning(request, 'Warning message.')
    messages.error(request, 'Error message.')
    return super().get(request, args, kwargs)
```

Start up the server and visit `http://127.0.0.1:8000/about-us/`. You should see a page like this one (You may need to do a hard refresh to get the CSS to reload):

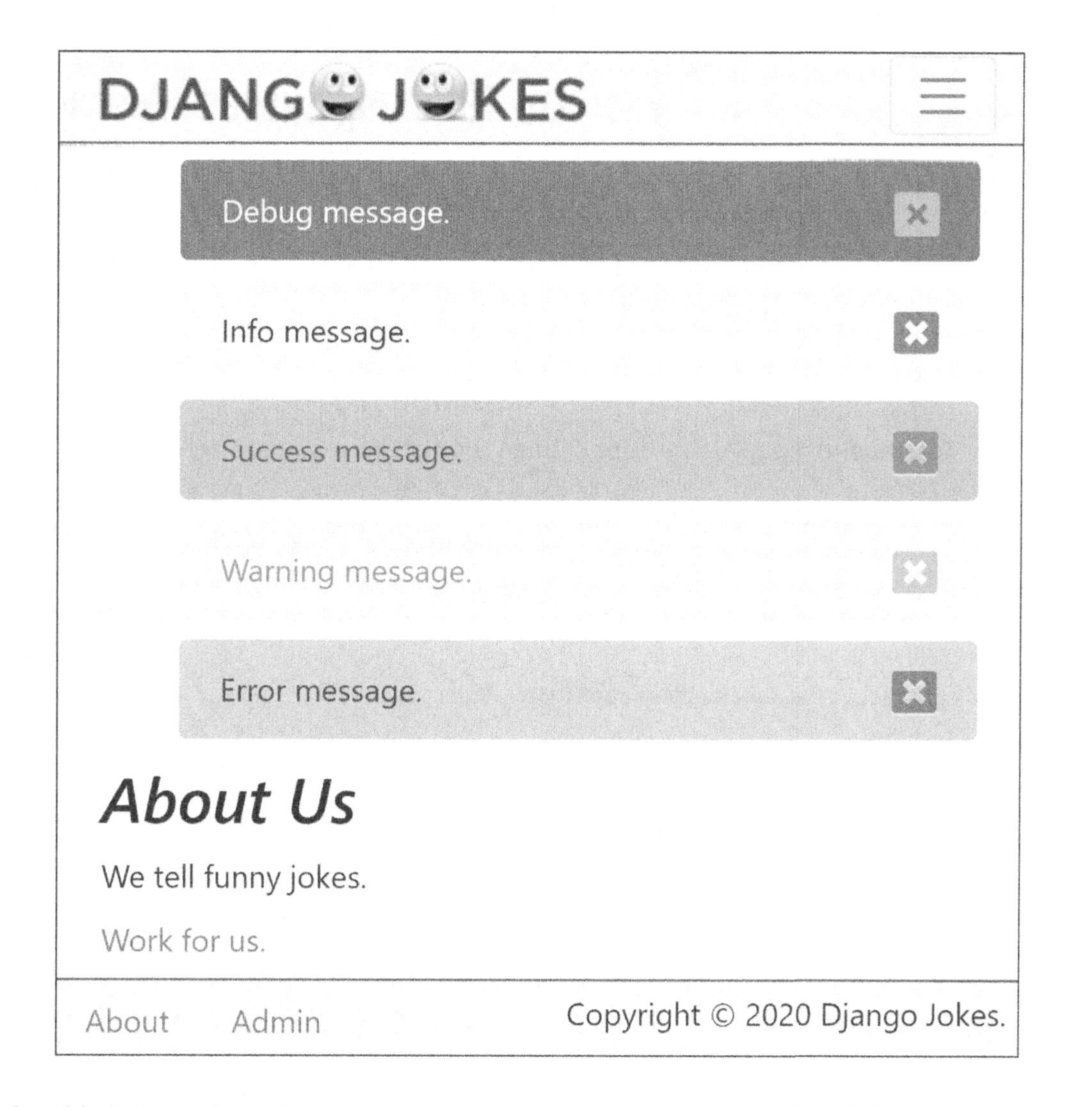

You only added this code to the `AboutUsView` view to learn how to add and display messages. When you are done, you can comment out or delete the `get()` method in the view.

Git Commit

Commit your code to Git.

Exercise 49: Using SuccessMessageMixin

10 to 15 minutes

The FormView, CreateView, and UpdateView classes can all inherit from SuccessMessageMixin, which provides a simple way for adding a success message.

The steps involved are:

1. Import SuccessMessageMixin from django.contrib.messages.views:

   ```
   from django.contrib.messages.views import SuccessMessageMixin
   ```

2. Inherit from SuccessMessageMixin:

   ```
   class MyUpdateView(SuccessMessageMixin, UpdateView):
       ...
   ```

3. Set success_message in the class:

   ```
   success_message = 'Update Successful'
   ```

Let's give it a try. Open users/views.py and add the following highlighted code:

Exercise Code 49.1: users/views.py

```
1.  from django.contrib.auth import get_user_model
2.  from django.contrib.auth.mixins import LoginRequiredMixin
3.  from django.contrib.messages.views import SuccessMessageMixin
    -------Lines 4 through 13 Omitted-------
14. class MyAccountPageView(SuccessMessageMixin, LoginRequiredMixin, UpdateView):
15.     model = get_user_model()
16.     form_class = CustomUserChangeForm
17.     success_message = 'Update Successful'
    -------Lines 18 through 21 Omitted-------
```

Start up the server and visit http://127.0.0.1:8000/account/my-account/. Submit the form. You should see an "Update Successful" message at the top of the page:

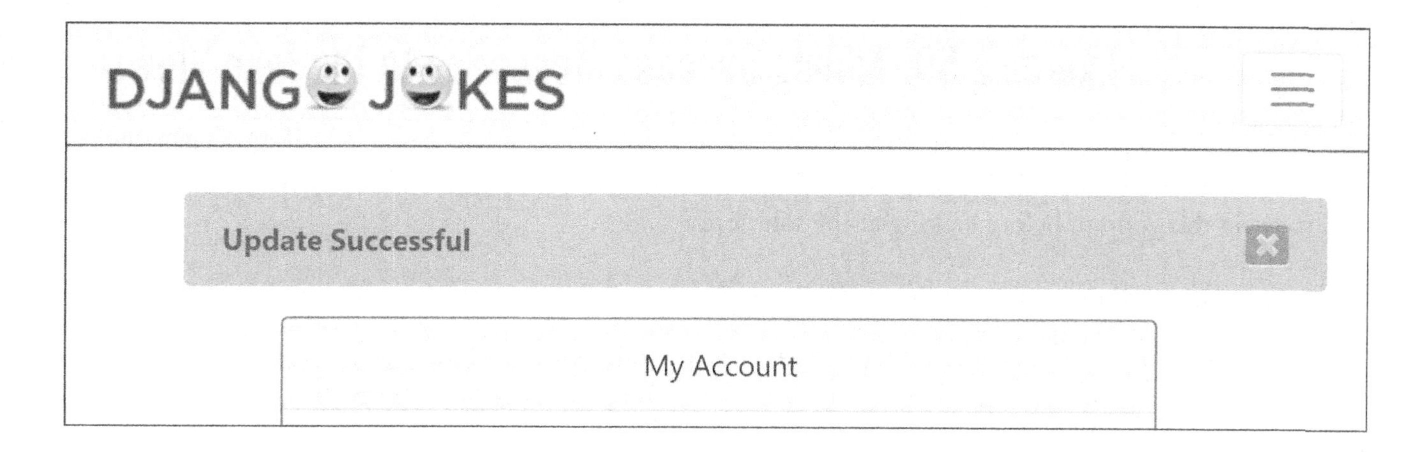

Git Commit

Commit your code to Git.

Exercise 50: Adding Success Messages to the Joke Views

10 to 15 minutes

Try to do this yourself before looking at the solution:

1. Open `jokes/views.py` in your editor.
2. Add success messages to `JokeCreateView` and `JokeUpdateView`.
3. Create a new joke. Did the success message you added to `JokeCreateView` show up?
4. Edit the joke. Did the success message you added to `JokeUpdateView` show up?

Solution: jokes/views.py

```
1.  from django.contrib.auth.mixins import LoginRequiredMixin, UserPassesTestMixin
2.  from django.contrib.messages.views import SuccessMessageMixin
3.  from django.urls import reverse_lazy
4.  from django.views.generic import (
5.      CreateView, DeleteView, DetailView, ListView, UpdateView
6.  )
7.
8.  from .models import Joke
9.  from .forms import JokeForm
    -------Lines 10 through 23 Omitted-------
24. class JokeCreateView(SuccessMessageMixin, LoginRequiredMixin, CreateView):
25.     model = Joke
26.     form_class = JokeForm
27.     success_message = 'Joke created.'
28.
29.     def form_valid(self, form):
30.         form.instance.user = self.request.user
31.         return super().form_valid(form)
    -------Lines 32 through 37 Omitted-------
38. class JokeUpdateView(SuccessMessageMixin, UserPassesTestMixin, UpdateView):
39.     model = Joke
40.     form_class = JokeForm
41.     success_message = 'Joke updated.'
42.
43.     def test_func(self):
44.         obj = self.get_object()
45.         return self.request.user == obj.user
```

Git Commit

Commit your code to Git.

 Exercise 51: Adding a Success Message to JokeDeleteView

10 to 15 minutes

DeleteView views cannot inherit from SuccessMessageMixin, so you have to write the code to add a message yourself. This is done by overriding the delete() method, like this:

```
def delete(self, request, *args, **kwargs):
    result = super().delete(request, *args, **kwargs)
    messages.success(self.request, 'Joke deleted.')
    return result
```

Note that before creating the message, you run the superclass's delete() method. That way, the message will not get added if an error occurs when trying to delete (e.g., due to a constraint that prevents the deletion).

If it is not already open, open jokes/views.py in your editor and modify the JokeDeleteView as follows:

Exercise Code 51.1: jokes/views.py

```
1.    from django.contrib.auth.mixins import LoginRequiredMixin, UserPassesTestMixin
2.    from django.contrib import messages
      -------Lines 3 through 11 Omitted-------
12.   class JokeDeleteView(UserPassesTestMixin, DeleteView):
13.       model = Joke
14.       success_url = reverse_lazy('jokes')
15.
16.       def delete(self, request, *args, **kwargs):
17.           result = super().delete(request, *args, **kwargs)
18.           messages.success(self.request, 'Joke deleted.')
19.           return result
      -------Lines 20 through 51 Omitted-------
```

Notice that you have imported messages from django.contrib. That isn't necessary when using the SuccessMessageMixin, but it is when you need to add messages on the messages object directly.

Try deleting a joke. You should be redirected to the joke-list page, and your "Joke deleted" message should show up at the top:

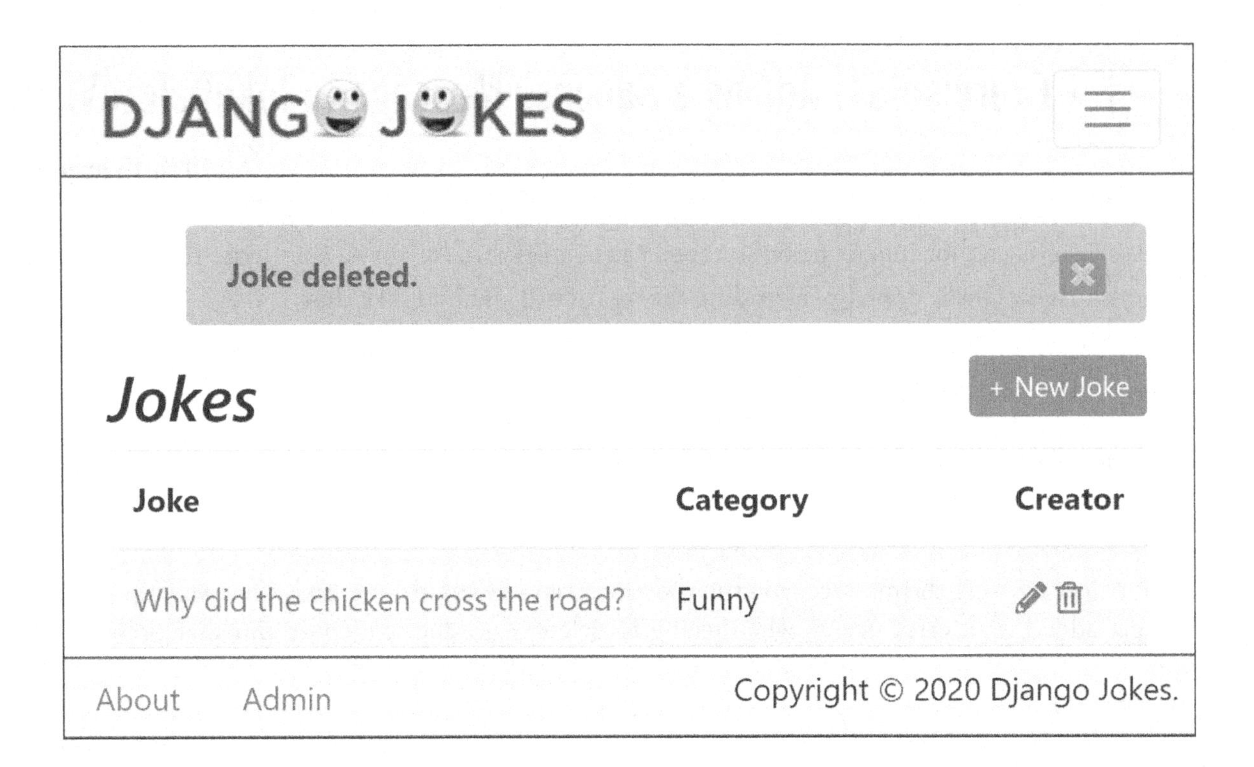

Git Commit

Commit your code to Git.

Conclusion

In this lesson, you have learned to use Django's built-in messages framework. See `https://docs.djangoproject.com/en/3.1/ref/contrib/messages/#creating-custom-message-levels` to learn how to create your own custom message levels.

LESSON 13

Media Files

Topics Covered

☑ Media files.

☑ Media settings.

☑ Uploading files.

☑ Cleaning form data.

☑ Safety concerns.

☑ The `filetype` library.

☑ Keeping uploaded files private.

☑ The `django-private-storage` library.

☑ `FileField` and `ImageField`.

☑ Displaying uploaded images.

☑ Amazon Simple Storage Service (Amazon S3).

> Oh, he struggled! he struggled! The wastes of his weary brain were haunted by shadowy **images** now – **images** of wealth and fame revolving obsequiously round his unextinguishable gift of noble and lofty expression.
>
> – *Heart of Darkness, Joseph Conrad*

Introduction

In this lesson, you will learn to let the user upload files, to make sure those files are safe, to keep private files private, and to display uploaded images in templates.

13.1. Media File Basics

In Django, *media* files are static files uploaded by users. Unlike Django's *static* files (see page 167), developers cannot trust media files to be safe. There are two major considerations related to user-uploaded files:

1. Is it safe? Is the content really what it purports to be and not some malicious file masquerading as a PDF?
2. Is it meant to be private? When a user uploads a **profile picture**, they may understand that it will be seen publicly, but when they upload a **resume**, they expect it to remain private.

Unfortunately, both of these issues are somewhat complex. In this lesson, we will cover the following through a series of exercises:

1. Adding media settings to `settings.py`.
2. Configuring media files to be served.
3. Providing a form field for uploading a resume and handling that upload.
4. Ensuring that the uploaded file is really a PDF.
5. Making URLs to resumes only accessible to staff. All others will get a `403: Permission Denied` error page.
6. Providing a form field for uploading an avatar (profile picture) on the My Account page.
7. Showing users' avatars on their My Account page and on joke-detail pages.

Exercise 52: Adding Media Settings

20 to 30 minutes

In this exercise, you will add media settings to `settings.py` and will configure media files to be served on development.

Before you can allow users to upload files, you need to determine:

1. The URL path to use to deliver media files on the website. The setting for this is `MEDIA_URL`.
2. Where those files will get uploaded. The setting for this is `MEDIA_ROOT`.

The general convention is to use "media" for both of these.

1. Add the following to your `settings.py` file:

   ```
   MEDIA_URL = '/media/'
   MEDIA_ROOT = BASE_DIR / 'media'
   ```

   A good place to add these settings is right below the static file settings.
2. Add a `media` directory at the root of the Django Jokes project.
3. Within the `media` directory, temporarily add a `temp.txt` file with some dummy text (e.g., "Hello, Media!").
4. Start up your server and visit `http://127.0.0.1:8000/media/temp.txt`. You should get a Page not found (404) error. That's because you have not yet configured media files to be served.

❖ E52.1. Serving Media Files

The way in which Django stores files depends on the `DEFAULT_FILE_STORAGE` setting, which defaults to `'django.core.files.storage.FileSystemStorage'`. If you leave this default in place, Django will store the files locally using the `MEDIA_URL` and `MEDIA_ROOT` settings that you just set. You'll learn how this configuration works first. Later in the lesson, you will switch to Amazon Simple Storage Service, which provides a more robust and possibly more secure way of storing files (see page 402).

1. Open `djangojokes/urls.py` for editing.

2. Import settings from django.conf and static from django.conf.urls.static:

```
from django.conf import settings
from django.conf.urls.static import static
```

3. Append the following highlighted code to the urlpatterns list:

```
urlpatterns = [
    ...
] + static(settings.MEDIA_URL, document_root=settings.MEDIA_ROOT)
```

The static() function is a helper function that only works when settings.DEBUG is set to True. So, you don't have to worry about removing this code when deploying to production. It will be ignored.

4. Visit http://127.0.0.1:8000/media/temp.txt again. It should now show your file:

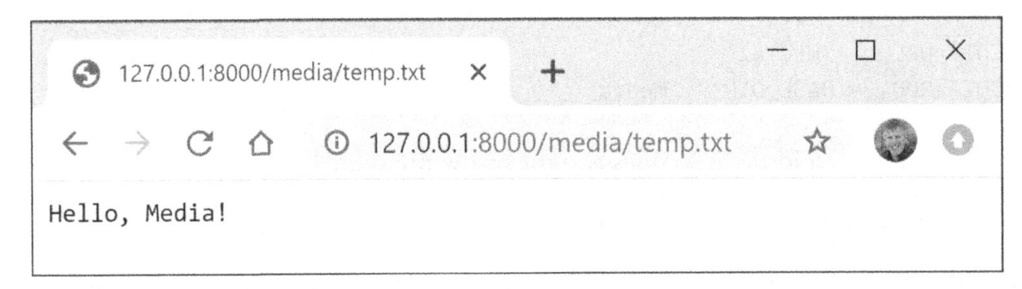

This demonstrates that the MEDIA_URL setting, which specifies the path used to serve media files, is correct and that you have the media folder in the right place. In the next exercise, you'll let the user upload a resume, which will demonstrate that the MEDIA_ROOT setting, which specifies where uploaded files get saved, is also correct.

Git Commit

Commit your code to Git.

Exercise 53: Uploading a Resume

20 to 30 minutes

In this exercise, you will provide a field for uploading a resume and handling that upload.

E53.1. The resumes Folder

In the `media` folder, create a `private` folder, and within that, create a `resumes` folder:

```
media
    private
        resumes
```

E53.2. The Model

1. From the `jobs` folder, open `models.py` for editing.
2. Below the `cover_letter` attribute of the `Applicant` class, add the following `resume` attribute:

```
resume = models.FileField(
    upload_to='private/resumes', blank=True, help_text='PDFs only'
)
```

   - The `upload_to` attribute holds the relative path below the path set in `settings.MEDIA_ROOT`, so resumes are set to upload to `/media/private/resumes/`.
   - Setting `blank` to `True` makes the field optional.

3. You know the drill. You changed the model, so you need to make and run migrations:

```
(.venv) …/projects/djangojokes.com> python manage.py makemigrations
(.venv) …/projects/djangojokes.com> python manage.py migrate
```

E53.3. The Form

1. From the `jobs` folder, open `forms.py` for editing.

2. In the META inner class of JobApplicationForm, add resume to the fields tuple right after cover_letter.
3. Below the cover_letter key in the widgets dictionary, add a key for resume:

```
'resume': forms.FileInput(attrs={'accept':'application/pdf'})
```

Setting the accept attribute in the widget tells the browser to only allow for PDFs. Not all browsers support this, but modern desktop browsers do. You can check out the status of browser support at https://caniuse.com/#feat=input-file-accept. As you shall soon see, this should be considered as helpful guidance to the user, not as protection to you.

❖ E53.4. The Template

1. From the templates/jobs folder, open applicant_form.html for editing.
2. In order to upload a file via an HTML form, the <form> tag must include an enctype="multipart/form-data" attribute. Add that to the <form> tag:

```
<form method="post" novalidate enctype="multipart/form-data">
```

Note that you are leaving the novalidate attribute in to bypass HTML validation, so that you see the Django-generated errors.
3. If your file is still using {{ form|crispy }} rather than the as_crispy_field filter we showed in the Forms and Widgets lesson (see page 268), then you don't have to change anything else.
4. If you updated the template to use the as_crispy_field filter, add this line after outputting form.cover_letter:

```
{{ form.resume|as_crispy_field }}
```

This will create the **Resume** file upload form control.

❖ E53.5. Try It Out

Note that different browsers and operating systems will handle file uploads differently. The screenshots below are using Google Chrome on Windows 10.

1. Start up your server and visit http://127.0.0.1:8000/jobs/job-app/. Notice the new **Resume** field:

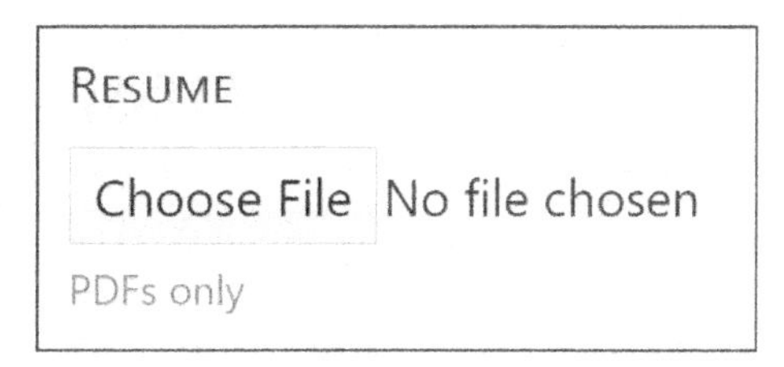

2. Fill out the form. When you click on the button to upload your resume, you are likely limited to PDFs:

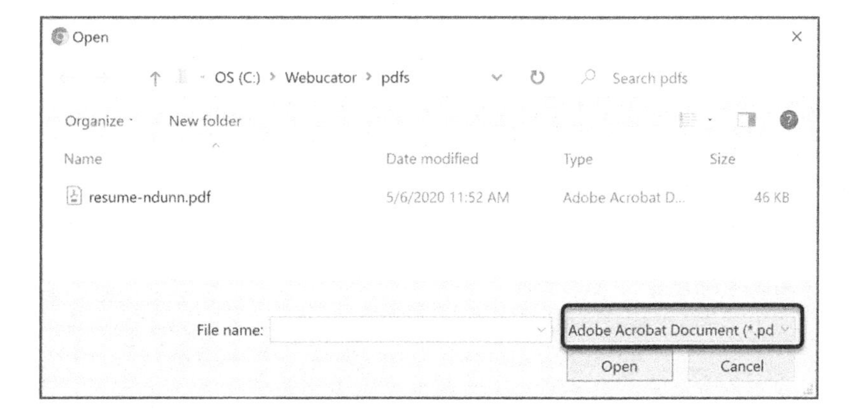

Choose a PDF file. If you don't have your own, you can use `resume-jangore.pdf` from `starter-code/media-files`.

3. Submit the form.
4. Look in the `media/private/resumes` folder. The PDF you uploaded should be there.
5. In Django admin...
    A. Click on **Applicants**. You should see the new applicant.
    B. Click on the applicant. The **Resume** field should look something like this:

    C. Click on the link to the PDF. It should open.

Git Commit

Commit your code to Git.

Exercise 54: Checking File Type

20 to 30 minutes

In this exercise, you will ensure that the uploaded resume file is really a PDF.

❖ E54.1. The Problem

There is a problem with your current resume upload field. The problem is two-fold:

1. Users could ignore the only-PDFs rule. The user can get around the file-type limitation set on the browser. To see this, return to the job-application page, and click on the button to upload a resume. Notice that you can choose to show **All Files** and that when you do, non-PDF files show up too.

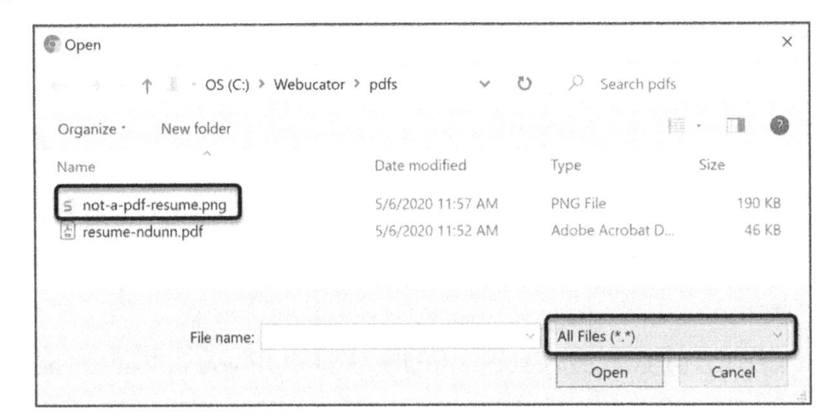

2. Worse, users could disguise a malicious file as a PDF by changing its extension.

For both of these reasons, you need to check to make sure that the file you're getting is really a PDF file.

❖ E54.2. The `filetype` Library

You are going to use the filetype[84] library to confirm that the uploaded file is really a PDF file. The library includes a `guess()` method, which takes a path to a file and returns an object with `extension` and `mime` attributes (or `None` if it cannot guess the MIME type). You shouldn't worry too much about the file extension as that doesn't *really* tell you what type of file it is. Instead, you should check the MIME type.

84. `https://pypi.org/project/filetype/`

Install `filetype`:

```
(.venv) …/projects/djangojokes.com> pip install filetype
```

Let's see how `filetype` works:

1. Open the shell and run the following code (if you uploaded a different PDF file, you will need to change the path):

   ```
   (.venv) …/projects/djangojokes.com> python manage.py shell
   >>> import filetype
   >>> from django.conf import settings
   >>> path_to_file = 'media/private/resumes/resume-jangore.pdf'
   >>> kind = filetype.guess(path_to_file)
   >>> if not kind:
   ...     print('Cannot guess file type!')
   ... else:
   ...     print(f'Extension: {kind.extension}')
   ...     print(f'MIME type: {kind.mime}')
   ...
   Extension: pdf
   MIME type: application/pdf
   ... exit()
   ```

Now, let's use `filetype` to validate PDF uploads.

You could validate the file type in the form, but then the validation is specific to that form. In Django admin, for example, you would still be able to upload non-PDF files. To make sure that only PDF files are uploaded to the resume field, you should add a validator to the model.

1. From the `jobs` folder, open `models.py` for editing.
2. At the top of the file, import `filetype`:

   ```
   import filetype
   ```

3. Add the following validator below the `validate_future_date()` validator:

```
def validate_pdf(value):
    kind = filetype.guess(value)
    if not kind or kind.mime != 'application/pdf':
        raise ValidationError("That's not a PDF file.")
```

   This will raise an error if `filetype` cannot guess the MIME type or if the MIME type is not `application/pdf`.

4. Add the `validate_pdf` validator to the resume field:

```
resume = models.FileField(
    upload_to='private/resumes', blank=True, help_text='PDFs only',
    validators=[validate_pdf]
)
```

❖ E54.3. Try It Out

In the `starter-code/media-files` folder, you will find a `not-a-pdf.pdf` file. This is a jpeg file with the extension changed to `pdf`. Fill out the application form at `http://127.0.0.1:8000/jobs/job-app/` and choose that file for your resume. When you submit, you should see the following error next to the resume field:

You will get the same error when trying to add a non-PDF file for this field in Django admin.

Git Commit

Commit your code to Git.

 Exercise 55: Keeping Resume Files Private

20 to 30 minutes

In this exercise, you will make URLs to resumes only accessible to staff. All other users who attempt to view a resume page will get a `403: Permission Denied` error page.

E55.1. The Problem

To see the problem, in Django admin...

1. Copy the link address of an uploaded resume:

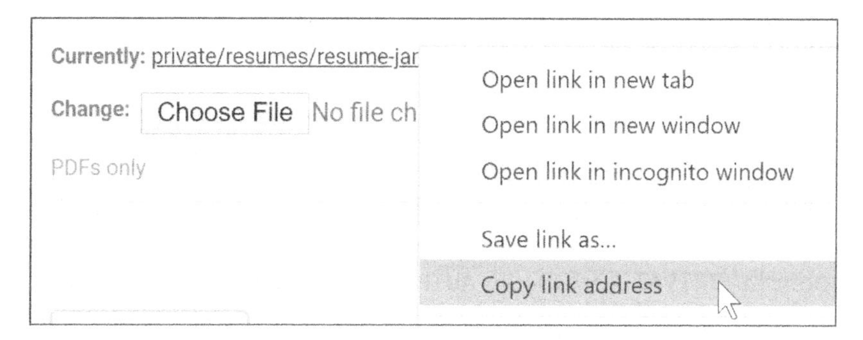

2. Log out of the website.
3. Paste the link address you copied in the browser's location bar and press Enter. Notice that the resume opens even though you are not logged into the site. This shows that anyone can get at that file.
4. Leave that page open, so that all you need to do is refresh it after making it so that the `private` folder is really private.

E55.2. The `django-private-storage` Library

There are many different ways to deal with this problem and the solution you use on a production site will depend largely on how and where you store media files. You are going to use the `django-private-storage`[85] library to demonstrate one way of protecting a directory from non-staff users. Later in this lesson, we will show you how to set up Amazon's Simple Storage Service, which will change the way you make files private.

85. `https://pypi.org/project/django-private-storage/`

1. Install django-private-storage:

```
(.venv) …/projects/djangojokes.com> pip install django-private-storage
```

2. Add private_storage to INSTALLED_APPS:

```
INSTALLED_APPS = [
    …
    # Third-party
    …
    'private_storage',
    …
]
```

3. Add the following additional settings to settings.py below the MEDIA_ROOT setting:

```
# private-storage settings
PRIVATE_STORAGE_ROOT = MEDIA_ROOT / 'private/'
PRIVATE_STORAGE_AUTH_FUNCTION = 'private_storage.permissions.allow_staff'
```

Other options for PRIVATE_STORAGE_AUTH_FUNCTION are:

```
private_storage.permissions.allow_authenticated
private_storage.permissions.allow_superuser
```

4. Open djangojokes/urls.py in your editor and add the following highlighted code:

```
import private_storage.urls

urlpatterns = [
    …

    # Private media
    path('media/private/', include(private_storage.urls)),

    # Local Apps

    …
] + static(settings.MEDIA_URL, document_root=settings.MEDIA_ROOT)
```

This tells Django to use the private_storage.urls URLConf for paths that begin with media/private.

5. Return to the browser tab that has the resume loaded and refresh the page. You should get a 403 Permission Denied page like this one:

Now, change the model so that all future resume files are put in the `private` directory as well. You don't really *have* to do this, as the field is already set up to store files in the `private` directory, but the advantage of making this change is that if you change where you are storing private files in settings, new files will automatically go to the destination.

1. From the `jobs` folder, open `models.py` for editing.
2. Import `PrivateFileField` from `private_storage.fields`:

```
from private_storage.fields import PrivateFileField
```

3. Change the `resume` field to a `PrivateFileField` and change the `upload_to` path to just `resumes` as the path is relative to the value in `settings.PRIVATE_STORAGE_ROOT`, which is `MEDIA_ROOT / 'private/'`:

```
resume = PrivateFileField(
    upload_to='private/resumes', blank=True, help_text='PDFs only',
    validators=[validate_pdf]
)
```

   Note that the `PrivateFileField` field also includes a `content_types` attribute, but it just checks the content-type sent by the browser in the request, which may not be the real content-type of the file, so you should continue to use the `validate_pdf` validator you wrote earlier.

4. To be sure everything is set up correctly, submit a new job application with a resume and check to make sure the resume landed in the `media/private/resumes` folder.

Again, there are different ways of keeping uploaded files private. Using `django-private-storage` is a good option if you are planning to store your files on the same server that is hosting your Django application.

Git Commit

Commit your code to Git.

 Exercise 56: Adding an ImageField to the Model

15 to 25 minutes

In this exercise, you will add an `ImageField` to the `CustomUser` model and provide a form field for uploading an avatar (profile picture) on the My Account page. You will also make sure the uploaded image is no taller or wider than 200 pixels.

The `Pillow` image-processing library[86] is required for working with `ImageField` in Django. Install that now:

```
(.venv) …/projects/djangojokes.com> pip install Pillow
```

`ImageField` inherits from `FileField`. It only allows for valid images and includes `height` and `width` attributes.

❖ E56.1. The Model

1. From the `users` folder, open `models.py` for editing.
2. Import `ValidationError` from `django.core.exceptions` and `get_image_dimensions` from `django.core.files.images`:

    ```
    from django.core.exceptions import ValidationError
    from django.core.files.images import get_image_dimensions
    ```

    You will use both of these in the validator function.

3. Add the following custom validator function above the `CustomUser` class:

    ```
    def validate_avatar(value):
        w, h = get_image_dimensions(value)
        if w > 200 or h > 200:
            raise ValidationError('Avatar must be no bigger than 200x200 pixels.')
    ```

86. `https://pypi.org/project/Pillow/`

4. Add the following field to CustomUser:

```
avatar = models.ImageField(upload_to='avatars/', blank=True,
    help_text='Image must be 200px by 200px.',
    validators=[validate_avatar]
)
```

Remember that the upload_to value for FileField is relative to the value of settings.MEDIA_ROOT. ImageField, which inherits from FileField, does not change this.

5. You changed the model, so you need to make and run migrations:

```
(.venv) …/projects/djangojokes.com> python manage.py makemigrations
(.venv) …/projects/djangojokes.com> python manage.py migrate
```

❖ E56.2. The Form

You now need to add the avatar field to the form. In users/forms.py, add 'avatar' to the fields tuple.

```
fields = (
    'email', 'username', 'first_name', 'last_name', 'dob', 'avatar'
)
```

❖ E56.3. The Template

Your HTML form needs to be capable of uploading files.

1. From the templates/account folder, open my_account.html for editing.
2. Add the enctype="multipart/form-data" attribute to the <form> tag so that the form can handle file uploading and add the novalidate attribute to bypass HTML validation, so that you see the Django-generated errors:

```
<form method="post" enctype="multipart/form-data" class="m-auto" novalidate>
```

❖ E56.4. Try It Out

You can find sample images in starter-code/media-files.

1. Log into the site and visit your account page. You should see a field for adding an avatar.
2. Try adding an image that is larger than 200px by 200px. It should give you an error:

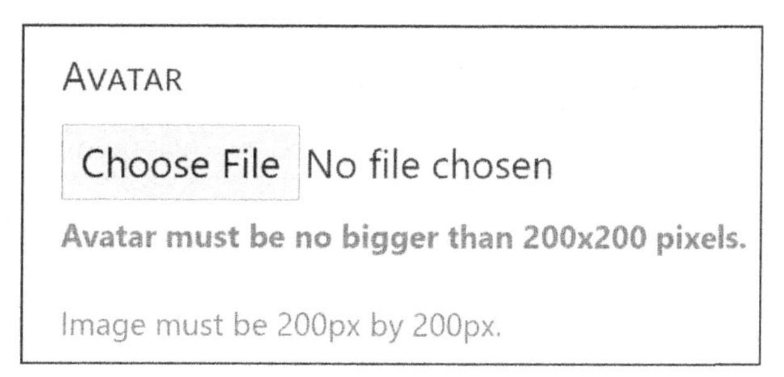

3. Try adding an image that is a valid size. It should upload the image. You will know it worked if it shows you an image path and a **CLEAR** checkbox:

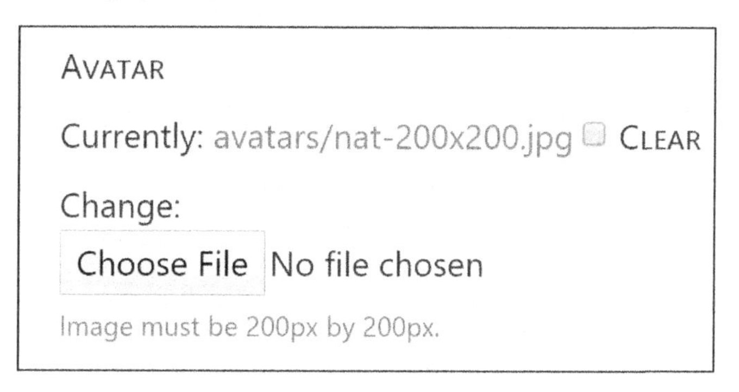

You should also find your profile picture in a new `avatars` folder within the `media` folder:

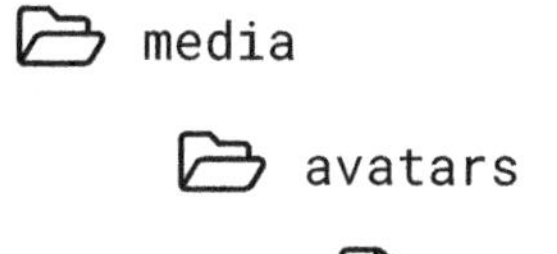

`profile-pic-200x200.png`

Git Commit

Commit your code to Git.

Exercise 57: Displaying the Avatar

15 to 25 minutes

In this exercise, you will update the templates to display users' avatars on their My Account page and on joke-detail pages.

❖ E57.1. My Account Template

1. If it's not still open in your editor, open `my_account.html` from the `templates/account` folder.
2. Add the following code at the top of the `card-body div` (above the form):

```
{% if user.avatar and not form.avatar.errors %}
  <img src="{{ user.avatar.url }}" alt="Avatar"
        class="img-thumbnail mx-auto d-block"/>
{% endif %}
```

   Notice that the `ImageFile` contains a `url` property that points to the relative path of the uploaded image. The generated HTML will be something like:

```
<img src="/media/avatars/nat-200x200.jpg" alt="Avatar"…>
```

3. Open your My Account page in the browser and upload an avatar (if you haven't already). You should see it at the top of the page:

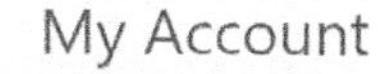

❖ E57.2. Joke Detail Template

1. From the `templates/jokes` folder, open `joke_detail.html` for editing.
2. Add the following highlighted code to the `<small>` text:

```
<small class="text-muted">
  {% if joke.user.avatar %}
    <img src="{{ joke.user.avatar.url }}" alt="{{ joke.user.username }}"
      class="mt-1 rounded float-right" width="50" height="50">
  {% endif %}
  Created on: {{ joke.created }} by {{ joke.user.username }}<br>
  Last updated: {{ joke.updated }}
</small>
```

3. Open a joke-detail page of one of the jokes written by a user with an avatar. You should see the user's avatar at the bottom of the joke:

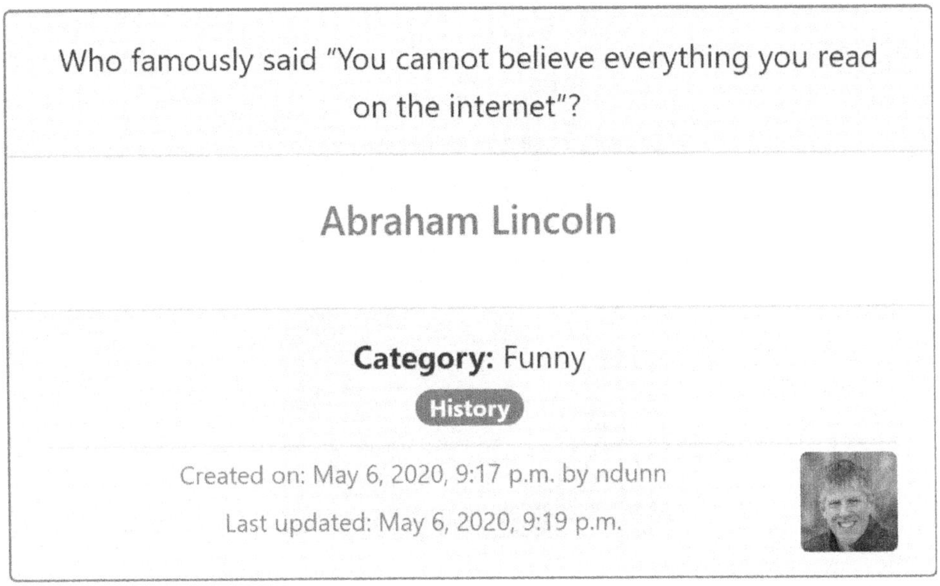

Who famously said "You cannot believe everything you read on the internet"?

Abraham Lincoln

Category: Funny

History

Created on: May 6, 2020, 9:17 p.m. by ndunn

Last updated: May 6, 2020, 9:19 p.m.

Git Commit

Commit your code to Git.

13.2. Amazon Simple Storage Service (Amazon S3)

Amazon **S**imple **S**torage **S**ervice, or S3 for short, is an object storage service. It provides a location for you to store static files (including media files), and gives you the ability to control permissions over those files. The free tier provides access to several gigs of space for a limited time[87] at no cost; however, their terms can change, so be sure to read the agreement and (if appropriate) create a reminder to cancel before they start charging you.

Buckets

S3 storage units are called buckets. You can think of a bucket as a top-level folder or a drive. Each bucket has permission settings, which by default are highly restricted. For a public website, you will generally store three types of files in your S3 buckets:

1. **Static files.** These are files created by developers to be used by the web pages (e.g., site images and CSS and JavaScript files). They must be publicly available.

87. 5 GB for a year at the time of this writing.

2. **Non-private media files.** These are files uploaded by users, but intended to be publicly accessible (e.g., profile pictures).
3. **Private media files.** These are files uploaded by users, but not intended to be publicly accessible (e.g., resumes).

S3 does not permit you to create public folders inside of private buckets. However, you can create private folders within public buckets. Because of this, for a public website, you need to make your buckets public and then add restrictions at the folder or file level.[88]

An AWS Account

You will need an AWS account, which you can get for free at `https://aws.amazon.com/free`.

In the following exercise, we will walk you through setting up S3 to store both the static files and the media files for the Django Jokes site.

Complexity Warning!

Amazon's *Simple* Storage Service isn't so simple. In fact, setting up S3 is pretty complex. If you are not storing media files on your site, there are generally simpler approaches you can take. However, if you are storing media files, you will very likely use Amazon's S3 service, or something similar, to do so.

Things Change!

Companies often change their registration and setup processes. Amazon is no exception. If the instructions here do not work, please visit `https://www.webucator.com/books/errata.cfm` to see if we have posted any updates. If we haven't posted any updates that help, please email us at actionable@webucator.com.

88. An alternative approach is to have multiple buckets with different restriction settings.

Exercise 58: Setting Up Amazon S3

60 to 120 minutes

In this exercise, you will set up S3 to store static and media files for the Django Jokes site. This involves:

1. Creating a free AWS account.
2. Creating an **I**dentity and **A**ccess **M**anagement (IAM) user.
3. Creating a group with full permissions to S3 buckets.
4. Creating an S3 bucket.
5. Installing `boto3` and `django-storages` with pip.
6. Changing and adding some settings.
7. Modifying the models to use the S3 buckets.

E58.1. Creating an AWS Account

Visit `https://aws.amazon.com/free` and follow the instructions to create a free AWS account.

E58.2. Creating an IAM User and Group

1. Log in to your AWS account.
2. On the AWS home page, under **Find Services**, enter "IAM" and select **IAM – Manage access to AWS resources**:

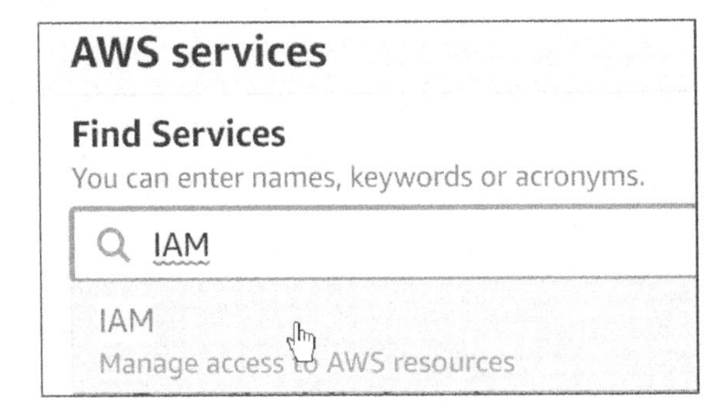

3. On the left sidebar, click **Users**:

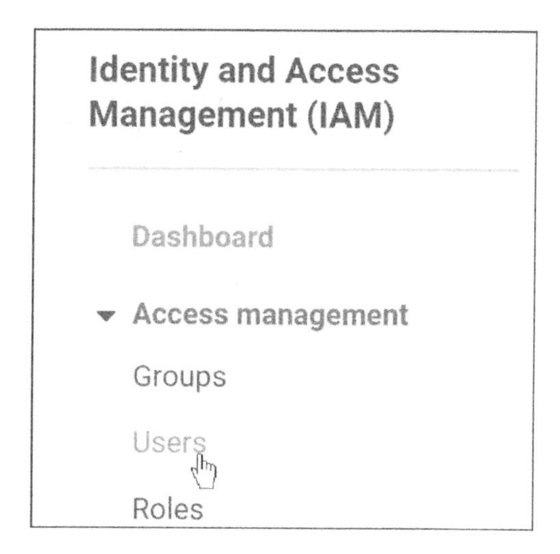

4. Click the **Add User** button:

5. Enter a user name, check **Programmatic access**, and click the **Next: Permissions** button:

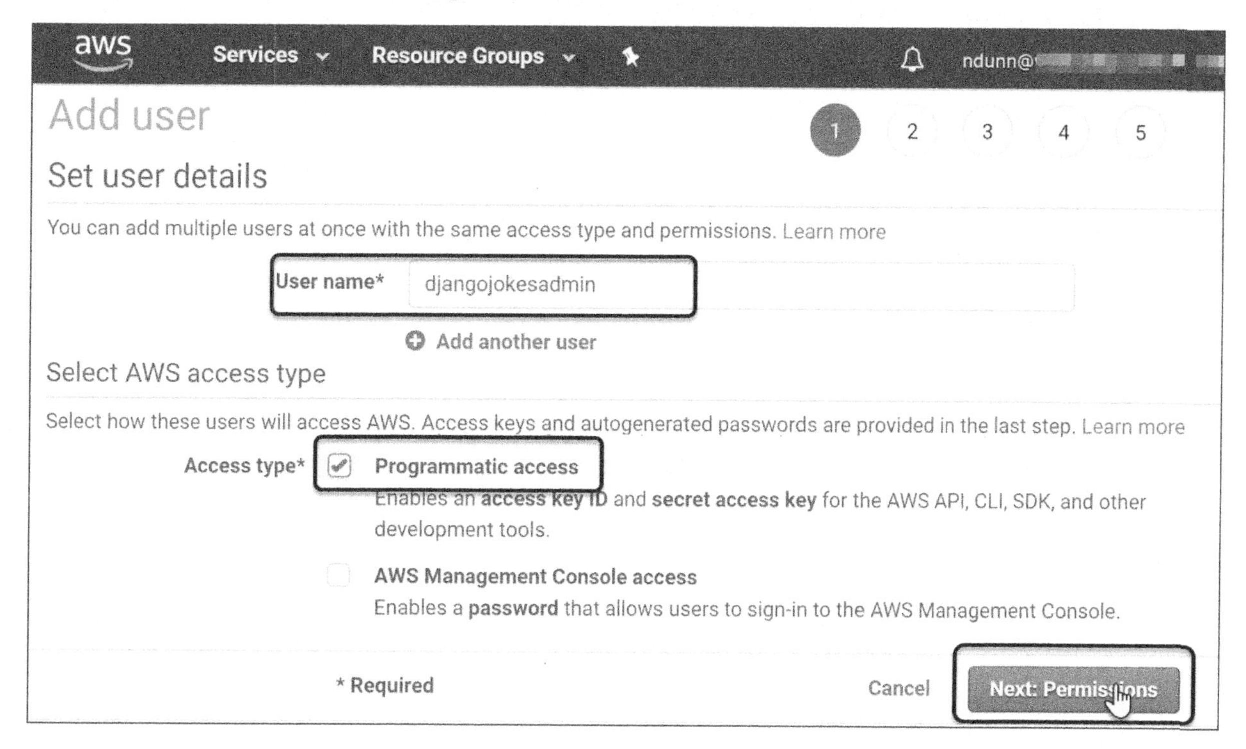

6. Select **Add user to group** and click **Create group**:

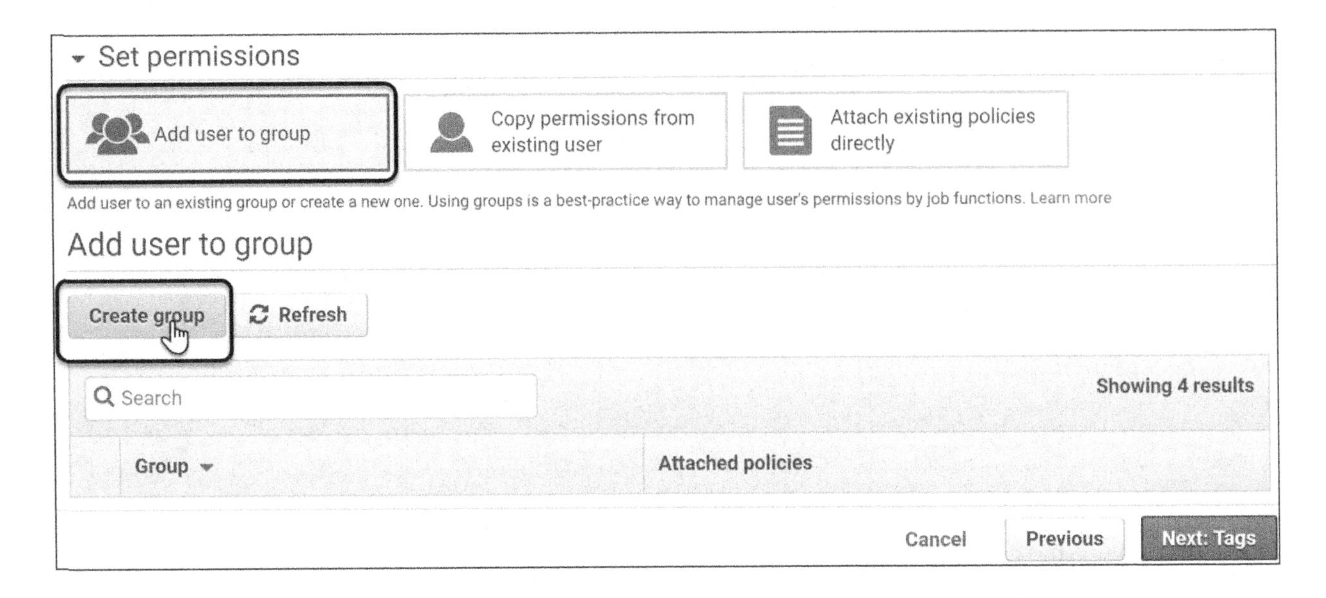

7. Enter a **Group name**. Then, scroll down through the policy types until you find "AmazonS3FullAccess" and check that policy. Then, click the **Create Group** button:

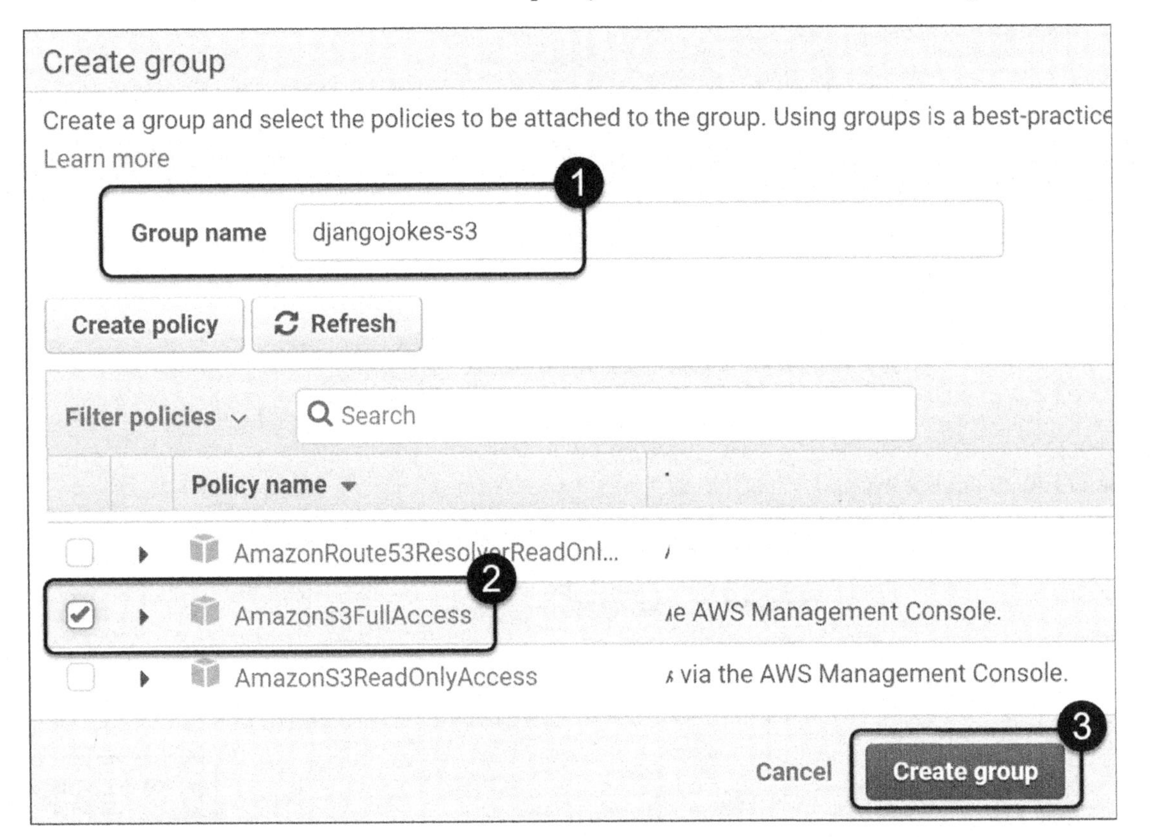

8. On the next screen, your new group should be checked. Click the **Next: Tags** button:

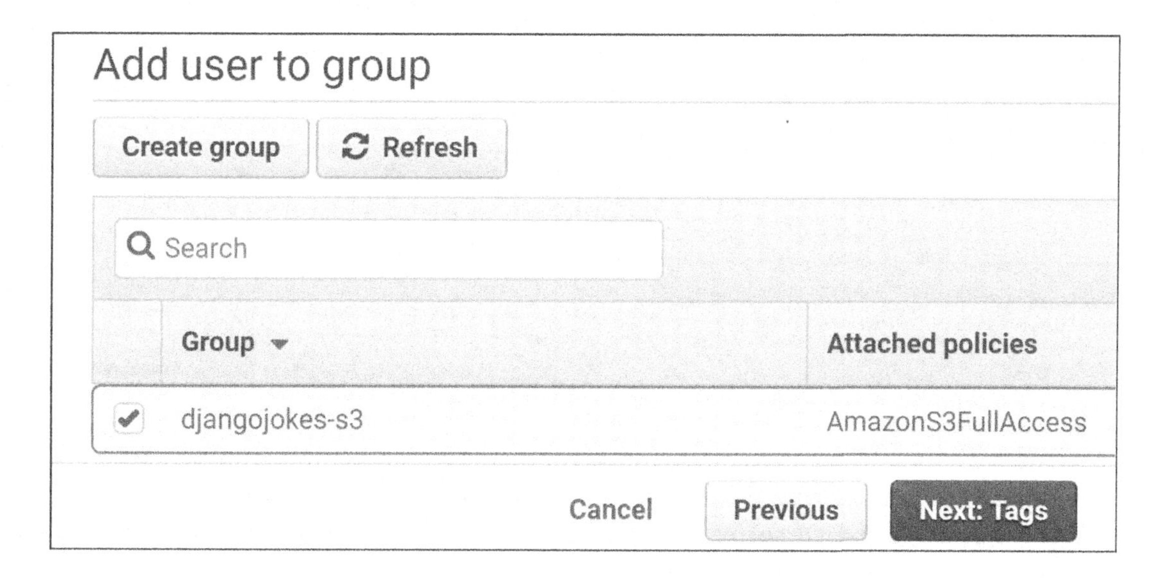

9. You don't need to add any tags. Click the **Next: Review** button:

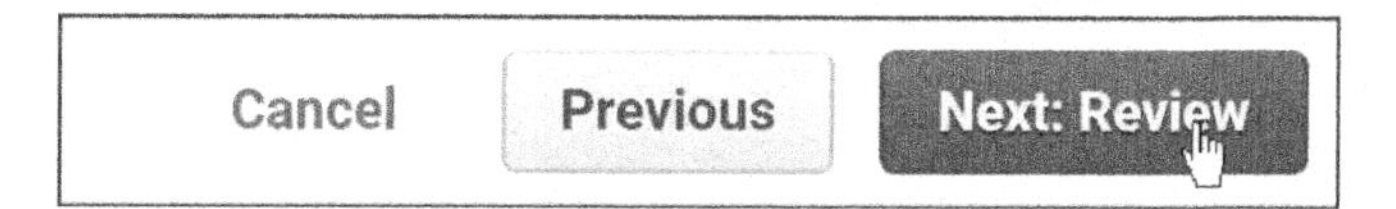

10. Finally, review your choices and click the **Create user** button:

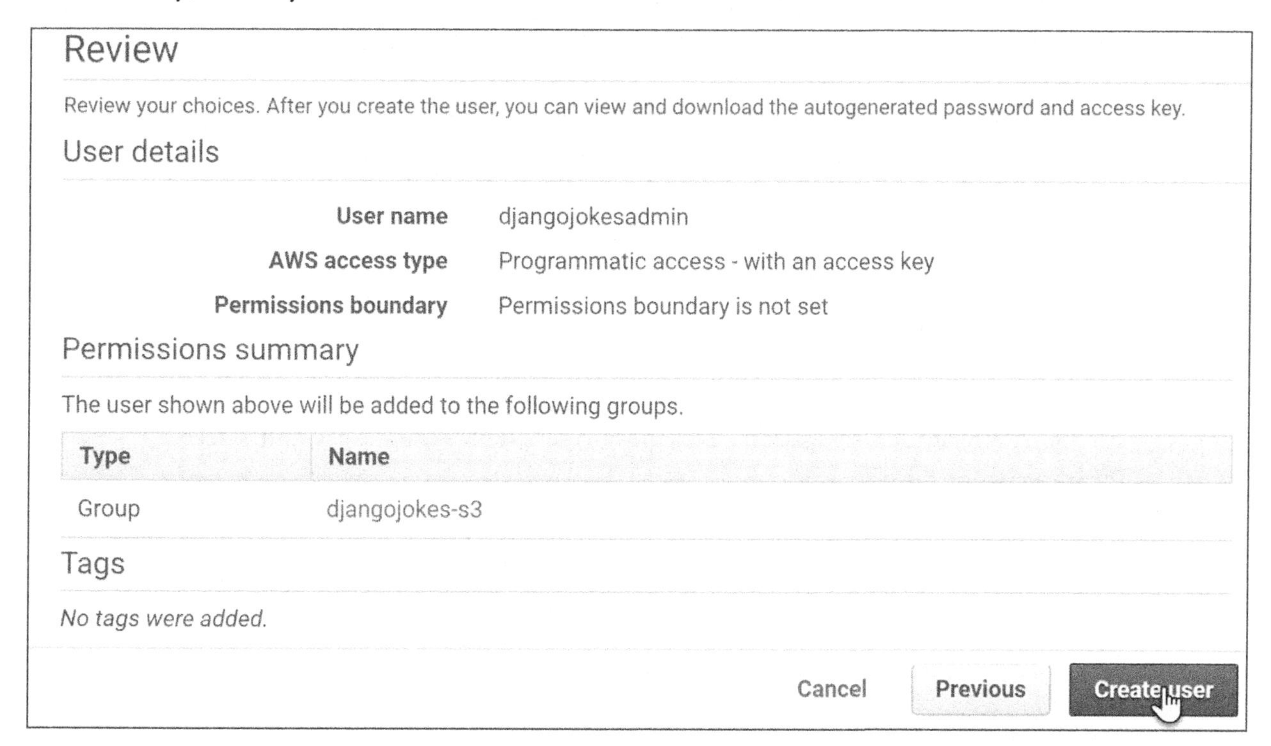

11. You should get a success message:

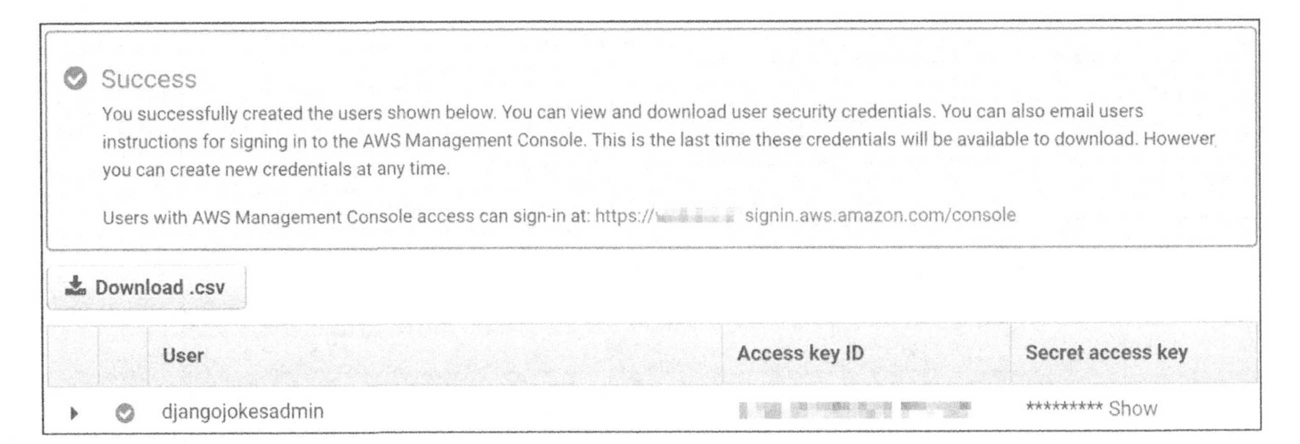

Important: Before leaving this screen, download the CSV into a safe place, and copy your **Access key ID** and your **secret access key**. Then, create the following two settings in your `djangojokes/local_settings.py>` file:

```
AWS_ACCESS_KEY_ID = 'YOUR_ACCESS_KEY_ID'
AWS_SECRET_ACCESS_KEY = 'YOUR_SECRET_ACCESS_KEY'
```

For example:

```
AWS_ACCESS_KEY_ID = 'AKVIMPFKGKEK6GX9IAUD'
AWS_SECRET_ACCESS_KEY = 'gZexvODaMlqhpzgSPGZYsG8Ja937v/QdNfLzZXYd'
```

Remember that the `local_settings.py` file does not get put to production. When you deploy to production, you will create environment variables to hold these settings.

❖ E58.3. Creating an S3 Bucket

Now that you have an IAM user account and a group setup, you need to create a bucket to store your files in.

1. In the AWS header navigation, click **Services**. Then, enter "S3", and select **S3 – Scalable Storage in the Cloud**:

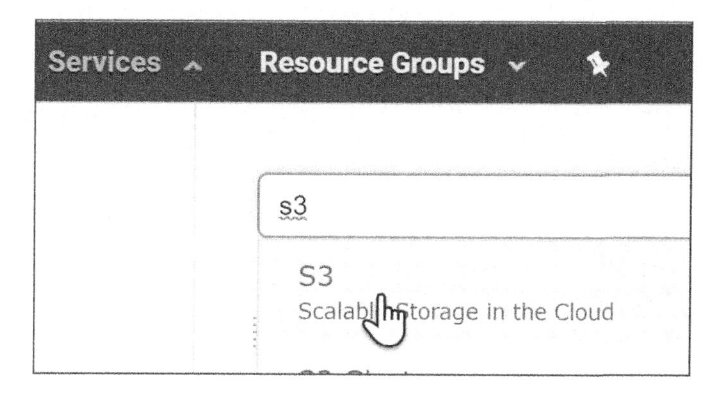

2. Click the **Create bucket** button.
3. Give the bucket a name and select a region:

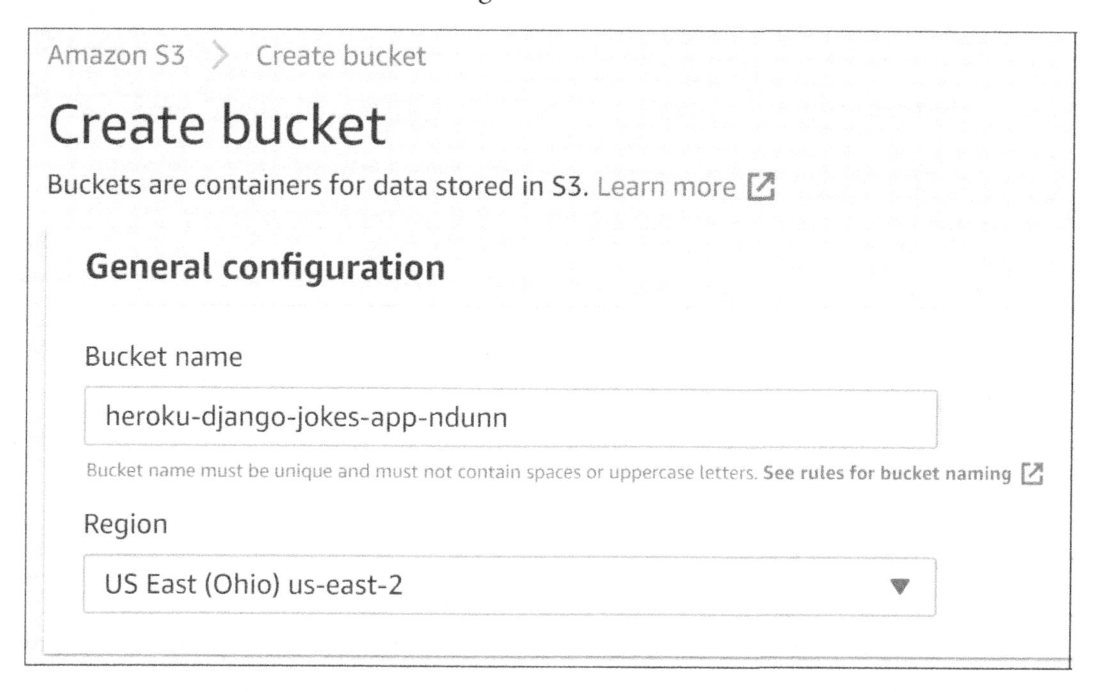

4. Uncheck **Block *all* public access**, check the "I acknowledge…" checkbox, and click the **Create bucket** button:

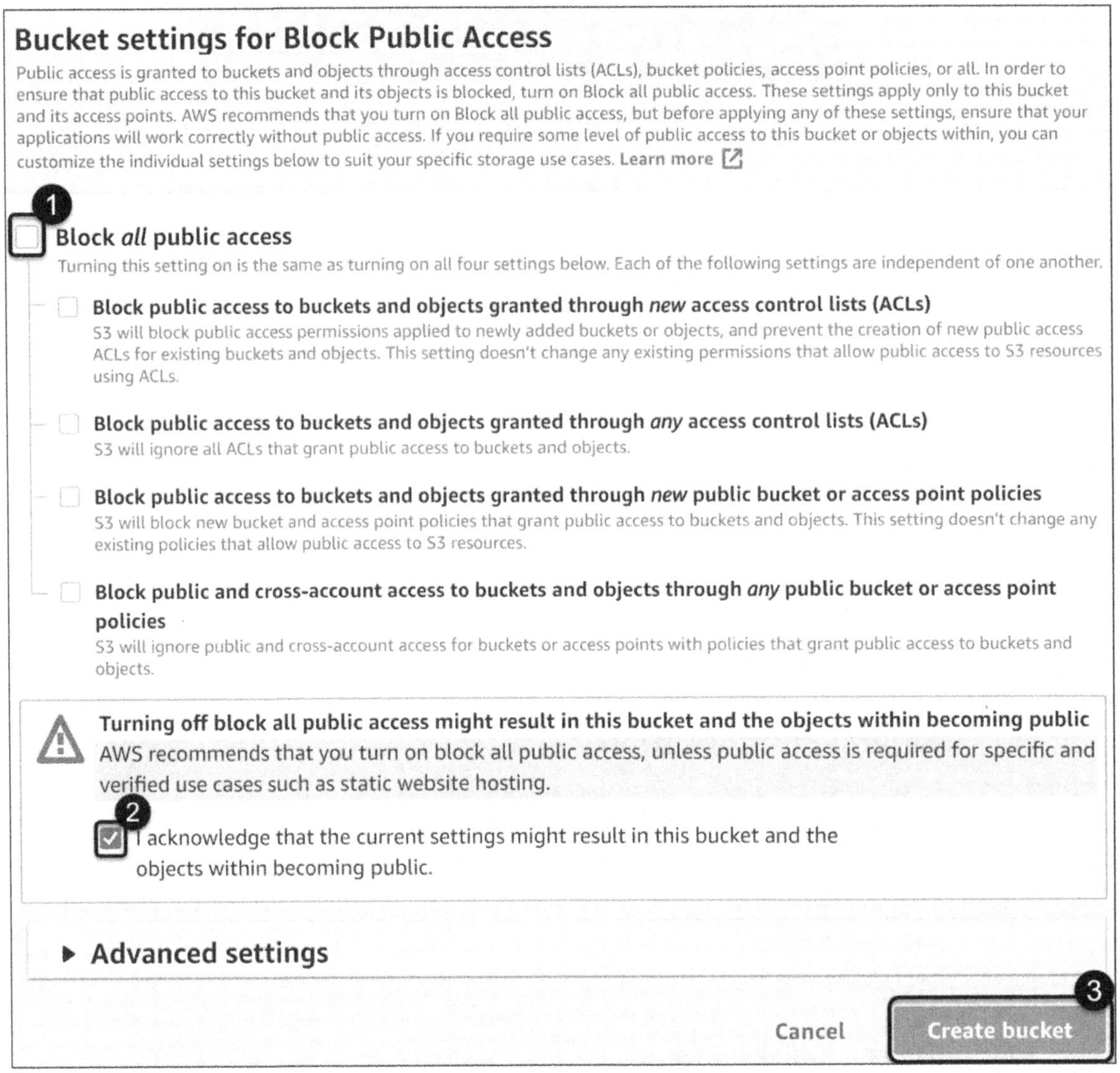

Bucket settings for Block Public Access

Public access is granted to buckets and objects through access control lists (ACLs), bucket policies, access point policies, or all. In order to ensure that public access to this bucket and its objects is blocked, turn on Block all public access. These settings apply only to this bucket and its access points. AWS recommends that you turn on Block all public access, but before applying any of these settings, ensure that your applications will work correctly without public access. If you require some level of public access to this bucket or objects within, you can customize the individual settings below to suit your specific storage use cases. Learn more

1

Block *all* public access

Turning this setting on is the same as turning on all four settings below. Each of the following settings are independent of one another.

Block public access to buckets and objects granted through *new* access control lists (ACLs)

S3 will block public access permissions applied to newly added buckets or objects, and prevent the creation of new public access ACLs for existing buckets and objects. This setting doesn't change any existing permissions that allow public access to S3 resources using ACLs.

Block public access to buckets and objects granted through *any* access control lists (ACLs)

S3 will ignore all ACLs that grant public access to buckets and objects.

Block public access to buckets and objects granted through *new* public bucket or access point policies

S3 will block new bucket and access point policies that grant public access to buckets and objects. This setting doesn't change any existing policies that allow public access to S3 resources.

Block public and cross-account access to buckets and objects through *any* public bucket or access point policies

S3 will ignore public and cross-account access for buckets or access points with policies that grant public access to buckets and objects.

Turning off block all public access might result in this bucket and the objects within becoming public

AWS recommends that you turn on block all public access, unless public access is required for specific and verified use cases such as static website hosting.

2

I acknowledge that the current settings might result in this bucket and the objects within becoming public.

▶ Advanced settings

3

Cancel Create bucket

Notice the warning: "AWS recommends that you turn on block all public access, **unless public access is required for specific and verified use cases such as static website hosting.**" – This "unless…" applies to you. You are storing files that need to be publicly accessible.

❖ E58.4. `boto3` and `django-storages`

You need `boto3` and `django-storages` to interact with S3. Install them both with pip:

```
(.venv) …/projects/djangojokes.com> pip install boto3
```

```
(.venv) …/projects/djangojokes.com> pip install django-storages
```

❖ E58.5. Settings

You now need to modify your settings to indicate that you are storing static and media files on S3 instead of the local server.

Open `djangojokes/settings.py` and delete the following settings:

```
STATIC_URL = '/static/'

STATICFILES_DIRS = [
    BASE_DIR / 'static',
]

MEDIA_URL = '/media/'
MEDIA_ROOT = BASE_DIR / 'media'

# private-storage settings
PRIVATE_STORAGE_ROOT = MEDIA_ROOT / 'private/'
PRIVATE_STORAGE_AUTH_FUNCTION = 'private_storage.permissions.allow_staff'
```

You do not delete the `STATICFILES_DIRS` setting, because that points to where static files are collected from, not to where they are stored.

In place of the settings you just deleted, add the following code:[89]

89. **Don't want to type?** Copy from `starter-code/media-files/settings.py`.

Exercise Code 58.1: djangojokes/settings.py

```
-------Lines 1 through 173 Omitted-------
174. # Static files (CSS, JavaScript, Images)
175. # https://docs.djangoproject.com/en/3.1/howto/static-files/
176.
177. AWS_ACCESS_KEY_ID = os.environ.get('AWS_ACCESS_KEY_ID')
178. AWS_SECRET_ACCESS_KEY = os.environ.get('AWS_SECRET_ACCESS_KEY')
179. AWS_STORAGE_BUCKET_NAME = 'YOUR_BUCKET_NAME' # REPLACE WITH YOUR BUCKET NAME
180. AWS_S3_CUSTOM_DOMAIN = f'{AWS_STORAGE_BUCKET_NAME}.s3.amazonaws.com'
181. AWS_S3_SIGNATURE_VERSION = 's3v4'
182. AWS_DEFAULT_ACL = None # Use S3 bucket's setting
183.
184. AWS_S3_OBJECT_PARAMETERS = {
185.     'CacheControl': 'max-age=86400',
186. }
187.
188. STATICFILES_STORAGE = 'djangojokes.storage_backends.StaticStorage'
189. DEFAULT_FILE_STORAGE = 'djangojokes.storage_backends.PublicMediaStorage'
190. PRIVATE_FILE_STORAGE = 'djangojokes.storage_backends.PrivateMediaStorage'
191.
192. STATIC_URL = f'https://{AWS_S3_CUSTOM_DOMAIN}/static/'
193. MEDIA_URL = f"https://{AWS_S3_CUSTOM_DOMAIN}/media/"
194.
195. STATICFILES_DIRS = [
196.     BASE_DIR / 'static',
197. ]
-------Lines 198 through 202 Omitted-------
```

Phew! That's a lot of settings. Following are explanations of what each is for:[90]

1. The `AWS_ACCESS_KEY_ID` and `AWS_SECRET_ACCESS_KEY` are set using environment variables. You will have to create those when you deploy to production. For the local server, you should have already created these in `local_settings.py`.
2. `AWS_STORAGE_BUCKET_NAME` – **Change this to the name you gave to the bucket.**
3. `AWS_S3_CUSTOM_DOMAIN` – The URL of the bucket.
4. `AWS_S3_SIGNATURE_VERSION` – The signature version used for generating *presigned URLs* – special URLs that are only available for a limited time. These are the URLs that give users with special permissions access to S3 files.

90. See `https://django-storages.readthedocs.io/en/latest/backends/amazon-S3.html#amazon-s3` for documentation on `django-storages` Amazon S3 settings.

5. `AWS_DEFAULT_ACL = None` – Setting this to `None` indicates that uploaded files should use the same access control settings as the S3 bucket.
6. `AWS_S3_OBJECT_PARAMETERS` – The cache-control setting specifies the number of seconds objects will be kept in cache.[91]
7. `STATICFILES_STORAGE` – This is a built-in Django setting pointing to the class responsible for handling static file storage. It defaults to:

   ```
   'django.contrib.staticfiles.storage.StaticFilesStorage'
   ```

   You are changing the value to:

   ```
   'djangojokes.storage_backends.StaticStorage'
   ```

   You will create that class shortly.
8. `DEFAULT_FILE_STORAGE` – This is the built-in Django setting we discussed earlier (see page 385). It points to the class responsible for handling uploaded files. It defaults to:

   ```
   'django.core.files.storage.FileSystemStorage'
   ```

   You are changing the value to:

   ```
   'djangojokes.storage_backends.PublicMediaStorage'
   ```

   You will create that class shortly also.
9. `PRIVATE_FILE_STORAGE` – This is **not** a built-in Django setting. You will have to reference it explicitly. You will create the class shortly and then will reference it in the `resume` field of the `jobs.Applicant` model.
10. You have changed `STATIC_URL` and `MEDIA_URL` to use the AWS `static` and `media` folders.
11. As you are no longer storing files on the server, you have removed the `STATIC_ROOT` and `MEDIA_ROOT` settings .
12. As you are no longer using `private-storage`, you have removed the `PRIVATE_STORAGE_ROOT` and `PRIVATE_STORAGE_AUTH_FUNCTION` settings.
13. Again, you have **not changed** the value of `STATICFILES_DIRS`. This setting tells Django where to *collect* static files from before moving them to storage. The settings you have added and changed have to do with where to *store* the collected files.

---

91. See `https://developer.mozilla.org/en-US/docs/Web/HTTP/Headers/Cache-Control` for information on Cache-Control.

The Storage Classes

Create a new file in the djangojokes folder and save it as storage_backends.py:[92]

Exercise Code 58.2: djangojokes/storage_backends.py

```
1.  from storages.backends.s3boto3 import S3Boto3Storage
2.
3.  class StaticStorage(S3Boto3Storage):
4.      """ Class for storing static files. """
5.      location = 'static'
6.      default_acl = 'public-read'
7.      file_overwrite = True
8.
9.  class PublicMediaStorage(S3Boto3Storage):
10.     """ Class for storing public media files. """
11.     location = 'media/public'
12.     default_acl = 'public-read'
13.     file_overwrite = False
14.
15. class PrivateMediaStorage(S3Boto3Storage):
16.     """ Class for storing private media files. """
17.     location = 'media/private'
18.     default_acl = 'private'
19.     file_overwrite = False
20.     custom_domain = False
```

In this file, you create three classes that inherit from S3Boto3Storage:

1. StaticStorage – For storing static files.
2. PublicMediaStorage – For storing public media files.
3. PrivateMediaStorage – For storing private media files.

These are the three classes referenced in settings.py by STATICFILES_STORAGE, DEFAULT_FILE_STORAGE, and PRIVATE_FILE_STORAGE. All three classes have the following attributes:

1. location – The path to which to upload the files.
2. default_acl – The default access control list. For StaticStorage and PublicMediaStorage, it is set to 'public-read', meaning everyone has read access to these files. For PrivateMediaStorage, it is set to 'private', meaning that special access is needed to read

92. **Don't want to type?** Copy from starter-code/media-files/storage_backends.py.

these files. That special access is given by setting custom_domain, which defaults to the value of the AWS_S3_CUSTOM_DOMAIN setting, to False.

3. file_overwrite – Whether or not to overwrite files. When you modify static files (e.g., add a rule to the CSS), you want to overwrite the existing files, so you set this to True for StaticStorage. For the other two, you never want to overwrite existing files, so you set it to False. If someone uploads a file with the same name as an existing file, the file name will be appended with a random string (e.g., my-resume_**o4GtK81**.pdf).

❖ E58.6. Models

1. Open jobs/models.py in your editor.
2. Import PrivateMediaStorage instead of PrivateFileField:

```
from private_storage.fields import PrivateFileField
from djangojokes.storage_backends import PrivateMediaStorage
```

3. In the Applicant model, change the field type back to models.FileField and set resume to use PrivateMediaStorage:

```
resume = models.FileField(
    storage = PrivateMediaStorage(),
    upload_to='resumes', blank=True, help_text='PDFs only',
    validators=[validate_pdf]
)
```

   Now, resumes will be uploaded to the media/private directory in the S3 bucket.

4. You don't need to change the avatar field in users.CustomUser because that already uses the default, which you changed to use S3 by setting DEFAULT_FILE_STORAGE in settings.py.
5. Because you changed the Applicant model, you need to make and run migrations:

```
(.venv) …/projects/djangojokes.com> python manage.py makemigrations
(.venv) …/projects/djangojokes.com> python manage.py migrate
```

❖ E58.7. Collect Static Files

Finally, because you have changed the location of static files, you need to collect them by running:

```
(.venv) …/projects/djangojokes.com> python manage.py collectstatic
```

This may take a little while to run as it needs to upload all your static files, including those used by Django admin, to the AWS bucket.

❖ E58.8. AWS S3

Visit `https://s3.console.aws.amazon.com/s3/` and open your bucket. It should contain a `static` folder:

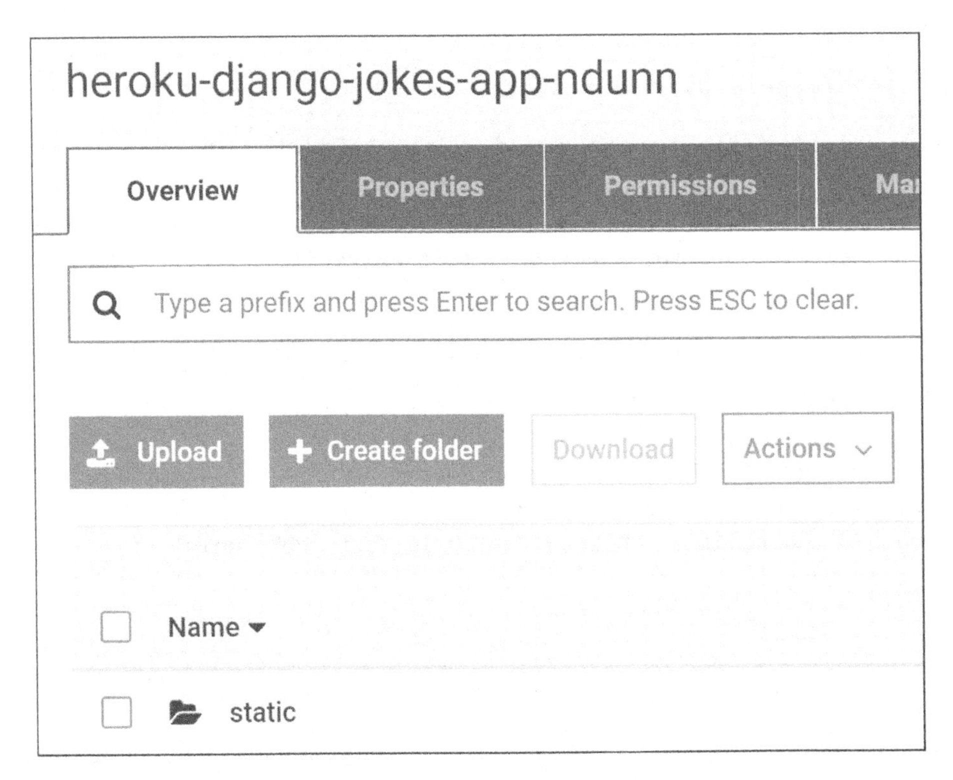

The `static` folder was created when `collectstatic` was run. The `media` folder and its subfolders will be created when files are first uploaded to them.

Disclaimer

You must keep your users' sensitive content private. While we believe the steps laid out here will do that, you should review Amazon S3 Bucket Public Access Considerations[93] and other resources, and test, test, test before allowing users to upload sensitive content.

93. `https://aws.amazon.com/articles/amazon-s3-bucket-public-access-considerations/`

❖ E58.9. Try It Out

Start up the server and try it out.

Upload an Avatar

1. Log in to the Django Jokes site.
2. Go to your My Account page.
3. Upload a profile picture and click **UPDATE**. Your profile picture should show up at the top of the form.
4. Right-click on your profile picture and select **Open image in new tab**:

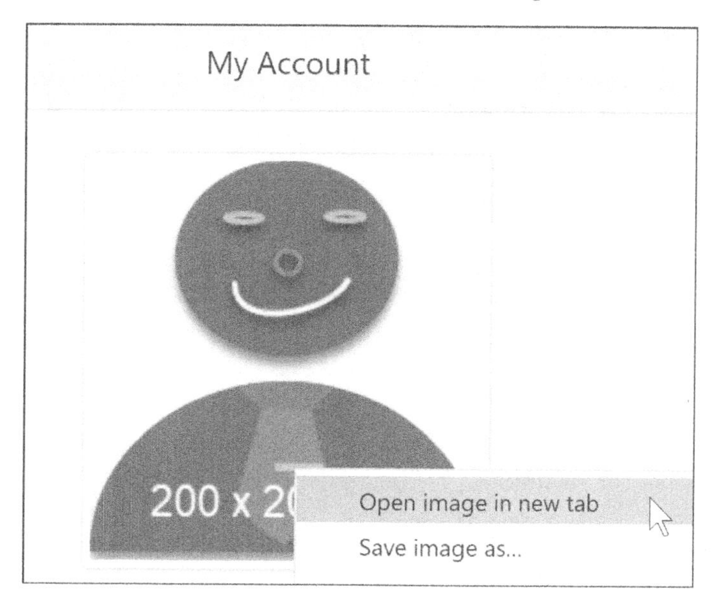

Notice the URL of the image. It will be something like:

```
https://your-bucket-name.s3.amazonaws.com/media/public/avatars/profile-pic-
200x200.png
```

5. Return to `https://s3.console.aws.amazon.com/s3/` and open your bucket. It should now contain a `media` folder with a `public` subfolder with an `avatars` subfolder with your image in it:

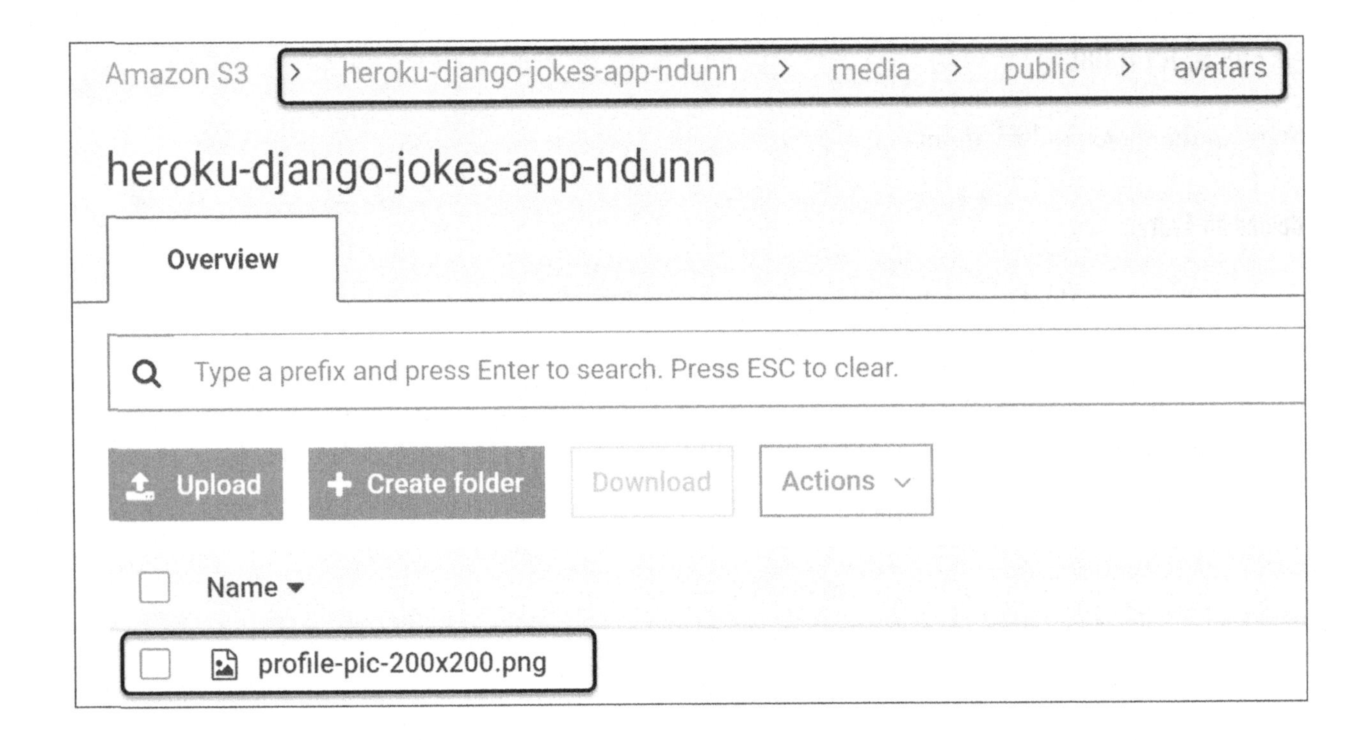

Apply for a Job

Back on your Django Jokes website:

1. Click on the **About** link in the footer.
2. Click on the **Work for us** link.
3. Fill out the job application and include a resume. You can use `starter-code/media-files/resume-jangore.pdf`.
4. In Django admin, click on **Applicants**.
5. Open the new applicant record and scroll down to the resume field.
6. Click on the resume link:

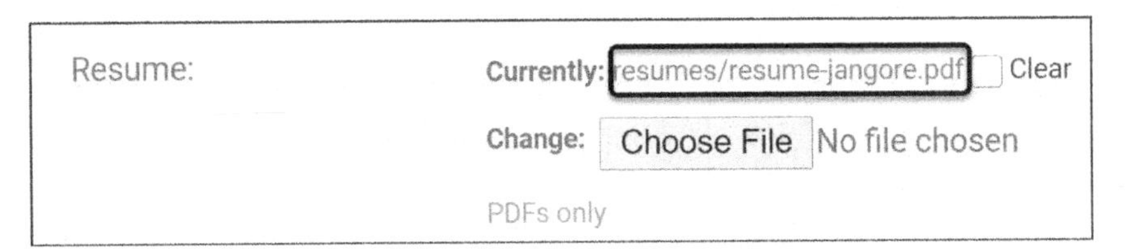

The resume should open up and the URL should be something like:

```
https://your-bucket-name.s3.amazonaws.com/media/private/resumes/resume-jan ↵↵
gore.pdf?AWSAccessKeyId=AKIILPF4KGEAUDVKE6GX&Signature=VvGOa ↵↵
JVBQ2HEUirQ1L%2Fpfvs5GX1%3D&Expires=1591221027
```

Those URL parameters are what make this URL private. Try removing them and pressing Enter. You should get an access denied error:

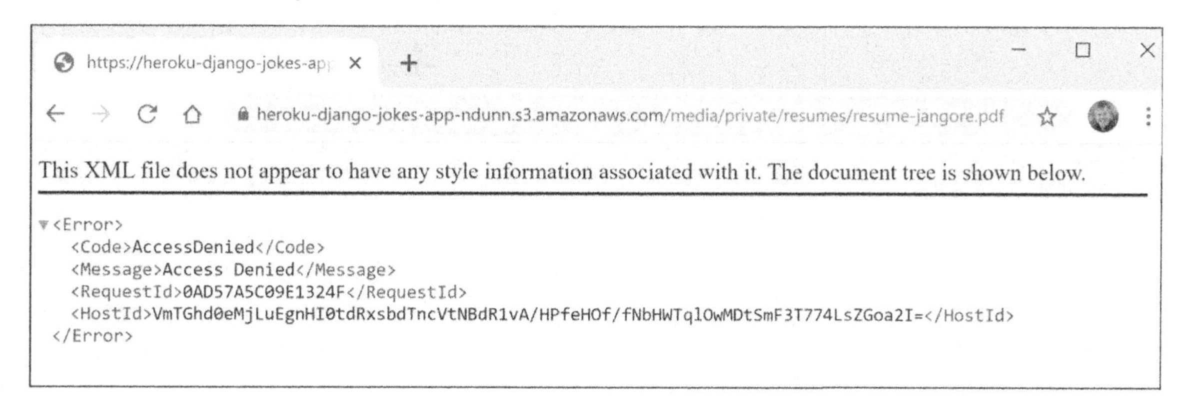

❖ E58.10. Cleanup

As you are no longer using `django-private-storage`, you can remove it from the project:

1. In `settings.py`, remove `'private_storage'` from `INSTALLED_APPS`:

```
# Third-party
'crispy_forms',
'allauth',
'allauth.account',
'allauth.socialaccount',
'private_storage',
```

2. In `djangojokes/urls.py`, remove the line of code importing `private_storage.urls` and the related path:

```
import private_storage.urls

urlpatterns = [
    ...
    # Private Media
    path('media/private/', include(private_storage.urls)),
    ...
```

Be careful uninstalling libraries!

Now that you are no longer using `django-private-storage`, it is tempting to uninstall it with `pip uninstall`; however, this is difficult to do. The problem is that you have already created and run migrations that use `django-private-storage`. If you uninstall the library, you will get an error when you try to migrate. You could try to clean up the related migration file, but that can lead to other problems. Our recommendation is to leave it alone.

Git Commit

Commit your code to Git.

Exercise 59: Static Settings in Development

5 to 10 minutes

It would be a pain to have to run `collectstatic` after every change to a static file during development. To avoid this, add the following settings to `local_settings.py`:

```
# Local Static File Settings
STATICFILES_STORAGE = 'django.contrib.staticfiles.storage.StaticFilesStorage'
STATIC_URL = '/static/'
```

This will set your local static settings back to the way they were before you started using Amazon S3. Your production settings will continue to use S3.

Git Commit

Commit your code to Git.

Conclusion

In this lesson, you have learned to set up media files and to allow users to upload files and images, both public and private, in a secure way both to the local computer and to Amazon's Simple Storage Service.

LESSON 14

Making Queries, Ajax, and View Functions

Topics Covered

☑ Querying models.

☑ Adding properties to models.

☑ Ajax.

☑ View functions.

☑ Model constraints.

> "**Query**," said Mr. Crawford, looking round him, "whether we may not find something to employ us here before we go farther? I see walls of great promise. Mr. Rushworth, shall we summon a council on this lawn?"
>
> – *Mansfield Park, Jane Austen*

Introduction

For every model you create in an app, Django creates at least one corresponding table in the database. While it is possible to query those tables directly using raw SQL,[94] it is rare that you will need to do so. Instead, you will use Django's database-abstraction layer, which allows you to perform SQL `SELECT`, `INSERT`, `UPDATE`, and `DELETE` statements without actually writing them.

❋

94. `https://docs.djangoproject.com/en/3.1/topics/db/sql/`

14.1. Useful Prerequisites

❖ 14.1.1. SQL

In this lesson, we show quite a bit of SQL to compare Django queries to raw SQL queries. While you don't need to have experience with SQL to learn Django (or to go through this lesson), it would certainly be helpful.

❖ 14.1.2. JavaScript and Ajax

We also use quite a bit of JavaScript and JSON in this lesson to show how to call a Django view without doing a page refresh using a technique known as Ajax. If you don't know JavaScript, just try to get an understanding of what the JavaScript is doing and how it interacts with the Django view and template.

14.2. Managers and `QuerySets`

SQL

SQL stands for **S**tructured **Q**uery **L**anguage and is pronounced either *ess-que-el* or *sequel.* It is the language used by relational database management systems (RDBMS) to access and manipulate data and to create, structure and destroy databases and database objects. Knowing SQL will give you a deeper understanding of how Django works with databases. In this lesson, we will make direct comparisons to SQL. Basic SQL statements are pretty easy to understand, so read through those SQL statements even if you have no prior experience with SQL.

Models have *managers*, and through those managers, you create `QuerySets`. The manager is held in the model class's `objects` attribute. Its main methods are:

1. `all()` – Retrieves all the objects in the model class. It is the equivalent of a SQL `SELECT` statement with no `WHERE` clause.
2. `filter(**kwargs)` – Retrieves objects in the model class that meet the conditions specified in the `kwargs`. Generally, it is the equivalent of a SQL `SELECT` statement with a `WHERE` clause.

3. `exclude(**kwargs)` – Like `filter()`, except that it retrieves all objects that *do not match* the conditions specified in `kwargs`. It is analogous to a SQL `SELECT` statement with a `WHERE NOT (...)` clause.

4. `get(**kwargs)` – Retrieves one and only one object (not a `QuerySet`). If no object is found that matches the conditions specified in `kwargs`, it will raise a `DoesNotExist` exception. If more than one object matches the conditions, it will raise a `MultipleObjectsReturned` exception.

Lookups

The `kwargs` passed to `filter()`, `exclude()`, and `get()` are called *lookups.*

From the `djangojokes.com` directory, open the Django shell (`python manage.py shell`) and run the following code:

Import the Tag Model

```
>>> from jokes.models import Tag
```

Get the Tag Manager

```
>>> Tag.objects
<django.db.models.manager.Manager object at 0x04227D60>
```

Get all the Tag objects with all()

```
>>> Tag.objects.all()
<QuerySet [<Tag: Animal>, <Tag: Bar>, <Tag: Birthday>, <Tag: Family>, <Tag: Grandparents>,
 <Tag: History>, <Tag: Nature>, <Tag: Pun>, <Tag: Sports>]>
```

The SQL query produced by `Tag.objects.all()` would look like this:

```
SELECT id, tag, slug, created, updated
FROM jokes_tag
ORDER BY tag ASC
```

Notice there is no `WHERE` clause – *all* records are returned.

```
Get a single Tag object with get()
>>> Tag.objects.get(pk=1)
<Tag: Animal>
```

The SQL query produced by `Tag.objects.get(pk=1)` would look like this:

```
SELECT id, tag, slug, created, updated
FROM jokes_tag
WHERE id = 1
```

```
Get specific Tag objects with filter()
>>> Tag.objects.filter(tag='Animal')
<QuerySet [<Tag: Animal>]>
```

The SQL query produced by `Tag.objects.filter(tag='Animal')` would look like this:

```
SELECT id, tag, slug, created, updated
FROM jokes_tag
WHERE tag = 'Animal'
```

```
Get all except specific Tag objects with exclude()
>>> Tag.objects.exclude(tag='Animal')
<QuerySet [<Tag: Bar>, <Tag: Birthday>, <Tag: Family>, <Tag: Grandparents>, <Tag: History>,
 <Tag: Nature>, <Tag: Pun>, <Tag: Sports>]>
```

The SQL query produced by `Tag.objects.exclude(tag='Animal')` would look like this:

```
SELECT id, tag, slug, created, updated
FROM jokes_tag
WHERE NOT (tag = 'Animal')
```

*

14.3. Indexing and Slicing `QuerySets`

Use Python's indexing syntax to get an object by position in a `QuerySet`:

```
>>> all_tags = Tag.objects.all()
>>> first_tag = all_tags[0]
>>> first_tag
<Tag: Animal>
```

Use Python's slicing syntax to get subsets of `QuerySets`:

```
>>> all_tags = Tag.objects.all()
>>> all_tags[2:5]
<QuerySet [<Tag: Birthday>, <Tag: Family>, <Tag: Grandparents>]>
```

Notice that this results in a brand new `QuerySet`. The original `all_tags` `QuerySet` remains untouched. The SQL for the new `QuerySet` would look like this:

```
SELECT id, tag, slug, created, updated
FROM jokes_tag
ORDER BY tag ASC
LIMIT 3 OFFSET 2
```

14.4. Checking for Existence

Creating a `QuerySet` does not cause a database query to be executed. The query will not be executed until the `QuerySet` is evaluated. If you want to check if the query would return results without actually getting those results, you can use the `QuerySet`'s `exists()` method. For example:

```
>>> from jokes.models import Tag
>>> if Tag.objects.filter(tag='History').exists():
...     print('We have history')
...
We have history
```

This is faster than performing the query and checking the results:

```
>>> history_tag = Tag.objects.filter(tag='History')
>>> if history_tag:
...     print('We have history.')
```

The `if history_tag:` line causes the query to get executed, which is slower than checking `exists()`; however, it isn't *a lot* slower, so if you are likely to use the results of the query, you're better off taking this second approach, so you don't have to hit the database twice:

```
if Tag.objects.filter(tag='History').exists(): # First database hit
    history_tag = Tag.objects.filter(tag='History')
    history_tag_created = history_tag.created # Second database hit
```

14.5. Creating, Updating, and Saving Model Instances

New model instances are created in the same way that new instances of any Python class are created: using the class constructor. You then call `save()` on the instance to save the record to the database:

```
>>> obnoxious_tag = Tag(tag='obnoxious')
>>> obnoxious_tag.save()
```

The SQL query that runs in the background is something like:

```
INSERT INTO jokes_tag
(tag, slug, created, updated)
VALUES ('obnoxious', 'obnoxious', datetime.now().time(), datetime.now().time())
```

To update the model instance, you:

1. Get the instance.
2. Set one or more of its attributes.
3. Save.

```
>>> obnoxious_tag = Tag.objects.get(tag='obnoxious')
>>> obnoxious_tag.tag = 'insufferable'
>>> obnoxious_tag.save()
```

The SQL query that runs in the background is something like:

```
UPDATE jokes_tag
SET tag = 'insufferable'
WHERE id = 10
```

Note that when creating and updating model instances, the database is not hit until `save()` is called.

14.6. `QuerySet` Methods that Don't Return `QuerySets`

The `all()`, `filter()`, and `exclude()` methods all return new `QuerySets`. The `get()` method returns a single model instance. `QuerySets` include additional methods that either return model instances or some other non-`QuerySet` type.

`earliest()` and `latest()`

The `earliest()` and `latest()` methods take one or more fields as arguments and return the record with the smallest (for `earliest()`) or largest (for `latest()`) values for the passed-in fields. Generally, they are used with date fields, but they can take fields of any type that can be ordered. For example, you can confirm that the "obnoxious" tag was saved using the following code:

```
>>> Tag.objects.latest('created')
<Tag: obnoxious>
```

`first()` and `last()`

The `first()` and `last()` methods return the first and last objects in a `QuerySet`.

```
>>> Tag.objects.first()
<Tag: Animal>
>>> Tag.objects.last()
<Tag: Work>
```

`count()`

The `count()` method returns the number of records in the `QuerySet`:

```
>>> Tag.objects.count()
10
```

❖ 14.6.1. The `all()` Assumption

Notice that some of these methods are used directly on the `objects` manager (e.g., `Tag.objects.count()`). This is equivalent to `Tag.objects.all().count()`. If no `QuerySet` is specified, it gets all the records.

See `https://docs.djangoproject.com/en/3.1/ref/models/querysets/#methods-that-do-not-return-querysets` for documentation on other methods that do not return `QuerySets`.

14.7. One-to-Many Relationships

Remember that the `Joke` model's `category` field is defined like this:

```
category = models.ForeignKey('Category', on_delete=models.PROTECT)
```

This creates a one-to-many relationship. Looking up one-to-many relationship with Django is straightforward:

```
>>> from jokes.models import Joke
>>> first_joke = Joke.objects.first()
>>> first_joke.category
<Category: Funny>
```

`first_joke.category` returns the category model instance. If you were to print that, it would print the value returned by the `Category` model's `__str__()` method, which is the `category` field value:

```
>>> print(first_joke.category)
Funny
```

To explicitly get the `category` field value, you need to do this:

```
>>> first_joke.category.category
'Funny'
```

The first occurrence of `category` (first_joke.*category*.category) gets the `category` model instance, and the second occurrence of `category` (first_joke.category.*category*) gets the `category` field on that instance.

This shows how to get the category of a joke, but how do you go the other way? How do you get all the jokes in a category?

Backward Relationships

Again, the relationship between the joke and the category is created by the `category` field in the `Joke` model:

```
category = models.ForeignKey('Category', on_delete=models.PROTECT)
```

In the Django Admin and the User Model lesson, you installed the Django admin documentation generator (see page 205). That can come in useful when looking at relationships between models.

1. Start up the server, log in as the superuser, and open up Django admin.
2. Click on the **Documentation** link in the top navigation and then click on **Models**.
3. Scroll down to the **Jokes** section, and click on **Joke**.
4. Notice the description of the `category` field is "the related `jokes.Category` object":

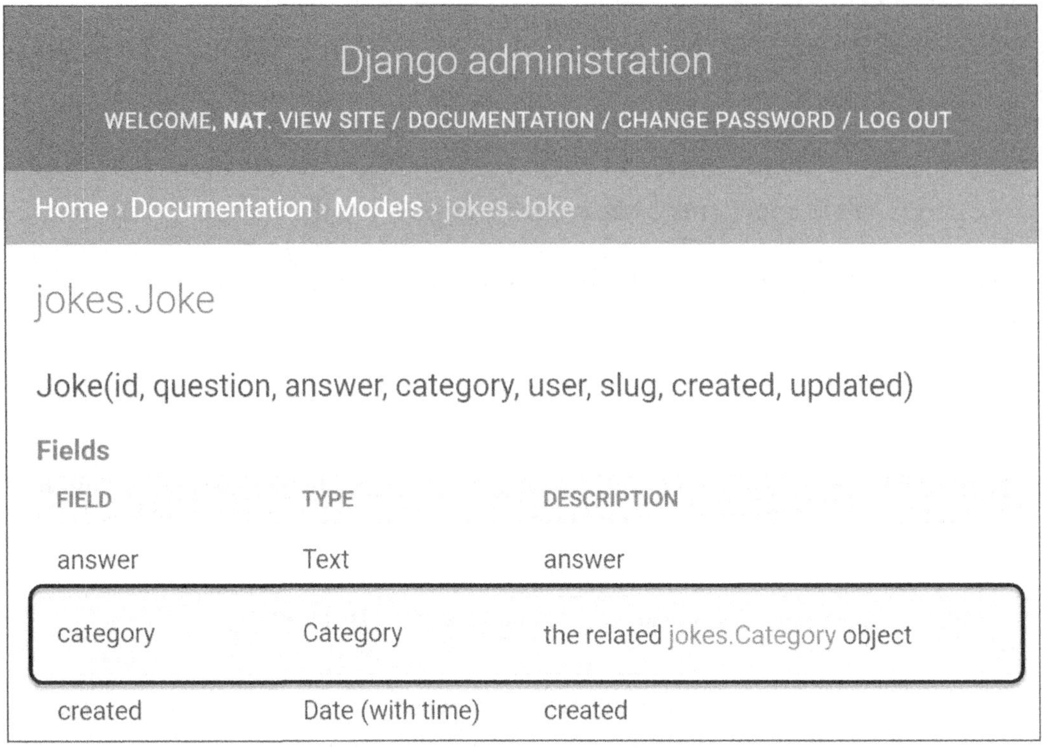

Django administration

WELCOME, **NAT**. VIEW SITE / DOCUMENTATION / CHANGE PASSWORD / LOG OUT

Home › Documentation › Models › jokes.Joke

jokes.Joke

Joke(id, question, answer, category, user, slug, created, updated)

Fields

FIELD	TYPE	DESCRIPTION
answer	Text	answer
category	Category	the related jokes.Category object
created	Date (with time)	created

5. Now, go back one page by clicking on the **Back** button and then click the **Category** link.
6. Notice the two `joke_set` entries:

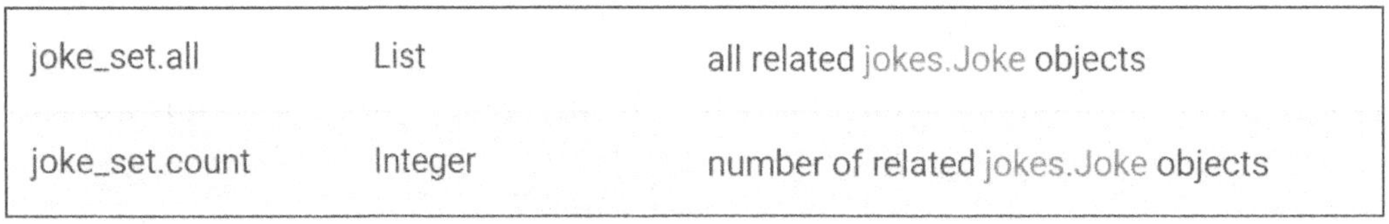

joke_set.all	List	all related jokes.Joke objects
joke_set.count	Integer	number of related jokes.Joke objects

Remember that the `Category` model has no `joke` field. But because it is referenced by the `Joke` model, its manager gets access to `Joke` instances through a *related manager*, which by default is named `joke_set` (the lowercase name of the referencing model appended with "_set").

7. To see the related manager object, run the following code at the Django shell:

```
>>> from jokes.models import Category
>>> first_category = Category.objects.first()
>>> first_category.joke_set
<django.db.models.fields.related_descriptors.create_reverse_many_to_one_manager.<lo ↵
cals>.RelatedManager object at 0x04C4AB38>
```

The related manager can be used in the same way as a model's `objects` manager. For example, you can use `count()` to get the number of jokes in a category:

```
>>> first_category.joke_set.count()
5
```

And, you can use `first()` to get the first joke in a category:

```
>>> first_category.joke_set.first()
<Joke: Why did the chicken cross the road?>
>>> first_category.joke_set.first().question
'Why did the chicken cross the road?'
>>> first_category.joke_set.first().answer
'To get to the other side.'
```

Renaming the Related Manager

If you don't like the default name given to the related manager (e.g., `joke_set`), you can use the `related_name` argument to provide a different name when you create the relationship. In `jokes/models.py`, make the following change to the `Joke` model:

```
category = models.ForeignKey(
    'Category', on_delete=models.PROTECT, related_name='jokes'
)
```

After doing so, you access the related manager using the new name. Note that you will need to exit and re-enter the shell for this change to take effect:

```
>>> from jokes.models import Category
>>> first_category = Category.objects.first()
>>> first_category.jokes
<django.db.models.fields.related_descriptors.create_reverse_many_to_one_manager.<locals>.Re ↵↵
latedManager object at 0x042E6070>
```

The change will also be reflected in the Django admin documentation:

jokes.all	List	all related jokes.Joke objects
jokes.count	Integer	number of related jokes.Joke objects

14.8. Many-to-Many Relationships

A couple of questions to start:

1. How many tags does the first joke have?
2. How many jokes are tagged with the "Animal" tag?

Remember that the `Joke` model's `tags` field is defined like this:

```
tags = models.ManyToManyField('Tag', blank=True)
```

When we first introduced `ManyToManyFields` (see page 291), we mentioned that the relationship could be defined on either model. For example, you could have defined this field on the `Tag` model:

```
jokes = models.ManyToManyField('Joke', blank=True)
```

We chose to do it the first way, because *jokes with tags* seems more intuitive than *tags with jokes*.

As a result of this choice, you access tags on a joke using the `tags` attribute, but you access jokes on a tag using the `joke_set` attribute. Run the following code to see this:

Get a joke's tags related manager

```
>>> from jokes.models import Joke, Tag
>>> first_joke = Joke.objects.first()
>>> first_joke.tags
<django.db.models.fields.related_descriptors.create_forward_many_to_many_manager.<lo ↵↵
cals>.ManyRelatedManager object at 0x04237040>
```

```
Get a tag's joke_set related manager
>>> first_tag = Tag.objects.first()
>>> first_tag.joke_set
<django.db.models.fields.related_descriptors.create_forward_many_to_many_manager.<lo ↵
cals>.ManyRelatedManager object at 0x04237D48>
```

As the choice of model to define the relationship on is somewhat arbitrary, it is a shame that you have to remember how you did it in order to know how to access the related manager. Fortunately, you don't. As with `ForeignKey` fields, you can override the default name of the related manager using the `related_name` argument. Make the following change to the `Joke` model:

```
tags = models.ManyToManyField('Tag', blank=True, related_name='jokes')
```

After making this change, you access the related manager using the new name. Note that you will need to exit and re-enter the shell for this change to take effect:

```
>>> from jokes.models import Tag
>>> first_tag = Tag.objects.first()
>>> first_tag.jokes
<django.db.models.fields.related_descriptors.create_forward_many_to_many_manager.<lo ↵
cals>.ManyRelatedManager object at 0x03D76040>
```

Answering the Questions

Now, you can answer the questions we asked at the beginning of this section. Note that your numbers may differ:

How many tags does the first joke have?

```
>>> from jokes.models import Joke
>>> first_joke = Joke.objects.first()
>>> first_joke.tags.count()
1
```

How many jokes are tagged with the "Animal" tag?

```
>>> from jokes.models import Tag
>>> animal_tag = Tag.objects.get(tag='Animal')
>>> animal_tag.jokes.count()
3
```

14.9. Spanning Relationships

Consider the following SQL query:

```
SELECT j.question, j.updated, u.username, c.category
FROM jokes_joke j
  JOIN jokes_category c ON c.id = j.category_id
  JOIN users_customuser u ON u.id = j.user_id
WHERE j.id = 1;
```

The query and its results are shown in the following screenshot:

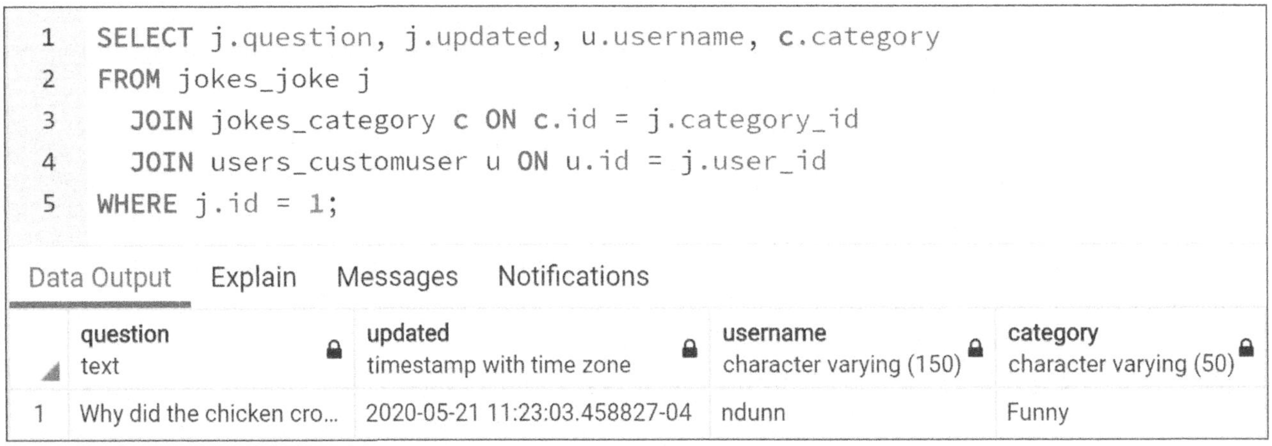

```
1  SELECT j.question, j.updated, u.username, c.category
2  FROM jokes_joke j
3    JOIN jokes_category c ON c.id = j.category_id
4    JOIN users_customuser u ON u.id = j.user_id
5  WHERE j.id = 1;
```

Data Output | Explain | Messages | Notifications

	question text	updated timestamp with time zone	username character varying (150)	category character varying (50)
1	Why did the chicken cro...	2020-05-21 11:23:03.458827-04	ndunn	Funny

This is essentially the query that is run when you execute the following:

```
>>> from jokes.models import Joke
>>> joke = Joke.objects.get(id=1)
>>> print(joke.question, joke.updated, joke.user, joke.category, sep='\n')
Why did the chicken cross the road?
2020-05-21 15:23:03.458827+00:00
ndunn
Funny
```

Notice that user and category are both attributes of joke and that their output is the user's username and the category's category. Recall how those models are connected to the Joke model:

```
user = models.ForeignKey(settings.AUTH_USER_MODEL, …)
category = models.ForeignKey('Category', …)
```

Also recall what the __str__() methods of those two models return:

```
# Category
def __str__(self):
    return self.category

# CustomUser (inherited from AbstractUser > AbstractBaseUser)
def __str__(self):
    return self.get_username()
```

If you were to change the return values of those __str__() methods, those changes would be reflected in the output of joke.user and joke.category. To make sure that the code always returns the values of the username and category fields, you should make the code explicit:

```
>>> joke.user.username
'ndunn'
>>> joke.category.category
'Funny'
```

Likewise, to get other fields on joined models, you must explicitly name those fields:

```
>>> joke.user.first_name
'Nat'
>>> joke.category.updated
datetime.datetime(2020, 5, 21, 15, 21, 21, 56735, tzinfo=<UTC>)
```

Lookups Across Relationships

Consider the following SQL query:

```
SELECT j.question, j.updated, u.username, c.category
FROM jokes_joke j
  JOIN jokes_category c ON c.id = j.category_id
  JOIN users_customuser u ON u.id = j.user_id
WHERE u.id = 1;
```

This query gets information on all the jokes created by a specific user, identified by their user `id`. The Django equivalent is:

```
>>> from jokes.models import Joke
>>> jokes = Joke.objects.filter(user=1)
>>> for j in jokes:
...     print(joke.question, joke.updated, joke.user, joke.category)
```

Now, consider this SQL query:

```
SELECT j.question, j.updated, u.username, c.category
FROM jokes_joke j
  JOIN jokes_category c ON c.id = j.category_id
  JOIN users_customuser u ON u.id = j.user_id
WHERE u.username = 'ndunn';
```

The only difference between this query and the previous one is that this time the user is identified by their `username` instead of their `id`. Again, the query could be generated with the `QuerySet`'s `filter()` method, but what would you pass to it?

You might try this:

```
Invalid
Joke.objects.filter(user='ndunn')
```

But that will result in a `ValueError`:

```
ValueError: Field 'id' expected a number but got 'ndunn'.
```

When a `ForeignKey` field is used in a lookup, it looks at the field referenced by the foreign key (usually the `id`), not the value returned by the model's `__str__()` method.

You might also try this:

Also Invalid

```
Joke.objects.filter(user.username='ndunn')
```

But that will result in a SyntaxError. In lookups, dots are not used to connect reference fields of related models. Instead, a double underscore (__) is used:

The Correct Way

```
>>> Joke.objects.filter(user__username='ndunn')
<QuerySet [<Joke: Why did the chicken cross the road?>, …]>
```

Some additional examples:

All Jokes by Nat Dunn

```
Joke.objects.filter(user__first_name='Nat', user__last_name='Dunn')
```

All Jokes by ndunn in the Funny Category

```
Joke.objects.filter(user__username='ndunn', category__category='Funny')
```

All Jokes with the Animal Tag

```
Joke.objects.filter(tags__tag='Animal')
```

A Gotcha with related_name

Consider again how you defined the relationships between the Joke model and the Category and CustomUser models:

```
user = models.ForeignKey(
    settings.AUTH_USER_MODEL, on_delete=models.PROTECT
)
category = models.ForeignKey(
    'Category', on_delete=models.PROTECT, related_name='jokes'
)
```

Notice that for `category`, you overrode the default name of the "backwards" relationship using `related_name`, but you didn't do that for `user`. That means that you would reference a category's jokes using `category.jokes` and you would reference a user's jokes using `user.joke_set`.

This difference comes into play again in lookup fields:

- If you **have not** used `related_name`, then you should use the lowercase name of the model in the "reverse" relationship:

  The User of a Joke by question

  ```
  User.objects.get(joke__question='What do you call a polar bear in the desert?')
  ```

- If you **have** used `related_name`, then you should use that `related_name` value in the "reverse" relationship:

  The Category of a Joke by question

  ```
  Category.objects.get(jokes__question='What do you call a polar bear in the desert?')
  ```

If this confuses you, it is because it is super confusing. The best way to avoid this confusion is to be consistent with how you handle related names: either use them always (our recommendation) or don't use them at all.

So, to be consistent, go ahead and update the `user` field in the `Joke` model:

```
user = models.ForeignKey(
    settings.AUTH_USER_MODEL, on_delete=models.PROTECT,
    related_name='jokes'
)
```

Summary

Backwards relationships and related names can be confusing. The following code shows the relevant fields of the `User`, `Category`, `Tag`, and `Joke` models:

```
class CustomUser(AbstractUser):
    ...


class Category(models.Model):
  ...


class Tag(models.Model):
  ...


class Joke(models.Model):
    ...
    user = models.ForeignKey(
        settings.AUTH_USER_MODEL, on_delete=models.PROTECT,
        related_name='jokes'
    )
    category = models.ForeignKey(
        'Category', on_delete=models.PROTECT, related_name='jokes'
    )
    tags = models.ManyToManyField('Tag', blank=True, related_name='jokes')
  ...
```

All the relationships are defined in the `Joke` class, so `Joke` objects will get the user, category, and tags using `joke.user`, `joke.category`, `joke.tags`. All the `related_name` arguments in the `Joke` fields have a value of `'jokes'`, so `User`, `Category`, and `Tag` objects will get related jokes using `user.jokes`, `category.jokes`, and `tag.jokes`.

When possible,[95] you recommend setting `related_name` to the lowercase plural form of the containing class name.

---

95. When two foreign keys point to the same model, they cannot both have the same `related_name`.

14.10. Joke Voting

In the remainder of this lesson, through a series of exercises, you will add functionality to the Django Jokes website that allows logged-in users to vote up or down on jokes. The interface looks like this:

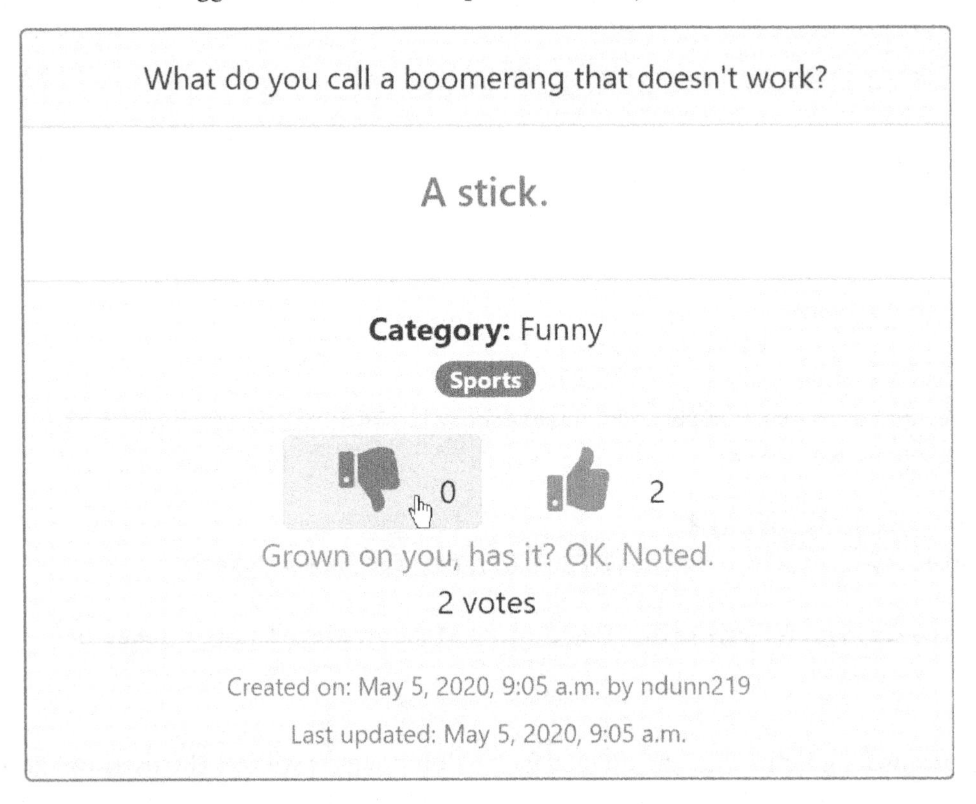

The user has just changed their vote from dislike to like and is about to change it back again.

Creating this functionality involves the following steps:

1. Adding a `JokeVote` model to hold the users' votes.
2. Registering the `JokeVote` model so that you can manage it in Django admin.
3. Adding "calculated fields" to the `Joke` model using properties.
4. Using Ajax to allow users to vote without a page refresh.
5. Adding a `vote()` view function.
6. Updating the URLConf to handle vote requests.
7. Updating the `_base.html` and `joke_detail.html` templates.

Exercise 60: Adding a JokeVote Model

15 to 25 minutes

Add the following model to `jokes/models.py`:[96]

Exercise Code 60.1: jokes/models.py

```
    -------Lines 1 through 84 Omitted-------
85.  class JokeVote(models.Model):
86.      user = models.ForeignKey(
87.          settings.AUTH_USER_MODEL, on_delete=models.CASCADE,
88.          related_name='jokevotes'
89.      )
90.      joke = models.ForeignKey(
91.          Joke, on_delete=models.CASCADE,
92.          related_name='jokevotes'
93.      )
94.      vote = models.SmallIntegerField()
95.      created = models.DateTimeField(auto_now_add=True)
96.      updated = models.DateTimeField(auto_now=True)
97.
98.      class Meta:
99.          constraints = [
100.             models.UniqueConstraint(
101.                 fields=['user', 'joke'], name='one_vote_per_user_per_joke'
102.             )
103.         ]
```

This model creates an intermediary `jokes_jokevote` table between the `jokes_joke` and `users_customuser` tables similar to the table created by the `ManyToManyField` `tag` field in the `Joke` model (see page 294):

```
tags = models.ManyToManyField('Tag', blank=True)
```

Let's look at that relationship again:

96. **Don't want to type?** Copy from `starter-code/making-queries/jokes_models.py`.

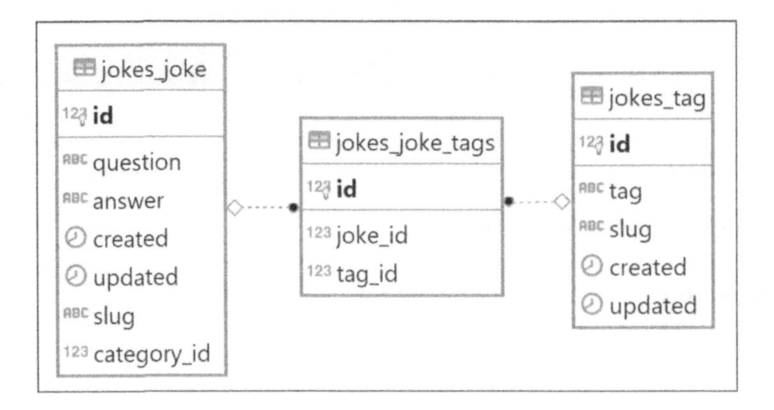

When you use a ManyToManyField, the intermediary table joins the two other tables, but doesn't provide any additional information about the relationship. For example, jokes can be related to many tags, and tags can be related to many jokes, but there is no way of getting additional information about those relationships from the intermediary table. The intermediary table doesn't tell you when the relationship began or when it was last updated. All you know is that they are related.

Now, take a look at the relationship created by the JokeVote model:

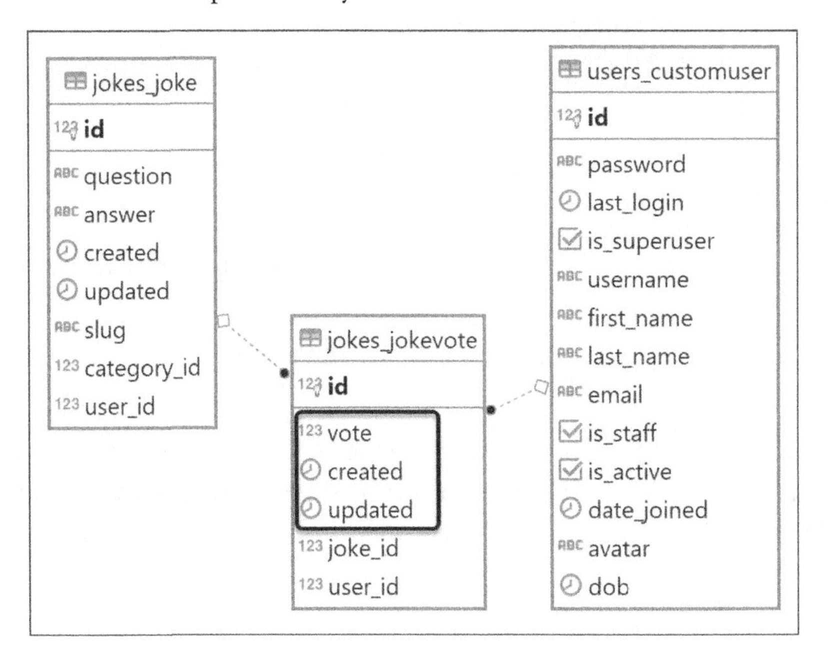

Notice the vote, created, and updated fields in the jokes_jokevote table. These fields give you information about the relationship:

1. How the user voted on this joke.
2. When the user first voted on this joke.
3. When the user last updated their vote on this joke.

The model also a constraint in the JokeVote model to prevent users from voting on the same joke more than once. We will cover constraints later (see page 465).

Make and run migrations:

```
(.venv) …/projects/djangojokes.com> python manage.py makemigrations
(.venv) …/projects/djangojokes.com> python manage.py migrate
```

❖ E60.1. Related Managers

Notice that both of the ForeignKey fields use the same value for related_name: 'jokevotes'.

```
user = models.ForeignKey(
    settings.AUTH_USER_MODEL, on_delete=models.CASCADE,
    related_name='jokevotes'
)
joke = models.ForeignKey(
    Joke, on_delete=models.CASCADE,
    related_name='jokevotes'
)
```

This means that Joke and CustomUser instances will be able to access their related JokeVote instances via the jokevotes property. For example:

- user.jokevotes.count() would get the number of votes a user has made.
- joke.jokevotes.count() would get the number of votes on a joke.

Git Commit

Commit your code to Git.

Exercise 61: Registering the JokeVote Model

5 to 10 minutes

You need to register the `JokeVote` model, so that you can manage it in Django admin. Open `jokes/admin.py`, import `JokeVote`, and create and register the `JokeVoteAdmin` class as follows:[97]

Exercise Code 61.1: jokes/admin.py

```
1.    from django.contrib import admin
2.
3.    from .models import Category, Joke, JokeVote, Tag
      -------Lines 4 through 26 Omitted-------
27.   @admin.register(JokeVote)
28.   class JokeVoteAdmin(admin.ModelAdmin):
29.       model = JokeVote
30.       list_display = ['joke', 'user', 'vote']
31.
32.       def get_readonly_fields(self, request, obj=None):
33.           if obj: # editing an existing object
34.               return ('created', 'updated')
35.           return ()
      -------Lines 36 through 46 Omitted-------
```

You can now manage joke votes in Django Admin:

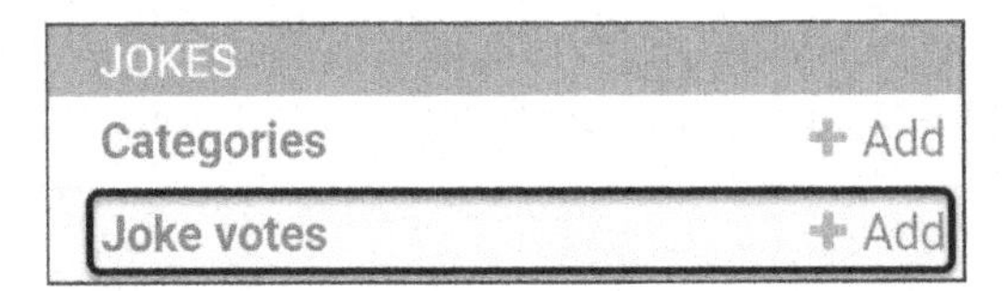

Git Commit

Commit your code to Git.

97. **Don't want to type?** Copy from `starter-code/making-queries/jokes_admin.py`.

Exercise 62: Adding Properties to the Joke Model

15 to 25 minutes

Class properties allow you to access a class method as if it were an attribute. You want to add the following calculated data to the `Joke` model, so that you can easily show this information in templates:

1. Number of likes.
2. Number of dislikes.
3. Number of votes.

Open `jokes/models.py` in your editor and add the following properties to the `Joke` model:

Exercise Code 62.1: jokes/models.py

```
    -------Lines 1 through 7 Omitted-------
8.  class Joke(models.Model):
9.      question = models.TextField(max_length=200)
    -------Lines 10 through 21 Omitted-------
22.     updated = models.DateTimeField(auto_now=True)
23.
24.     @property
25.     def num_votes(self):
26.         return self.jokevotes.count()
27.
28.     @property
29.     def num_likes(self):
30.         return self.jokevotes.filter(vote=1).count()
31.
32.     @property
33.     def num_dislikes(self):
34.         return self.jokevotes.filter(vote=-1).count()
    -------Lines 35 through 111 Omitted-------
```

Let's see how these properties work. From the `djangojokes.com` directory, open the Django shell (`python manage.py shell`) and run the following code:

```
Import Models
>>> from jokes.models import Joke, Category, JokeVote
>>> from django.contrib.auth import get_user_model
>>> User = get_user_model()


Create Objects
>>> question='What do you a call a camel with no hump?'
>>> answer='Humphrey'
>>> creator = User.objects.first() # A user to create the new joke
>>> category = Category.objects.first() # A category for the new joke
>>> joke = Joke(question=question, answer=answer, user=creator, category=category)
>>> joke.save()


>>> user = User.objects.last() # A user to vote on the new joke
>>> joke_vote = JokeVote(user=joke_voter, joke=joke, vote=1)
>>> joke_vote.save()
>>> joke.num_likes
1
>>> joke.num_dislikes
0
>>> joke.num_votes
1
```

Now that you have added these properties to the model, you can access them in templates as attributes of the `Joke` instance.

Git Commit

Commit your code to Git.

Exercise 63: Rating Jokes Using Ajax

15 to 25 minutes

You will use Ajax to let users vote on jokes without causing a complete page refresh. Ajax is a technique that uses JavaScript to make requests of the server and then update the page based on the server response. The beauty of Ajax is that it doesn't require a full page refresh.

The following JavaScript file is available to copy from `starter-code/making-queries/jokes.js`. It should be saved as `jokes.js` in a `js` folder within the `static` folder:

```
static
    js
        jokes.js
```

Exercise Code 63.1: static/js/jokes.js

```
1.  window.addEventListener('load', () => {
2.    const likeButton = document.getElementById('like-button');
3.    const dislikeButton = document.getElementById('dislike-button');
4.    likeButton.addEventListener('click', () => { register(1); })
5.    dislikeButton.addEventListener('click', () => { register(-1); })
6.  })
7.
8.  function register(vote) {
9.    const csrfInput =  document.querySelector("input[name='csrfmiddlewaretoken']");
10.   const csrfToken = csrfInput.value;
11.   const likes = Number(document.getElementById('likes').innerHTML);
12.   const dislikes = Number(document.getElementById('dislikes').innerHTML);
13.   const data = {
14.     'vote': vote,
15.     'likes': likes,
16.     'dislikes': dislikes
17.   }
18.   fetch(ajaxURL, {
19.     method: 'POST',
20.     headers: {
21.       'Content-Type': 'application/json',
22.       'X-CSRFToken': csrfToken
23.     },
24.     body: JSON.stringify(data),
25.   })
26.     .then(response => response.json())
27.     .then(data => {
28.       const numVotes = data.dislikes + data.likes;
29.       let voteText = `${numVotes} vote`;
30.       if (numVotes !== 1) voteText += 's';
31.       document.getElementById('output').innerHTML = data.msg;
32.       document.getElementById('likes').innerHTML = data.likes;
33.       document.getElementById('dislikes').innerHTML = data.dislikes;
34.       document.getElementById('num-votes').innerHTML = voteText;
35.     });
36. }
```

We are not going to cover Ajax in detail, but **there are a few things we want to point out:**

1. The code is fetching from a URL stored in a constant named `ajaxURL`:

   ```
   fetch(ajaxURL, {…
   ```

The `ajaxURL` variable is not defined in this JavaScript file. That's because you want to populate the variable using Django and you cannot use Django to modify static files on the fly. The solution is to populate the variable in a preceding `script` element in the `joke_detail.html` template. You will do that soon.

2. You are using the "POST" method to send data to the server. Any time you are changing state (e.g., updating a database), you should use `POST`. Because you are using `POST`, you need to pass in the appropriate `X-CSRFToken` token. In HTML forms in Django templates, you add a `hidden input` using the `{% csrf_token %}` tag, which produces HTML like this:

```
<input type="hidden" name="csrfmiddlewaretoken"
value="RcOQcEfjA40fCIYVCiwVnzadkuoCYCFdrmkz0rEQ06q8LxGUum8iOwaCH0aoi3Er">
```

Django requires such an `input` element to handle CSRF Validation, so you will include it in the template even though there is no form on the page. You then use JavaScript to get its value:

```
const csrfInput = document.querySelector("input[name='csrfmiddlewaretoken']");
const csrfToken = csrfInput.value;
```

And then you pass that value in the `Request` headers:

```
headers: {
'Content-Type': 'application/json',
'X-CSRFToken': csrfToken
}
```

This essentially opens up the communication gateway between JavaScript and Django. You can then pass JSON data back and forth between the two.

Git Commit

Commit your code to Git.

Exercise 64: Adding a vote() View Function

20 to 30 minutes

In this exercise, you will add a view for the Ajax request. Up until this point, you have been working with class-based views. This will be your first *view function*. View functions are passed a request and possibly some keyword arguments from the URL pattern in the URLConf. They then return a web response to be sent to the client. In this case, you will be sending JSON, but view functions can be used to send HTML, image files, PDFs, a redirect to another web page, or any valid web response.

1. From the `jokes` folder, open `views.py` for editing.
2. You will need Python's `json` library to convert the JSON string passed in the request body to a Python object. Import that at the top of the file:

   ```
   import json
   ```

3. You will also need `JsonResponse` from `django.http` to return JSON to the browser. Import that too:

   ```
   from django.http import JsonResponse
   ```

4. Import the `JokeVote` model:

   ```
   from .models import Joke, JokeVote
   ```

5. At the bottom of the file, write the `vote` view function as shown in the following file. You do not need to include a ll the comments, but you should read them carefully.[98]

98. **Don't want to type?** Copy from `starter-code/making-queries/jokes_views.py`.

Exercise Code 64.1: jokes/views.py

```
1.  import json
2.  from django.contrib.auth.mixins import LoginRequiredMixin, UserPassesTestMixin
3.  from django.contrib import messages
4.  from django.contrib.messages.views import SuccessMessageMixin
5.  from django.http import JsonResponse
6.  from django.urls import reverse_lazy
7.  from django.views.generic import (
8.      CreateView, DeleteView, DetailView, ListView, UpdateView
9.  )
10.
11. from .models import Joke, JokeVote
12. from .forms import JokeForm
    -------Lines 13 through 55 Omitted-------
56. def vote(request, slug):
57.     user = request.user # The logged-in user (or AnonymousUser).
58.     joke = Joke.objects.get(slug=slug) # The joke instance.
59.     data = json.loads(request.body) # Data from the JavaScript.
60.
61.     # Set simple variables.
62.     vote = data['vote'] # The user's new vote.
63.     likes = data['likes'] # The number of likes currently displayed on page.
64.     dislikes = data['dislikes'] # The number of dislikes currently displayed.
65.
66.     if user.is_anonymous: # User not logged in. Can't vote.
67.         msg = 'Sorry, you have to be logged in to vote.'
68.     else: # User is logged in.
69.         if JokeVote.objects.filter(user=user, joke=joke).exists():
70.             # User already voted. Get user's past vote:
71.             joke_vote = JokeVote.objects.get(user=user, joke=joke)
72.
73.             if joke_vote.vote == vote: # User's new vote is the same as old vote.
74.                 msg = 'Right. You told us already. Geez.'
75.             else: # User changed vote.
76.                 joke_vote.vote = vote # Update JokeVote instance.
77.                 joke_vote.save() # Save.
78.
79.                 # Set data to return to the browser.
80.                 if vote == -1:
81.                     likes -= 1
82.                     dislikes += 1
83.                     msg = "Don't like it after all, huh? OK. Noted."
84.                 else:
85.                     likes += 1
86.                     dislikes -= 1
```

```
87.                     msg = 'Grown on you, has it? OK. Noted.'
88.             else: # First time user is voting on this joke.
89.                 # Create and save new vote.
90.                 joke_vote = JokeVote(user=user, joke=joke, vote=vote)
91.                 joke_vote.save()
92.
93.                 # Set data to return to the browser.
94.                 if vote == -1:
95.                     dislikes += 1
96.                     msg = "Sorry you didn't like the joke."
97.                 else:
98.                     likes += 1
99.                     msg = "Yeah, good one, right?"
100.
101.        # Create object to return to browser.
102.        response = {
103.            'msg': msg,
104.            'likes': likes,
105.            'dislikes': dislikes
106.        }
107.        return JsonResponse(response) # Return object as JSON.
```

Read through the view function carefully, paying particular attention to the comments.

Things to notice:

1. The function expects two arguments:
    A. `request` – The web request.
    B. `slug` – The joke slug, which is passed in from a URL pattern in the URLConf, which you will add shortly.
2. Using the passed-in `slug`, you get the joke:

```
joke = Joke.objects.get(slug=slug)
```

3. In the JavaScript (in `jokes.js`), you created a JSON string from a JavaScript object and passed the string to the server in the body of the message:

JavaScript Object to JSON

```
fetch(ajaxURL, {
  method: 'POST',
  headers: {
    'Content-Type': 'application/json',
    'X-CSRFToken': csrfToken
  },
  body: JSON.stringify(data),
})
```

In the Python (in `views.py`, you convert that string to a Python object using `json.loads()`:

JSON to Python Object

```
data = json.loads(request.body)
```

Based on that incoming data, you create a `response` object and send it back to the browser as JSON:

```
response = {
    'msg': msg,
    'likes': likes,
    'dislikes': dislikes
}
return JsonResponse(response)
```

4. If you knew the user was logged in and had never voted, you could jump right to the last `else` block with the "First time user is voting on this joke." comment:

```
else: # First time user is voting on this joke.
    # Create and save new vote.
    joke_vote = JokeVote(user=user, joke=joke, vote=vote)
    joke_vote.save()

    # Set data to return to the browser.
    if vote == -1:
        num_dislikes += 1
        msg = "Sorry you didn't like the joke."
    else:
        num_likes += 1
        msg = "Yeah, good one, right?"
```

   This code creates and saves a new `JokeVote` instance and then sets the `num_likes`, `num_dislikes`, and `msg` variables to return to browser. JavaScript will use those values to decide how to update the web page.

5. But you don't know that the user is logged in, so you first have to check that using `user.is_anonymous`:

```
if user.is_anonymous: # User not logged in. Can't vote.
    msg = 'Sorry, you have to be logged in to vote.'
```

6. And, if the user is logged in, you don't know that they haven't voted before. If they have, you cannot have them vote again as there is a `one_vote_per_user_per_joke` constraint on the model. Note that we chose to use `exists()` to check if a `JokeVote` already exists for this user and joke combination:

```
JokeVote.objects.filter(user=user, joke=joke).exists()
```

   If such a `JokeVote` instance does exist, then you have to get that `JokeVote` instance, which means hitting the database again with:

```
joke_vote = JokeVote.objects.get(user=user, joke=joke)
```

An alternative approach would be to skip the `exists()` check and just try to get the `JokeView` instance using `filter()` (not `get()` as that will result in a `DoesNotExist` exception if there is no matching `JokeVote` instance):

```
joke_votes = JokeVote.objects.filter(user=user, joke=joke)
if joke_votes: # User already voted.
    joke_vote = joke_votes[0]
    # Check if vote is different and respond accordingly.
else: # First time user is voting on this joke.
    # Create and save new vote.
```

Either approach is fine. We chose the first approach, because we assume most people will not try to vote more than once. Using `exists()` is the fastest way to check to confirm that, so that you can quickly move on to creating the new `JokeView` instance. Note that this type of design decision is mostly academic. Unless you're dealing with complex queries and a lot of data, both approaches will be lightning fast.

Git Commit

Commit your code to Git.

Exercise 65: Updating the URLConf

5 to 10 minutes

Open `jokes/urls.py` for editing, import the `vote` view and add the URL pattern shown in the following code:

Exercise Code 65.1: jokes/urls.py

```
1.    from django.urls import path
2.
3.    from .views import (
4.        JokeCreateView, JokeDeleteView, JokeDetailView, JokeListView,
5.        JokeUpdateView, vote
6.    )
7.
8.    app_name = 'jokes'
9.    urlpatterns = [
10.       path('joke/<slug>/update/', JokeUpdateView.as_view(), name='update'),
11.       path('joke/<slug>/delete/', JokeDeleteView.as_view(), name='delete'),
12.       path('joke/create/', JokeCreateView.as_view(), name='create'),
13.       path('joke/<slug>/', JokeDetailView.as_view(), name='detail'),
14.       path('joke/<slug>/vote/', vote, name='ajax-vote'),
15.       path('', JokeListView.as_view(), name='list'),
16.   ]
```

Code Explanation

When a URL matching this pattern is requested, the `vote()` view function will be called and passed the slug from the URL.

Git Commit

Commit your code to Git.

Exercise 66: Updating the Templates

30 to 45 minutes

❖ E66.1. The _base.html Template

Open templates/base.html in your editor and add the following block tag somewhere in the head:

```
{% block javascript %}{% endblock %}
```

Templates that extend _base.html will be able to include JavaScript in the head by putting the code in this new block tag.

❖ E66.2. The joke_detail.html Template

1. Open templates/jokes/joke_detail.html in your editor. Add the following block tag immediately above the title block tag:

   ```
   {% block javascript %}
     <script>
       const ajaxURL = "{% url 'jokes:ajax-vote' joke.slug %}";
     </script>
     <script src="{% static 'js/jokes.js' %}"></script>
   {% endblock %}
   ```

   A. The first script element sets the ajaxURL constant that is used in jokes.js (see page 450). You set this in the template so that you can get a dynamic URL based on the slug of the Joke instance.

   B. The second script element uses the {% static %} tag to get the path to js/jokes.js. The {% static %} tag only works if it has been loaded. Add this to the top of the document, below the {% extends "_base.html" %} tag:

   ```
   {% load static %}
   ```

2. You are now going to add the code that:

   A. Shows how many likes, dislikes, and votes a joke has gotten.

B. Allows users to vote on jokes.

You are not going to let users vote on their own jokes. In the if block that checks if the logged-in user is the creator of the joke, you will add a joke-voting report showing the user how their joke is doing. In addition, you will add an `else` block for holding the voting area for the users who didn't write the joke:

A. Move the `if` condition that checks if the current logged-in user created the joke inside of the `div` element, so that:

```
{% if joke.user == user %}
  <div class="border-bottom border-faded m-2 pb-2">
    <a href="{% url 'jokes:update' joke.slug %}"
      class="btn btn-info btn-sm mr-2">Update</a>
    <a href="{% url 'jokes:delete' joke.slug %}"
      class="btn btn-danger btn-sm mr-2">Delete</a>
  </div>
{% endif %}
```

... becomes:

```
<div class="border-bottom border-faded m-2 pb-2">
  {% if joke.user == user %}
    <a href="{% url 'jokes:update' joke.slug %}"
      class="btn btn-info btn-sm mr-2">Update</a>
    <a href="{% url 'jokes:delete' joke.slug %}"
      class="btn btn-danger btn-sm mr-2">Delete</a>
  {% endif %}
</div>
```

B. After the two link buttons and before the `{% endif %}` tag, add a joke-voting report:

```
<p>
  Your joke has
  <span id="num-votes">
    {{ joke.num_votes|default:'no' }}
    vote{{ joke.num_votes|pluralize }}</span>{% if num_votes %}:
  <span id="likes">{{ joke.num_likes }}
    like{{ joke.num_likes|pluralize }}</span> and
  <span id="dislikes">
    {{ joke.num_dislikes }}
    dislike{{ joke.num_dislikes|pluralize }}</span>{% endif %}.
</p>
```

That block shows what the user who created the joke will see when they are logged in.

C. Below the joke-voting report, add an `else` block to hold the voting buttons:

```
{% else %}
  {% csrf_token %}
  <button id="dislike-button" class="btn btn-light">
    <i class="fas fa-thumbs-down fa-2x text-danger mx-3"></i>
    <span id="dislikes">{{ joke.num_dislikes }}</span>
  </button>
  <button id="like-button" class="btn btn-light">
    <i class="fas fa-thumbs-up fa-2x text-success mx-3"></i>
    <span id="likes">{{ joke.num_likes }}</span>
  </button>
  <div id="output" class="text-info"></div>
  <span id="num-votes">{{ joke.num_votes }}
    vote{{ joke.num_votes|pluralize }}</span>
{% endif %}
```

The completed `div` element will look like this:

Exercise Code 66.1: templates/jokes/joke_detail.html

```
-------Lines 1 through 24 Omitted-------
25.        <div class="border-bottom border-faded m-2 pb-2">
26.          {% if joke.user == user %}
27.            <a href="{% url 'jokes:update' joke.slug %}"
28.              class="btn btn-info btn-sm mr-2">Update</a>
29.            <a href="{% url 'jokes:delete' joke.slug %}"
30.              class="btn btn-danger btn-sm mr-2">Delete</a>
31.            <p>
32.              Your joke has
33.              <span id="num-votes">
34.                {{ joke.num_votes|default:'no' }}
35.                vote{{ joke.num_votes|pluralize }}</span>{% if num_votes %}:
36.              <span id="likes">{{ joke.num_likes }}
37.                like{{ joke.num_likes|pluralize }}</span> and
38.              <span id="dislikes">
39.                {{ joke.num_dislikes }}
40.                dislike{{ joke.num_dislikes|pluralize }}</span>{% endif %}.
41.            </p>
42.          {% else %}
43.            {% csrf_token %}
44.            <button id="dislike-button" class="btn btn-light">
45.              <i class="fas fa-thumbs-down fa-2x text-danger mx-3"></i>
46.              <span id="dislikes">{{ joke.num_dislikes }}</span>
47.            </button>
48.            <button id="like-button" class="btn btn-light">
49.              <i class="fas fa-thumbs-up fa-2x text-success mx-3"></i>
50.              <span id="likes">{{ joke.num_likes }}</span>
51.            </button>
52.            <div id="output" class="text-info"></div>
53.            <span id="num-votes">{{ joke.num_votes }}
54.              vote{{ joke.num_votes|pluralize }}</span>
55.          {% endif %}
56.        </div>
-------Lines 57 through 67 Omitted-------
```

Things to notice:

A. The template code makes use of the properties that you added to the `Joke`: `num_likes`, `num_dislikes`, and `num_votes`.

B. When the joke creator and the logged-in user are one and the same, they'll see a report on the voting, which will read something like this:

```
Your joke has 1 vote: 1 like and 0 dislikes.
```

If there haven't been any votes yet, it will just say:

```
Your joke has no votes.
```

C. In the `else` block, you include the voting buttons. The `id`s of these `button`s, of the `span`s that follow them, and of the empty "output" `div` are important as your JavaScript uses them to capture clicks and to change the page:

```
const likeButton = document.getElementById('like-button');
const dislikeButton = document.getElementById('dislike-button');

document.getElementById('output').innerHTML = data.msg;
document.getElementById('likes').innerHTML = data.likes;
document.getElementById('dislikes').innerHTML = data.dislikes;
document.getElementById('num-votes').innerHTML = voteText;
```

D. You also include the `{% csrf_token %}` tag in the `else` block. Again, that will produce HTML, which JavaScript will use to get the token to send to the server:

```
<input type="hidden" name="csrfmiddlewaretoken"
  value="RcOQcEfjA4OfCIYVCiwVnzadkuoCYCFdrmkz0rEQ06q8LxGUum8iOwaCH0aoi3Er">
```

❖ E66.3. Try It Out

1. Start up the server and navigate to a joke that the logged-in user wrote. You should see something like this:

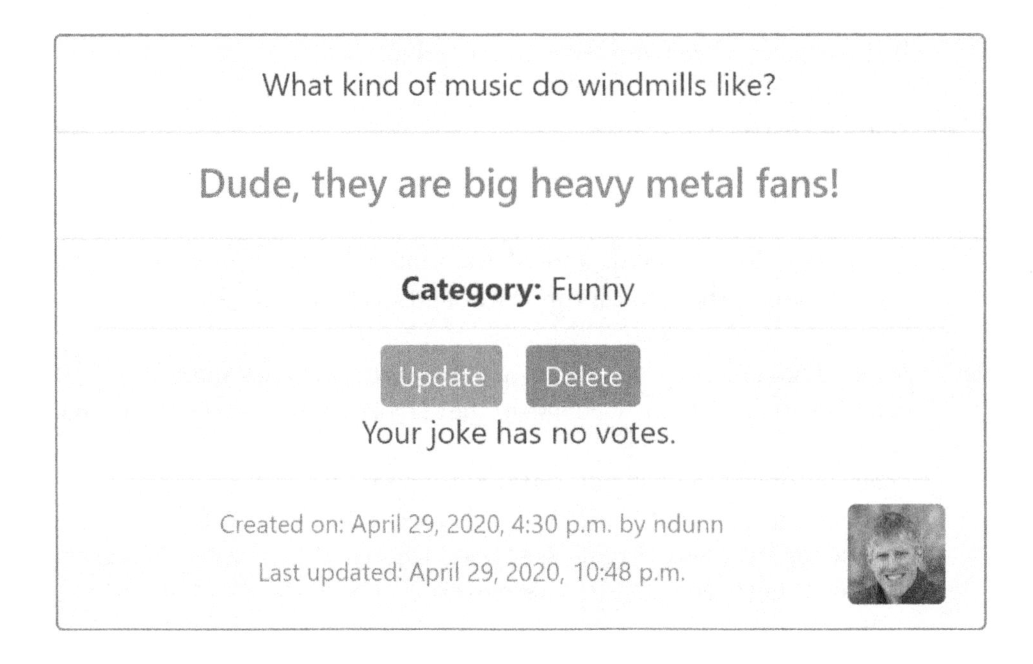

2. Log out, and then visit the same joke. You should see something like this:

Try to vote. You should get a "Sorry, you have to be logged in to vote." message. Note that it would probably be better to handle this scenario client-side. The browser knows that the user is not logged in, so it is not necessary to roundtrip to the server to check that. We explain how to do that later in this lesson (see page 468).

3. Log in as a different user (not the one who created that joke) and visit the same joke. Then, vote. You should see something like this:

Vote again the same way you just voted. You should get a "Right. You told us already. Geez." message. Change your vote several times. The message should toggle between "Don't like it after all, huh? OK. Noted." and "Grown on you, has it? OK. Noted."

Git Commit

Commit your code to Git.

14.11. Model Constraints

Model field definitions control the type of data that can be entered in the field. For example, `models.URLField` must contain a valid URL, `models.PositiveIntegerField` must contain a positive integer, `models.DateField` must contain a valid date. You can pass arguments (e.g., `max_length`, `unique`, and `choices`) to further limit the type of content that can be entered for the field. Sometimes, however, you want to add additional constraints on field values.

Additional constraints are added to a model in the models `Meta` inner class:

```
class MyModel(models.Model):
    field_name = models.TextField()
    ...

    class Meta:
        constraints = [
            models.UniqueConstraint(
                fields=['user', 'joke'], name='one_vote_per_user_per_joke'
            )
        ]
```

There are two types of constraints:

1. `UniqueConstraint`
2. `CheckConstraint`

❖ 14.11.1. `UniqueConstraint`

In the Adding a `JokeVote` Model (see page 443) exercise, you added this `JokeVote` class:

```
class JokeVote(models.Model):
    user = models.ForeignKey(
        settings.AUTH_USER_MODEL, on_delete=models.CASCADE,
        related_name='jokevotes'
    )
    joke = models.ForeignKey(
        Joke, on_delete=models.CASCADE,
        related_name='jokevotes'
    )
    vote = models.SmallIntegerField()
    created = models.DateTimeField(auto_now_add=True)
    updated = models.DateTimeField(auto_now=True)

    class Meta:
        constraints = [
            models.UniqueConstraint(
                fields=['user', 'joke'], name='one_vote_per_user_per_joke'
            )
        ]
```

This prevents the same user from voting on the same joke more than once. In other words, `joke` and `user` must be unique together. `UniqueConstraint` must take a `fields` argument listing the fields that must be unique together, and a `name` argument, which will be output in the error message when this constraint is violated.

`UniqueConstraint` can take additional arguments. See the documentation[99] for more information.

❖ 14.11.2. CheckConstraint

`CheckConstraint` gives you a lot of control over the content of a field or multiple fields. It takes a `check` argument with a `Q` object, which we will cover later (see page 501). Any content that fails to pass the tests in the `Q` object will be rejected. For example, if you wanted to prevent this author from creating an account on your site, you could use the following constraint:

```
class Meta:
    constraints = [
        models.CheckConstraint(
            check=~Q(first_name='Nat') & ~Q(last_name='Dunn'),
            name='no_nat_dunn'
        )
    ]
```

After adding this constraint (and running migrations), if you try to add the user "Nat Dunn," you will get this error:

```
django.db.utils.IntegrityError: new row for relation "users_customuser" violates check
constraint "no_nat_dunn"
```

As of Django 3.1, `CheckConstraint` can also take a boolean `Expression`. See the documentation[100] for more information.

99. https://docs.djangoproject.com/en/3.1/ref/models/constraints/#uniqueconstraint
100. https://docs.djangoproject.com/en/3.1/ref/models/constraints/#checkconstraint

14.12. Letting JavaScript Know if the User is Logged In

Earlier (see page 464), we mentioned that you don't need to roundtrip to the server to let JavaScript know that the user is not logged in. You can handle that in the template using a JavaScript constant that is set to `{{ user.is_authenticated|lower }}`. It is import to lowercase the value of `user.is_authenticated`, because Python's booleans are `True`/`False` and JavaScript's booleans are `true`/`false`.

So, in `templates/jokes/joke-detail.html`, you would add the following highlighted code:

```
{% block javascript %}
  <script>
    const ajaxURL = "{% url 'jokes:ajax-vote' joke.slug %}";
    const isAuthenticated = {{ user.is_authenticated|lower }};
  </script>
  <script src="{% static 'js/jokes.js' %}"></script>
{% endblock %}
```

And then in `static/js/jokes.js`, you would check the value of `isAuthenticated`. If the user is not authenticated, you would set the message of the "output" `div` and leave the function:

```
function register(vote) {
  if (!isAuthenticated) {
    const outputDiv = document.getElementById('output');
    outputDiv.innerHTML = 'Sorry, only logged-in users can vote.';
    return false;
  }
```

❖ 14.12.1. `@login_required` Decorator

If you are handling non-authenticated users client-side, you no longer have to give them access to the `vote` method at all. You can add the `@login_required` decorator to the `vote` function (or any view function) to make the view only accessible to logged-in users:

```
@login_required
def vote(request, slug):
    …
```

This is to prevent scoundrels from adding votes by posting directly to the voting URL.

Conclusion

In this lesson, you have learned to query models across relationships, to add "calculated fields" to models via properties, to create view functions, and to use Ajax with Django.

LESSON 15

Pagination and Ordering

Topics Covered

☑ Loading data with fixtures.

☑ Pagination.

☑ Sorting.

> After he had left me, I placed all my words, with their interpretations, in alphabetical **order**. And thus, in a few days, by the help of a very faithful memory, I got some insight into their language.
>
> – *Gulliver's Travels, Jonathan Swift*

Introduction

You are finished with your models. Now, we have bunch of data for you to load into the database. Once you have loaded that data, you will add pagination and ordering to your joke-list template.

15.1. Fixtures

You will use *fixtures* to load initial data into the database, so that you can test pagination and sorting, advanced querying, and search. A fixtures is just a collection of structured data that Django can import into the database. The data can be JSON, XML, or YAML[101]. You will be using JSON.

`dumpdata`

Although you won't need to create any fixtures for the Django Jokes website, we will give you a quick overview of how fixtures are created with the `dumpdata` command:

```
python manage.py dumpdata
```

Without any arguments or flags, this command will output all the data in all the apps in the `INSTALLED_APPS` setting of the project settings.

To limit the dump to the specific apps you want to include, list those apps, separated by spaces, after the `dumpdata` command:

```
python manage.py dumpdata app_name1 app_name2
```

To exclude certain apps, use the `--exclude` flag, like this:

```
python manage.py dumpdata --exclude app_name1 --exclude app_name2
```

You can also specify the models you want to dump:

```
python manage.py dumpdata app_name.Model1 app_name.Model2
```

To write the output to a file instead of to the standard output, use the `-o` flag:

```
python manage.py dumpdata app_name1 -o datadump.json
```

---

101. `https://yaml.org/`

By default, the output will all be on a single line, which is fine if you are just getting this data to load somewhere else. But if you want to be able to read the data, you can format the JSON using the `--indent` flag followed by the number of spaces you want to indent:

```
python manage.py dumpdata app_name1 --indent 2 -o datadump.json
```

`loaddata`

To load data from fixtures, use the `loaddata` command:

```
python manage.py loaddata path/to/my/fixture.json
```

If you don't specify a path, Django will look in each installed app folder for a `fixtures` folder. You can also set the `FIXTURE_DIRS` setting in `settings.py` to specify a directory that Django should search for fixtures.

Fixtures are meant to be used with initial data, so, if you're planning to use them, you should use them before adding any real data into the database.

Exercise 67: Loading Data from a Fixture

20 to 30 minutes

The fixture we have created uses JSON data, which includes:

1. 50 users, including one superuser, and five additional staff. The superuser data is:

    ```
    first_name: Jane
    last_name: Gould
    username: jgould
    email: jgould@example.com
    ```

    All users, including the superuser, have the same password: `DjangoP@$$`

2. Verified email addresses for all users.
3. Four categories:
    A. Funny
    B. Brain Teaser
    C. Play on Words
    D. Uncategorized
4. 34 tags.
5. 595 jokes.
6. 10,000 votes.

Before you import this data though, you need to make sure the current database doesn't contain any conflicting data. The only safe way to do this is to remove all data that might conflict, and the easiest way to do that is to start with a new database, which is what you will do:

❖ E67.1. Recreating the Database

1. Stop your server if it is running.
2. Open pgAdmin.
    A. Right-click on the **Jokes** database and select **Properties**:

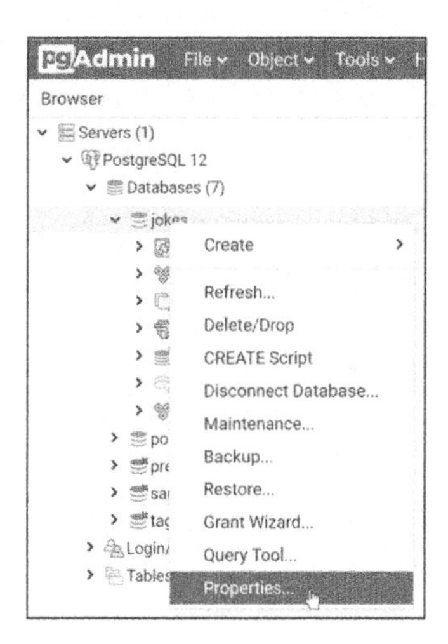

If you get an error, try disconnecting the database first by right-clicking and selecting **Disconnect Database...**

B. Rename "jokes" to "jokes_old" and click **Save**:

Later, when you're sure you don't need any of the data in the old database, you can delete it:

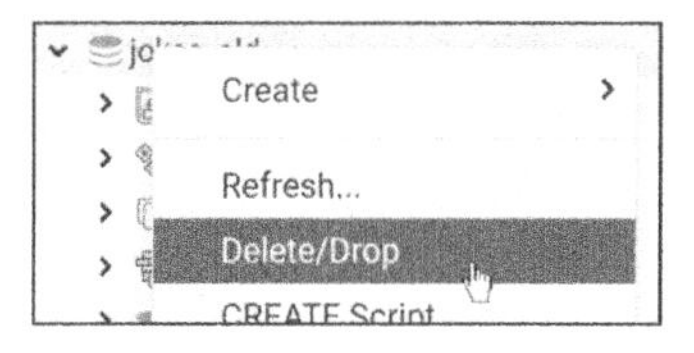

C. Right-click on **Databases** and select **Create > Database**:

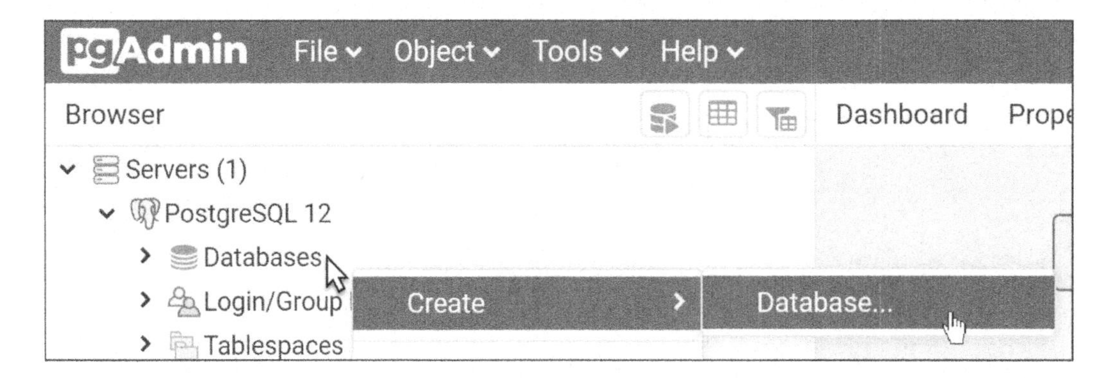

D. Enter "jokes" for the **Database** and click **Save**:

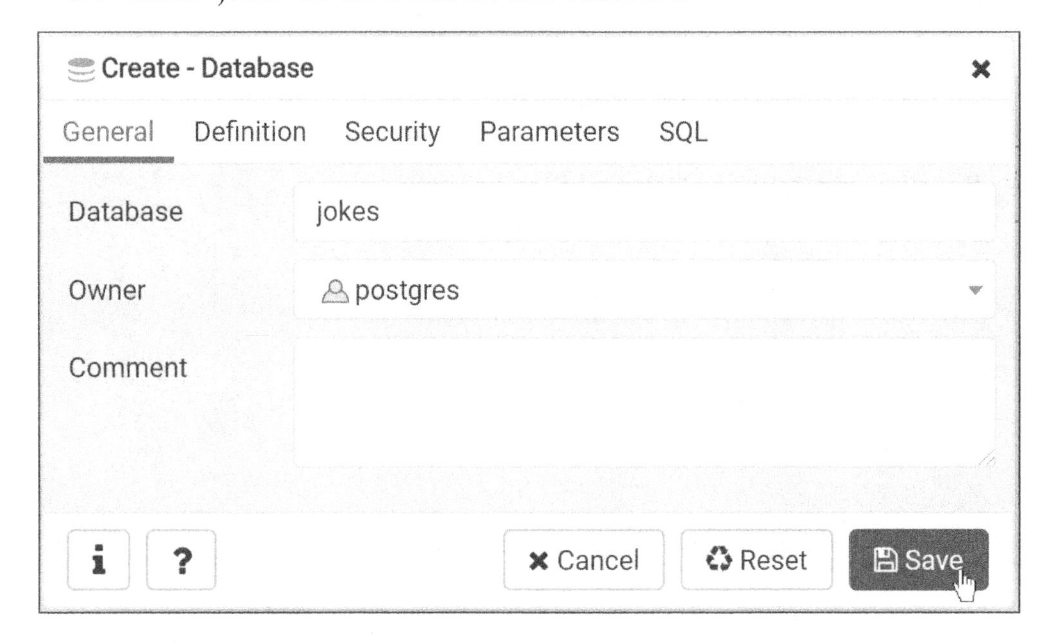

3. Now, you need to re-create the database structure by re-running all migrations:

```
(.venv) …/projects/djangojokes.com> python manage.py migrate
```

❖ E67.2. Populating the Database

It is now time to populate the database using the fixture:

1. Create a `fixtures` folder in the `djangojokes.com` folder.
2. Copy the `fixture_jokes.json` file from `starter-code/pagination-and-ordering` and paste it in the `fixtures` folder you just created.

3. Run the following command at the terminal:

```
(.venv) …/projects/djangojokes.com>
python manage.py loaddata fixtures/fixture_jokes.json
```

After a little bit, you should get a message like this one:

```
Installed 10733 object(s) from 1 fixture(s)
```

❖ E67.3. Try it Out

1. Start up the server and visit the site.
2. Click on the **Jokes** link in the header. This may take a few moments to load as it will show all the jokes on the same page. You'll add pagination soon.
3. Open the site and log in as the superuser using the following credentials:
    - Email: `jgould@example.com`
    - Password: `DjangoP@$$`
4. Change your email to your real email, and if you would prefer a different password, update your password. You can do this on the My Account page or in Django admin.

Git Commit

Commit your code to Git.

Exercise 68: Pagination

20 to 30 minutes

Django makes adding pagination to a `ListView` super easy.

1. Open `jokes/views.py` in your editor.
2. Add to `JokeListView`:

```
class JokeListView(ListView):
    model = Joke
    paginate_by = 10
```

3. Visit `http://127.0.0.1:8000/jokes/`. Notice that only ten jokes show up on the page.
4. Visit `http://127.0.0.1:8000/jokes/?page=2`. Notice a different ten jokes show up.
5. You need to update the template to add links to previous and next pages to allow users to go from page to page. Open `templates/jokes/joke_list.html` in your editor.
6. Add the following code right above the closing `{% endblock %}` tag:[102]

102. **Don't want to type?** Copy from `starter-code/pagination-and-ordering/joke_list_pagination.html`.

Exercise Code 68.1: templates/joke_list.html

```
-------Lines 1 through 100 Omitted-------
101.   <nav aria-label="pagination">
102.     <ul class="pagination justify-content-center">
103.       {% if page_obj.has_previous %}
104.         <li class="page-item">
105.           <a class="page-link" href="?page=1">&laquo; 1…</a>
106.         </li>
107.         {% if page_obj.previous_page_number != 1 %}
108.           <li class="page-item">
109.             <a class="page-link"
110.               href="?page={{ page_obj.previous_page_number }}">
111.               {{ page_obj.previous_page_number }}
112.             </a>
113.           </li>
114.         {% endif %}
115.       {% endif %}
116.       <li class="page-item active">
117.         <span class="page-link">
118.           {{ page_obj.number }}
119.         </span>
120.       </li>
121.       {% if page_obj.has_next %}
122.         {% if page_obj.next_page_number != page_obj.paginator.num_pages %}
123.           <li class="page-item">
124.             <a class="page-link" href="?page={{ page_obj.next_page_number }}">
125.               {{ page_obj.next_page_number }}
126.             </a>
127.           </li>
128.         {% endif %}
129.         <li class="page-item">
130.           <a class="page-link" href="?page={{ page_obj.paginator.num_pages }}">
131.             …{{ page_obj.paginator.num_pages }} &raquo;
132.           </a>
133.         </li>
134.       {% endif %}
135.     </ul>
136.   </nav>
137. {% endblock %}
```

When you add the paginate_by attribute to the ListView, you get access to a new page_obj in the context. The page_obj object includes the following properties:

A. page_obj.has_previous – True if the current page is not the first page.

B. page_obj.previous_page_number – The number of the previous page.

C. `page_obj.has_next` – `True` if the current page is not the last page.

D. `page_obj.next_page_number` –The number of the next page.

E. `page_obj.number` – The current page number.

F. `page_obj.paginator.num_pages` – The total number of pages.

The code in the template uses nested if conditions so that `page_obj.previous_page_number` and `page_obj.next_page_number` only show up if `page_obj.has_previous` and `page_obj.has_next`, respectively, are `True`.

❖ E68.1. Try it Out

Go to the **Jokes** page on the website. At the bottom of the page, you should see a pagination navbar like this one:

❖ E68.2. Making Pagination Template Code Reusable

There is nothing in your pagination template code that is specific to the joke-list page. You may want to use it for other apps that you create in the project. As such, it makes sense to move it into a separate file and include it on the page via the `{% include %}` tag.

1. Create a new `includes` folder in the `templates` folder.
2. Within the `includes` folder, create a new `pagination.html` file.
3. Cut the pagination `nav` from `joke_list.html` and paste it into `pagination.html`.
4. In `joke_list.html`, add the following `include` tag where the pagination `nav` was:

   ```
   {% include 'includes/pagination.html' %}
   ```

5. Refresh the joke-list page. It should work exactly the same as it did before.

Git Commit

Commit your code to Git.

Exercise 69: Ordering

60 to 120 minutes

To allow the user to sort jokes, you need to update the `ListView` and the joke-list template.

E69.1. The `ListView`

You can control the ordering of `ListViews` using the `ordering` attribute. To see how it works:

1. Navigate to `http://127.0.0.1:8000/jokes/` and notice the order of the questions.
2. Open `jokes/views.py` in your editor and update the `JokeListView` to look like this:

```
class JokeListView(ListView):
        model = Joke
        paginate_by = 10
        ordering = ['question']
```

3. Back in the browser, refresh the joke-list page. Notice that it is now ordered by the joke question.
4. Return to the editor and change the `JokeListView` to order by `question` in descending order by adding a `-` before `question`:

```
ordering = ['-question']
```

5. Back in the browser, refresh the joke-list page again. Notice that it now sorts by the joke question in descending order.

Notice that `ordering` is a list. You can order by multiple fields. For example:

```
ordering = ['last_name', 'first_name']
```

This works great if you always want to sort in the same way, but not if you want dynamic sorting.

The `get_ordering()` Method

The `get_ordering()` method of `ListViews` makes it possible to change the ordering based on values passed in over the querystring. At its simplest, it can look like this:

```
class JokeListView(ListView):
    model = Joke
    paginate_by = 10

    def get_ordering(self):
        # default ordering will be '-updated'
        ordering = self.request.GET.get('order', '-updated')
        return ordering
```

The `get()` method will return the value of the `order` URL parameter if it exists; otherwise, it will return `'-updated'`.

Go ahead and replace the `ordering` attribute in `JokeListView` with that `get_ordering()` method and then visit `http://127.0.0.1:8000/jokes/?order=user__username`. Notice that jokes are sorted by the joke creator.

In the URL, add a - before `user__username`:

```
http://127.0.0.1:8000/jokes/?order=-user__username
```

Press Enter to load the page. Now, the jokes should be sorted by joke creator in reverse order.

This works well as long as the passed-in `order` parameter contains a valid value. But try visiting `http://127.0.0.1:8000/jokes/?order=abc`. You'll get a "Cannot resolve keyword 'abc' into field." error. You will need to write code so that the `get_ordering()` method knows the valid ordering fields. You will also write some code so that the values used for the `order` parameter in the template are friendlier (e.g., `creator` and `category` instead of `user__username` and `category__category`).

get_order_fields()

Add the following `get_order_fields()` method to `JokeListView`:

```
def get_order_fields(self):
    """
    Returns a dict mapping friendly names to field names and lookups.
    """
    return {
        'joke': 'question',
        'category': 'category__category',
        'creator': 'user__username',
        'created': 'created',
        'updated': 'updated',
        'default_key': 'updated'
    }
```

This method returns a dictionary:

- The dictionary keys are friendly names, which you will use in the template.
- The dictionary values are field names (and lookups), which you will use to set the ordering.
- The final key, `'default_key'`, holds the default field to order by if `order_key` is either unspecified or invalid.

Note that `get_order_fields()` is not a built-in method of `ListView`. It is a custom method that you have added to `JokeListView`.

Update `get_ordering()`

Soon, you will add both a sorting form and sorting links to the joke-list template. These will pass in two parameters:

1. `order` – The order key. In the view, you will get this value using:

   ```
   order_fields = self.get_order_fields()
   default_order_key = order_fields['default_key']
   order_key = self.request.GET.get('order', default_order_key)
   ```

   If the `order` parameter is not passed in, `order_key` will get the default order key.

2. `direction` – The order direction: `'asc'` or `'desc'`. In the view, you will get this value using:

   ```
   direction = self.request.GET.get('dir', 'desc')
   ```

   If the `dir` parameter is not passed in, `direction` will get `'desc'`.

Update `get_ordering()` as follows:

```
def get_ordering(self):
    order_fields = self.get_order_fields()
    default_order_key = order_fields['default_key']
    order_key = self.request.GET.get('order', default_order_key)
    direction = self.request.GET.get('direction', 'desc')

    # If order_key is invalid, use default
    if order_key not in order_fields:
        order_key = default_order_key

    ordering = order_fields[order_key]

    # if direction is 'desc' or is invalid use descending order
    if direction != 'asc':
        ordering = '-' + ordering

    return ordering
```

Review this method. Notice that it doesn't contain anything specific to jokes. You can reuse it along with a custom `get_order_fields()` method in any `ListView`.

get_context_data()

The options in the *sorting form* in the template will be generated from the list of order keys, so you need to make those keys available in the `context`. You learned how to add context in the Template Filters and Tags lesson (see page 118).

You need to add three keys to the context:

1. `order_fields` - So the template can generate the options for the sorting form.
2. `order` – So the current order key can be pre-selected in the sorting form.
3. `direction` – So the current direction can be pre-selected in the sorting form.

Review the following `get_context_data()` method, but don't add it yet.

```
def get_context_data(self, **kwargs):
    context = super().get_context_data(**kwargs)

    order_fields = self.get_order_fields()
    default_order_key = order_fields['default_key']
    order_key = self.request.GET.get('order', default_order_key)
    direction = self.request.GET.get('direction', 'desc')

    # If order_key is invalid, use default
    if order_key not in order_fields:
        order_key = default_order_key

    context['order'] = order_key
    context['direction'] = direction

    # get all but the last order key, which is 'default'
    context['order_fields'] = list(order_fields.keys())[:-1]

    return context
```

Notice that the highlighted section also appears in the `get_ordering()` method. To follow the DRY[103] principle, move that functionality into a separate method:

```
def get_order_settings(self):
    order_fields = self.get_order_fields()
    default_order_key = order_fields['default_key']
    order_key = self.request.GET.get('order', default_order_key)
    direction = self.request.GET.get('direction', 'desc')

    # If order_key is invalid, use default
    if order_key not in order_fields:
        order_key = default_order_key

    return (order_fields, order_key, direction)
```

The `get_order_settings()` method returns a tuple, which you can assign to `order_fields`, `order_key`, and `direction` in both the `get_ordering()` and the `get_context_data()` methods like this:

103. **D**on't **R**epeat **Y**ourself

```
order_fields, order_key, direction = self.get_order_settings()
```

The tuple returned from `get_order_settings()` will be unpacked and the items will be assigned to the individual variables.

Update `jokes/views.py` as shown in the following code:[104]

[104]. **Don't want to type?** Copy from `starter-code/pagination-and-ordering/jokes_views.py`.

Exercise Code 69.1: jokes/views.py

```
    -------Lines 1 through 41 Omitted-------
42.  class JokeListView(ListView):
43.      model = Joke
44.      paginate_by = 10
45.
46.      def get_context_data(self, **kwargs):
47.          context = super().get_context_data(**kwargs)
48.
49.          order_fields, order_key, direction = self.get_order_settings()
50.
51.          context['order'] = order_key
52.          context['direction'] = direction
53.
54.          # get all but the last order key, which is 'default'
55.          context['order_fields'] = list(order_fields.keys())[:-1]
56.
57.          return context
58.
59.      def get_ordering(self):
60.          order_fields, order_key, direction = self.get_order_settings()
61.
62.          ordering = order_fields[order_key]
63.
64.          # if direction is 'desc' or is invalid use descending order
65.          if direction != 'asc':
66.              ordering = '-' + ordering
67.
68.          return ordering
69.
70.      def get_order_settings(self):
71.          order_fields = self.get_order_fields()
72.          default_order_key = order_fields['default_key']
73.          order_key = self.request.GET.get('order', default_order_key)
74.          direction = self.request.GET.get('direction', 'desc')
75.
76.          # If order_key is invalid, use default
77.          if order_key not in order_fields:
78.              order_key = default_order_key
79.
80.          return (order_fields, order_key, direction)
81.
82.
83.      def get_order_fields(self):
84.          # Returns a dict mapping friendly names to field names and lookups.
```

```
85.             return {
86.                 'joke': 'question',
87.                 'category': 'category__category',
88.                 'creator': 'user__username',
89.                 'created': 'created',
90.                 'updated': 'updated',
91.                 'default_key': 'updated'
92.             }
-------Lines 93 through 156 Omitted-------
```

Test your code out by visiting the following pages:

1. `http://127.0.0.1:8000/jokes/?order=category&direction=asc` – Sorted by joke category in ascending order.
2. `http://127.0.0.1:8000/jokes/?order=creator&direction=desc` – Sorted by joke creator in descending order.
3. `http://127.0.0.1:8000/jokes/?order=joke&direction=asc` – Sorted by joke question in ascending order.

Of the four methods that you have added to `JokeListView`, only `get_order_fields()` is specific to your application. The other three methods (`get_context_data()`, `get_ordering()`, and `get_order_settings()`) can be used without modification (or at least as starting points) with any `ListView`.

❖ E69.2. Adding Sorting Controls to the Template

The HTML page should have *sorting links*, usually in column headers (`th`), and/or a *sorting form*, which send parameters to the server via a `GET` request. You will learn how to implement both.

Clickable Header Links

If the fields that you want to order by are all showing as headers, you can turn those headers into links that pass the ordering parameter on the querystring, like this:

```
{% if request.GET.order == 'joke' and request.GET.direction == 'asc' %}
  <th><a href="?order=joke&direction=desc">Joke</a></th>
{% else %}
  <th><a href="?order=joke&direction=asc">Joke</a></th>
{% endif %}
```

The code checks `request.GET.order` to see if it is currently sorting by this field in ascending order. If it is, then you create a link to sort by the field in descending order. Otherwise, you create a link to sort by the field in ascending order.

Sorting Form

Another option is to add a form that uses the `GET` method, which is the default method, to pass in the ordering parameters:

```
<form>
  <label for="order">Order By:</label>
  <select name="order" id="order">
    {% for field in order_fields %}
      <option value="{{ field }}" {% if order == field %}selected{% endif %}>
        {{ field|title }}
      </option>
    {% endfor %}
  </select>
  <input type="radio" name="direction" id="asc" value="asc"
    {% if direction == 'asc' %}checked{% endif %}
  >
  <label for="asc">ASC</label>
  <input type="radio" name="direction" id="desc" value="desc"
    {% if direction == 'desc' %}checked{% endif %}
  >
  <label for="desc">DESC</label>
  <button type="submit">Sort</button>
</form>
```

Things to notice:

1. You use a `for` loop to loop through the `order_fields` list, which you added to the `context` of `JokeListView`, to create the options for `order`.

- You check each field to see if you are currently sorting by that field, and if you are, you add the `selected` attribute so that the field will show as selected:

  ```
  <option value="{{ field }}" {% if order == field %}selected{% endif %}>
  ```

2. You create two radio buttons to hold the direction, and you check the current value of `direction` to decide which one to pre-check (using the `checked` attribute):

   ```
   <input type="radio" name="direction" id="asc" value="asc"
     {% if direction == 'asc' %}checked{% endif %}
   >

   <input type="radio" name="direction" id="desc" value="desc"
     {% if direction == 'desc' %}checked{% endif %}
   >
   ```

Add the completed sorting code to the joke-list template as shown:[105]

105. **Don't want to type?** Copy from `starter-code/pagination-and-ordering/joke_list_ordering.html`.

Exercise Code 69.2: templates/jokes/joke_list.html

```
-------Lines 1 through 4 Omitted-------
5.    <div class="row">
6.      <div class="col-12 col-md-2 col-lg-3">
7.        <h2>Jokes</h2>
8.      </div>
9.      <div class="col-12 col-md-8 col-lg-6">
10.       <form class="form-inline my-2 mx-auto" style="max-width: 30rem;">
11.         <label class="my-1 mr-2" for="order">Order By:</label>
12.         <select class="form-control mr-sm-2" name="order" id="order">
13.           {% for field in order_fields %}
14.             <option value="{{ field }}"
15.               {% if order == field %}selected{% endif %}
16.             >{{ field|title }}</option>
17.           {% endfor %}
18.         </select>
19.         <div class="form-check form-check-inline">
20.           <input class="form-check-input" type="radio" name="direction"
21.             id="asc" value="asc"
22.             {% if direction == 'asc' %}checked{% endif %}
23.           >
24.           <label class="form-check-label" for="asc">ASC</label>
25.         </div>
26.         <div class="form-check form-check-inline">
27.           <input class="form-check-input" type="radio" name="direction"
28.             id="desc" value="desc"
29.             {% if direction == 'desc' %}checked{% endif %}
30.           >
31.           <label class="form-check-label" for="desc">DESC</label>
32.         </div>
33.         <button class="btn btn-primary btn-sm m-2" type="submit">
34.           Sort
35.         </button>
36.       </form>
37.     </div>
38.     <div class="col-12 col-md-2 col-lg-3 text-right">
39.       <a class="btn btn-success btn-sm m-2" href="{% url 'jokes:create' %}">
40.         + New Joke
41.       </a>
42.     </div>
43.   </div>
44.
45.   <div class="table-responsive">
46.     <table class="table table-striped" style="min-width: 500px">
47.       <thead>
```

```
48.         {% with order=request.GET.order dir=request.GET.direction %}
49.           <tr>
50.             {% if order == 'joke' and dir == 'asc' %}
51.               <th><a href="?order=joke&direction=desc">Joke</a></th>
52.             {% else %}
53.               <th><a href="?order=joke&direction=asc">Joke</a></th>
54.             {% endif %}
55.             {% if order == 'category' and dir == 'asc' %}
56.               <th><a href="?order=category&direction=desc">Category</a></th>
57.             {% else %}
58.               <th><a href="?order=category&direction=asc">Category</a></th>
59.             {% endif %}
60.             {% if order == 'creator' and dir == 'asc' %}
61.               <th><a href="?order=creator&direction=desc">Creator</a></th>
62.             {% else %}
63.               <th><a href="?order=creator&direction=asc">Creator</a></th>
64.             {% endif %}
65.           </tr>
66.         {% endwith %}
67.       </thead>
    -------Lines 68 through 102 Omitted-------
```

The new code uses the sorting mechanisms we have discussed, but there are some other changes as well:

1. You have restructured the content above the table to create a nice three-column layout using Bootstrap classes.
2. You have used Bootstrap classes to style the sorting form.
3. You have used `{% with order=request.GET.order dir=request.GET.direction %}` so that you don't have to repeatedly type out `request.GET.order` and `request.GET.direction`.

❖ E69.3. Updating the Pagination

The final thing you need to do is make sure that your pagination links retain the ordering. Currently, they will not, because they don't pass in the `order` and `direction` parameters.

Open `templates/includes/pagination.html` in your editor and update the links as shown.

Note that there should be no break in the code where the ↵↵ symbols appear. When you see:

```
dir ↵↵
ection
```

…, you should type:

```
direction
```

The links:

```
<a class="page-link"
  href="?page=1&order={{ order }}&direction={{ direction }}">
  &laquo; 1…
</a>

<a class="page-link"
  href="?page={{ page_obj.previous_page_number }}&order={{ order }}&dir ↵↵
ection={{ direction }}">
  {{ page_obj.previous_page_number }}
</a>

<a class="page-link"
  href="?page={{ page_obj.next_page_number }}&order={{ order }}&dir ↵↵
ection={{ direction }}">
  {{ page_obj.next_page_number }}
</a>

<a class="page-link"
  href="?page={{ page_obj.paginator.num_pages }}&order={{ order }}&dir ↵↵
ection={{ direction }}">
  …{{ page_obj.paginator.num_pages }} &raquo;
</a>
```

❖ E69.4. Try it Out

Visit the joke-list page and sort using the form or one of the header links. Then, click through the pagination. It should retain the sorting.

Git Commit

Commit your code to Git.

Conclusion

In this lesson, you have learned to add pagination and ordering to a `ListView`. You have also learned to load data from fixtures.

LESSON 16

Advanced Querying and Search

Topics Covered

☑ Advanced querying.

☑ Field Lookups.

☑ Q Objects.

☑ Search.

☑ Aggregation.

☑ Annotation.

☑ The Django Debug Toolbar.

☑ Prefetching queries.

> We had reached Baker Street and had stopped at the door. He was **search**ing his pockets for the key when someone passing said: "Good-night, Mister Sherlock Holmes."
>
> *– A Scandal in Bohemia, Arthur Conan Doyle*

Introduction

In this lesson, you will learn to use advanced querying, to implement search, and to get joke ratings by averaging aggregate data. You will also learn to optimize your code using a third-party app called Django Debug Toolbar.

❋

16.1. Field Lookups

All the lookups you have used so far have looked for exact matches. For example:

```
Joke.objects.filter(tags__tag='Animal')
```

They are the equivalent of `WHERE field = value` in SQL.

Django field lookups have a *lookup type*, which is appended to the field with two underscores, like this:

```
field__lookuptype
```

Thus far, you haven't had to specify the lookup type, because it defaults to `exact`. The two following QuerySets are equivalent:

```
Joke.objects.filter(tags__tag='Animal')
Joke.objects.filter(tags__tag__exact='Animal')
```

The lookup types are:

- `exact` / `iexact`
- `contains` / `icontains`
- `startswith` / `istartswith`
- `endswith` / `iendswith`
- `regex` / `iregex`
- `lt` / `lte` / `gt` / `gte`
- `in`
- `range`
- `isnull`
- `date` / `year` / `month` / `day` / `week` / `week_day` / `quarter` / `iso_year`[106]
- `time` / `hour` / `minute` / `second`

---

106. See `https://en.wikipedia.org/wiki/ISO_week_date` for information on the ISO week dates system.

Case Sensitivity and the Database

Lookup types that have the `i` prefix will do case-**i**nsensitive comparisons.

While PostgreSQL fully supports case sensitivity "out of the box," not all databases do. If you find that case is always being ignored even with the lookup types that are not prefixed with `i`, you may need to tweak some settings in your database.

In the following section, we show examples of the different lookup types and their SQL equivalents (or near equivalents).

exact / iexact

Generally, you will leave off `exact` when looking for exact matches:

Django

```
Joke.objects.filter(question='...')
Joke.objects.filter(question__exact='...')
```

SQL

```
SELECT *
FROM jokes_joke
WHERE question = '...';
```

Use `iexact` for an exact match that ignores case:

Django

```
Joke.objects.filter(question__iexact='...')
```

SQL

```
SELECT *
FROM jokes_joke
WHERE lower(question) = lower('...');
```

contains / icontains

Django

```
Joke.objects.filter(question__contains='...')
```

SQL

```
SELECT *
FROM jokes_joke
WHERE question LIKE '%...%';
```

startswith / istartswith

Django

```
Joke.objects.filter(question__startswith='...')
```

SQL

```
SELECT *
FROM jokes_joke
WHERE question LIKE '...%';
```

endswith / iendswith

Django

```
Joke.objects.filter(question__endswith='...')
```

SQL

```
SELECT *
FROM jokes_joke
WHERE question LIKE '%...';
```

lt / lte / gt / gte

Django

```
import datetime
start_date = datetime.datetime(2020, 1, 1, tzinfo=datetime.timezone.utc)
Joke.objects.filter(created__gte=start_date)
```

SQL

```
SELECT *
FROM jokes_joke
WHERE created >= '2020-01-01 00:00:00+00:00';
```

in

Django

```
Tag.objects.filter(tag__in=['...', '...', '...'])
```

SQL

```
SELECT *
FROM jokes_tag
WHERE tag IN ('...', '...', '...');
```

range

Django

```
import datetime
start_date = datetime.datetime(2020, 1, 1, tzinfo=datetime.timezone.utc)
end_date = datetime.datetime(2021, 1, 1, tzinfo=datetime.timezone.utc)
Joke.objects.filter(created__range=(start_date, end_date))
```

SQL

```
SELECT *
FROM jokes_joke
WHERE created BETWEEN '2020-01-01 00:00:00+00:00' AND '2021-01-01 00:00:00+00:00';
```

isnull

Django

```
User.objects.filter(dob__isnull=False)
```

SQL

```
SELECT *
FROM users_customusers
WHERE dob IS NOT NULL;
```

regex / iregex

Django

```
Joke.objects.filter(question__regex=r'^(Why?|How) .+')
```

SQL

```
SELECT *
FROM jokes_joke
WHERE question ~ '^(Why?|How) .+';
```

date / year / etc.

```
Joke.objects.filter(created__date=datetime.date(2020, 1, 1))
```

```
Joke.objects.filter(created__year=2020)
```

The date and time field lookups allow chaining of additional field lookups.

```
Joke.objects.filter(created__date__gt=datetime.date(2020, 1, 1))
```

```
Joke.objects.filter(created__year__gte=2020)
```

16.2. Q Objects

The lookup types cover most cases, but they do not handle some compound conditions. For example, you cannot create the following SQL query with lookup types alone:

```
SELECT *
FROM jokes_joke
WHERE question ILIKE '%dog%' OR answer ILIKE '%dog%';
```

To create such compound queries, you need to import `Q` from `django.db.models`:

```
from django.db.models import Q
```

The `Q` operators are:

- `|` – OR
- `&` – AND
- `~` – NOT

To find jokes that contain "dog" in **either** the question or the answer, use the "or" operator (`|`):

```
Joke.objects.filter(Q(question__icontains='dog') | Q(answer__icontains='dog'))
```

To find jokes that contain "dog" in **both** the question and the answer, use the "and" operator (`&`):

```
Joke.objects.filter(Q(question__icontains='dog') & Q(answer__icontains='dog'))
```

To find jokes that contain "dog" in the question, **but not** in the answer, use the "not" operator (`~`):

```
Joke.objects.filter(Q(question__icontains='dog') & ~Q(answer__icontains='dog'))
```

 Exercise 70: Limiting Results by Category, Tag, or Creator

20 to 30 minutes

In this exercise, you will add paths to the URLConf to list jokes in a specific category, with a specific tag, or created by a specific user. You will then use the `get_queryset()` method of the `ListView` to appropriately limit the `QuerySet`.

❖ E70.1. URLConf

Open `jokes/urls.py` and add the following three paths to the end of `urlpatterns`:

```
path('category/<slug>/', JokeListView.as_view(), name='category'),
path('tag/<slug>/', JokeListView.as_view(), name='tag'),
path('creator/<username>/', JokeListView.as_view(), name='creator'),
```

Notice that all the paths use `JokeListView.as_view()`. You will need to modify that view so that it returns the appropriate `QuerySet` for the given path.

❖ E70.2. `JokeListView`

The default `QuerySet` for a `ListView` is `*model*.objects.all()` where model is the value of the `model` attribute. For example, `JokeListView` begins with:

```
class JokeListView(ListView):
    model = Joke
```

The implied `QuerySet` for the view is `Joke.objects.all()`.

The `QuerySet` can be changed using the `get_queryset()` method. In `jokes/views.py`, add the following method to `JokeListView`:

```
def get_queryset(self):
    ordering = self.get_ordering()
    qs = Joke.objects.all()

    if 'slug' in self.kwargs: # Filter by category or tag
        slug = self.kwargs['slug']
        if '/category' in self.request.path_info:
            qs = qs.filter(category__slug=slug)
        if '/tag' in self.request.path_info:
            qs = qs.filter(tags__slug=slug)
    elif 'username' in self.kwargs: # Filter by joke creator
        username = self.kwargs['username']
        qs = qs.filter(user__username=username)

    return qs.order_by(ordering)
```

Things to notice:

1. You use the view's `get_ordering()` method that you wrote earlier to get the ordering.
2. You assign `Joke.objects.all()` to `qs` to get the unfiltered queryset.
3. If `'slug'` is in `self.kwargs`, then the path is one of these two:

   ```
   path('category/<slug>/', JokeListView.as_view(), name='category'),
   path('tag/<slug>/', JokeListView.as_view(), name='tag'),
   ```

   To figure out which one it is, you look in `self.request.path_info`, which is a string containing the full path from the web root (e.g., `/jokes/tag/animal/`). And then you filter accordingly:

   ```
   if '/category' in self.request.path_info:
       qs = qs.filter(category__slug=slug)
   if '/tag' in self.request.path_info:
       qs = qs.filter(tags__slug=slug)
   ```

4. Otherwise, you check to see if `'username'` is in `self.kwargs`, which will be `True` for this path:

   ```
   path('creator/<username>/', JokeListView.as_view(), name='creator')
   ```

In this case, you limit the QuerySet to jokes created by the specified creator:

```
username = self.kwargs['username']
qs = qs.filter(user__username=username)
```

5. If neither 'slug' nor 'username' show up in self.kwargs then you leave the default query as is and it will return all the jokes.

6. Finally, you return the ordered QuerySet:

```
return qs.order_by(ordering)
```

❖ E70.3. The Templates

1. Open templates/_base.html in your editor.

2. Modify the link with the text "My Django Jokes" as follows:

```
<a class="dropdown-item"
  href="{% url 'jokes:creator' user.username %}?order={{ order }}&dir ↵↵
ection={{ direction }}">
  My Django Jokes
</a>
```

Now, when you visit that link, it will list the jokes you have created. Notice that the URL in the link includes the order and direction parameters, so that the sorting is maintained when the link is clicked.

3. Open templates/jokes/joke_list.html in your editor.

4. Wrap {{ joke.category.category }}, {{ tag.tag }}, and {{ joke.user.username }} in links:

```
<a href="{% url 'jokes:category' joke.category.slug %}?order={{ order }}&dir ↵↵
ection={{ direction }}">
  {{ joke.category.category }}
</a>
```

For the tag link, replace the existing span element with an a element:

```
<a href="{% url 'jokes:tag' tag.slug %}?order={{ order }}&dir ↵
ection={{ direction }}"
  class="badge badge-pill badge-secondary">{{ tag.tag }}</a>
```

```
<a href="{% url 'jokes:creator' joke.user.username %}?order={{ order }}&dir ↵
ection={{ direction }}">
  {{ joke.user.username }}
</a>
```

❖ E70.4. Try it Out

From the jokes-list page, click on a category, tag, or username. The jokes should be filtered accordingly. If there is an error or the jokes do not appear to be filtering correctly, examine the URL. These are some examples of valid URLs:

1. `http://127.0.0.1:8000/jokes/creator/nbeasley/?order=updated&direction=desc`
2. `http://127.0.0.1:8000/jokes/tag/animal/?order=category&direction=asc`
3. `http://127.0.0.1:8000/jokes/category/brain-teaser/?order=joke&direction=desc`

Git Commit

Commit your code to Git.

Exercise 71: Implementing Search

45 to 60 minutes

You will now add search to the Django Jokes website. The search path will also use `JokeListView`, but it will limit jokes to those with a question or answer that contains the searched text. We have included instructions below, but you may want to try this one on your own first, and then come back to the instructions if you need help. You will need to modify the `get_queryset()` method in the view and the search form in the base template.

1. Open `jokes/views.py` in your editor.
2. As the search will use a compound query, import `Q` from `django.db.models`:

```
from django.db.models import Q
```

3. In the `get_queryset()` method of `JokeListView`, add a new `if` block to check if `'q'` is in `self.request.GET`:

```
def get_queryset(self):
    ordering = self.get_ordering()
    qs = Joke.objects.all()

    if 'q' in self.request.GET: # Filter by search query
        q = self.request.GET.get('q')
        qs = qs.filter(
            Q(question__icontains=q) | Q(answer__icontains=q)
        )

    if 'slug' in self.kwargs: # Filter by category or tag
        …
```

4. Open `templates/_base.html` in your editor.

5. Modify the search form to look like this:

```
<form class="form-inline my-2 my-lg-0" action="{% url 'jokes:list' %}">
  <input class="form-control mr-sm-2" type="search"
    placeholder="Search" aria-label="Search" name="q"
    value="{{ request.GET.q }}">
  <button class="btn btn-outline-success my-2 my-sm-0" type="submit">
    Search
  </button>
</form>
```

   Notice that you use `{{ request.GET.q }}` for the `value` of the `'q' input`. That's so the last search will appear in the form.

6. Start up the server, visit the site, and do a search. The results should be limited to jokes whose question or answer contains the searched text.

The following screenshot shows the result:

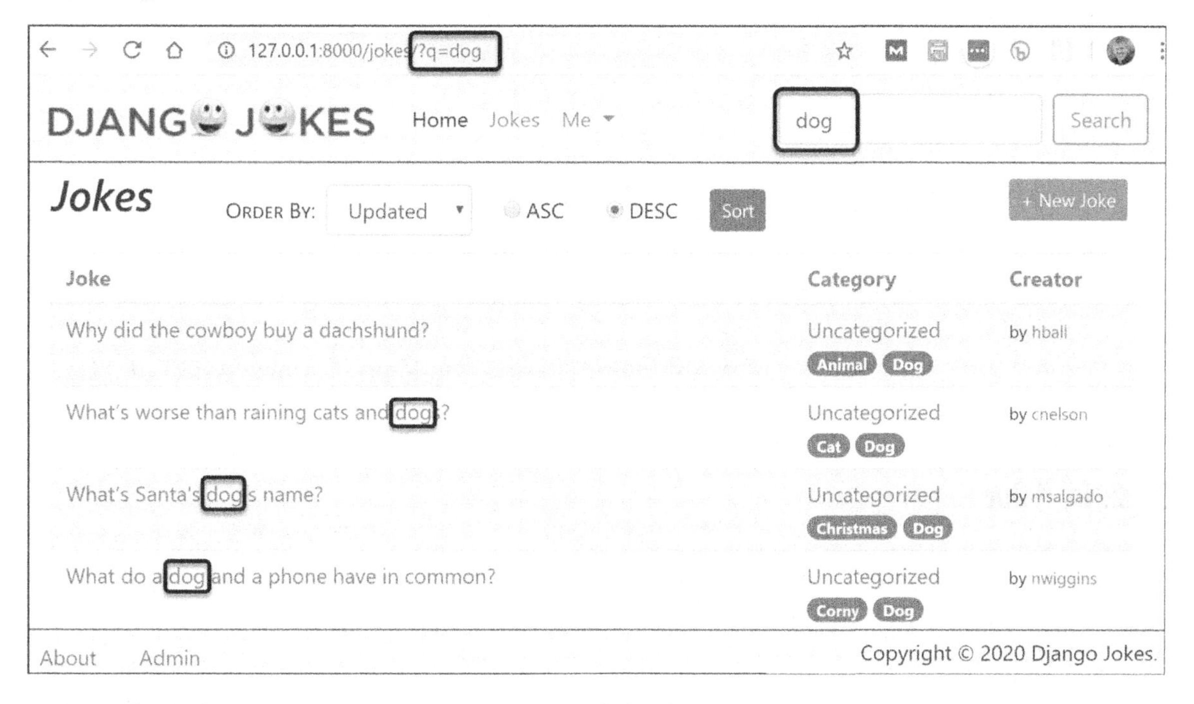

Note that "dog" does not appear in the question of the first joke shown. Therefore, it must appear in the answer, which it does: "Someone told him to get a long little *dog*gie."

❖ E71.1. Updating Other Templates

After a user searches, you want the pagination and sorting to stay within the searched text. For example, if a user searches on "dog" and then sorts the page using a header link or the form, you still want the results limited to jokes about dogs. And when the user uses the paginator at the bottom of the page, you want it to paginate through the jokes about dogs. To make this work, you need to update `templates/jokes/joke-list.html` and `templates/includes/pagination.html`.

1. Open `templates/jokes/joke-list.html` in your editor.
2. Add the following hidden `input` as the first child of the sorting form:

    ```
    <input type="hidden" name="q" value="{{ request.GET.q }}">
    ```

    When the form is submitted, it will pass the `q` parameter on the query string.
3. In the row in the `thead` of the table, append `&q={{ request.GET.q }}` to the URL of each sorting link. For example, the `href` value of the first **Joke** link should be:

    ```
    ?order=joke&direction=desc&q={{ request.GET.q }}
    ```

4. Open `templates/includes/pagination.html` in your editor.
5. Append `&q={{ request.GET.q }}` to the URL in all four pagination links. For example, the `href` value of the first link should be:

    ```
    ?page=1&order={{ order }}&direction={{ direction }}&q={{ request.GET.q }}
    ```

❖ E71.2. Try it Out

Test the page by visiting `http://127.0.0.1:8000/jokes/` in your browser, doing a search, and then sorting and navigating with the paginator. When you move from page to page or sort, the results should remain limited by the search.

Git Commit

Commit your code to Git.

16.3. Aggregation

The most commonly used aggregate functions in SQL are:

- COUNT
- SUM
- AVG
- MAX
- MIN

Django QuerySets include an aggregate() method to create aggregate queries. To use it, you must first import the aggregate methods you want to use from django.db.models. Open the Django shell and run the following code:

```
(.venv) …/projects/djangojokes.com> python manage.py shell
>>> from django.db.models import Avg, Count, Max, Min, Sum
```

Now, import JokeVote:

```
>>> from jokes.models import JokeVote
```

The following code gets the average vote for all JokeVotes:

```
>>> JokeVote.objects.aggregate(Avg('vote'))
{'vote__avg': -0.0106}
```

The generated SQL would look something like this:

```
SELECT AVG(vote) AS vote__avg
FROM jokes_jokevote;
```

Notice that the aggregate() method returns a dictionary, so it is terminal, meaning that you cannot chain additional filters after it. Default names for the dictionary keys are created using the field name and the lowercase aggregate method name separated by a double underscore (e.g., "vote__avg"). However, you can assign key names like this:

```
>>> JokeVote.objects.aggregate(average_vote=Avg('vote'))
{'average_vote': -0.0106}
```

You can get multiple aggregate fields at a time:

```
>>> JokeVote.objects.aggregate(average_vote=Avg('vote'), num_votes=Count('vote'))
{'average_vote': -0.0106, 'num_votes': 10000}
```

The generated SQL would look something like this:

```
SELECT AVG(vote) AS average_vote, COUNT(vote) AS num_votes
FROM jokes_jokevote;
```

Here are some more examples followed by the SQL they would generate:

1. Get the average vote and number of votes in the "Funny" category:

   Django

   ```
   >>> JokeVote.objects.filter(joke__category__category='Funny').aggregate(
   ...     average_vote=Avg('vote'), num_votes=Count('vote')
   ... )
   {'average_vote': -0.010682559316316204, 'num_votes': 8893}
   ```

   SQL

   ```
   SELECT AVG(vote) AS average_vote, COUNT(vote) AS num_votes
   FROM jokes_jokevote v
     JOIN jokes_joke j ON j.id = v.joke_id
     JOIN jokes_category c ON c.id = j.category_id
   WHERE c.category='Funny';
   ```

2. Get the average vote and number of votes that are tagged with "Animal":

```
>>> JokeVote.objects.filter(joke__tags__tag='Animal').aggregate(
...     average_vote=Avg('vote'), num_votes=Count('vote')
... )
{'average_vote': 0.005574136008918618, 'num_votes': 897}
```

SQL

```
SELECT AVG(vote) AS average_vote, COUNT(vote) AS num_votes
FROM jokes_jokevote v
  JOIN jokes_joke j ON j.id = v.joke_id
  JOIN jokes_joke_tags jt ON j.id = jt.joke_id
  JOIN jokes_tag t ON t.id = jt.tag_id
WHERE t.tag='Animal';
```

3. Get the average vote and number of votes on a specific joke:

Django

```
>>> JokeVote.objects.filter(joke=2).aggregate(avg=Avg('vote'), num=Count('vote'))
{'avg': 0.047619047619047616, 'num': 21}
```

SQL

```
SELECT AVG(vote) AS average_vote, COUNT(vote) AS num
FROM jokes_jokevote
WHERE joke_id = 2;
```

Note that if you just want to get the number of results, you can use a `QuerySet`'s `count()` method:

Total Number of Votes

```
>>> JokeVote.objects.count()
10000
```

Number of Likes

```
>>> JokeVote.objects.filter(vote=1).count()
4947
```

Number of Dislikes

```
>>> JokeVote.objects.filter(vote=-1).count()
5053
```

There are not equivalent methods to `count()` for `sum()`, `avg()`, `max()`, and `min()`, because they require specific fields.

Exercise 72: Getting Joke Ratings

30 to 45 minutes

In this exercise, you will add a `rating` property to the `Joke` model and you will display the rating using a bar, like this:

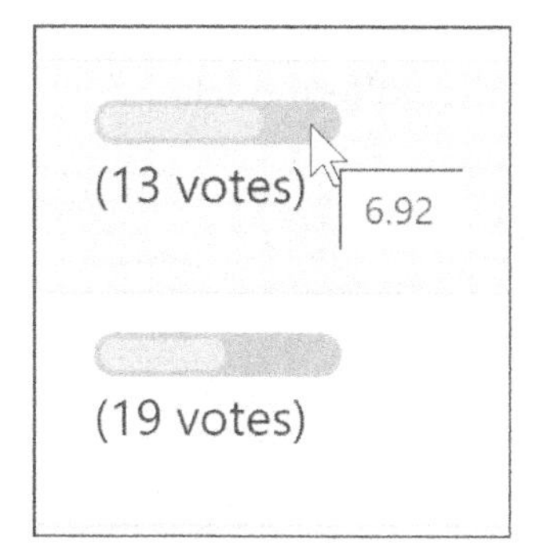

You can get the average rating for a specific joke like this:

```
JokeVote.objects.filter(joke=2).aggregate(average=Avg('vote'))
```

Remember that a vote is `-1` for a dislike and `1` for a like. That means that the average will be somewhere in between `-1` and `1`. You will use a 10-point scale for the rating. The formula you will use for that is:

```
rating = 5 + (average * 5)
```

If everyone likes the joke, the average will be `1`, so the rating is calculated as:

```
5 + (1 * 5) = 10
```

If everyone dislikes the joke, the average will be `-1`, so the rating is calculated as:

```
5 + (-1 * 5) = 0
```

If the joke has the same number of likes as dislikes, the average will be `0`, so the rating is calculated as:

```
5 + (0 * 5) = 5
```

❖ E72.1. The Model

1. Open `jokes/models.py` in your editor.
2. Import `Avg` from `django.db.models`:

```
from django.db.models import Avg
```

3. Add the following property to the `Joke` model:

```
@property
def rating(self):
    if self.num_votes == 0: # No jokes, so rating is 0
        return 0

    r = JokeVote.objects.filter(joke=self).aggregate(average=Avg('vote'))

    # Return the rounded rating.
    return round(5 + (r['average'] * 5), 2)
```

Things to note:

A. You return `0` for the rating if there are not yet any jokes.

B. You filter the `JokeVote` queryset using `joke=self`. That will return `JokeVote` object for given `Joke` instance.

❖ E72.2. The Template

1. Open `templates/jokes/joke_list.html` in your editor.
2. Add a "Rating" heading to the table row in the `thead` right before the closing `</tr>` tag:

```
<th>Rating</th>
```

3. Add the following table cell at the end of the table row in the `tbody`:

```
<td>
  <div id="rating-container" title="{{ joke.rating }}">
    <div id="rating"
      style="width:{% widthratio joke.rating 10 100 %}%;"></div>
  </div>
  ({{ joke.num_votes }} vote{{ joke.num_votes|pluralize }})
</td>
```

This code uses the `widthratio` template tag to create a bar. We explain how the `widthratio` tag works in Template Tags and Filters (see page 149).

❖ E72.3. CSS

Open `static/css/main.css` and the following rules to style the rating bar:

```
/* RATING BAR */
#rating-container {
  background-color:silver;
  border-radius: .5em;
  max-width: 5rem;
  padding: 2px;
}

#rating {
  background-color: gold;
  border-radius: .5em;
  height: 10px;
}
```

❖ E72.4. Try It Out

Start up the server and visit the joke list. You should see the rating bars in the right-most column. You may need to do a hard refresh to get the CSS to reload.

Git Commit

Commit your code to Git.

16.4. Code Optimization

Take a look at the joke-list page and think about how many times the database is being hit to create this page. It turns out that it is a lot of queries that get run, including:

1. The query that gets all the jokes that show up on the page.
2. The queries that get information about the joke's category – one query for each joke.
3. The queries that get information about the joke's tags – one query for each joke.
4. The queries that get information about the joke's creator – one query for each joke.
5. The queries that get information about voting – several queries for each joke as a result of the `num_votes`, `num_likes`, `num_dislikes`, and `rating` properties of the `Joke` model.

❖ 16.4.1. Django Debug Toolbar

The Django Debug Toolbar is a third-party app that provides a set of debugging panels, including a SQL panel that provides details about the queries run when a page loads:

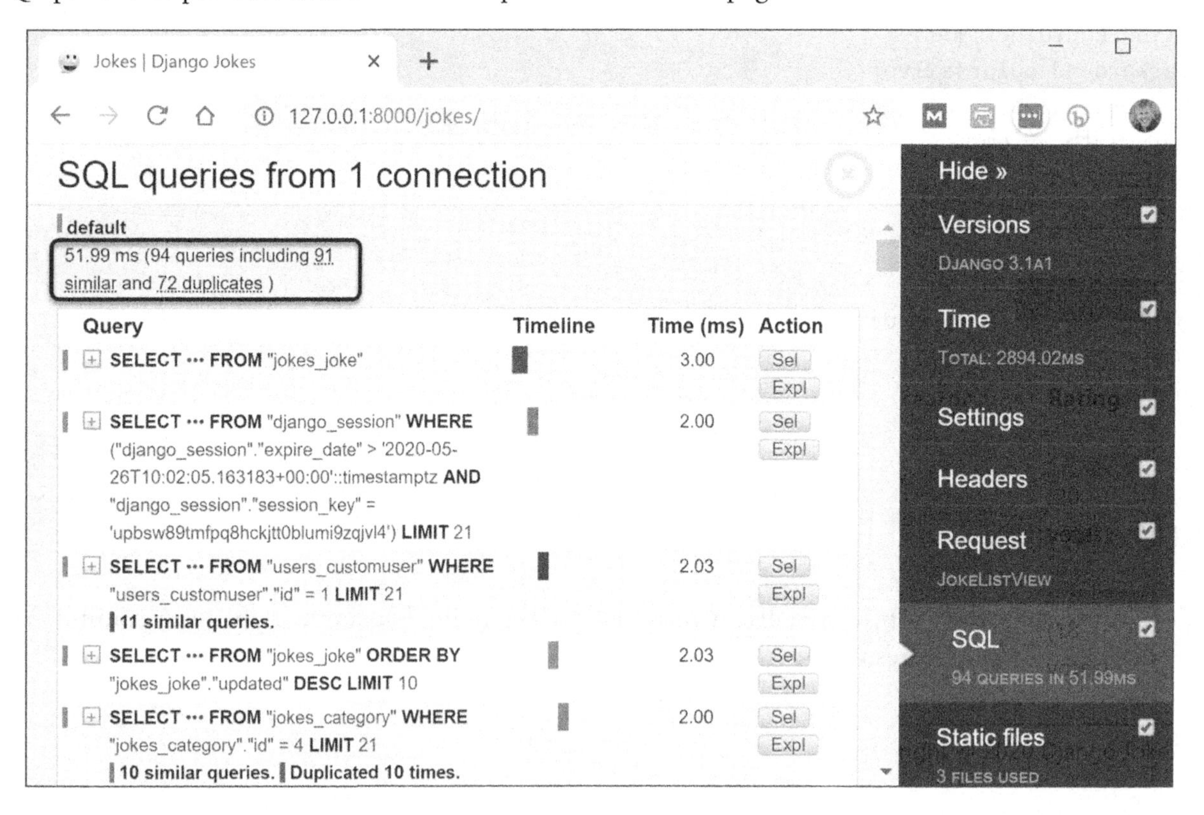

In the upper-left of the report, it shows how long it took to run all the queries, how many queries were run, how many are similar, and how many are exact duplicates. In our case, the duplicates result from getting information about the same category, tags, or creator more than once.

The `prefetch_related()` Method

The `prefetch_related()` method of `QuerySets` is used to get data about the related objects at the same time as it gets the data for the main object, thereby reducing the number of separate queries.

In the next exercise, you will install and use the Django Debug Toolbar and use `prefetch_related()` to reduce the number of times the database is hit.

Exercise 73: Installing and Using the Django Debug Toolbar

60 to 90 minutes

1. Install the Django Debug Toolbar:

```
pip install django-debug-toolbar
```

2. Open `settings.py` in your editor:

   A. Add `'debug_toolbar'` to `INSTALLED_APPS`:

   ```
   INSTALLED_APPS = [
       …
       # Third-party
       …
       'debug_toolbar',
       …
   ]
   ```

   B. Add the `DebugToolbarMiddleware` middleware to the beginning of the list:

   ```
   MIDDLEWARE = [
       'debug_toolbar.middleware.DebugToolbarMiddleware', # The Debug Toolbar

       …
   ]
   ```

   C. Add an `INTERNAL_IPS` setting below the `ALLOWED_HOSTS` setting:[107]

   ```
   INTERNAL_IPS = [ # Necessary for the Debug Toolbar
       '127.0.0.1',
   ]
   ```

   This setting is not specific to the Django Debug Toolbar, but it is required by it.

3. Open `urls.py` from the `djangojokes` folder.

107. It doesn't have to go right there, but it seems to fit well alongside `ALLOWED_HOSTS`.

4. At the top of the file, import `settings` from `django.conf`:

```
from django.conf import settings
```

5. Add the following to the bottom to import `debug_toolbar` and add its path only in `DEBUG` mode:

```
if settings.DEBUG:
    import debug_toolbar
    urlpatterns = [
        path('__debug__/', include(debug_toolbar.urls)),
    ] + urlpatterns
```

Start up the server and visit the joke list. Then, sort by category. You should see the Django Debug Toolbar panels on the right side. If it is collapsed, click on the **DjDT** tab to open it up:

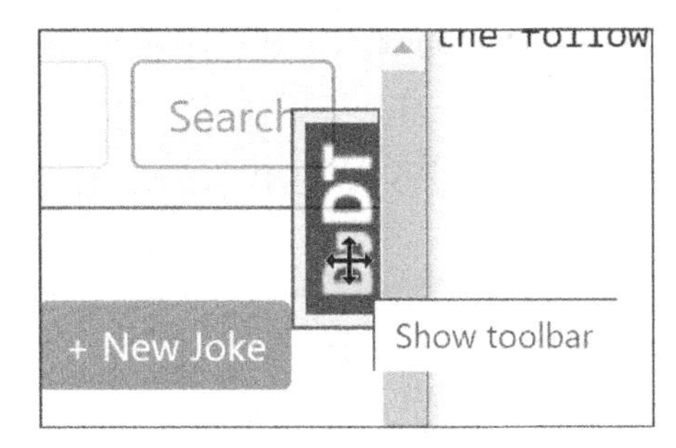

Click on the SQL panel and notice the summary report in the top-left:

```
50.98 ms (92 queries including 90 similar and 73 duplicates )
```

Note that your numbers may be somewhat different.

❖ E73.1. Reducing Duplicates

All the queries are listed on the page and can be expanded by clicking on the + icon. Look for the query from `jokes_category` and expand it:

```
SELECT "jokes_category"."id",
       "jokes_category"."category",
       "jokes_category"."slug",
       "jokes_category"."created",
       "jokes_category"."updated"
  FROM "jokes_category"
 WHERE "jokes_category"."id" = 2
 LIMIT 21
10 similar queries. Duplicated 10 times.
```

Notice that the query is duplicated 10 times. Let's fix that.

1. Open `jokes/views.py` in your editor.
2. In the `get_queryset()` method of `JokeListView`, add `prefetch_related('category')` to the returned queryset:

    ```
    return qs.prefetch_related('category').order_by(ordering)
    ```

3. Refresh the joke-list page and open the SQL panel again. The summary report should read something like:

    ```
    44.93 ms (83 queries including 80 similar and 63 duplicates )
    ```

    Notice that the number of duplicate queries was reduced by ten and the time to execute all the queries was reduced a bit.

4. Close the Debug report by clicking on the circled X:

5. Sort by **Creator**. The same username should show up on the page ten times, resulting in ten duplicate queries. Open the SQL panel again. The summary report should read something like:

    ```
    45.03 ms (83 queries including 80 similar and 70 duplicates )
    ```

6. Add `'user'` to the `prefetch_related()`:

    ```
    return qs.prefetch_related('category', 'user').order_by(ordering)
    ```

Refresh the joke-list page and re-open the SQL panel. Things should have improved even more:

```
39.95 ms (74 queries including 70 similar and 60 duplicates )
```

You have optimized quite a bit already, shaving a bunch of database hits and reducing the total query execution speed, but you can do more.

❖ E73.2. Consolidating Model Properties

Notice the many queries on the `jokes_jokevote` table:

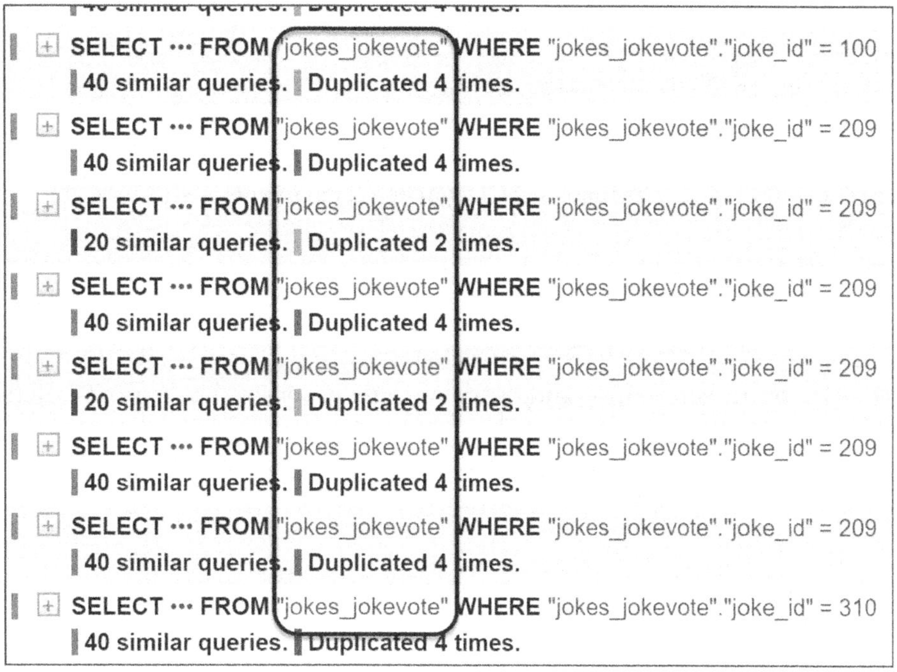

```
SELECT ··· FROM "jokes_jokevote" WHERE "jokes_jokevote"."joke_id" = 100
40 similar queries. Duplicated 4 times.
SELECT ··· FROM "jokes_jokevote" WHERE "jokes_jokevote"."joke_id" = 209
40 similar queries. Duplicated 4 times.
SELECT ··· FROM "jokes_jokevote" WHERE "jokes_jokevote"."joke_id" = 209
20 similar queries. Duplicated 2 times.
SELECT ··· FROM "jokes_jokevote" WHERE "jokes_jokevote"."joke_id" = 209
40 similar queries. Duplicated 4 times.
SELECT ··· FROM "jokes_jokevote" WHERE "jokes_jokevote"."joke_id" = 209
20 similar queries. Duplicated 2 times.
SELECT ··· FROM "jokes_jokevote" WHERE "jokes_jokevote"."joke_id" = 209
40 similar queries. Duplicated 4 times.
SELECT ··· FROM "jokes_jokevote" WHERE "jokes_jokevote"."joke_id" = 209
40 similar queries. Duplicated 4 times.
SELECT ··· FROM "jokes_jokevote" WHERE "jokes_jokevote"."joke_id" = 310
40 similar queries. Duplicated 4 times.
```

These queries are a result of this code in the template:

```
<td>
  <div id="rating-container" title="{{ joke.rating }}">
    <div id="rating"
      style="width:{% widthratio joke.rating 10 100 %}%;"></div>
  </div>
  ({{ joke.num_votes }} vote{{ joke.num_votes|pluralize }})
</td>
```

… which calls these methods in the Joke model:

```
@property
def num_votes(self):
    return self.jokevotes.count()

@property
def num_likes(self):
    return self.jokevotes.filter(vote=1).count()

@property
def num_dislikes(self):
    return self.jokevotes.filter(vote=-1).count()

@property
def rating(self):
    if self.num_votes == 0: # No jokes, so rating is 0
        return 0

    r = JokeVote.objects.filter(joke=self).aggregate(average=Avg('vote'))

    # Return the rounded rating.
    return round(5 + (r['average'] * 5), 2)
```

Open `jokes/models.py` in your editor and create a single property that returns a dictionary with all that data, like this:

```
@property
def votes(self):
    result = JokeVote.objects.filter(joke=self).aggregate(
        num_votes=Count('vote'),
        sum_votes=Sum('vote')
    )

    # If there aren't any votes yet, return a dictionary with values of 0.
    if result['num_votes'] == 0:
        return {'num_votes': 0, 'rating': 0, 'likes': 0, 'dislikes': 0}

    # Otherwise, calculate the dict values using num_votes and sum_votes.
    result['rating'] = round(
        5 + ((result['sum_votes']/result['num_votes'])*5), 2
    )
    result['dislikes'] = int((result['num_votes'] - result['sum_votes'])/2)
    result['likes'] = result['num_votes'] - result['dislikes']

    return result
```

Notice the query uses `Count()` and `Sum()`. Change the import statement at the top of the file to import those in addition to `Avg`:

```
from django.db.models import Avg, Count, Sum
```

That's it for the model. On to the template…

❖ E73.3. The `joke_list.html` Template

1. Open `joke_list.html` from `templates/jokes`.
2. Modify the "rating-container" `div` to use the new `votes` property dictionary in the model:

```
<td>
  {% with votes=joke.votes %}
  <div id="rating-container" title="{{ votes.rating }}">
    <div id="rating"
      style="width:{% widthratio votes.rating 10 100 %}%;"></div>
  </div>
  ({{ votes.num_votes }} vote{{ votes.num_votes|pluralize }})
  {% endwith %}
</td>
```

   Notice how this code uses the `with` tag to save the results of `joke.votes` into a local variable, so that the template doesn't repeatedly go back to the model (and then to the database) to get the votes.

With these changes in place, visit `http://127.0.0.1:8000/jokes/` again. You should notice a dramatic reduction in the number of queries run:

```
24.84 ms (24 queries including 20 similar )
```

❖ E73.4. The `joke_detail.html` Template

You need to update the `joke_detail.html` template to use your new `votes` property:[108]

108. **Don't want to type?** Copy from `starter-code/advanced-querying-and-search/joke_detail.html`.

Exercise Code 73.1: templates/jokes/joke_detail.html

```
-------Lines 1 through 24 Omitted-------
25.       <div class="border-bottom border-faded m-2 pb-2">
26.         {% if joke.user == user %}
27.           <a href="{% url 'jokes:update' joke.slug %}"
28.             class="btn btn-info btn-sm mr-2">Update</a>
29.           <a href="{% url 'jokes:delete' joke.slug %}"
30.             class="btn btn-danger btn-sm mr-2">Delete</a>
31.           {% with votes=joke.votes %}
32.             <p>Your joke has
33.             <span id="num-votes">{{ votes.num_votes|default:'no' }}
34.             vote{{ votes.num_votes|pluralize }}</span>{% if votes.num_votes %}:
35.             <span id="likes">{{ votes.likes }}
36.               like{{ votes.likes|pluralize }}</span> and
37.             <span id="dislikes">{{ votes.dislikes }}
38.               dislike{{ votes.dislikes|pluralize }}</span>{% endif %}.</p>
39.           {% endwith %}
40.         {% else %}
41.           {% csrf_token %}
42.           {% with votes=joke.votes %}
43.             <button id="dislike-button" class="btn btn-light">
44.               <i class="fas fa-thumbs-down fa-2x text-danger  mx-3"></i>
45.               <span id="dislikes">{{ votes.dislikes }}</span>
46.             </button>
47.             <button id="like-button" class="btn btn-light">
48.               <i class="fas fa-thumbs-up fa-2x text-success mx-3"></i>
49.               <span id="likes">{{ votes.likes }}</span>
50.             </button>
51.             <div id="output" class="text-info"></div>
52.             <span id="num-votes">
53.               {{ votes.num_votes }}
54.               vote{{ votes.num_votes|pluralize }}
55.             </span>
56.           {% endwith %}
-------Lines 57 through 69 Omitted-------
```

Git Commit

Commit your code to Git.

16.5. Brief Introduction to Annotation

The QuerySet's annotate() method is used to group data using SQL's GROUP BY clause. For example, to get the average rating on every joke using just a single query, you would use:

```
Joke.objects.values('question').annotate(
    avg_vote=Avg('jokevotes__vote'), num_votes=Count('jokevotes__vote')
).order_by('-avg_vote')
```

The generated SQL query would look something like this:

```
SELECT j.question, AVG(v.vote) AS avg_vote, COUNT(v.vote) AS num_votes
    FROM jokes_joke j
      LEFT JOIN jokes_jokevote v ON j.id = v.joke_id
    GROUP BY j.question
    ORDER BY avg_vote DESC;
```

A few things to note:

1. You can include one or more values in the values() method. These will be the fields that go in the SQL GROUP BY clause.
2. Unlike aggregate(), annotate() is not terminal, which is why you can use order_by() after it.
3. You can use filter() after annotate() like this:

   ```
   Joke.objects.values('question').annotate(
       avg_vote=Avg('jokevotes__vote'), num_votes=Count('jokevotes__vote')
   ).filter(num_votes__gt=0).order_by('-avg_vote')
   ```

   This will add a HAVING clause to the generated SQL statement:

   ```
   SELECT j.question, AVG(v.vote) AS avg_vote, COUNT(v.vote) AS num_votes
   FROM jokes_joke j
     LEFT JOIN jokes_jokevote v ON j.id = v.joke_id
   GROUP BY j.question
   HAVING COUNT(v.vote) > 0
   ORDER BY avg_vote DESC;
   ```

16.6. Viewing SQL Used in QuerySets

When debugging queries, it can be helpful to view the raw SQL used to generate a query. You can print the `query` attribute of a `QuerySet` to see a representation of the SQL used to generate it:

```
>>> q_all = Tag.objects.all()
>>> print(q_all.query)
SELECT "jokes_tag"."id", "jokes_tag"."tag", "jokes_tag"."slug", "jokes_tag"."created",
"jokes_tag"."updated"
FROM "jokes_tag"
ORDER BY "jokes_tag"."tag" ASC
```

It is important to note that the SQL held in the `query` attribute is not always valid SQL. It can be useful for debugging, but don't ever try to execute it.

For more complex queries, the SQL returned by printing the query attribute can be pretty ugly. We use a simple utility function to print a prettified version of it:

Demo 16.1: common/utils/queries.py

```
1.   import re
2.
3.   def pretty_sql(queryset):
4.       query = str(queryset.query)
5.       query = query.replace('"', '')
6.       table_name = re.search('SELECT (\w+)\.', query).group(1)
7.       query = query.replace(f'{table_name}.', '')
8.       sql_clauses = ['FROM', 'WHERE', 'ORDER BY', 'LIMIT', 'GROUP BY']
9.       for clause in sql_clauses:
10.          query = query.replace(clause, '\n' + clause)
11.      print(query)
```

Copy this file from `starter-code/advanced-querying-and-search/queries.py` to the `com mon/utils` folder.

The following code shows how to make use of the `pretty_sql()` function:

```
>>> from jokes.models import Tag
>>> from common.utils.queries import pretty_sql
>>> q_exclude = Tag.objects.exclude(tag='Animal')
>>> pretty_sql(q_exclude)
SELECT id, tag, slug, created, updated
FROM jokes_tag
WHERE NOT (tag = Animal)
ORDER BY tag ASC
```

Again, this is just for debugging. Notice that the string `Animal` is not in single quotes, making the SQL invalid. You need to clean that up if you want to run the query:

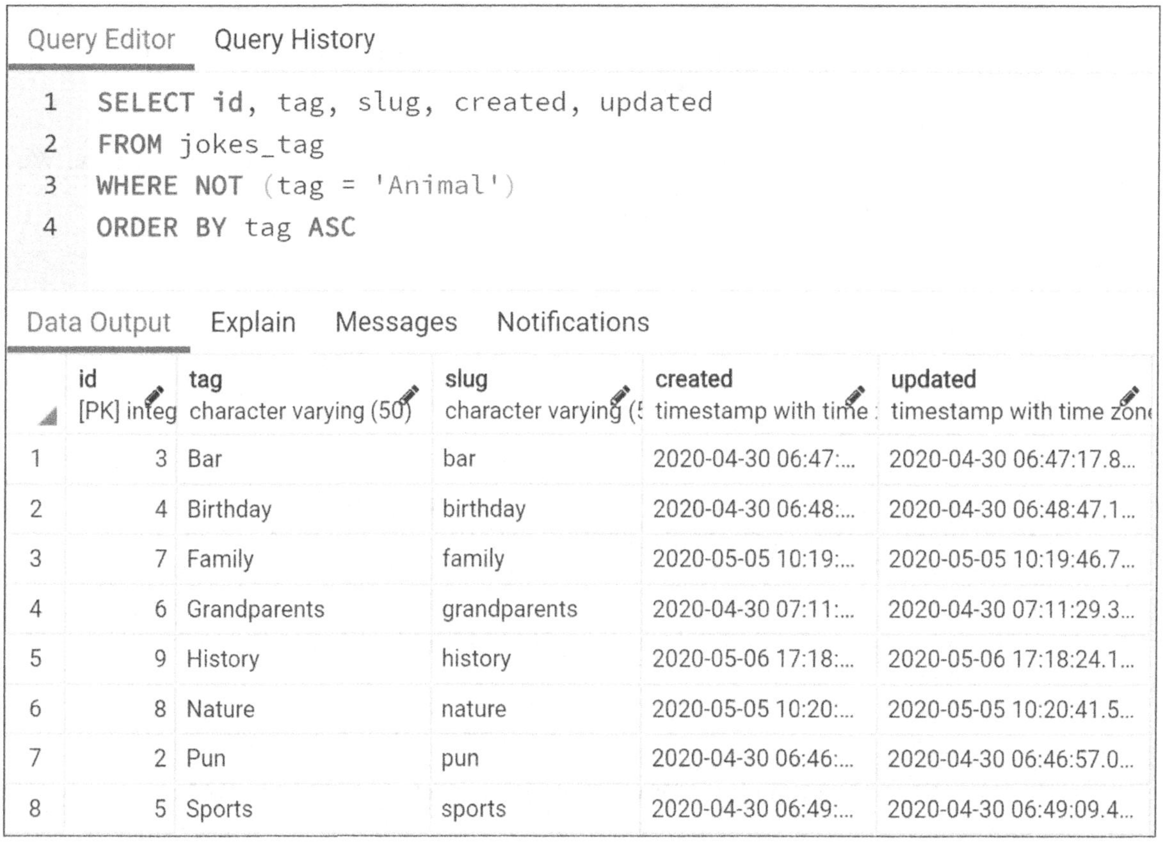

Query Editor | Query History

```
1 SELECT id, tag, slug, created, updated
2 FROM jokes_tag
3 WHERE NOT (tag = 'Animal')
4 ORDER BY tag ASC
```

Data Output | Explain | Messages | Notifications

	id [PK] integ	tag character varying (50)	slug character varying (5	created timestamp with time	updated timestamp with time zone
1	3	Bar	bar	2020-04-30 06:47:...	2020-04-30 06:47:17.8...
2	4	Birthday	birthday	2020-04-30 06:48:...	2020-04-30 06:48:47.1...
3	7	Family	family	2020-05-05 10:19:...	2020-05-05 10:19:46.7...
4	6	Grandparents	grandparents	2020-04-30 07:11:...	2020-04-30 07:11:29.3...
5	9	History	history	2020-05-06 17:18:...	2020-05-06 17:18:24.1...
6	8	Nature	nature	2020-05-05 10:20:...	2020-05-05 10:20:41.5...
7	2	Pun	pun	2020-04-30 06:46:...	2020-04-30 06:46:57.0...
8	5	Sports	sports	2020-04-30 06:49:...	2020-04-30 06:49:09.4...

Conclusion

In this lesson, you have learned to implement search, to write advanced queries with Django, and to optimize the code to reduce the number of times the database is hit.

LESSON 17

Deploying your Website to Production

Topics Covered

☑ Deploying to Heroku.

"If the wind only held, little doubt had they, that chased through these Straits of Sunda, the vast **host** would only **deploy** into the Oriental seas to witness the capture of not a few of their number.

– Moby Dick, Herman Melville

Introduction

In this lesson, you will learn to deploy the Django Jokes website to production using Heroku, a popular Platform as a Service (PaaS) for hosting Django websites.

17.1. Where to Host Your Django Site

When it's time to go live with your website, you need to decide where to host it. There are plenty of options, including big ones like AWS Elastic Beanstalk, Google Cloud, and Microsoft Azure. We have chosen to use Heroku, because…

1. It is relatively easy to set up.
2. It has a free tier.
3. It integrates nicely with GitHub.
4. It gives you full control over the environment.

Exercise 74: Deploying to Heroku

90 to 120 minutes

First, you need to prepare your local environment to work with Heroku. Then, you will create a Heroku account, log into it, and set it up to pull from the GitHub repository.

Warning!

> Setting up a production environment is tricky. The hosting sites are picky to begin with and always making changes/improvements to their systems. Heroku is no exception. Follow along closely with the instructions here, and be prepared to use Google and StackOverflow[109] to debug. If you find anything that has changed since this was published, please check out `https://www.webucator.com/books/errata.cfm` to see if we have posted any updates. If we haven't posted any updates that help, please email us at actionable@webucator.com.

❖ E74.1. Setting Up Heroku

1. Sign up for a free Heroku account at `https://signup.heroku.com/dc`.
2. Download and install the appropriate Heroku Command Line Interface (CLI) for your operating system at `https://devcenter.heroku.com/articles/heroku-cli`
3. Test your installation by running `heroku --version`:

    ```
    (.venv) …/projects/djangojokes.com> heroku --version
    heroku/7.41.1 win32-x64 node-v12.16.2
    ```

4. Log in to Heroku:

    ```
    heroku login
    ```

    You will be prompted to open a browser and log in to the following URL:

    ```
    https://cli-auth.heroku.com/auth/browser/
    ```

109. `https://www.stackoverflow.com`

When you log in via the browser, you will be logged in to the CLI as well:

```
(.venv) …/projects/djangojokes.com> heroku login
heroku: Press any key to open up the browser to login or q to exit:
Opening browser to https://cli-auth.heroku.com/auth/cli/browser/308b15e3-a6c…
Logging in... done
Logged in as ndunn@example.com
```

If you have any trouble, see `https://devcenter.heroku.com/articles/authentication` for additional details on Heroku authentication.

5. Create the Heroku app, which will be your website. We named ours "djangojokes," but you will have to use a different name as all names must be unique:

```
(.venv) …/projects/djangojokes.com> heroku create your_unique_name
```

6. In your browser, open `https://dashboard.heroku.com/` and make sure you're logged in.
7. Click on your app name, then click on **Deploy** and click the **Connect to GitHub** link/button:

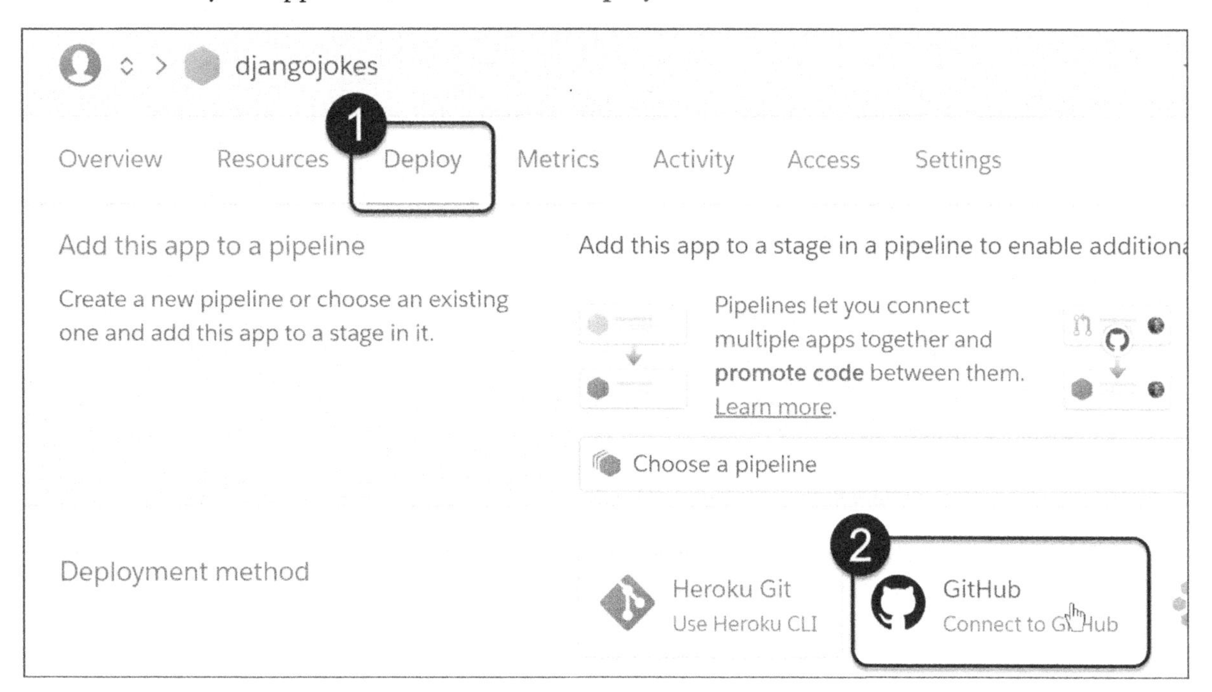

On the next page, click the **Connect to GitHub** button:

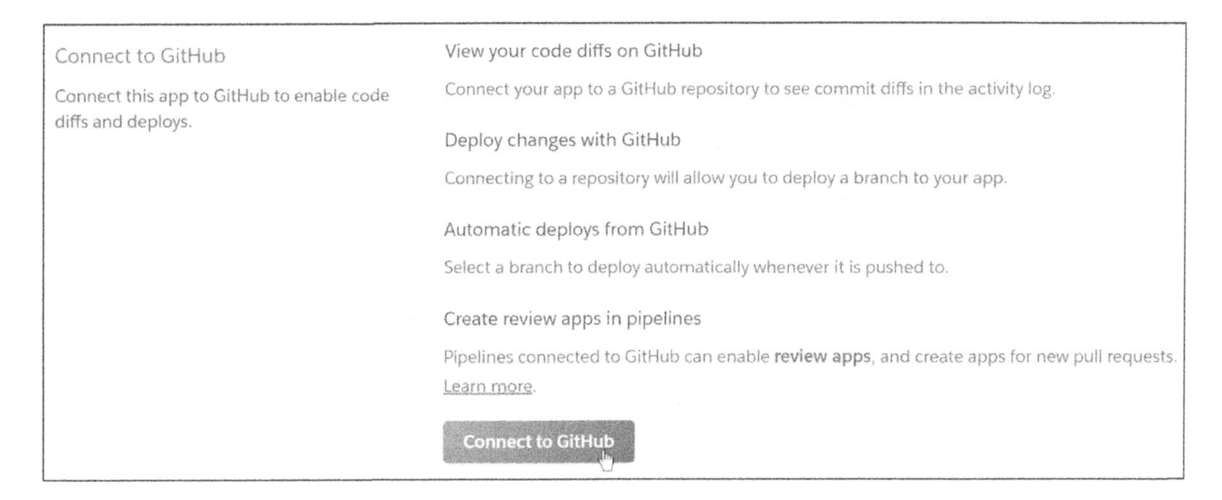

If your GitHub repository is in an organization, you will need to first grant access to Heroku:

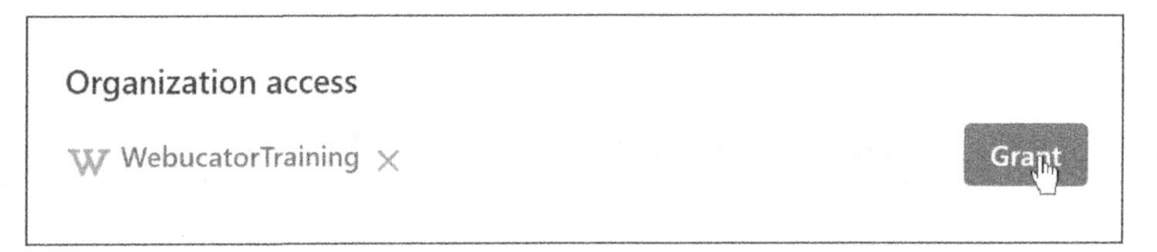

Click **Authorize heroku** to give Heroku authorization to your GitHub account:

On the **Deploy** tab of your Heroku dashboard, click the **Connect** button to connect to your GitHub account:

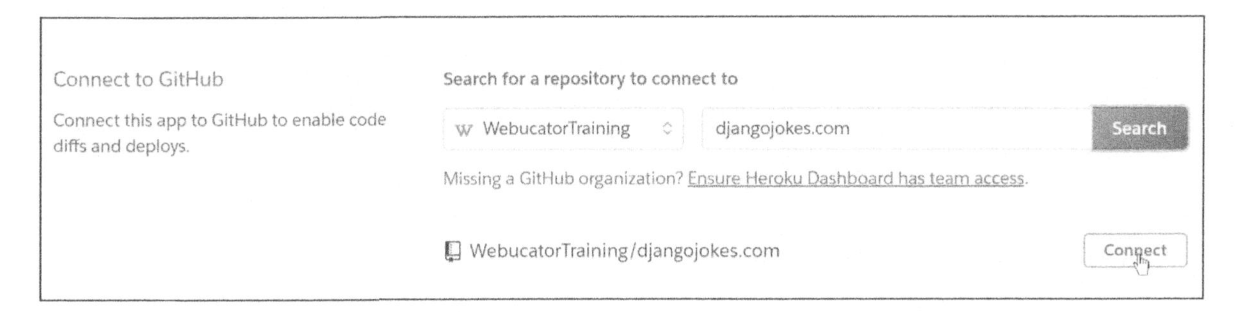

Click the **Enable Automatic Deploys** button so that Heroku will deploy your app every time you push to GitHub:

Automatic deploys

Enables a chosen branch to be automatically deployed to this app.

Enable automatic deploys from GitHub

Every push to the branch you specify here will deploy a new version of this app. **Deploys happen automatically:** be sure that this branch is always in a deployable state and any tests have passed before you push. Learn more.

Choose a branch to deploy

master

Wait for CI to pass before deploy

Only enable this option if you have a Continuous Integration service configured on your repo.

Enable Automatic Deploys

8. On the **Resources** tab under **Add-ons**, enter "post", and then select **Heroku Postgres:**

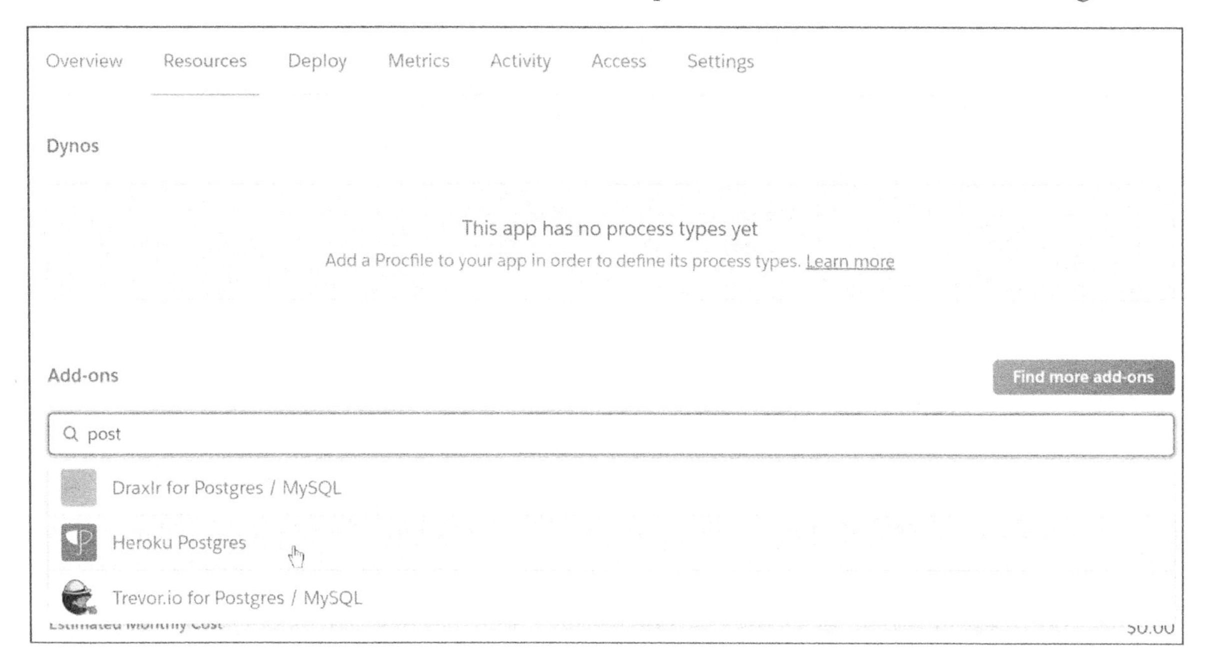

In the resulting dialog, select "Hobby Dev - Free" and click **Provision:**

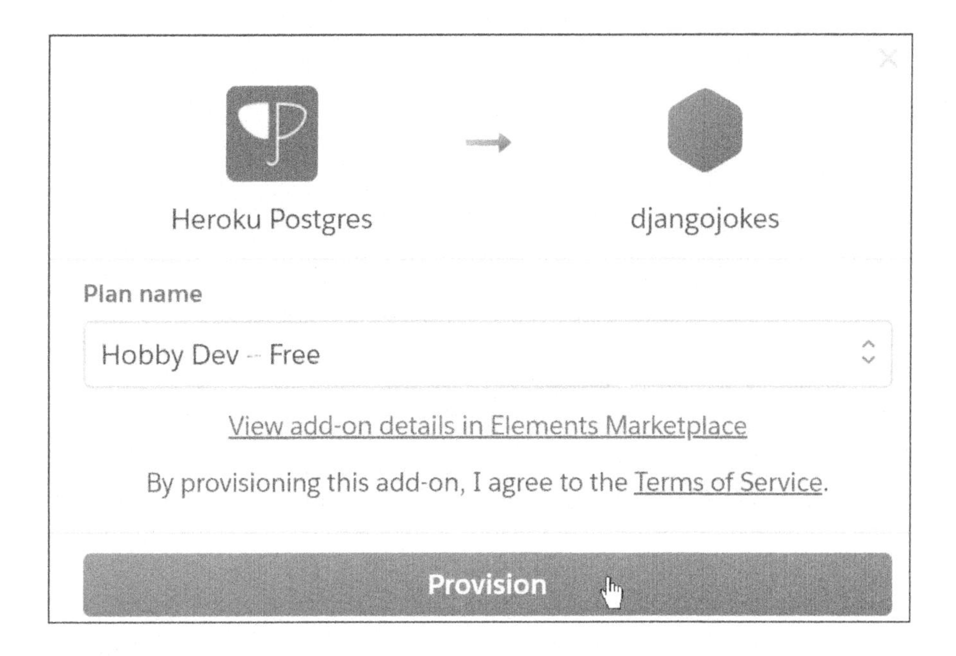

9. On the **Settings** tab, click **Reveal Config Vars**:

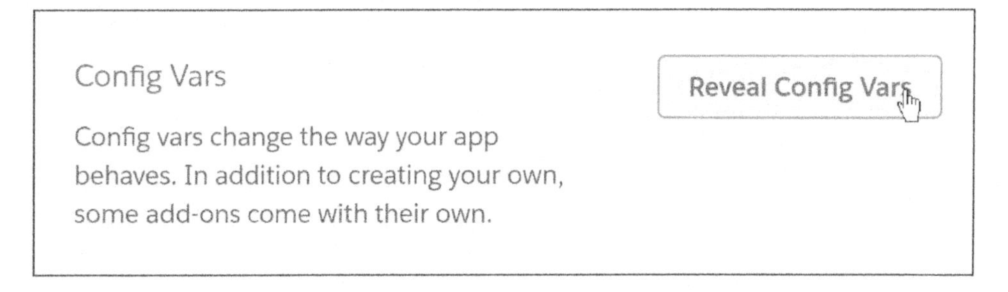

You will see a `DATABASE_URL` config var. That's a result of adding PostgreSQL. Add the following new config vars:

A. `AWS_ACCESS_KEY_ID`: The `AWS_ACCESS_KEY_ID` stored in your `local_settings.py` file.

B. `AWS_SECRET_ACCESS_KEY`: The `AWS_SECRET_ACCESS_KEY` stored in your `local_settings.py` file.

C. `ENVIRONMENT`: `production`

D. `SENDGRID_API_KEY`: The `SENDGRID_API_KEY` stored in your `local_settings.py` file.

❖ E74.2. Preparing to Deploy to Heroku

1. The web server used by Heroku for Django sites is Green Unicorn WSGI HTTP Server (Gunicorn). Install Gunicorn with pip:

```
(.venv) …/projects/djangojokes.com> pip install gunicorn
```

2. Create a `Procfile` file (with no extension) directly within the project folder (`djangojokes.com`) and add these two lines of text specifying that Gunicorn should be used as the web server:

djangojokes.com/Procfile

```
release: python manage.py migrate
web: gunicorn djangojokes.wsgi
```

The `Procfile` specifies the commands that the app should execute when it starts up. You are indicating that it should:

A. Run migrations.

B. Use gunicorn to start up the `wsgi` application in the `djangojokes` folder.

3. Run `python -V` at the terminal to check what version of Python you are running locally. To make sure Heroku uses that same version, create a `runtime.txt` file directly within the project folder (`djangojokes.com`) and add just one line of text with the version of Python that you are running. For example:

   djangojokes.com/runtime.txt

   ```
   python-3.8.5
   ```

4. Heroku uses the `dj-database-url` utility for setting up the database environment. Install that with pip:

   ```
   pip install dj-database-url
   ```

5. Run the following command to create the `requirements.txt` file that Heroku should use to set up the environment:

   ```
   (.venv) …/projects/djangojokes.com> pip freeze > requirements.txt
   ```

   Open the `requirements.txt` file in Visual Studio Code. It will look something like this:

Exercise Code 74.1: requirements.txt

```
1.  asgiref==3.2.10
2.  boto3==1.14.38
3.  botocore==1.17.38
4.  certifi==2020.6.20
5.  chardet==3.0.4
6.  defusedxml==0.6.0
7.  dj-database-url==0.5.0
8.  Django==3.1
9.  django-allauth==0.42.0
10. django-crispy-forms==1.9.2
11. django-debug-toolbar==2.2
12. django-private-storage==2.2.2
13. django-storages==1.9.1
14. docutils==0.15.2
15. filetype==1.0.7
16. gunicorn==20.0.4
17. idna==2.10
18. jmespath==0.10.0
19. oauthlib==3.1.0
20. Pillow==7.2.0
21. psycopg2==2.8.5
22. python-dateutil==2.8.1
23. python-http-client==3.2.7
24. python3-openid==3.2.0
25. pytz==2020.1
26. requests==2.24.0
27. requests-oauthlib==1.3.0
28. s3transfer==0.3.3
29. sendgrid==6.4.5
30. six==1.15.0
31. sqlparse==0.3.1
32. starkbank-ecdsa==1.0.0
33. urllib3==1.25.10
```

Heroku uses this to know how to set up the environment. Any other developers working on this project with you will also use this file to set up their own environments.

❖ E74.3. Settings

You will need to make some updates to `settings.py` and `local_settings.py`.

local_settings.py

Open local_settings.py in your editor.

1. Add:

   ```
   DEBUG = True

   ALLOWED_HOSTS = ['127.0.0.1']
   ```

2. Copy the DATABASE settings from settings.py and paste it in local_settings.py.

Your local_settings.py looks like this:

Exercise Code 74.2: djangojokes/local_settings.py

```
1.  DEBUG = True
2.
3.  ALLOWED_HOSTS = ['127.0.0.1']
4.
5.  DATABASES = {
6.      'default': {
7.          'ENGINE': 'django.db.backends.postgresql',
8.          'NAME': 'jokes',
9.          'USER': 'postgres',
10.         'PASSWORD': 'YOURPASSWORD',
11.         'HOST': 'localhost',
12.         'PORT': 5432
13.     }
14. }
15.
16. SENDGRID_API_KEY = 'YOURSENDGRIDAPIKEY'
17. EMAIL_HOST_PASSWORD = SENDGRID_API_KEY
18.
19. AWS_ACCESS_KEY_ID = 'YOUR_ACCESS_KEY_ID'
20. AWS_SECRET_ACCESS_KEY = 'YOUR_SECRET_ACCESS_KEY'
21.
22. # Local Static File Settings
23. STATICFILES_STORAGE = 'django.contrib.staticfiles.storage.StaticFilesStorage'
24. STATIC_URL = '/static/'
```

Be sure to replace YOURPASSWORD, YOURSENDGRIDAPIKEY, YOUR_ACCESS_KEY_ID, and YOUR_SECRET_ACCESS_KEY with your database password, SendGrid API Key, and AWS settings.

settings.py

Make the following changes/additions to `settings.py`:

1. Set `DEBUG` to `False`:

   ```
   DEBUG = False
   ```

2. Add your herokuapp.com URL to `ALLOWED_HOSTS`:

   ```
   ALLOWED_HOSTS = ['your_unique_name.herokuapp.com']
   ```

   Replace "your_unique_name" with the name you chose for your Heroku app.

3. Replace your `DATABASES` setting with the following:

   ```
   import dj_database_url

   DATABASES = { 'default' : dj_database_url.config()}
   ```

   Heroku will manage your database settings for you, so you don't have to put sensitive information (e.g., the database username and password) in the `settings.py` file.

4. You may want to change your `DEFAULT_FROM_EMAIL` to a real email address. To do so, you will have to give SendGrid permission to send email on your behalf.[110]

In the Static Files lesson (see page 169), we mentioned that you would need to run `python manage.py collectstatic` to collect all the static files into one location. Heroku takes care of collecting the static files as part of the build process, so you don't have to worry about doing it explicitly.

❖ E74.4. Deploy

You are now ready to deploy. Because you have connected Heroku to GitHub, this is just a matter of committing and pushing your changes to GitHub and then saying a little prayer.

1. Stage, commit, and push your changes to GitHub.
2. Notice the progress bar above message box:

110. https://sendgrid.com/docs/ui/account-and-settings/how-to-set-up-domain-authentication/

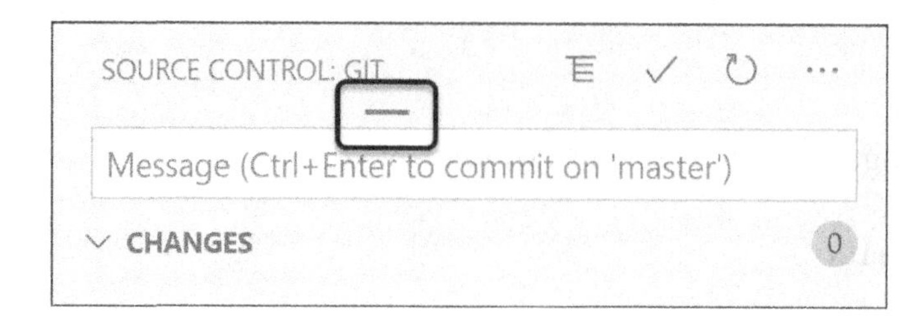

When that bar disappears, go to the Heroku dashboard, and click the **Activity** tab. You should see a "Build in progress" message.

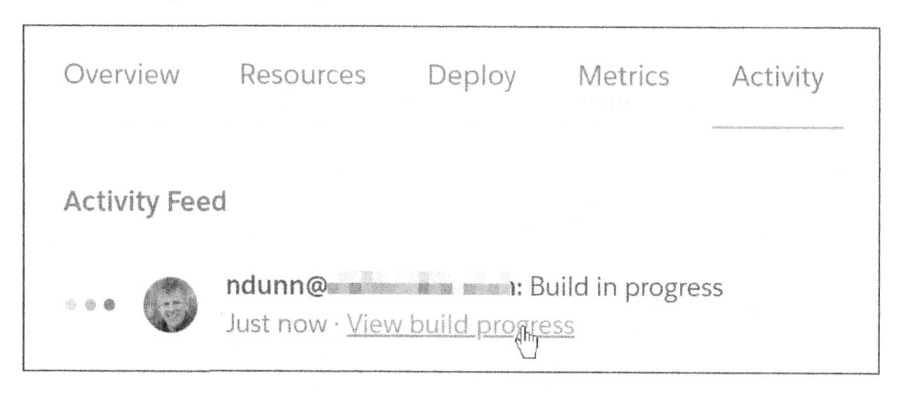

Now is the time to say that short prayer. If all goes well, you will get a "Build succeeded" message followed shortly by a "Deployed" message (most recent message show on top):

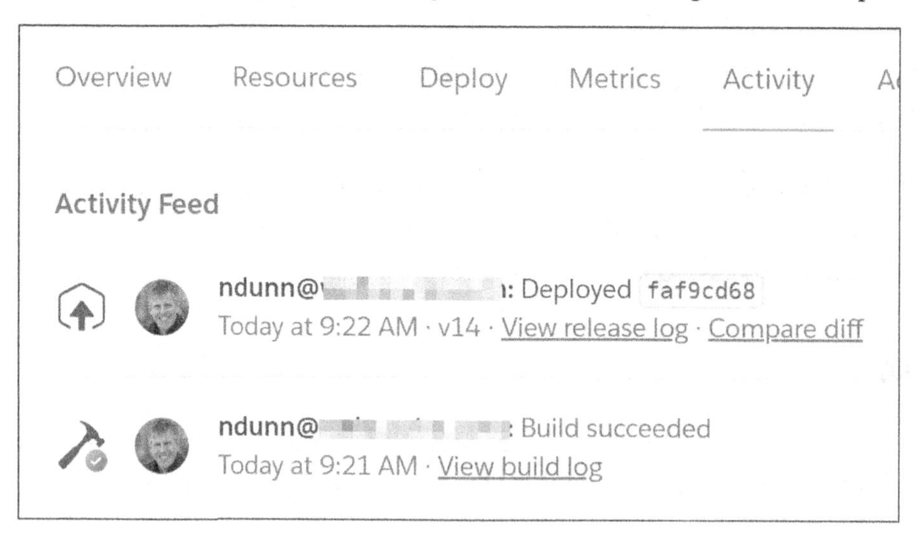

If the build or deployment fails, troubleshoot by clicking on the "View build log" or "View release log" links. Read through the log from the bottom up and find out where things went wrong. If you don't understand the error, try Googling it to see if you can find a solution.

3. Assuming all went well, you can now visit your website. On the **Settings** tab, scroll down to the **Domains** heading:

Click the URL where it says "Your app can be found at…" Your site should load:

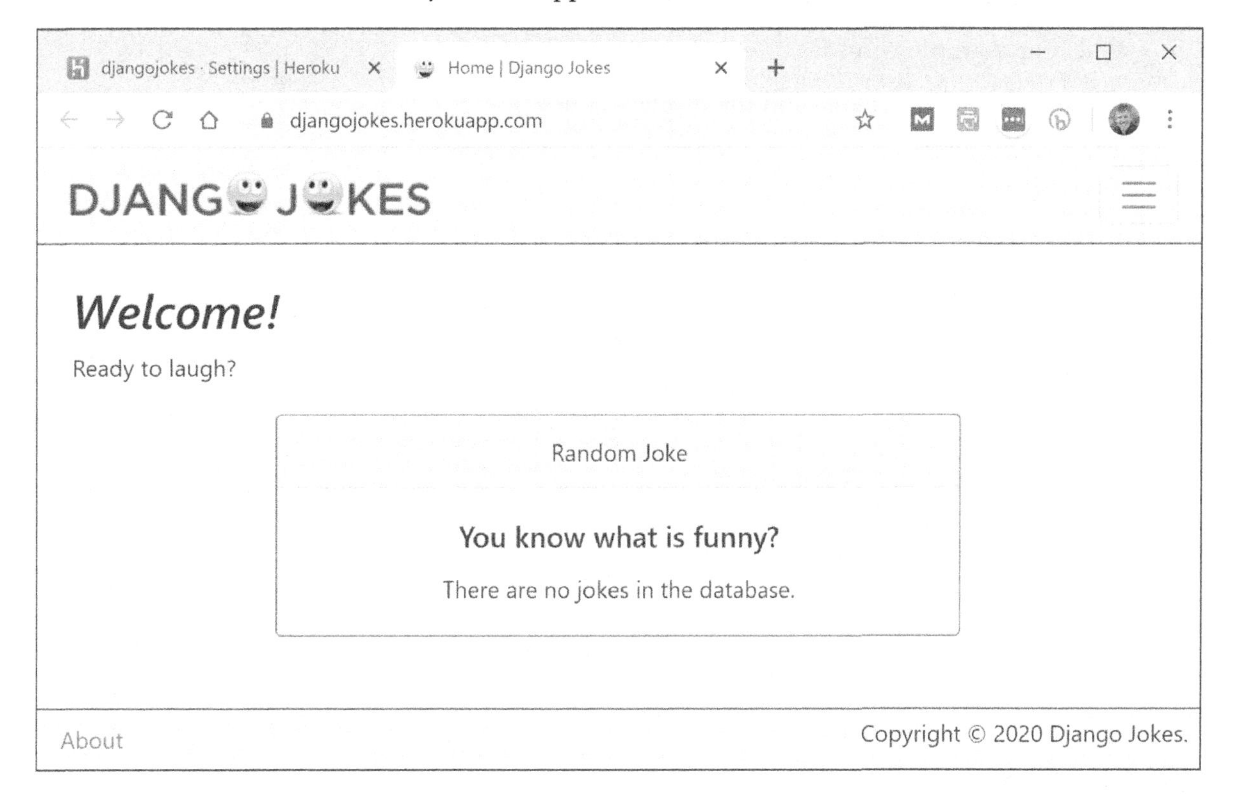

❖ E74.5. Creating a Superuser

It's time to create the superuser on Heroku, so you can log in to Django admin. In the terminal, run:

```
(.venv) …/projects/djangojokes.com> heroku run python manage.py createsuperuser
```

Enter whatever username and password you like, and make sure the email you enter is valid, as you will need to confirm your account by email.

Return to your website and log in. You will be prompted to verify your email address. Do so. Then, log back into the site.

❖ E74.6. Changing the Site Name and URL

You may have noticed that the email you receive starts with "Hello from example.com!" That comes from the site name. You can change that in Django admin:

1. Log in to Django admin.
2. Under the **SITES** heading, click on the **Sites** link.
3. Click on **example.com**.
4. Change the domain name and the display name:

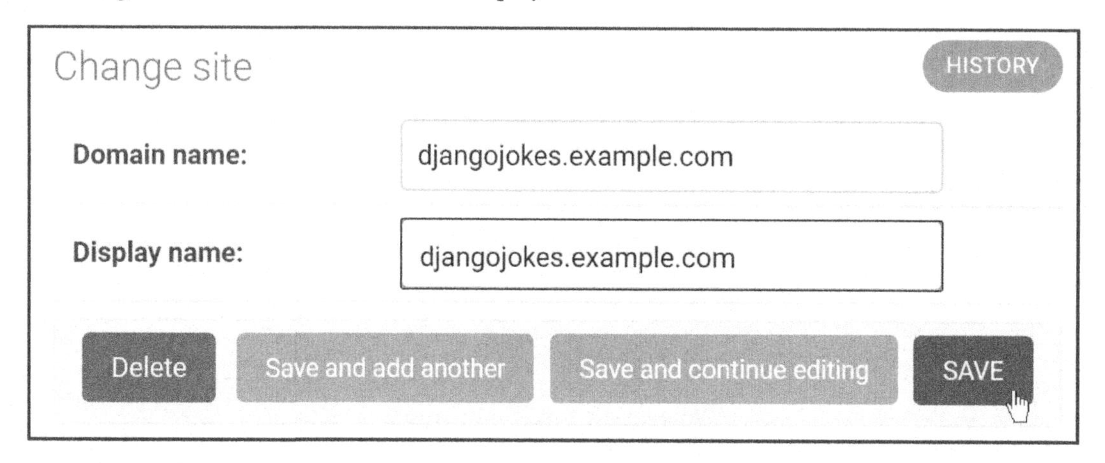

See `https://devcenter.heroku.com/articles/custom-domains` to learn how to add a custom domain to your Heroku app.

❖ E74.7. Have Some Fun

You are live! It took a lot of work to get here, and we imagine that it was pretty frustrating at times. There are a lot of moving parts, and it's easy to make mistakes. Sometimes, things even go wrong even when you do everything right. In any case, you've come a long way! Congratulations! Play around with the site. Add and remove jokes. Invite your friends to create accounts and add their own jokes.

Conclusion

In this lesson, you have learned to deploy your Django application to Heroku.

LESSON 18

Customizing Django Admin

Topics Covered

☑ Django admin views.

☑ Customizing title text, change lists, forms, and fieldsets.

☑ Unregistering models.

☑ Groups and permissions.

> I would thou wert a man's tailor, that thou mightst mend him and make him fit to go.
>
> – *Henry IV, William Shakespeare*

Introduction

In this lesson, you will learn to customize Django admin for your project.

18.1. Django Admin Views

The most important views used in Django admin are:

1. `changelist_view` – the view for listing model instances.
2. `change_view` – the view for changing an existing model instance.
3. `add_view` – the view for adding a new model instance.

There are other views as well, but these are the ones you are most likely to want to customize. For simplicity, we will refer to the `changelist_view` as the Django admin list view and to `change_view` and `add_view` as the Django admin form views.

Exercise 75: Customizing Titles and Headers

10 to 15 minutes

The default home-page (index) title is “Site administration,” the default site title is “Django site administration,” and the default Django admin header is “Django administration”:

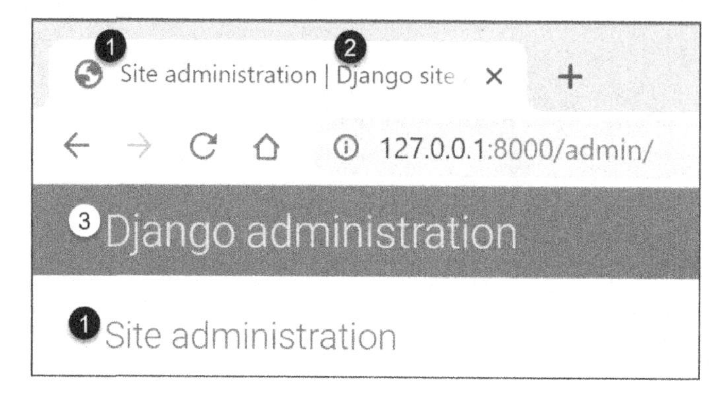

1. Home-page (index) title.
2. Site title.
3. Site header.

These can be changed in any app’s `admin.py` file.

1. Open `common/admin.py` in your editor, and add the following lines of code:

```
admin.site.index_title = 'Home'
admin.site.site_title = 'Django Jokes Admin'
admin.site.site_header = 'Django Jokes Admin'
```

2. Open Django admin to see the new custom header:

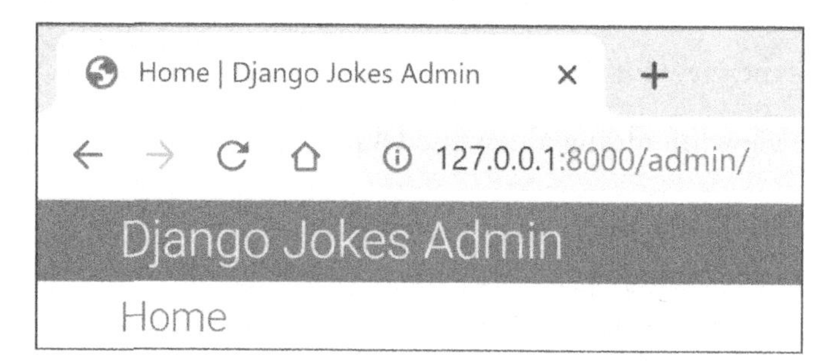

18.2. `ModelAdmin` Attributes that Affect the List View

The following attributes of the `ModelAdmin` class are used to change list views in Django admin.

1. `list_display` – A list setting the fields to display.
2. `list_display_links` – A list setting the fields to link to the object.
3. `list_per_page` – An integer setting the number of objects per page. The default is `100`.
4. `list_max_show_all` – An integer setting the maximum number of objects to be shown in a single "show-all" list. The default is `200`. If the number of objects is less than or equal to `list_max_show_all`, a **Show all** link will be displayed along with the pagination:

5. `ordering` – A list setting the fields to order by.
6. `search_fields` – A list of fields to search. When this attribute is present, a search form will appear above the list:

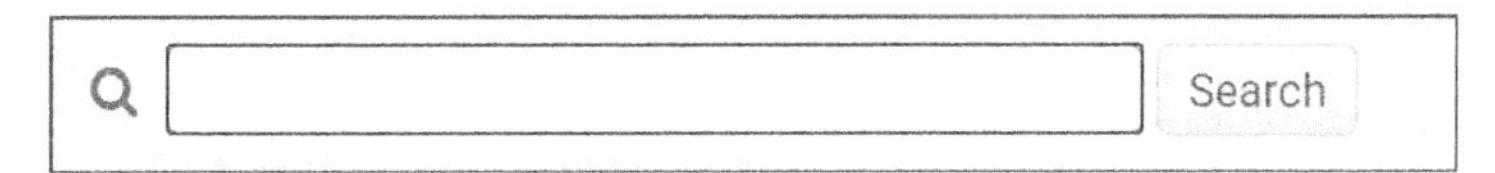

7. `list_filter` – A list of fields to filter by. When this attribute is present, one or more filter forms will appear to the right of the list:

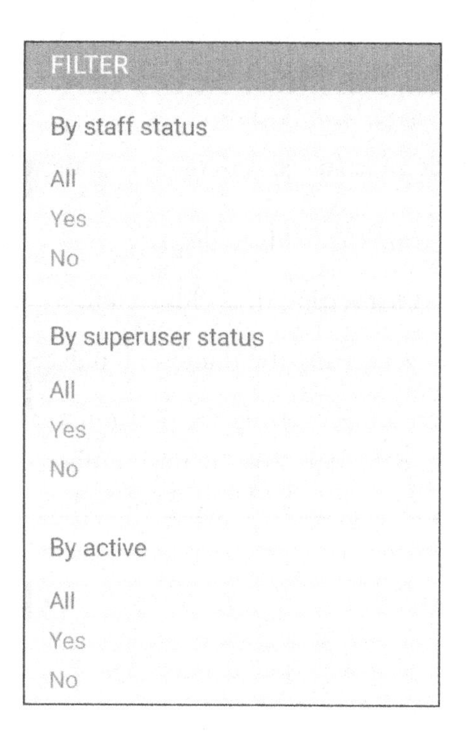

8. `date_hierarchy` – A `DateField` or `DateTimeField` in the model. When this attribute is present, a date-based drilldown navigation bar will appear above the list. It will start by showing years:

When you click on a year, it will show months:

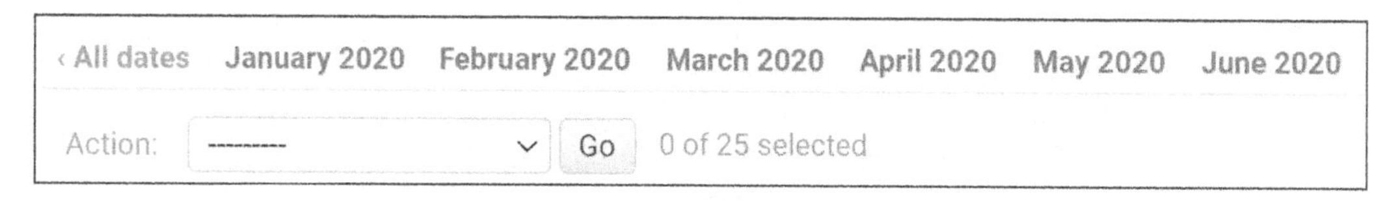

Exercise 76: Creating a Custom ModelAdmin Base Class

10 to 15 minutes

You may want to have more control over default values for `ModelAdmin` attributes. A good way to handle this is to create a custom `ModelAdmin` class that all of your other `ModelAdmin` classes inherit from.

1. Start up the server and open Django admin.
2. On the side navigation, click **Jokes**.
3. Notice that it shows 100 jokes per page. You can tell by looking at the paginator, which shows 595 jokes broken into six pages (your numbers may differ):

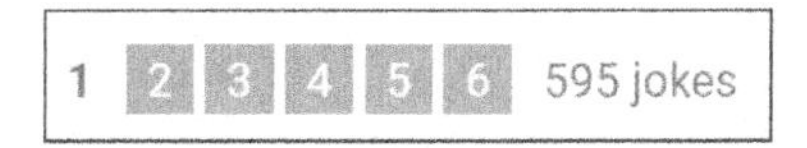

4. On the side navigation, click on **Users**.
5. Notice that all 50 users show up on a single page.
6. Open `common/admin.py` in your editor, and add the following `DjangoJokesAdmin` class:

```
class DjangoJokesAdmin(admin.ModelAdmin):
    list_per_page = 25
```

   You will set all your other `ModelAdmin` classes to inherit from this class.

7. Open `users/admin.py` in you editor:
   A. Import the `DjangoJokesAdmin` class you just created:

   ```
   from common.admin import DjangoJokesAdmin
   ```

   B. Make `CustomUserAdmin` inherit from `DjangoJokesAdmin` in addition to `UserAdmin`:

   ```
   class CustomUserAdmin(DjangoJokesAdmin, UserAdmin):
   ```

8. In the browser, refresh the **Custom user** list view. Scroll to the bottom. You should see that it shows 25 users per page (50 users broken into two pages), and there should be a **Show all** link:

   Click on the **Show all** link to show all 50 users at once.

9. Open `jokes/admin.py` in you editor:

   A. Import the `DjangoJokesAdmin` class you just created:

   ```
   from common.admin import DjangoJokesAdmin
   ```

   B. Make `JokeAdmin` inherit from `DjangoJokesAdmin` instead of `admin.ModelAdmin`:

   ```
   class JokeAdmin(DjangoJokesAdmin):
   ```

10. Back in the browser, on the side navigation, click **Jokes**.
11. Scroll down to the paginator and notice that the joke list is now broken into 24 pages of 25 jokes per page:

    Also, notice that there is no **Show all** link. That's because the default value of `list_max_show_all` is `200`.

12. Open `common/admin.py` in your editor and change the value of `list_max_show_all` in the `DjangoJokesAdmin` class:

```
class DjangoJokesAdmin(admin.ModelAdmin):
    list_per_page = 25
    list_max_show_all = 1000
```

13. In the browser, refresh the **Jokes** list view. Scroll to the bottom. The **Show all** link should now be there:

    Click on the **Show all** link to show all the jokes at once.

The `DjangoJokesAdmin` class should now look like this:

Exercise Code 76.1: common/admin.py

```
1.  from django.contrib import admin
2.
3.  admin.site.index_title = 'Home'
4.  admin.site.site_title = 'Django Jokes Admin'
5.  admin.site.site_header = 'Django Jokes Admin'
6.
7.  class DjangoJokesAdmin(admin.ModelAdmin):
8.      list_per_page = 25
9.      list_max_show_all = 1000
```

Exercise 77: Customizing the Django Admin List View

45 to 60 minutes

In this exercise, you will add more attributes to `JokeAdmin` that affect the Django admin list view.

1. Open `jokes/admin.py` in your editor and modify all the admin classes, so that they inherit from `DjangoJokesAdmin` instead of `admin.ModelAdmin`.
2. Make the following changes to the `JokeAdmin` class:

   A. Add the `search_fields` attribute:

   ```
   search_fields = ['question', 'answer']
   ```

   Refresh the jokes list in Django admin and try some searches. Notice that it searches both the question and answer fields of jokes.

   B. Add the `ordering` attribute to show the most recently updated first by default:

   ```
   ordering = ['-updated']
   ```

   C. Add the `list_filter` attribute to add some filters:

   ```
   list_filter = ['updated', 'category', 'tags']
   ```

   Refresh the jokes list in Django admin. The **By category** and **By tags** filters just list out category and tag links, but **By updated** is a date filter, and date filters provide segments of time:

   By updated
   Any date
   Today
   Past 7 days
   This month
   This year

   Try clicking on some of the filter links to filter the joke list.

D. Set the `date_hierarchy` attribute to `'updated'`:

```
date_hierarchy = 'updated'
```

Refresh the jokes list in Django admin. Notice that you can drill down into date segments.

The `JokeAdmin` class should now include the following highlighted attributes:

```
class JokeAdmin(DjangoJokesAdmin):
    model = Joke

    # List Attributes
    date_hierarchy = 'updated'
    list_display = ['question', 'category', 'updated']
    list_filter = ['updated', 'category', 'tags']
    ordering = ['-updated']
    search_fields = ['question', 'answer']

    def get_readonly_fields(self, request, obj=None):
        if obj: # editing an existing object
            return ('slug', 'created', 'updated')
        return ()
```

Git Commit

Commit your code to Git.

18.3. Lists vs. Tuples

You have the option of using lists or tuples for many of the `ModelAdmin` attributes. For example, in the last exercise, you set `list_display` like this:

```
list_display = ['question', 'category', 'updated']
```

You could have used a tuple instead:

```
list_display = ('question', 'category', 'updated')
```

It doesn't much matter which you use, but there are a couple of gotchas you need to be aware of:

1. **Single-item tuples.** Consider the `ordering` attribute from the last exercise:

   ```
   ordering = ['-updated']
   ```

   That can be changed to a tuple like this:

   ```
   ordering = ('-updated',)
   ```

   If you leave off the trailing comma, it's just a string in parentheses, and it will result in an error:

   ```
   (admin.E031) The value of 'ordering' must be a list or tuple.
   ```

2. **Inheriting from a class.** When inheriting from a class, you can append to the superclass's class attributes. To do that correctly, you must know whether the superclass defined those attributes as lists or tuples. Consider the `CustomUserAdmin` class, which inherits from Django's built-in `UserAdmin` class. The `UserAdmin` class defines `list_display` like this:

   ```
   list_display = ('username', 'email', 'first_name', 'last_name', 'is_staff')
   ```

   As it is defined as a tuple, to add a field (e.g., `'is_superuser'`) to that sequence, you must append a tuple:

   ```
   list_display = UserAdmin.list_display + ('is_superuser',)
   ```

   If you try to append a list, you will get a `TypeError`:

   ```
   TypeError: can only concatenate tuple (not "list") to tuple
   ```

Which should you use for your own `ModelAdmin` classes? We don't have a recommendation. Use whichever you prefer. Internally, Django usually uses tuples, but in the documentation,[111] it uses both. If you get bit by the single-item tuple gotcha enough, you may prefer to use lists.

111. `https://docs.djangoproject.com/en/3.1/ref/contrib/admin/`

18.4. ModelAdmin Attributes that Affect Forms

The following attributes of the `ModelAdmin` class are used to change form fields in Django admin:

1. `radio_fields` – By default, `ForeignKey` fields are updated in forms using a select menu:

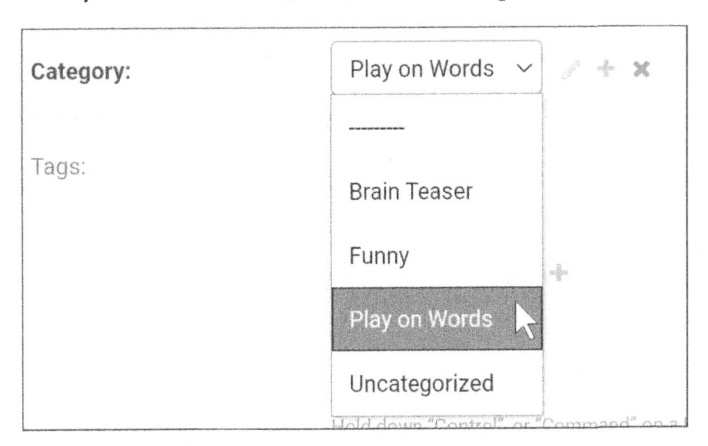

When there are only a few options, it can be more convenient to edit with radio buttons. The `radio_fields` attribute takes a dictionary, in which the keys are the fields that should use radio buttons in place of select lists. You can set the fields to use `admin.HORIZONTAL` or `admin.VERTICAL`:

```
radio_fields = {
    'favorite_vegetable': admin.HORIZONTAL,
    'favorite_fruit': admin.VERTICAL,
}
```

<u>`admin.HORIZONTAL`</u>

Favorite vegetable: Corn Eggplant Squash Zucchini

<u>`admin.VERTICAL`</u>

Favorite fruit:
Apple
Banana
Cherry
Pear

2. By default, `ManyToManyFields` are updated in forms using a `SelectMultiple` widget:

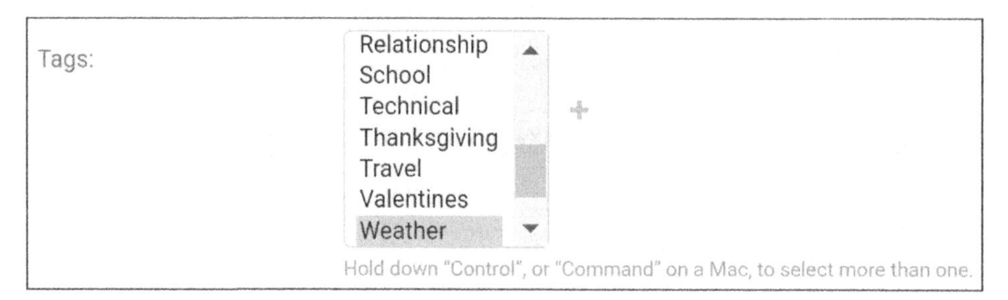

Multiple select form controls can be difficult to use. Django admin provides a few alternatives, all of which take lists of fields:

A. `filter_horizontal`

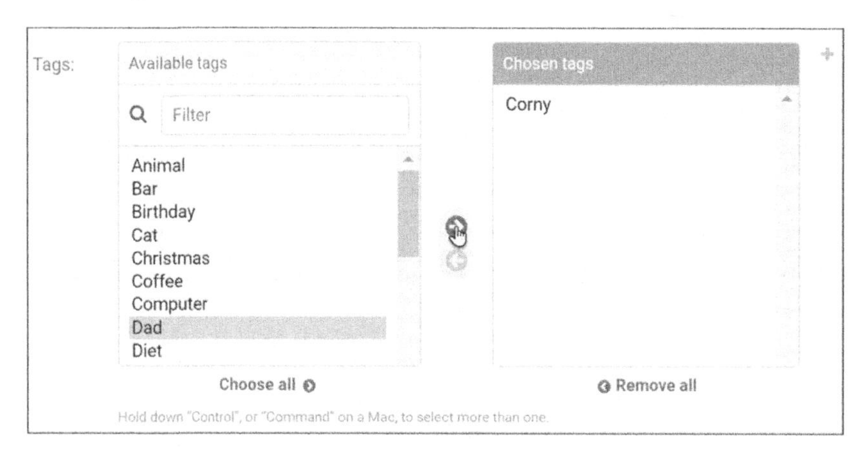

B. `filter_vertical`

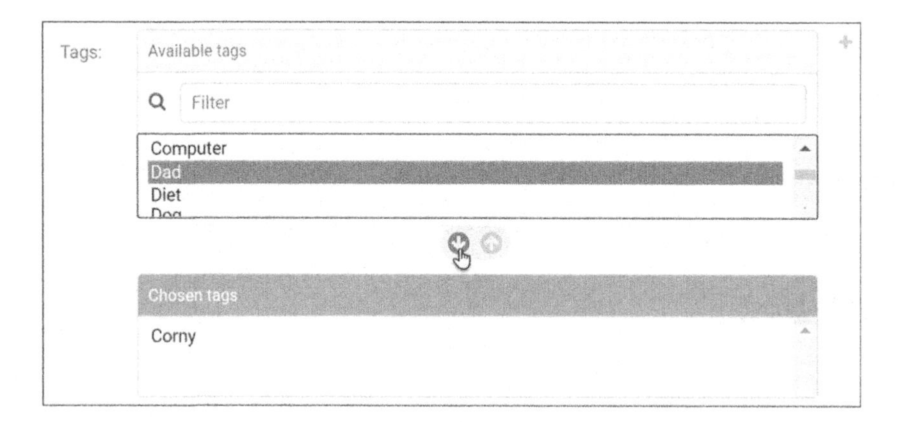

C. `autocomplete_fields` – This can be used for `ForeignKey` fields as well as `ManyToManyField` fields. It is, in our opinion, the best control to use when there are many options to choose from. It requires that the `ModelAdmin` class for the object being searched includes a `search_fields` attribute, as it uses that to decide which fields to search:

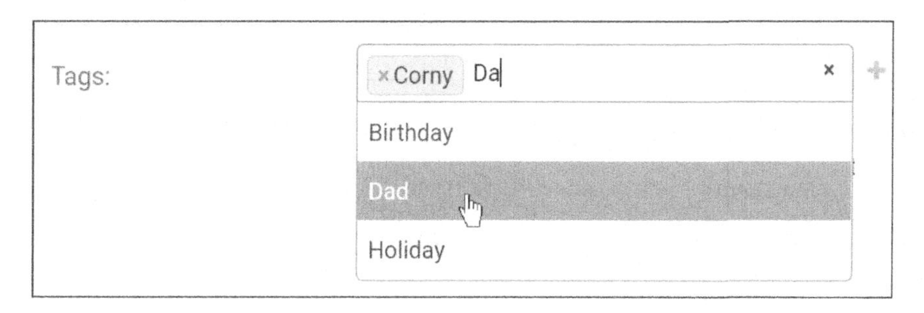

3. `save_as` – By default, Django admin's update forms have the following three save buttons:

Set the `save_as` attribute to `True` to replace the **Save and add another** button with a **Save as new** button, which will make a copy of the current object, but with a new primary key:

4. `save_on_top` – By default, the save buttons only appear at the bottom of the form. For long forms, it can be annoying to have to scroll to the bottom to save. Set `save_on_top` to `True` to add save buttons at the top of the form as well.

You will make these customizations in the next exercise.

 Exercise 78: Customizing Django Admin Form Views

20 to 30 minutes

1. Start up the server and open Django admin.
2. On the side navigation, click **Jokes** and then click on any joke.
3. Open `common/admin.py` in your editor, and add the following attribute to `DjangoJokesAdmin`:

   ```
   save_as = True
   ```

   Now, all of your admin forms that inherit from `DjangoJokesAdmin` will include a **Save as new** button unless you override `save_as` in the inheriting class.
4. Open `jokes/admin.py` in your editor.
5. Add the following attributes to the `JokeAdmin` class:

   ```
   # Form Attributes
   autocomplete_fields = ['tags', 'user']
   radio_fields = { 'category': admin.HORIZONTAL}
   ```

6. In the `TagAdmin` class in the same file, add the following attribute:

   ```
   search_fields = ['tag']
   ```

   This is required in order to add `'tags'` to the `autocomplete_fields` list in `JokeAdmin`.

   - You do not need to do the same to add `'user'` because the class it inherits from (`django.contrib.auth.admin.UserAdmin`) already defines `search_fields` as:

     ```
     search_fields = ('username', 'first_name', 'last_name', 'email')
     ```

7. Open `users/models.py` in your editor and add the following `__str__()` method to the `CustomUser` class:

   ```
   def __str__(self):
       return f'{self.first_name} {self.last_name} ({self.username})'
   ```

   This will be used to populate the `user` dropdown in the joke form.

8. Refresh the joke in Django admin. The three fields affected by your changes are `user`, `category`, and `tags`. They should appear as follows:

User:	Roland Trejo (rtrejo)
Category:	◯ Brain Teaser ◯ Funny ◉ Play on Words ◯ Uncategorized
Tags:	× Weather

You should also have a **Save as new** button in the bottom navigation.

18.5. Customizing Fieldsets

In Django Admin and the User Model (see page 194), we showed how you can customize the forms in Django admin. Django admin forms are broken into fieldsets. When inheriting from a model, you sometimes want to append fields to an existing fieldset, to move fields from one fieldset to another, or to add a new fieldset. For example, you appended an "Optional Fields" fieldset to the `UserAdmin` class like this:

```
add_fieldsets = UserAdmin.add_fieldsets + (
    ('Optional Fields', {
        'classes': ('wide',),
        'fields': ('email', 'first_name', 'last_name'),
    }),
)
```

The following utility functions make it easier to make such changes. The complete file is available at `starter-code/customizing-django-admin/utils_admin.py`. In the `common/utils` directory, create a new `admin.py` file and paste the content from `utils_admin.py` in it.

Read through the docstrings. You will use these functions in the next exercise:

Demo 18.1: common/utils/admin.py

```
1.  def append_fields(fieldsets, fieldset, fields):
2.      """Appends new fields to a fieldset in fieldsets.
3.
4.      Args:
5.          fieldsets (tuple): The fieldsets to append to.
6.              - fieldsets for editing existing objects
7.              - add_fieldsets for adding new objects
8.          fieldset (str or None): The title of the fieldset.
9.              None for the titleless fieldset.
10.         fields (tuple): The fields to append.
11.
12.     Returns:
13.         tuple: The modified fieldsets.
14.     """
15.     for _fieldset in fieldsets:
16.         if _fieldset[0] == fieldset:
17.             _fieldset[1]['fields'] += fields
18.             break
19.     else: # Fieldset doesn't exist yet. Add new fieldset.
20.         fieldsets = fieldsets + (
21.             (fieldset, {
22.                 'classes': ('wide',),
23.                 'fields': fields
24.             }),
25.         )
26.
27.     return fieldsets
28.
29.
30. def remove_fields(fieldsets, fieldset, fields):
31.     """Removes fields from fieldset in fieldsets.
32.
33.     Args:
34.         fieldsets (tuple): The fieldsets to modify.
35.             - fieldsets for editing existing objects
36.             - add_fieldsets for adding new objects
37.         fieldset (str or None): The title of the fieldset from which to
38.             remove the field.
39.         fields (tuple): The fields to remove.
40.
41.     Returns:
42.         tuple: The modified fieldsets.
43.     """
44.     for _fieldset in fieldsets:
```

```
45.             if _fieldset[0] == fieldset:
46.                 field_list = list(_fieldset[1]['fields'])
47.                 for field in fields:
48.                     field_list.remove(field) # raises exception if field not found
49.                 _fieldset[1]['fields'] = tuple(field_list)
50.                 break
51.         else:
52.             raise Exception(f'No such fieldset: {fieldset}')
53. 
54.         return fieldsets
55. 
56. 
57.     def move_fields(fieldsets, from_fieldset, to_fieldset, fields):
58.         """Moves fields from from_fieldset to to_fieldset in fieldsets.
59. 
60.         Args:
61.             fieldsets (tuple): [description]
62.             from_fieldset (str or None): The title of the fieldset from which to
63.                 remove the field.
64.             to_fieldset (str or None): The title of the fieldset in which to
65.                 add the field.
66.             fields (tuple): The fields to remove.
67. 
68.         Returns:
69.             tuple: The modified fieldsets.
70.         """
71.         remove_fields(fieldsets, from_fieldset, fields)
72.         append_fields(fieldsets, to_fieldset, fields)
73. 
74.         return fieldsets
```

 Exercise 79: Modifying the CustomUserAdmin Class

45 to 60 minutes

Currently, the `CustomUserAdmin` class looks like this:

Exercise Code 79.1: users/admin.py

```
1.  from django.contrib import admin
2.  from django.contrib.auth import get_user_model
3.  from django.contrib.auth.admin import UserAdmin
4.
5.  from common.admin import DjangoJokesAdmin
6.
7.  CustomUser = get_user_model()
8.
9.  @admin.register(CustomUser)
10. class CustomUserAdmin(DjangoJokesAdmin, UserAdmin):
11.     model = CustomUser
12.
13.     add_fieldsets = UserAdmin.add_fieldsets + (
14.         ('Optional Fields', {
15.             'classes': ('wide',),
16.             'fields': ('email', 'first_name', 'last_name'),
17.         }),
18.     )
```

In this exercise, you will make the following modifications to the `CustomUserAdmin` class:

1. Add `list_display` and `list_display_links` attributes.
2. Use the admin utility functions to add, move, and remove fields in the **Add user** and **Change user** forms.
3. Add a link to the **Password change** form.
4. Make it so that the save buttons show up at the top of the **Change user** form, but not at the top of the **Add user** form.

❖ E79.1. List Attributes

You will start with the list attributes, and then modify the forms.

1. Start up the server and open Django admin.

2. On the side navigation, click **Users**.
3. Notice that:
   A. **SUPERUSER STATUS** is not included in the table columns.
   B. Only the username field is linked to the change form page.
4. Open `users/admin.py` in your editor.
5. Add the following attributes to `CustomUserAdmin`:

```
# List Attributes
list_display = UserAdmin.list_display + ('is_superuser',)
list_display_links = ('username', 'email', 'first_name', 'last_name')
```

6. Back in the browser, refresh the user list. Notice that **SUPERUSER STATUS** is now included, and all text fields are links to the change form page:

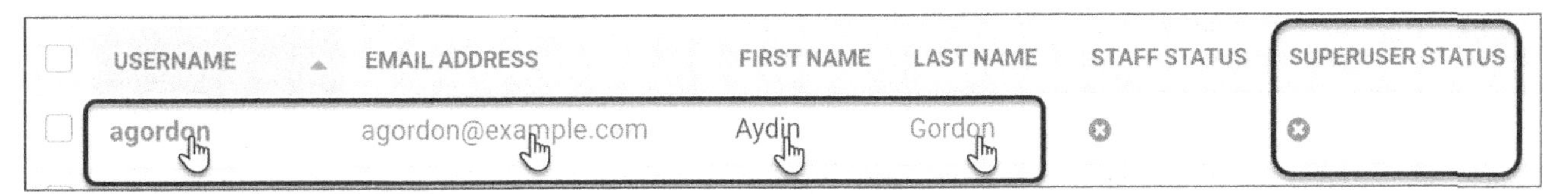

❖ E79.2. Change User Form

1. On the user list in Django admin, click any user to open the change form.
2. Notice that the form is broken into these fieldsets:
   A. **Unlabelled**
      i. Username
      ii. Password
   B. **Personal info**
      i. First name
      ii. Last name
      iii. Email address
   C. **Permissions**
      i. Active
      ii. Staff status
      iii. Superuser status

iv. Groups

v. User permissions

D. **Important dates**

i. Last login

ii. Date joined

Use the admin utility functions in `common/utils/admin.py` to customize the **Change user** form:

1. Import the utility functions:

```
from common.utils.admin import append_fields, move_fields, remove_fields
```

2. Delete the `add_fieldsets` attribute:

```
add_fieldsets = UserAdmin.add_fieldsets + (
        ('Optional Fields', {
            'classes': ('wide',),
            'fields': ('email', 'first_name', 'last_name'),
        }),
    )
```

You will add those fields back soon using the utility functions.

3. Add the `dob` and `avatar` fields to the "Personal info" fieldset:

```
# Fields for editing existing user.
new_fields = ('dob', 'avatar')
# Add new fields to 'Personal info' fieldset.
append_fields(UserAdmin.fieldsets, 'Personal info', new_fields)
```

4. Move the `email` field to the unlabelled fieldset:

```
# Move email field from 'Personal info' fieldset to unlabelled fieldset
move_fields(UserAdmin.fieldsets, 'Personal info', None, ('email',))
```

The form for editing an existing user should now look like this:

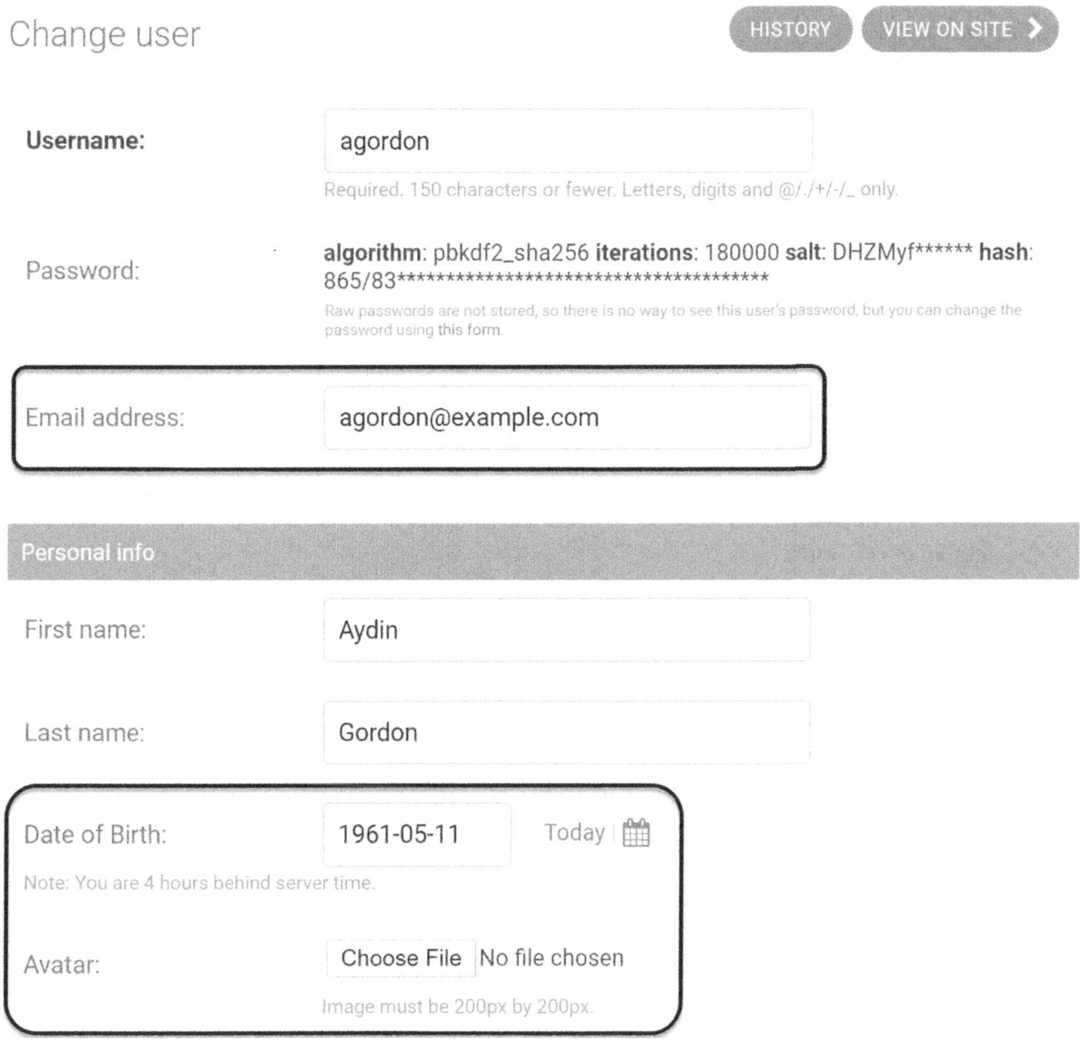

Change user

HISTORY VIEW ON SITE

Username: agordon

Required. 150 characters or fewer. Letters, digits and @/./+/-/_ only.

Password: **algorithm**: pbkdf2_sha256 **iterations**: 180000 **salt**: DHZMyf****** **hash**: 865/83**

Raw passwords are not stored, so there is no way to see this user's password, but you can change the password using this form.

Email address: agordon@example.com

Personal info

First name: Aydin

Last name: Gordon

Date of Birth: 1961-05-11 Today

Note: You are 4 hours behind server time.

Avatar: Choose File No file chosen

Image must be 200px by 200px.

Notice that the `email` field has been moved to the unlabelled fieldset and the `dob` and `avatar` fields have been added to the "Personal info" fieldset.

❖ E79.3. The Password Field

The password field takes up a lot of space and the only useful part of it is the **this form** link, which links to a password-change form:

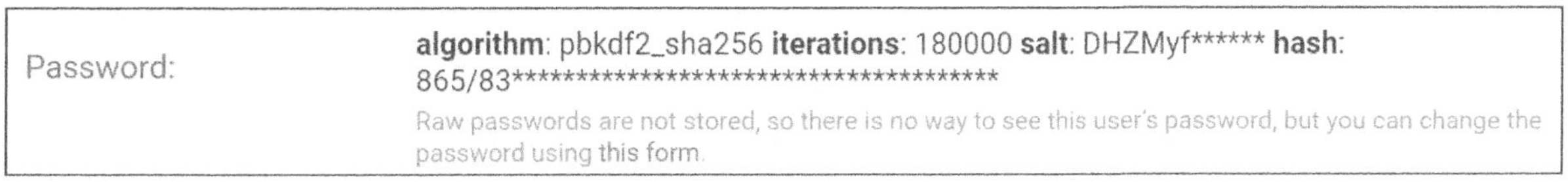

Password: **algorithm**: pbkdf2_sha256 **iterations**: 180000 **salt**: DHZMyf****** **hash**: 865/83**

Raw passwords are not stored, so there is no way to see this user's password, but you can change the password using this form.

Remove the password field using the `remove_fields()` method:

```
# Remove password field.
remove_fields(UserAdmin.fieldsets, None, ('password',))
```

That removes the password field, but it also removes the link to the password form. You will add that back shortly.

❖ E79.4. New User Form

Now, use the admin utility functions to make the following changes to the **Add user** form:

1. Add the `email` field to the unlabelled fieldset:

    ```
    # Fields for adding new user.
    new_fields = ('email', )
    # Add new fields to unlabelled fieldset.
    append_fields(UserAdmin.add_fieldsets, None, new_fields)
    ```

2. Add the `first_name`, `last_name`, and `dob` fields to a new "Optional Fields" fieldset:

    ```
    # Add optional fields to new 'Optional Fields' fieldset.
    optional_fields = ('first_name', 'last_name', 'dob')
    append_fields( UserAdmin.add_fieldsets, 'Optional Fields', optional_fields)
    ```

The form for adding a new user should now look like this:

Add user

First, enter a username and password. Then, you'll be able to edit more user options.

Username:

Required. 150 characters or fewer. Letters, digits and @/./+/-/_ only.

Password:

Your password can't be too similar to your other personal information

Your password must contain at least 8 characters.

Your password can't be a commonly used password.

Your password can't be entirely numeric.

Password confirmation:

Enter the same password as before, for verification.

Email address:

Optional Fields

First name:

Last name:

Date of Birth: Today

Note: You are 4 hours behind server time.

Notice that the `email` field has been added to the unlabelled fieldset and the `first_name`, `last_name`, and `dob` fields have been added a new "Optional Fields" fieldset.

❖ E79.5. Save Buttons Placement

The **Change user** form is pretty long, so it would be convenient to have save buttons at both the top and bottom of the form. The **Add user** form, however, is not that long, so it only needs save buttons on the bottom.

The `get_form()` method of the `ModelAdmin` class gets the form used in both the `add_view` and the `change_view`. You can override this method to conditionally change the value of `save_on_top`:

```
def get_form(self, request, obj=None, **kwargs):
    self.save_on_top = obj is not None
    return super().get_form(request, obj, **kwargs)
```

This will set `save_on_top` to `True` when `obj` exists and to `False` when it does not. Add the method to the `CustomUserAdmin` class.

The modified code in the `CustomUserAdmin` class follows:

Exercise Code 79.2: users/admin.py

```
    -------Lines 1 through 4 Omitted-------
5.  from common.admin import DjangoJokesAdmin
6.  from common.utils.admin import append_fields, move_fields, remove_fields
7.
8.  CustomUser = get_user_model()
9.
10. @admin.register(CustomUser)
11. class CustomUserAdmin(DjangoJokesAdmin, UserAdmin):
12.     model = CustomUser
13.
14.     # List Attributes
15.     list_display = UserAdmin.list_display + ('is_superuser',)
16.     list_display_links = ('username', 'email', 'first_name', 'last_name')
17.
18.     # Fields for editing existing user.
19.     new_fields = ('dob', 'avatar')
20.     # Add new fields to 'Personal info' section.
21.     append_fields(UserAdmin.fieldsets, 'Personal info', new_fields)
22.     # Move email field from 'Personal info' section to unlabelled section
23.     move_fields(UserAdmin.fieldsets, 'Personal info', None, ('email',))
24.     # Remove password field.
25.     remove_fields(UserAdmin.fieldsets, None, ('password',))
26.
27.     # Fields for adding new user.
28.     new_fields = ('email', )
29.     # Add new fields to unlabelled section.
30.     append_fields(UserAdmin.add_fieldsets, None, new_fields)
31.
32.     # Add optional fields to new 'Optional Fields' section.
33.     optional_fields = ('first_name', 'last_name', 'dob')
34.     append_fields(UserAdmin.add_fieldsets, 'Optional Fields', optional_fields)
35.
36.     # Add Save buttons to the top of the change user form
37.     def get_form(self, request, obj=None, **kwargs):
38.         self.save_on_top = obj is not None
39.         return super().get_form(request, obj, **kwargs)
```

The complete file is available at `starter-code/customizing-django-admin/users_admin_1.py`.

18.6. Adding Calculated Read-only Fields

In addition to including fields from the model, read-only fields can also include values returned from the model's method or from a `ModelAdmin` method.

For example, in `jokes/admin.py`, add the following method to `JokeAdmin`:

```
def vote_summary(self, obj):
    return f'{obj.num_votes} votes. Rating: {obj.rating}.'
```

And add `'vote_summary'` to the returned value of `get_readonly_fields`:

```
def get_readonly_fields(self, request, obj=None):
    if obj: # editing an existing object
        return ('slug', 'created', 'updated', 'vote_summary')
    return ()
```

Then, open any joke in Django admin and you will see a "Vote summary" field:

```
Vote summary:    17 votes. Rating: 5.88.
```

In the next exercise, you will use this technique to add a link in the user form to the password-change form.

Exercise 80: Adding a Link to the Change Password Form

10 to 15 minutes

In this exercise, you will add a link in the user form to the password-change form.

1. Open `users/admin.py` in your editor.
2. Import `mark_safe` from `django.utils.safestring`. You need this method to output HTML.

```
from django.utils.safestring import mark_safe
```

3. Import `reverse` from `django.urls`. You need this method to get the URL to the password-change form:

```
from django.urls import reverse
```

4. Add the following method to `CustomUserAdmin` right before the `get_form()` method:

```
def password_form(self, obj):
    url = reverse('admin:auth_user_password_change', args=[obj.pk])
    return mark_safe(f'<a href="{url}">Change Password</a>')
```

   `admin:auth_user_password_change` is the named URL pattern of the password-change form used by the `UserAdmin` class.[112]

5. Add the following `readonly_fields` attribute below the list attributes:

```
readonly_fields = ['password_form']
```

6. Use the `append_fields()` utility method to add `'password_form'` to the unlabelled fieldset:

```
append_fields(UserAdmin.fieldsets, None, ('password_form',))
```

   You can add this line right below the line where you remove the `password` field.

7. In Django admin, open any user record to see the new **Password form** field and **Change Password** link:

112. See `https://docs.djangoproject.com/en/3.1/ref/contrib/admin/#reversing-admin-urls` for documentation on reversing admin URLs.

Username: agordon

Required. 150 characters or fewer. Letters, digits and @/./+/-/_ only.

Email address: agordon@example.com

Password form: Change Password

The modified code in the `CustomUserAdmin` class is shown below:

Exercise Code 80.1: users/admin.py

```
    -------Lines 1 through 3 Omitted-------
4.  from django.utils.safestring import mark_safe
5.  from django.urls import reverse
    -------Lines 6 through 11 Omitted-------
12. @admin.register(CustomUser)
13. class CustomUserAdmin(DjangoJokesAdmin, UserAdmin):
14.     model = CustomUser
15.
16.     # List Attributes
17.     list_display = UserAdmin.list_display + ('is_superuser',)
18.     list_display_links = ('username', 'email', 'first_name', 'last_name')
19.
20.     readonly_fields = ['password_form']
    -------Lines 21 through 27 Omitted-------
28.     # Remove password field from 'Personal info'
29.     remove_fields(UserAdmin.fieldsets, None, ('password',))
30.     append_fields(UserAdmin.fieldsets, None, ('password_form',))
    -------Lines 31 through 40 Omitted-------
41.     def password_form(self, obj):
42.         url = reverse('admin:auth_user_password_change', args=[obj.pk])
43.         return mark_safe(f'<a href="{url}">Change Password</a>')
    -------Lines 44 through 48 Omitted-------
```

The complete file is available at `starter-code/customizing-django-admin/users_admin_2.py`.

Exercise 81: Unregistering Models

5 to 10 minutes

Sometimes, some of the third-party apps you install, register models that you don't end up using. For example, `django-allauth` includes apps for authenticating with social accounts. It registers these apps by default, so they show up in Django admin:

You're not currently using those, so you can unregister them using `admin.site.unregister()`.

1. Open `users/admin.py` in your editor.
2. Import the social apps from `allauth.socialaccount.models`:

   ```
   from allauth.socialaccount.models import SocialApp, SocialAccount, SocialToken
   ```

3. At the bottom of the file, add these lines of code to deregister the three apps:

   ```
   admin.site.unregister(SocialApp)
   admin.site.unregister(SocialAccount)
   admin.site.unregister(SocialToken)
   ```

4. Open Django admin and notice that the social apps no longer appear in the sidebar.

The modified code in the `CustomUserAdmin` class is shown below:

Exercise Code 81.1: users/admin.py

```
        -------Lines 1 through 6 Omitted-------
7.      from allauth.socialaccount.models import SocialApp, SocialAccount, SocialToken
        -------Lines 8 through 13 Omitted-------
14.     @admin.register(CustomUser)
15.     class CustomUserAdmin(DjangoJokesAdmin, UserAdmin):
16.         model = CustomUser
        -------Lines 17 through 52 Omitted-------
53.     admin.site.unregister(SocialApp)
54.     admin.site.unregister(SocialAccount)
55.     admin.site.unregister(SocialToken)
```

The complete file is available at `starter-code/customizing-django-admin/users_admin_3.py`.

Exercise 82: Django Admin Groups and Permissions

10 to 15 minutes

Log in to the website as a Clyde Cortez, who is a staff member. Clyde's login credentials are:

- Email: ccortez@example.com
- Password: DjangoP@$$

Notice that, although Clyde can log in, he does not have permissions to do anything:

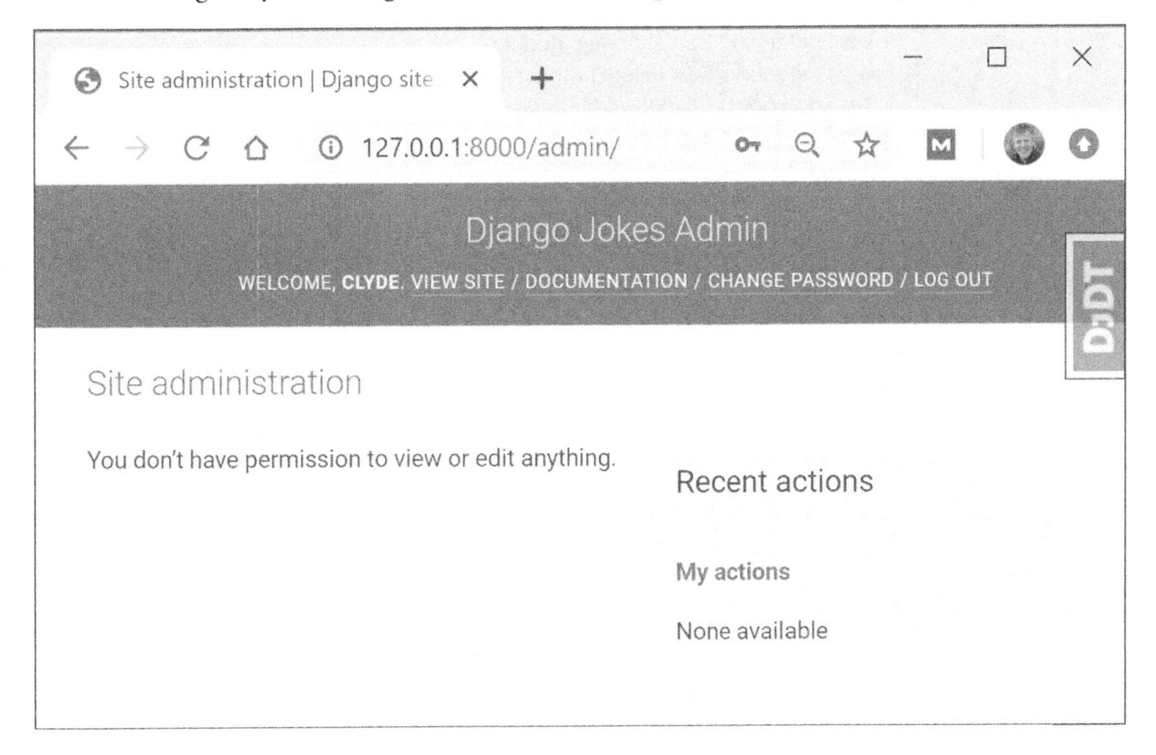

There are two ways to give users permissions in Django admin:

1. Give them permissions directly via their user record:

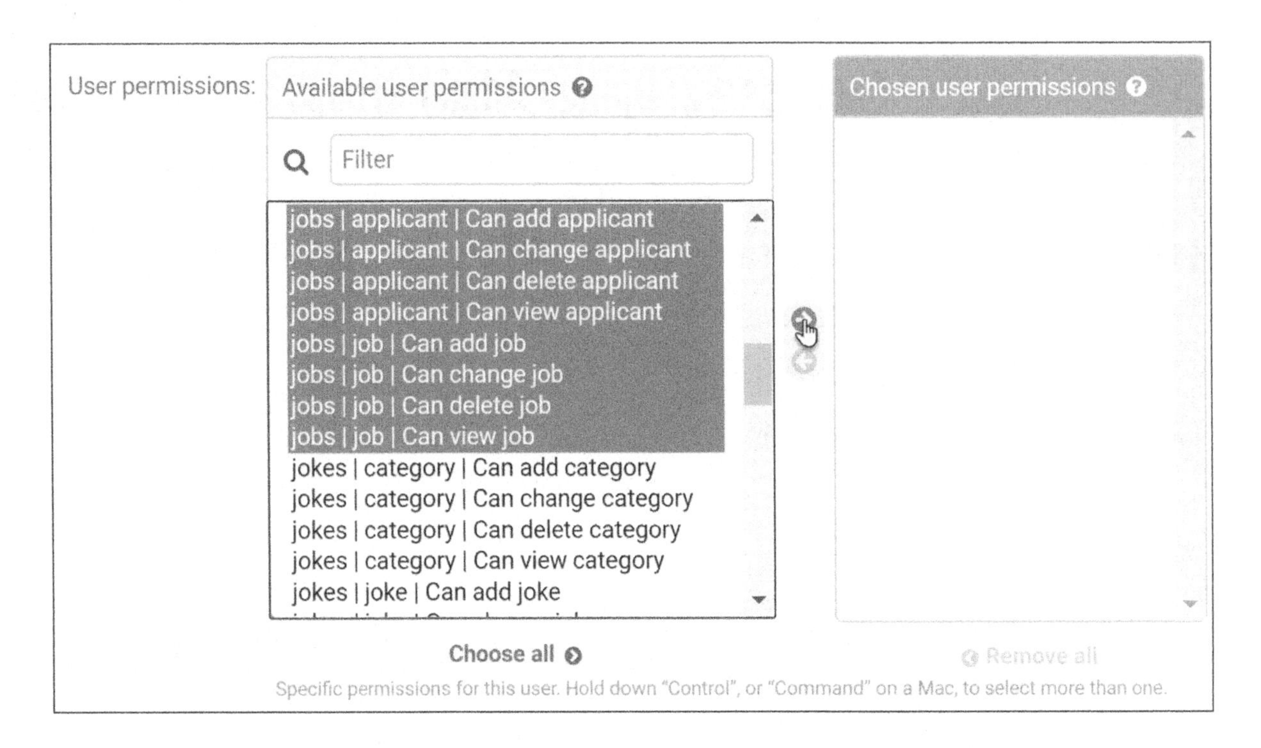

2. Create a group with permissions and add the user to the group.

You will take the second approach:

1. Log in to Django admin as the superuser.
2. Under **AUTHENTICATION AND AUTHORIZATION** on the sidebar of Django admin, click **Groups**.
3. Click **Add group**.
4. Enter "HR" for **Name**.
5. Under **Permissions**, select all of the items that begin with "jobs," and then click the right arrow:

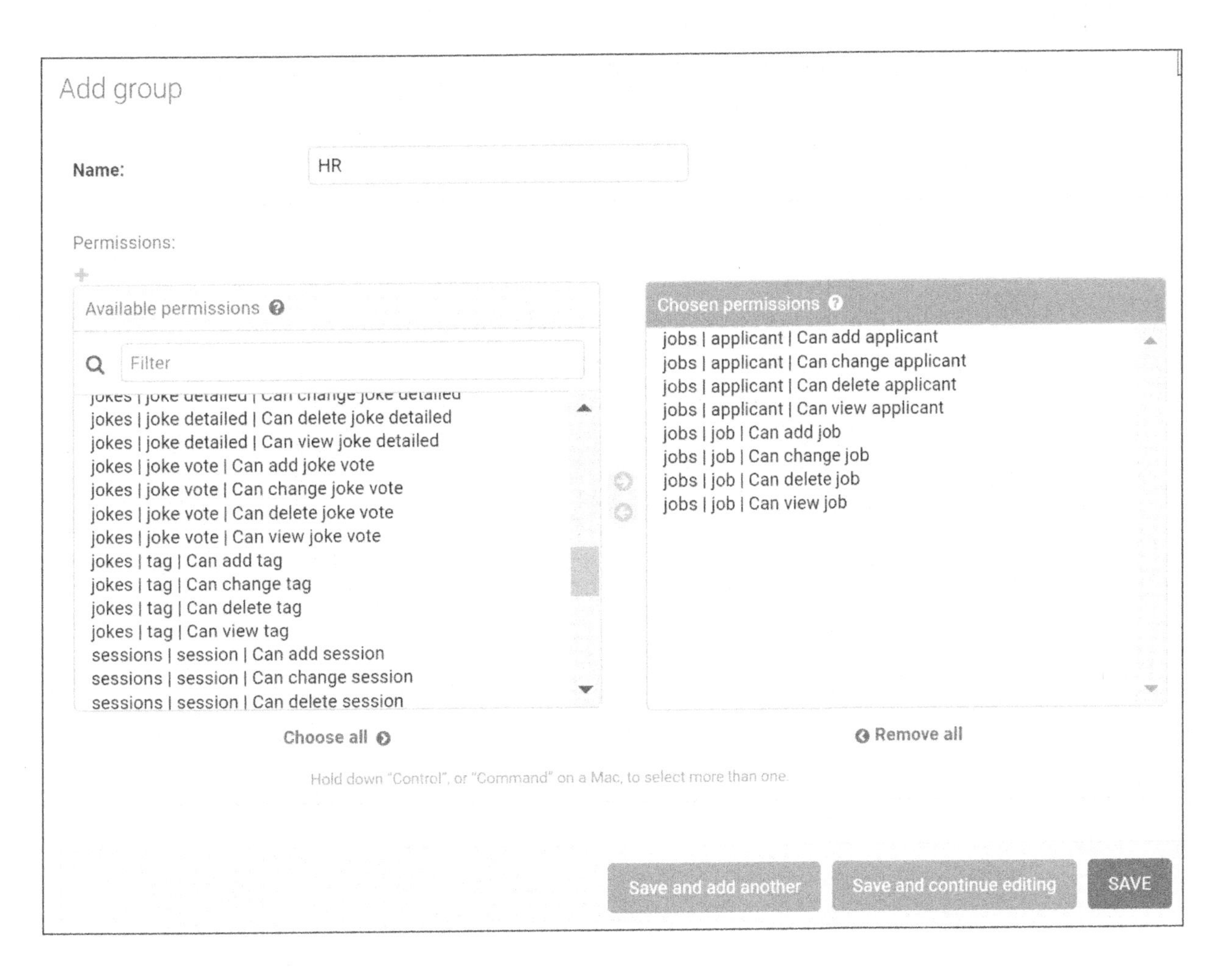

6. Click **SAVE** to save.
7. Under **USERS** on the sidebar of Django admin, click **Users**.
8. Find and open Clyde Cortez's record:

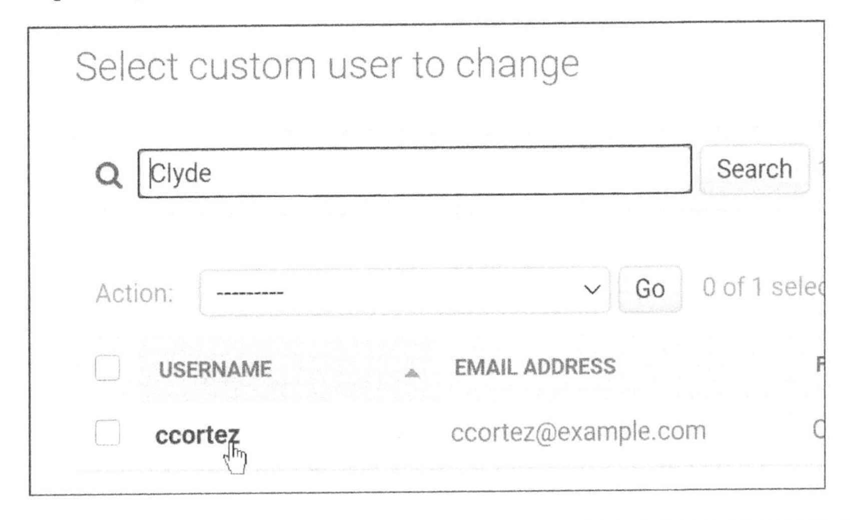

9. Under **Permissions**, move "HR" from **Available groups** to **Chosen groups**.
10. Click **SAVE** to save.
11. Log out of Django admin, and log back in again as Clyde Cortez:
    - Email: ccortez@example.com
    - Password: DjangoP@$$

    Notice that he now has access to applicants and jobs:

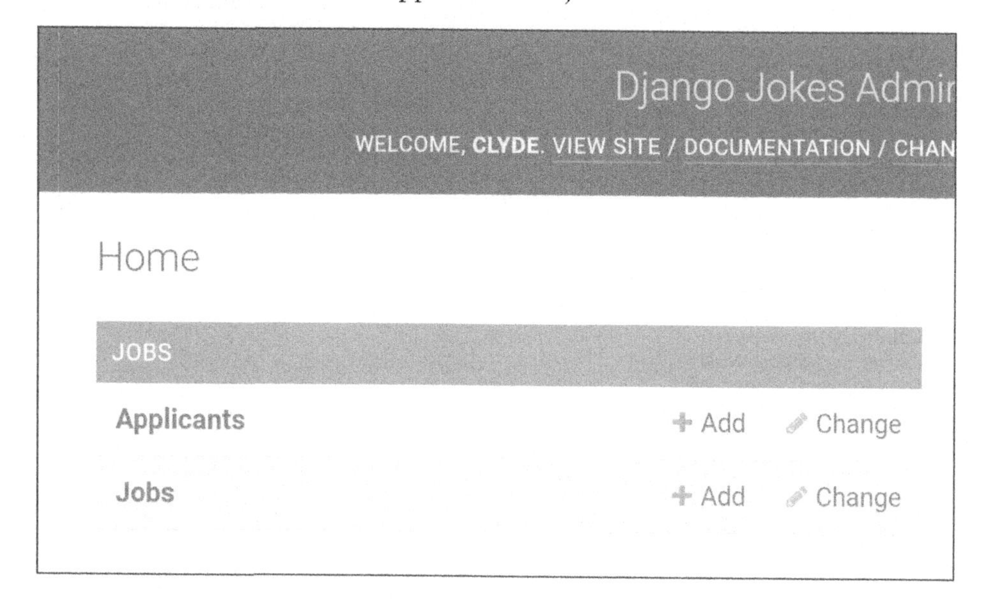

Conclusion

In this lesson, you have learned some ways to customize Django admin. For additional information, see `https://docs.djangoproject.com/en/3.1/ref/contrib/admin/`

LESSON 19

Additional Topics

Topics Covered

☑ Additional learning.

☑ Projects for practice.

> My sensations had by this time become distinct, and my mind received every day **additional** ideas. My eyes became accustomed to the light and to perceive objects in their right forms; I distinguished the insect from the herb, and by degrees, one herb from another. I found that the sparrow uttered none but harsh notes, whilst those of the blackbird and thrush were sweet and enticing.
>
> – *Frankenstein, Mary Wollstonecraft*

Introduction

In this lesson, we give you some ideas for additional learning and some project ideas you can do to practice your skills.

19.1. Additional Learning

❖ 19.1.1. Testing

As a rule, developers should write tests for every new feature they add. So, your development process looks something like this:

1. Decide to add a feature.
2. Write a test to test the feature you're about to add.
3. Run the test. It should fail, because you haven't added the feature yet.
4. Add the feature.

5. Run the test again. If it fails, keep working on the feature until the test passes.
6. Decide to add another feature…

But writing good tests is an art, and writing bad tests can lead to disaster. There should be a book dedicated to test-driven development with Django. And, luckily, there is: Harry Percival's *Test-Driven Development with Python*. You can read it online for free at `https://www.obeythetestinggoat.com` or purchase a print version on Amazon.

See `https://docs.djangoproject.com/en/3.1/topics/testing/` for Django's documentation on testing, which uses Python's `unittest` module.

❖ 19.1.2. Caching

As your site grows, you may find it slows down. You may be able to use caching to speed it up.

See `https://docs.djangoproject.com/en/3.1/topics/cache/` to learn about Django's cache framework.

❖ 19.1.3. Logging

Heroku gives you access to your app logs via **More > View logs**:

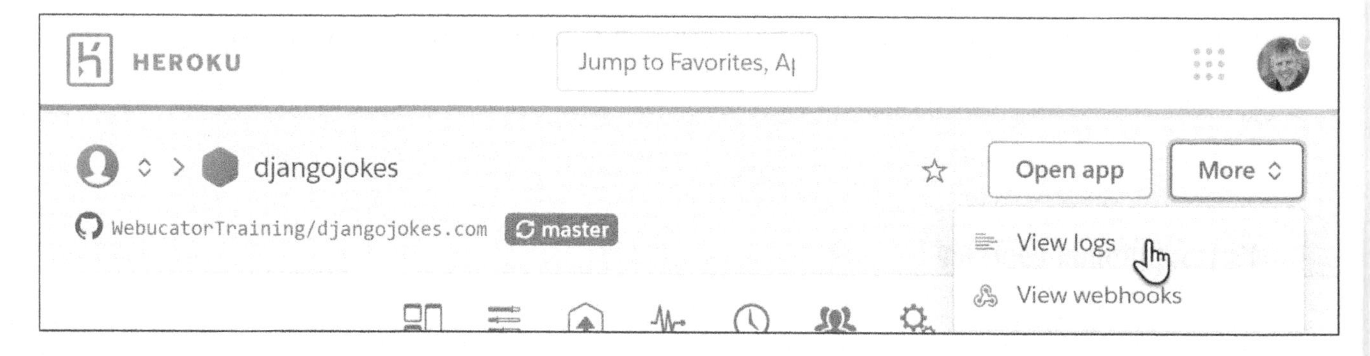

Django uses Python's built-in logging module, which provides the following log levels:

- `DEBUG`
- `INFO`
- `WARNING`
- `ERROR`
- `CRITICAL`

Generally, you configure logging in `settings.py`. A sample configuration follows:

```
LOGGING = {
    'version': 1,
    'disable_existing_loggers': False,
    'handlers': {
        'warning': {
            'level': 'WARNING',
            'class': 'logging.FileHandler',
            'filename': BASE_DIR / 'logs/error.log',
        },
        'info': {
            'level': 'INFO',
            'class': 'logging.FileHandler',
            'filename': BASE_DIR / 'logs/info.log',
        },
        'debug': {
            'level': 'DEBUG',
            'class': 'logging.FileHandler',
            'filename': BASE_DIR / 'logs/debug.log',
        },
    },
    'loggers': {
        'django': {
            'handlers': ['warning', 'info', 'debug'],
            'level': 'DEBUG',
            'propagate': True,
        },
    },
}
```

You can add messages to the log using a logger. First, import `logging` and get the `logger`:

```
import logging

logger = logging.getLogger(__name__)
```

Then, add messages using:

- `logger.debug()`
- `logger.info()`

- `logger.warning()`
- `logger.error()`
- `logger.critical()`

For detailed information on logging, see:

- `https://docs.djangoproject.com/en/3.1/topics/logging/`
- `https://docs.python.org/3/library/logging.html`

❖ 19.1.4. Internationalization and localization

Internationalization is the process of preparing software for localization. It is the job of developers. *Localization* is the process of creating the translations and local formats. It is the job of translators.

See `https://docs.djangoproject.com/en/3.1/topics/i18n/` to learn about internationalization and localization in Django.

19.2. Additional Projects

There is a lot more you can do with the `Django Jokes` website to practice your new Django skills. Here are some ideas:

❖ 19.2.1. Use Favicon to Distinguish Between Dev and Production

We'll start with a relatively easy one. Sometimes, as you're working, you will have both your live site and your development site open in the browser at the same time. It can be helpful to be able to distinguish between the two by looking at their browser tabs. One way to do this is to show different favicons for development and production. For example, you could create a `favicon-dev.png` file with a border on it and show that one on development:

Django templates have access to a boolean `debug` variable. Use that to display different favicons for development and production.

❖ 19.2.2. Dynamically Create Small Profile Pics

We display a small profile picture of the joke creator on a joke-detail page:

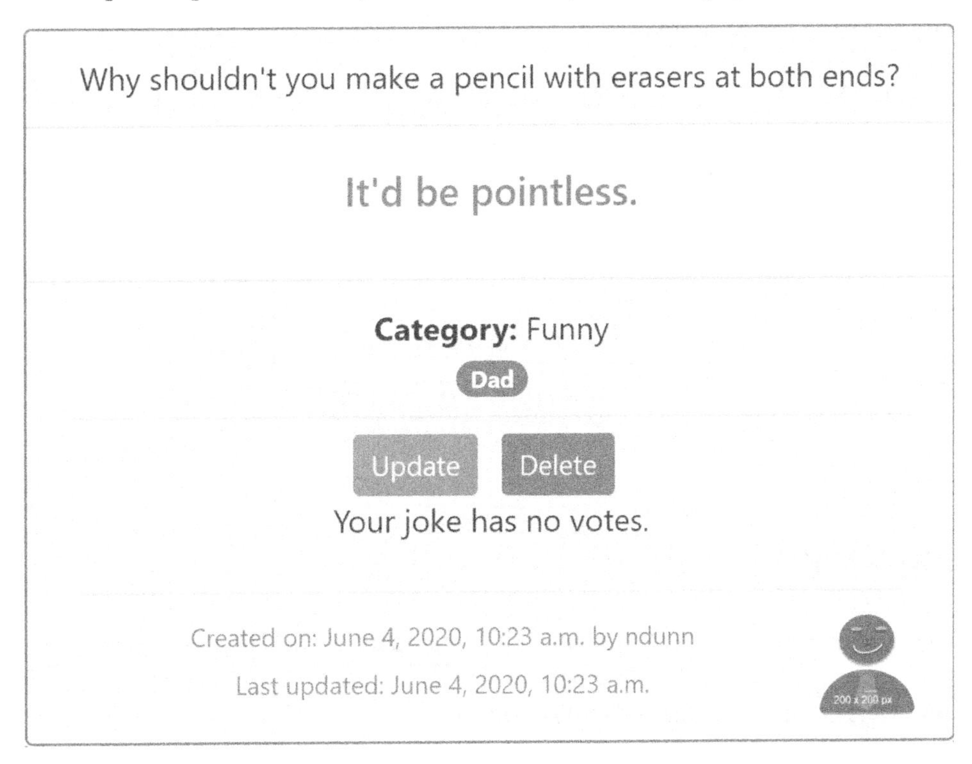

We currently use the `height` and `width` attributes of the `img` element to "shrink" the image:

```
<img src="{{ joke.user.avatar.url }}" alt="{{ joke.user.username }}"
  class="mt-1 rounded float-right" width="50" height="50">
```

It would be better to use Python to create and save a 50px-by-50px version of the image and use that instead of the 200px-by-200px image. The smaller image will download faster.

See `https://pillow.readthedocs.io/en/stable/reference/Image.html#PIL.Image.Image.resize` to learn how to do this.

❖ 19.2.3. Add a Joke Approval Process

You probably don't want user-entered content going live immediately. Here are some ideas for creating an approval process:

1. Add an `approved` field to the `Joke` model that holds the date and time the joke was approved. It should default to `null`.
2. When a user creates a new joke, an email gets sent to a person or group of people who are responsible for approving jokes.

If you want to go further with this one, read about adding actions in Django admin,[113] so that you can easily approve multiple jokes at one time:

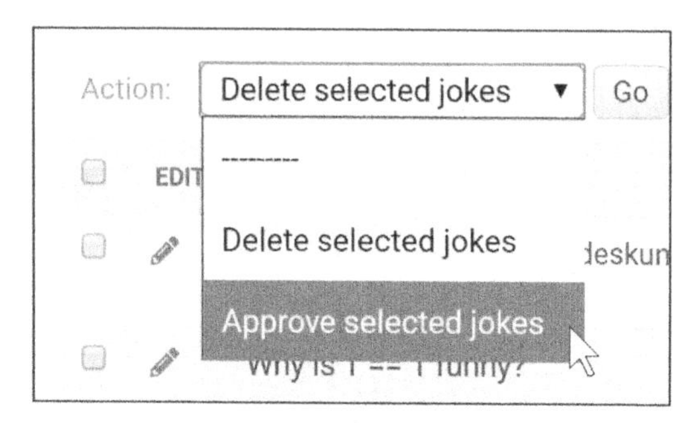

❖ 19.2.4. Advanced Search

Many sites provide an advanced search option. Some examples:

1. `https://github.com/search/advanced`
2. `https://www.amazon.com/Advanced-Search-Books/b?node=241582011`
3. https://www.google.com/advanced_search

You could set up an advanced search page that allowed users to search by:

- Joke question.
- Joke answer.
- Joke creator.
- Joke category.
- Joke tag.
- Updated since.
- Created since.

113. `https://docs.djangoproject.com/en/3.1/ref/contrib/admin/actions/`

❖ 19.2.5. Allow Users to Save As...

We showed you how you can add a **Save as new** button to a form in Django admin (see page 555). This allows an admin user to create a copy of an existing object. Add this same functionality for end users. For example, you could add a copy icon to the joke-detail page, like this:

When a logged-in user clicked the icon, it should create an exact copy of the joke and take the user to the new joke's update form.

Conclusion

In this lesson, we have provided you with further learning resources and some ideas for projects to practice what you have learned. We hope you have enjoyed learning Django and wish you the best of luck!

Made in the USA
Middletown, DE
31 August 2020

17162986R00331